Failures

of State

The Inside Story of Britain's Battle with Coronavirus

Jonathan Calvert
George Arbuthnott

MUDLARK

Mudlark
An imprint of HarperCollins*Publishers*
1 London Bridge Street
London SE1 9GF

www.harpercollins.co.uk

HarperCollins*Publishers*
1st Floor, Watermarque Building, Ringsend Road
Dublin 4, Ireland

First published by HarperCollins Publishers 2021

1 3 5 7 9 10 8 6 4 2

© Jonathan Calvert and George Arbuthnott 2021

Jonathan Calvert and George Arbuthnott assert the
moral right to be identified as the authors of this work

Sunday Times graphics on coronavirus (p15, p30, p218, p251, p252,
p264, p362, p378) © *The Sunday Times*/News Licensing

Picture credits for plate section: p1 (top) © JOHANNES EISELE/AFP via Getty
Images; p1 (bottom) © HECTOR RETAMAL/AFP via Getty Images; p2 (t), p7
(b) © BEN STANSALL/AFP via Getty Images; p2 (b) © Mark Pain/Alamy Stock
Photo; p3 (t) © PA Images/Alamy Stock Photo; p3 (b) © Richard Pohle/The
Times/News Licensing; p4 (t) © PA Video/PA Archive/PA Images/Alamy Stock
Photo; p4 (b) © Jacob King/Pool/AFP via Getty Images; p5 (t) © John Keeble/
Getty Images; p5 (b) © Joel Goodman/The Times/News Licensing; p6 (t)
© Donna Grove; p6 (b) © Jonathan Brady/Pool/AFP via Getty Images; p7 (t)
© HM Treasury/Flickr (https://www.flickr.com/photos/hmtreasury); p8 (t)
© REUTERS/Simon Dawson/Alamy Stock Photo; p8 (b) © Jane Wellington

A catalogue record of this book is
available from the British Library

ISBN 978-0-00-843052-8

Printed and bound in Great Britain by
CPI Group (UK) Ltd, Croydon

MIX
Paper from
responsible sources
FSC™ C007454

This book is produced from independently certified FSC™ paper
to ensure responsible forest management.

For more information visit: www.harpercollins.co.uk/green

To all the bright sparks, the friends and lovers lost,
and the hearts broken by this wretched pestilence.
And to the doctors, nurses and carers who
held their hands.

Contents

PART THREE – THE RECKONING

24 March 2020 to 26 April 2020

PART FOUR – THE SAME MISTAKE TWICE

27 April 2020 to 2 December 2020

PART FIVE – THE FINAL RECKONING

3 December 2020 to January 2021

Prologue

You must stay at home

The last Monday before the clocks went back in March 2020 had been a day for brisk walks in the sunshine under flawless azure skies. But the freshness and promise of a fine spring day at the end of a long rainy winter did little to temper the collective sense of unease being felt across Britain. As darkness fell, people hunkered down in their homes, unsure about what would happen next. Like participants in an all-too-real Doomsday film, the nation tuned in to radios, switched on their televisions and flicked through their smartphones, awaiting that evening's important announcement on the only issue of the moment: the virus. It was a crisis unlike any other in modern Britain and it now gripped the country. People feared for their lives. Outside, beneath the stars, the flashing blue lights of ambulances strafed through empty city streets, their wailing sirens amplified in the stillness.

It had been almost three months since the stealthy killer had crept into the country and it was now replicating itself with alarming speed. The virus had already embedded itself in the lungs of more than a million people in the UK and many of them would perish in the grim weeks that followed. One hospital had been forced to turn away patients because it could not cope with such a large number of infections and France was threatening

1

to close its borders to England. The French were horrified by the way the virus had been allowed to run rampant without tougher control measures being introduced by their English neighbours a few miles across the Channel. The crisis was beginning to look desperate and finally something had to be done. The prime minister was guaranteed an immense and captive audience for his address to the nation, which had been scheduled at 8.30 p.m. – a later time than his now familiar daily press conferences, which signified that something serious was about to be announced.

This was the kind of historic moment that Alexander Boris de Pfeffel Johnson believed he had been born for. As a young child with supreme self-confidence, Johnson had told his family he would be a 'world king' – although he eventually lowered his sights to settle for prime minister. His adolescent role model had been Winston Churchill, the doughty leader who had rallied Britain through the last great national emergency, the Second World War. In his 2014 biography of his illustrious predecessor, *The Churchill Factor*, Johnson describes how 'thrusting young Tories' regarded Churchill as a 'divinity' and sported posters of their pin-striped cigar-chomping idol on teenage walls. He was, no doubt, referring to a particular teenager with a shot of blond shaggy hair and a comparably large ego. One of the key arguments in Johnson's biography is that Adolf Hitler would have won the war and Nazism would have prevailed throughout Europe had it not been for his hero prime minister.

This was now Johnson's moment to rally the nation in its darkest hour. Could he summon his inner Churchill and save Britain from the threat of the coronavirus pandemic? Twenty-eight million people tuned in to watch Johnson's address from Downing Street that evening. The camera had framed the doorway of the White Drawing Room – the great state reception overlooking the No. 10 gardens, which has hosted US presidents from Ronald Reagan to Barack Obama and was once used by Churchill himself as his bedroom. In the middle of the frame was Johnson looking his most headmasterly as he earnestly leant forward towards the camera with clasped hands – his elbows resting on a polished antique desk. Such was the gravity of the moment, he had even combed his haystack hair into something resembling neatness.

'The coronavirus is the biggest threat this country has faced for decades – and this country is not alone. All over the world we are seeing the devastating impact of this invisible killer,' his address began. 'Without a huge national effort to halt the growth of this virus, there will come a moment when no health service in the world could possibly cope; because there won't be enough ventilators, enough intensive care beds, enough doctors and nurses.

'The time has now come for us all to do more. From this evening I must give the British people a very simple instruction: you must stay at home.'

Those final five words will probably stick in our collective memory for decades. Never before had such an extraordinary instruction been given to the people of Britain. We were told to remain in our homes indefinitely. People would only be allowed out of the house for a limited set of activities: to buy food or medical supplies; to visit the doctor or hospital; to help someone vulnerable; and to exercise once a day. Some people would still be permitted to travel to work, but only if their job was absolutely necessary. Meetings with friends or family members who lived outside the household were forbidden. That evening, there were tears in many homes as people began to realise that they would be parted from loved ones in such uncertain times when everyone's life appeared to be in danger.

The clampdown on civil liberties was far-reaching. Johnson made clear: 'We will stop all gatherings of more than two people in public – excluding people you live with; and we'll stop all social events, including weddings, baptisms and other ceremonies, but excluding funerals.' Anyone who disobeyed would be breaking the law. 'If you don't follow the rules the police will have the powers to enforce them,' Johnson added. The immediate effects on the British economy would be enormous. In a stroke the prime minister had brought trade and commerce to a great shuddering halt, and this decision would, no doubt, have ramifications for many years to come. 'No prime minister wants to enact measures like this. I know the damage that this disruption is doing and will do to people's lives, to their businesses and to their jobs,' he said.

Johnson had come a long way in the six weeks leading up to his lockdown speech on the evening of Monday 23 March 2020. He had initially been dismissive of the 'irrational' panic about the virus when others were warning that this could be the much-feared plague-like contagion, in an era of mass world travel, that scientists had predicted for years. It had only been a few months earlier that Johnson had risen to power taking advantage of the fissure in his party caused by the Brexit vote. He had promised his fellow Conservatives he would deliver a departure from the European Union that would unshackle the British economy – heralding a new era of free trade and prosperity. While many argued that Brexit might actually have the opposite effect and would wreak havoc with the economy, Johnson was determined to prove them wrong. It was his mission as prime minister and it was his destiny – or so he believed before the virus came along. The virus changed everything.

Churchill drew his strength from the moral authority of having taken a consistent position on the threat of Nazi Germany before and after he became prime minister. While others had dithered over appeasement to Hitler, Churchill had for years been a siren voice warning of the serious danger posed by the rejuvenated military might of Germany and its fanatical chancellor. But Johnson could claim no such unwavering stance when he first faced the crisis that will now inevitably define his premiership. In fact, he belittled those who were warning that the virus might become a problem that would require serious economic intervention. Six weeks before lockdown, Johnson's first act on the Monday morning after signing the withdrawal treaty from the European Union on Friday 31 January was to give a speech in the Painted Hall of the Old Royal Naval College in Greenwich.

The venue had been chosen for its symbolism. The examples of early maritime technology surrounding Johnson harkened back to an era when Britain's mastery of the seas led to an explosion in global trade. The PM drew parallels with the high-point of British power during the colonial era and Britain's new beginning after Brexit. But he argued that protectionism was once again a real issue dragging at the heels of free trade. 'From Brussels to China to Washington, tariffs are being waved around like cudgels even in debates on foreign policy where frankly they have no place,' he told the invited audience.

He then produced an example of the type of protectionism he would fight tooth and nail to prevent. He said: 'When barriers are going up, and when there is a risk that new diseases such as coronavirus will trigger a panic and a desire for market segregation that go beyond what is medically rational to the point of doing real and unnecessary economic damage, then at that moment humanity needs some government somewhere that is willing at least to make the case powerfully for freedom of exchange, some country ready to take off its Clark Kent spectacles and leap into the phone booth and emerge with its cloak flowing as the supercharged champion, of the right of the populations of the earth to buy and sell freely among each other. And here in Greenwich in the first week of February 2020, I can tell you in all humility that the UK is ready for that role.'

Johnson, of course, would never squeeze into Superman's tight-fitting suit, and six weeks later he was forced to do exactly the thing that he vowed he would save the world from. He almost completely shut down the economy and trade. But the viewpoint exhibited in the Painted Hall speech goes to the heart of why Britain would be hit by one of the worst outbreaks of coronavirus in the world and our death toll would be so tragically high. The one-eyed obsession with Brexit had left the UK in a poor state of preparation for a pandemic and blinded its leaders to the imminent threat because they were so focused on an issue that – although of huge magnitude – would become secondary in the new post-Covid-19 world.

As investigative reporters for *The Sunday Times*, we produced a series of articles throughout 2020 examining the UK government's reaction to the coronavirus crisis and attempting to understand how this country – which prided itself on its pandemic defences – managed to get it so badly wrong. Our first article was published on Sunday 19 April 2020 when Johnson still enjoyed a relatively high degree of public confidence, according to the polls. But there was growing unease at the time about why Britain seemed to be consistently slower to act in tackling the virus in comparison to the rest of Europe. The article struck a chord. That Sunday it became the most read online piece in *The Sunday Times* and *The Times*'s history. It was described by Andrew Marr on the BBC as 'a devastating piece of journalism'; ITV's Robert Peston said he was 'literally gobsmacked' by the article; the *Guardian* columnist Owen Jones said it was 'one of the most important things you've read'; the broadcaster Piers Morgan called it straightforwardly 'a scandal'; and the writer Caitlin Moran said it read like 'the obituary of Boris Johnson's government'. The *Press Gazette* said the article was 'the first major national press investigation to cast serious doubt over the government's handling of the pandemic'.

The article did not please everyone, however. It elicited a furious response from government ministers and their spin doctors, who issued a remarkable 2,000-word blog defending their actions, which was tweeted out by most of the leading members of the cabinet. It was filled with the kind of sleights of hand that would become an increasingly familiar hallmark of the government's approach as it battled through problem after problem with its handling of the virus crisis. Two phrases in particular would become government fall-back mantras to absolve ministers of any blame: 'we were following the science' and 'we have taken the right steps at the right time.' But were they and had they? The decisions were taken ultimately by politicians, and the buck stopped with Johnson. Over the months that followed, we continued exposing the scandalous death toll caused by government incompetence, and at the same time the public's trust in Johnson's administration began to collapse. Of the world's seven largest economies, no other government saw trust in its handling of the virus slump to the same degree as in Britain.

One day there will be an inquiry into the lack of preparations from those first days when the virus stole into the country from China, and there will be many serious questions for the politicians to answer. In researching this book and for our articles in *The Sunday Times*, we have spoken to hundreds of witnesses, including scientists, academics, doctors, paramedics, bereaved families, care home workers, emergency planners, public officials, Downing Street whistle-blowers and politicians about the causes of the debacle in the UK. We asked them whether Britain was equipped to fight a pandemic and if the politicians understood the severity of the threat. We wanted to know what the scientists told ministers and why so little was done to equip the National Health Service for the difficult days ahead. Why was it that the government failed to act more swiftly to kick-start the Whitehall machine and put the NHS onto a war footing, and what were the consequences?

They told us that, contrary to the official line, Britain was not in a state of readiness for the pandemic. Emergency stockpiles of personal protective equipment (PPE) had severely dwindled and were out of date because they had become a low priority in the years of austerity cuts. The training to prepare key workers for a pandemic had been put on hold for two years while contingency planning was diverted to deal with a possible no-deal Brexit. This made it doubly important that the government hit the ground running in late January and early February.

The scientists gave clear warnings that there was a coming storm. In particular, the government's key advisory committee was given a dire prediction many weeks before the lockdown about the prospect of having to deal with mass casualties as a result of the government's strategy, and yet too little was done. It was a message repeated throughout February, and it became all the louder as deaths started to ramp up elsewhere in Europe in early March and neighbouring countries began taking drastic action. But the wise voices and advance warnings fell on deaf ears within the British government. The need, for example, to boost emergency supplies of protective masks and gowns for health workers was pressing, but little progress was made in obtaining the items from manufacturers, mainly in China. Instead, the government sent supplies the other way – shipping hundreds of thousands of items from its depleted stockpile of protective equipment to China during this period in response to a request for help from the authorities there. It would take the government months before it was able to buy its donation back.

There will also be grave questions for the prime minister, who was so fixated by Brexit and developing trade relationships that he only came to appreciate the extreme danger posed by the virus when it was too late. He did not attend any of the first five meetings of Cobra, the key national crisis committee that commanded the UK's response to the pandemic. The first Cobra meeting Johnson attended was on 2 March and by then the virus had already firmly gained its foothold in the country. As many commentators would point out after our first article: this was an extraordinary dereliction of his duty as a prime minister, which would have enormous consequences.

* * *

This book will chart the coronavirus crisis from its origins in China, raising serious questions about how the first outbreak emerged in the city of Wuhan and why the country's government attempted to conceal the severity of the contagion. It will examine how our politicians and scientists responded to the virus when it first entered Britain and show how infections were allowed to spread too widely before Johnson's lockdown speech on that Monday in March. His prevarication over taking decisive action had devastating consequences that have continued to reverberate throughout the year, and those days in the lead-up to lockdown were especially important. The virus had been doubling every three days, which meant that any small delay in bringing in the lockdown would cause a huge increase in infections, and ultimately deaths. Johnson's closest advisers are said to have lobbied to bring in the lockdown a week earlier, but the prime minister's libertarian instincts and concerns for the economy made him hold back. It was a fatal decision – for thousands of people.

A study by Imperial College London's pandemic modellers and Oxford University's department of statistics has estimated that coronavirus infections across the UK rocketed from an estimated 200,000 to 1.5 million in the nine days before lockdown as the prime minister agonised over whether to act. Johnson and his team of ministers and scientists justified the delay by telling one of the most illogical untruths in British political history. They argued that the late lockdown was the correct decision because it meant that the strict controls would need to be in place for less time. But, of course, the opposite was true. The delay in making the decision until 23 March resulted in the UK suffering more cases of infection when it went into lockdown than Italy, Spain, Germany and France.

The results were catastrophic. Many people died unnecessarily because the prime minister allowed infections to spread so widely across the country as he dithered over lockdown. Between March and August 2020, there were 51,000 more deaths outside hospitals in Britain than in normal years. To put that into context, fewer than 3,000 members of the UK's armed forces died in the wars in Afghanistan, Iraq, Northern Ireland and the Falklands combined. Among those infected was the prime minister, who almost certainly already had the virus on that Monday evening when he announced Britain was shutting down.

It was an exceptional year, unlike any other. There was much fear and also great sadness for the many mothers, fathers, friends, sons and daughters who were lost. The nation was hugely grateful for the heroism of those in our health service and care homes who risked their own lives to save countless others. It was a time of loneliness and isolation, and yet a country split asunder by Brexit somehow managed to recapture its community spirit and single purpose. Neighbours helped those less able with shopping and chores, volunteers sewed surgical gowns in their homes, comic memes became a daily currency between friends, and every Thursday evening we would all come together and clap as one. Facemasks became a part of our everyday life, as did Perspex barriers in shops and bars, arrow markings on floors, long segregated queues outside supermarkets, hand washing, and alcohol-based hand rubs. There was a revolution in home working, and Britain's parks and public spaces were used more than ever before.

But most of all, it was a year of seismic political decisions demanding wisdom and leadership. Some people will say it is easy to criticise our politicians in hindsight when the country was facing an unparalleled crisis with a unique set of problems that had never been tackled before in the modern age. Yet the fact that the UK suffered the highest number of deaths from the virus in Europe during the first wave tells its own story. Its economy was also hit harder than any of its global peers in the G7 group of developed nations. Many other leaders across the world faced the same challenges yet saved more of their citizens' lives, while also managing to protect their economies more effectively. Some were able to suppress the virus almost completely and thereby reduced the chances of a second deadly wave later on in the year, buying their countries time as scientists around the world worked furiously to develop a vaccine. Britain, on the other hand, did not escape a second wave, and Johnson and his government went on to repeat many of the same mistakes that had caused so many deaths in the first outbreak. The experts we talked to found this simply 'unforgivable'. It was a year of tough decisions, and tragically the UK politicians seemed to make the wrong ones.

PART ONE

ORIGINS

24 April 2012 to 23 January 2020

1
The Best Clue to the Origins

Tuesday 24 April 2012 to Saturday 30 November 2019

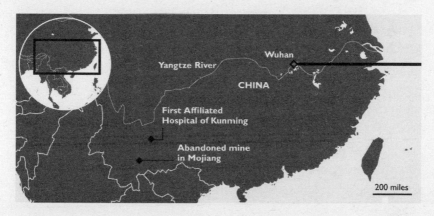

In a sense, the world had been waiting for this moment. The possibility that a deadly virus might one day emerge from the zoological melting pots in temperate climes had been foreshadowed in a series of outbreaks in which animals had passed viruses to humans over the last 20 years. It seemed only a matter of time before one of these killers would acquire the potency to leap easily from human to human and cause destruction to lives and livelihoods in a way that had not been witnessed since the Spanish flu pandemic more than a hundred years ago. But like other natural disasters such as earthquakes, volcanos and rising sea levels, it appeared to be mostly a distant problem to governments in the West. This was especially true in Britain. In 2019 the UK was still suffering from an extreme form of myopia, which had left the government unable to see beyond the domestic drama of Brexit. A pandemic virus was listed as the top threat to the country on paper for the purposes of emergency planning, but it had slipped to the bottom of the government's list of actual concerns. It had been many years since an emerging virus from across the globe had severely impacted on Britain and there was an insular self-confidence – some might say arrogance – that our island nation with its sea borders had the best pandemic plan in the world.

There was no such complacency in China. The Communist-controlled country had experienced a tragically painful wake-up call 17 years earlier. The 2002 Severe Acute Respiratory Syndrome (Sars) pandemic had infected 5,300 people in China and killed 349 after first surfacing in the wild-animal markets in the south of the country. Sars was a coronavirus – from a group of viruses that look like they have a crown (corona) when viewed under a microscope because of the spikes protruding from their surface. Before Covid-19 appeared in 2019 there were six types of coronavirus known to infect humans, but mostly they caused mild respiratory symptoms with the exception of the Middle East Respiratory Syndrome in 2012 and Sars, which were both killers.

Covid-19 is from the same evolutionary branch as Sars, which is why the virus causing the disease is named Sars-CoV-2. The original Sars virus – or Sars-CoV-1 as it is now officially called – is thought to have been passed to humans by masked palm civets, which are eaten in China as a delicacy. The animal's flesh in combination with snake meat are the main ingredients of an exotic wildlife dish called 'dragon-tiger-phoenix soup', which is flavoured with chrysanthemum petals and sells at expensive restaurants in Guangdong province, southern China. Sars, first emerged in Foshan, a city south-west of Guangzhou in Guangdong province, in the middle of November 2002. It went on to reach 29 countries across the world and caused a major outbreak far away in Toronto, Canada. There were four suspected cases in the UK. By the time the virus fizzled out in 2004, it had infected 8,096 people in 29 countries and killed 774.

The Chinese authorities did not cover themselves in glory when the virus was first discovered. There were several reports about a 'strange disease' made by regional health officials to the central government over the following months, but there was a blanket of secrecy placed over the news. The authorities are alleged to have ordered doctors to downplay the scale of the epidemic to a team from the World Health Organization (WHO). At one stage, 30 patients with the virus are claimed to have been driven around Beijing in ambulances while another 40 were moved out of a hospital into a hotel in order to hide their existence from WHO scientists.[1] The WHO would not be officially informed about the outbreak until the beginning of April 2003 – five months after its emergence. Stung by criticism that it had allowed the virus to flourish, the Chinese government beefed up public health surveillance by increasing its network of centres for disease control and laboratory systems.

One of the main challenges for the scientists was to hunt down the original source of the Sars virus to try to prevent such an outbreak happening again. In 2004 this task fell on the slim shoulders of a 39-year-old virologist called Dr Shi Zhengli, who would later earn the nickname 'Bat Woman'. Her work would be inextricably linked to the discovery of the Covid-19 virus, which was, in effect, a new supercharged and much more lethal version of Sars. Courageous and dedicated, she has provided the biggest leads so far to one of the most pressing questions facing humankind today: where and how did our current pandemic come into existence? And yet, Shi's research has also sparked great controversy because of the secrets she and her colleagues have kept back from the world.

As a young student Shi had taken a degree in hereditary biology at Wuhan University in the central Chinese city of that name. She was hired by the city's virology institute in the early 1990s and went on to gain a doctorate from the Montpellier II University in France. Following the Sars outbreak, Shi took a leading role in the virology institute's investigation into the theory that the virus may have originated in one of south China's many bat caves. The Sars virus might have passed from a bat to a civet to humans, according to the theory. Shi was dispatched to the subtropical south of China along with an international team to see whether they could find any evidence to support this hypothesis. Later, in the course of this work, she would find the best clue to the origins of the Covid-19 pandemic – years before it began.

When the Wuhan Institute's south China work on Sars began in 2004, there was developing research that would link bats to many viruses that affected humans, including the world's most deadly, Ebola, which took its name from the river in the Democratic Republic of Congo where it was found. These types of viruses were usually transmitted via an intermediary animal. The Hendra virus that broke out in Australia in 1994 and the Nipah virus that first hit Malaysia in 1998 were both shown to have originated in bats. The Hendra virus – which was relatively rare, killing only four people – had passed from bats to horses to humans. The Nipah virus spread widely through South East Asia and had caused hundreds of fatalities after being passed on to humans by pigs, which had probably caught it from bats. Four different species of bat had been found to be carrying Sars-like viruses by 2004.

Bats are the second most common order of mammal in the world after rodents and are known to carry a diverse range of viruses that spread quickly in their crowded cave habitats, where they mingle with other animals. The caves are breeding grounds for viruses that can pass from species to species and mutate into hundreds of new forms that might randomly become infectious to humans. As bats can contract more than one strain at a time, they become mammalian blenders for viruses. As the only flying mammal, they are also ideal hosts to disperse diseases far beyond the caves where they are incubated.

In an interview with *Scientific American* magazine, Shi described how the team scoured the mountainous terrain of Guangxi autonomous region, on China's border with Vietnam, seeking out bat caves. When they found bats, they placed a net across the entrance to the cave at dusk and captured the animals as they flew out to find food. Faecal samples were then taken from the bats and sent back in frozen containers to the laboratories in Wuhan for testing. The first eight months of the search proved fruitless and the team were on the brink of giving up. 'Eight months of hard work seemed to have gone down the drain,' Shi told the magazine.[2] 'We thought maybe bats had nothing to do with Sars.' But the breakthrough came when they were given a diagnostic test kit for Sars antibodies in humans that they could use on the bats. These tests were able to determine whether the bats had been infected with the virus at some point in the past – whereas previously they had been forced to rely on discovering an infection in the animal at the very moment they were tested. It therefore significantly increased the scope of the scientists' surveillance programme. The new technique proved a success. Three samples from horseshoe bats were found to have Sars antibodies. 'It was a turning point for the project,' said Shi.

Shi's team then used the antibody test to narrow down the list of locations that her team would target. By 2010 they had decided to concentrate on a cave called Shitou in remote mountains south-west of Yunnan's capital Kunming, on the far eastern edge of the Himalayas. They began a five-year study that would find a strain of coronavirus with similar genetic building blocks to Sars. Evidence gathered there would later be used as clinching proof that Sars began in bats. However, it was while they were conducting this research that they were called upon to investigate an incident in a copper mine 200 miles away. Their findings have major ramifications for the Covid-19 pandemic, but at the time they were hushed up even though three people died from a mysterious pneumonia-type illness with links to bats. It all began with an extraordinary series of admissions to a hospital near to the caves where Shi and her team were searching for the origin of Sars.

The sprawling high-rise buildings of the First Affiliated Hospital tower over the ancient city of Kunming, which is known as 'the city of eternal spring' because its unique climate encourages flowers to bloom all year. On Tuesday 24 April 2012, a 45-year-old man with the surname of Guo was admitted to the hospital's intensive care unit suffering from severe pneumonia. The next day a 42-year-old man with the surname Lv was taken to the hospital with the same life-threatening symptoms, and by Thursday three more cases – Zhou, 63, Liu, 46, and Li, 32 – had joined him in intensive care. A sixth man called Wu, 30, was taken into intensive care the following Wednesday.

All of the men were linked. They were part of a group of 10 miners who had been tasked with clearing out piles of bat faeces in the abandoned copper mine in the hills south of the town of Tongguan in the Mojiang region. Some had worked for two weeks before falling ill, and others just a few days. The illness confounded the doctors. The men had raging fevers of above 39°C, coughs and aching limbs. All but one had severe difficulty breathing.

The first man to die, on 7 May 2012, was Zhou – the oldest of the group. Zhou had been admitted to the hospital 11 days earlier, after working in the mine for a fortnight. Lv, who had been clearing out the mine alongside Zhou, also lost his life to the mystery illness days later. The remaining four men were given a barrage of tests for haemorrhagic fever, dengue fever, Japanese encephalitis and influenza, but they all came back negative. They were also tested to check whether they had the Sars virus, but that also proved negative.

Initially, a respiratory specialist from another hospital suggested that the cause might be an infection from fungus in the mine and the men were treated with antifungal drugs, but the evidence was inconclusive as to whether this was effective. So the doctors sought the opinion of Professor Zhong Nanshan, a British-educated respiratory specialist and a former president of China's medical association who had spearheaded his country's efforts to combat the Sars pandemic nine years earlier. Aware the men might be suffering from another Sars-related coronavirus, he advised they be tested for antibodies against Sars, which would have shown whether the men had previously contracted the virus.

These tests were undertaken on the remaining four of the patients. The doctors also wanted to carry out tests on the bodies of the two dead men, but their families were unwilling to give permission to carry out autopsies. The four tests, however, produced remarkable findings. While none of the men tested positive for Sars itself, all four had antibodies against another, previously unknown Sars-like coronavirus. Furthermore, the two patients who recovered and went home showed greater levels of antibodies to this novel coronavirus than the two who were still patients in hospital at the time of the tests. This led the doctors to conclude that the deaths were likely to have been caused by the coronavirus. By September 2012, three out of six of the miners had died and three were discharged. Two of the men who recovered had spent more than a hundred days in hospital and would still be reporting symptoms resulting from the damage to their lungs more than a year later.

News of this emergence of a potentially deadly Sars-like coronavirus would have rung alarm bells across China if it had been allowed to get out. But there was a news blackout. There is no known contemporaneous reporting in the national or local media of the tragedy in the mine and its aftermath. We have, however, pieced together what little is known about these cases from two pieces of academic research that were produced shortly after the incident. The most detailed is a master's thesis by a young medic at the Kunming Hospital called Li Xu, which we had translated into English. Li Xu's thesis supervisor was Professor Qian Chuanyun, who headed the emergency department that treated the men. The other is a doctoral thesis by a student of the director of the Chinese Centre for Disease Control and Prevention, which was on constant watch for the emergence of a new threatening virus. There has been no official acknowledgement of the incident by the Chinese authorities to date.

Both pieces of research accept that it is difficult to be conclusive as to the actual cause of the miners' illness given the available evidence. But Li Xu's thesis argues that it was most likely to have been a Sars-like coronavirus that the men had caught from a bat while working in the cave. 'This makes the research of the bats in the mine where the six miners worked and later suffered from severe pneumonia caused by an unknown virus a significant research topic,' Li concluded. That research was already underway, led by 'Bat Woman'. It would lead to the discovery of the virus that is now recognised to be the closest known relative of Sars-CoV-2, which caused the pandemic.

Monsoon season had arrived by the time the small team of scientists from the Wuhan Institute of Virology travelled to investigate the mine. They were already familiar with the region as they were in the midst of their five-year research project monitoring the Shitou caves a little over two hundred miles away searching for the origin of Sars. The last leg of their journey by car took them through the fertile lands south of the town of Tongguan where the famous green terraces of the tea plantations flow across the contours of rolling hills, which had been made more verdant by the daily downpours. The team were fully equipped with their best protective equipment, as they were aware that whatever was lurking in the murky crevices of the mine had already claimed three lives.

When the scientists cautiously ventured into the darkness of the mine – dressed from head to toe in white suits, respirator facemasks and thick gloves – they were instantly struck by the repellent stench. Before them was a breeding ground crawling with mutated and as yet undiscovered microorganisms. In its derelict state, the former copper mine had been taken over by a large colony of roosting bats, which mingled with the rats and shrews that scurried along man-made floors made soft underfoot with thick layers of foul-smelling guano. It was the perfect environment for the intermingling of dangerous pathogens that might one day make the leap to human hosts. The scientists set about sampling the animals in the cave.

Between August 2012 and July 2013 they visited the mine four times. Shi led a team of six scientists from the Wuhan Institute, who were aided by researchers from the local Yunnan and Mojiang Centres for Disease Control. The bats were captured in large nets, as was now routine practice for Shi's team. In total they took faecal samples from 276 different bats, which were quickly stored at −80°C in liquid nitrogen and were then dispatched in small freezer containers back to Wuhan where the molecular study work and analysis were conducted in the virology institute's laboratories. The analysis work found that the fetid mine was infested with viruses – especially coronaviruses. Exactly half the bats carried coronaviruses and several were carrying more than one virus at a time – an illustration of just how easy it was for potentially harmful new strains to develop within the bloodstream of a single bat.

The first public mention of the mine was in a scientific paper by Shi and her team three years later in 2016 entitled 'Coexistence of multiple coronaviruses in several bat colonies in an abandoned mineshaft'. The paper reported on the coronaviruses found during the one-year investigation in the mine by her team. One of the most striking things about the paper is that there is not a single mention of the reason that the Wuhan scientists went there in the first place. There was no reference at all to the deaths of the miners. This was puzzling because her team's main work had been to discover the source of Sars – a pneumonia-type illness caused by a coronavirus. Yet the paper ignored the fact that the miners suffered from a pneumonia illness and had been exposed to multiple coronaviruses. This may well have been because there was still a news blackout imposed by the Chinese government over the tragedy. It was certainly very odd.

The paper says that a total of 152 genetic sequences of coronavirus were found in the six species of bats in the mineshaft and two were of the strand that had caused Sars. One of them stood out because it was a 'new strain' of coronavirus, which, while being far from an exact match for Sars, came from the same family as the 2003 killer. The small faecal sample of this new strain had been collected from a *Rhinolophus affinis*, commonly known as a horseshoe bat, during the scientists' last visit to the mine on 24 July 2013. It was listed in the storage vaults as RaBtCoV/4991 – not a catchy name, but this would later become important when the worldwide significance of this virus strain became clear.

It is not known what happened to the mine after the scientists left in 2013. Neither the Chinese authorities nor the Wuhan Institute have ever said what became of it. Were the infected bats allowed to continue breeding viruses in the mine or were they evicted? Was the mine boarded up? These would become important questions. Meanwhile, RaBtCoV/4991 would apparently remain just an interesting discovery in a scientific paper until January 2020, when the Sars-CoV-2 pandemic began in Wuhan – the same city where it was being stored in the virology institute's vaults. It would then be identified as the closest known match in the world to the new killer virus.

Today Wuhan is a modern metropolis – a ubiquitous skyline of concrete. To the casual onlooker it might appear to be like any other city if it wasn't for the distinctive Yellow Crane Tower, a five-storey pagoda that surveys the bustle below from its perch on top of the city's Snake Mountain. Although destroyed 10 times since it was first built in AD 223, the tower is a singular visual reminder of an ancient city with a proud past stretching back more than 3,000 years. Located at the very centre of China, Wuhan grew around an inland port on the banks of the Yangtze, the world's third largest river behind the Nile and the Amazon. The dusty orange waters of the river cleave the city in two as it flows west to east from the Tibetan plateau to the coast at Shanghai.

Wuhan was one of the great engines of China's industrial revolution, kick-starting the country's steel industry and becoming a major manufacturing centre for textiles, machinery and consumer products. But it is also a place of much political symbolism as the birthplace of the Chinese Republic, which was formed after an uprising in its Wuchang district in 1911. The revolution overthrew the Qing dynasty, the country's last imperial rulers, and led finally to the abdication of the six-year-old Puyi, who became known as the 'last' Emperor. When, in 1966, Chairman Mao chose to signal his return as the country's 'Great Helmsman' aged 72, before launching the Cultural Revolution after a year in the shadows, he went to Wuhan to swim in the Yangtze. There is now an annual swim across the river to commemorate the infamous despot's rejuvenation.

Today Wuhan is China's ninth-largest city with a population of 11 million people. It has become the international centre for the study of coronaviruses as a result of the work of the city's virology institute, which is why it is a remarkable fact that Wuhan, of all the places in the world, was where the Covid-19 pandemic began. Could such an extraordinary coincidence be possible or was there another reason?

While Shi had been publishing her 2016 paper on the findings from the mine, a new facility was taking shape on the campus of her virology institute, which is situated on the west side of the Yangtze in Wuhan. The construction of the new facility was being controlled by the People's Liberation Army under strict secrecy because it was to be a top-security laboratory for handling deadly human pathogens. The building was finally finished and opened the following year. There were 31 such laboratories in the world at the time, but this was China's first. The new lab had been certified by the Chinese authorities as fit for containing pathogens that required BSL-4, the highest biosafety level. But it was raising eyebrows internationally. Scientists and biosafety experts were concerned that the closed nature of the Chinese state and the emphasis on hierarchy would prove incompatible with running such a dangerous facility. 'Diversity of viewpoint, flat structures where everyone feels free to speak up and openness of information are important,' Tim Trevan, a consultant in biosecurity, told the scientific journal *Nature* when the lab opened. Some of the cultural concerns about the institute mirror those raised about the management of the Soviet Union's Chernobyl Nuclear Power Plant before the catastrophic accident in 1986, considered to be the worst nuclear disaster in history.

Laboratory leaks are not uncommon. In the past, Ebola and the fatal bat disease Marburg, which kills nine out of ten people infected, have escaped from BSL-4 laboratories in the US. American health authorities recorded 749 laboratory safety breaches in the six years to 2015. Indeed, nine people were infected by Sars in 2004 after safety breaches at China's National Institute of Virology in Beijing. One of them died of the disease.

The need for a secure facility in Wuhan was obvious. Shi and her team had already collected hundreds of samples of the coronavirus – including RaBtCoV/4991 from the mine – in the course of their work on bats across Yunnan province, and they were running high-risk experiments to find out how these pathogens might mutate to become more infectious to humans. Papers released by the Wuhan Institute of Virology between 2015 and 2017 describe how Shi's team combined snippets of different coronaviruses to see if they could be made more transmissible to humans. They called them 'virus infectivity experiments'. This type of 'gain-of-function' work was controversial because it had the potential to turn bat coronaviruses into human pathogens that could cause an outbreak of a deadly disease, or even a pandemic, if they leaked out. In 2014 the US government issued a ban on funding similar scientific experimentation that would make a virus more contagious.

The rationale for the gain-of-function work carried out by Shi's team was that it increased general understanding of how an ordinary coronavirus might one day transform into a killer such as Sars. Others disagreed. 'The debate is whether in fact you learn more by helping to develop vaccines or even drugs by replicating a more virulent virus than currently exists, versus not doing that,' said Deenan Pillay, Professor of Virology at University College London. 'And I think the consensus became that the risk was too much.'

In January 2018 the US Embassy in Beijing took the unusual step of sending scientists with diplomatic status to Wuhan to find out what was going on in the institute's new biosafety laboratories. They met Shi and members of her team. Details of the diplomats' findings have been found in US diplomatic cables that were leaked to the *Washington Post*[3] and other news media. 'Most importantly,' states a cable from 19 January 2018, 'the researchers also showed that various Sars-like coronaviruses can interact with ACE2, the human receptor identified for Sars-coronavirus. This finding strongly suggests that Sars-like coronaviruses from bats can be transmitted to humans to cause Sars-like diseases.' The Americans were evidently worried about safety. 'During interactions with scientists at the Wuhan Institute of Virology laboratory, they noted the new lab has a serious shortage of appropriately trained technicians and investigators needed to safely operate this high-containment laboratory,' the cable added.

Shi and her team at the Wuhan Institute have never explained what happened to the novel coronavirus RaBtCoV/4991 over the years it was stored in the laboratory, but some of the gaps have been filled in by a British scientist who is one of their close collaborators. Manchester-born Peter Daszak had been working alongside Shi's team hunting down viruses in Chinese caves for

15 years as part of his role as president of the New York-based wildlife and conservation charity EcoHealth Alliance. He had first become interested in zoonotic diseases – those that jump from animals to humans – when he studied parasites during his zoology degree at the University of North Wales. Ever since the Sars outbreak of 2002–03 he has been visiting China several times a year to research coronaviruses, and he is a fierce defender of the Wuhan Institute, dismissing all suggestions that Covid-19 could have leaked from a laboratory.

He describes RaBtCoV/4991 as '[from] just one of the 16,000 bats we sampled' in 2013. He said: 'It was a faecal sample; we put it in a tube, put it in liquid nitrogen, took it back to the lab [in Wuhan].' The laboratory team had run the sample through a polymerase chain reaction process to amplify the amount of genetic material so it could be studied, Daszak said. 'We sequenced a short fragment … And we looked at that, and we found that it did have coronaviruses,' he went on. 'But they weren't close to Sars. And we were looking for the 99 per cent match to Sars. And it wasn't that. So we didn't do any more work on it. And it's only after Sars-CoV-2 [the Covid-19 virus] emerged that we found that it was close to Sars-2.'

Other scientists find this indifference to a new strain of a potentially deadly coronavirus hard to believe. Nikolai Petrovsky, Professor of Medicine at Flinders University in Adelaide, South Australia, and secretary-general of the International Immunomics Society, has led a team of researchers studying the virus. He said it was 'simply not credible' that the Wuhan Institute of Virology would have failed to carry out any further analysis on RaBtCoV/4991, especially as it had been linked to the deaths of three miners. 'If you really thought you had a novel virus that had caused an outbreak that killed humans then there is nothing you wouldn't do – given that was their whole reason for being [there] – to get to the bottom of that, even if that meant exhausting the sample and then going back to get more,' he said.

Despite Daszak's assertion that RaBtCoV/4991 was left untouched until early 2020, evidence was uncovered that showed that the Wuhan laboratory may have indeed been working on Covid-19's sister virus in the intervening years. Records held by the United States National Center for Biotechnology Information suggest the Wuhan Institute was mapping the virus's genetic identity between June 2017 and October 2018. The genetic information was uploaded to the public data repository in 2020 after the pandemic had begun, but each of their file names contained the earlier dates. This suggests that the Wuhan laboratory analysed 33 different parts of the virus's genetic sequence during that 15-month period. Indeed in November 2020 the institute eventually bowed to pressure and confirmed that it had sequenced the virus's genome in 2018. This raises the key question: was the Wuhan laboratory conducting any further experimentation on the virus in the run-up to the Covid-19 pandemic? The Wuhan Institute has refused to answer any questions on the subject.

Shi was at a conference in Shanghai in December 2019 when she first heard about the emerging pandemic. She received a call to say there was a new coronavirus on the loose – and it had surfaced in Wuhan, of all places. Since her work had established that such viruses were most likely to originate in south China, she found the news puzzling and extremely worrying. 'I wondered if [the local health authority] got it wrong,' she said in the *Scientific American* interview. 'I had never expected this kind of thing to happen in Wuhan, in central China.' Inevitably, as she prepared to return to immediately analyse the virus, her initial reaction was to jump to the most logical conclusion. Could it 'have come from our lab?' she asked herself.

2
Outbreak and Cover-Up

Sunday 1 December 2019 to Thursday 23 January 2020
UK government's risk assessment: Very low

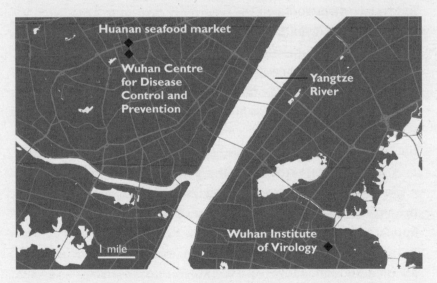

Improbable coincidences do sometimes happen. But if there really is no link between Wuhan being both the place where Covid-19 was first located and also the world centre for the study and storage of such coronaviruses, then it really is an extraordinarily freakish occurrence. It is a two-hour and thousand-mile flight away from the areas in the province of Yunnan in the south-west of China that Shi and her team had identified as the breeding ground for the types of animal viruses that might one day infect humans, and that are considered to have been the likely place of origin for Covid-19. The distance between Wuhan and the caves in Yunnan is similar to that between London and Belgrade, the Serbian capital. And yet of all the 662 cities in China, the first cases emerged in Wuhan. The strongest link between the two areas is the Wuhan Institute of Virology itself. For almost 16 years, teams from the institute led by Shi had been visiting remote caves in Yunnan hunting for coronaviruses carried by bats that might be infectious to humans. They returned with hundreds of samples that were analysed and experimented on in the institute's fast-growing laboratory complex. This has led to serious questions about whether the scientists' well-intentioned work may have inadvertently introduced the Covid-19 virus into their own city. But is that what really happened?

The precise point at which Covid-19 stole into Wuhan and began infecting people may never be known. There have been various academic reports and speculative claims that suggest the virus may have entered the city as early as the summer of 2019, but, while fascinating, they should be taken with a pinch of salt.

A study by Harvard University used satellite images of the car parks in selected Wuhan hospitals to advance an argument that the virus had taken hold in August that year. The car parks appeared busier in the summer and autumn than they had the year before, suggesting that more people were visiting hospitals all of a sudden. However, the study's many detractors have pointed out that several of the photos are taken at different angles and a larger proportion of the cars were obscured by buildings or trees in the later photos. The study backed up its findings by pointing out that there was an increase in online searches for a Chinese term that translates as 'symptoms of diarrhoea' on the popular Chinese internet search engine Baidu between August and December 2019. This was undermined by BBC analysis that found that searches for the single word 'diarrhoea' on its own actually decreased during the same period and it is, anyway, one of the less common symptoms of Covid-19. The most obvious Covid-19 search term, 'cough', had much less traffic during the autumn than it had earlier in the year.[1]

There was also a theory – propagated chiefly in China's government-controlled media – that the virus might have been introduced into the country by foreign athletes competing in the Military World Games in Wuhan during October 2019. Athletes from all over the world descended on the city and many were struck down with a debilitating flu-type illness. They included the French former world champion pentathlete Élodie Clouvel and the Italian Olympic gold medallist fencer Matteo Tagliariol, who were laid low by fever during the Games. Few of the athletes were later tested to find out whether they carried antibodies to Covid-19, but those who were, such as the Swedish team, turned out to have no trace of the virus. Melina Westerberg, a pentathlete, who was one of several Swedish team members who became sick during the games, believes the illness 'was just a coincidence'.[2]

The earliest possible case in Wuhan may have been in late September. Yu Chuanhua, vice president of the Hubei Province Health Statistics and Information Society and an epidemiology professor at Wuhan University, told Chinese media that one man was admitted to hospital in the city on 29 September with Covid-19-like symptoms. It will never be known for certain whether he had the virus, because he died of his illness long before tests for Covid-19 were developed. There were two more suspected early carriers of the virus between 14 and 21 November in the city's 47,000-strong database of cases, but they too are unconfirmed.

The first confirmed case was a 70-year-old man with Alzheimer's disease, whose family had told researchers from Wuhan Jinyintan Hospital that his symptoms had begun on 1 December. This is the point when the virus seems to have taken hold and accelerated. There were about 60 identifiable cases by 20 December, according to government research data reported in the *South China Morning Post*.[3] However, it would not be until a week later that Dr Zhang Jixian, of the Hospital of Integrated Traditional Chinese and Western Medicine in Hubei province, became the first person to report a suspected outbreak to the provincial government.

By then it had already spread as far as Europe, probably via regular flights from Wuhan. The virus may have been in Italy as early as 18 December, as the country's National Institute of Health reported finding traces of Covid-19 in sewage water collected in Milan and Turin on that date. It was certainly in France that month. A 43-year-old fishmonger called Amirouche Hammar was admitted to the Jean-Verdier Hospital in Paris on 27 December. He had pneumonia of unknown cause and was coughing up blood. His samples later revealed the presence of Covid-19. His wife worked at a supermarket used by shoppers leaving Charles de Gaulle airport, where there were direct flights from Wuhan. She suffered only a slight cough that lasted just three days, but Amirouche was admitted to hospital, where he was saved by doctors after going into intensive care. He made a complete recovery.

In Wuhan itself the first cluster of cases included traders and shoppers at the Huanan seafood market, a maze of small trading stores opening on to crowded alleys in the centre of the city. Despite its name, the market also sold meat and vegetables, and there was an exotic wildlife section on its west side. The Chinese authorities acted swiftly and closed down the market on 1 January 2020. Scientists pored over its empty stalls looking for evidence. They took 585 samples, of which 33 tested positive for the new coronavirus – 31 of these being found in the area of the market where wild animals were sold. It seemed like an open-and-shut case. Since the 2002 Sars outbreak was believed to have passed to humans from masked palm civet cats in wildlife markets, it seemed entirely logical that the virus could have entered the city through an animal being sold for its meat. When the outcome of the tests inside the market was released later that month, the Chinese state news agency Xinhua reported: 'The results suggest that the novel coronavirus outbreak is highly relevant to the trading of wild animals.'

However, the picture was far more complicated than it first seemed. An early study published in *The Lancet* in January made clear that of the 41 patients who contracted Covid-19 in Wuhan, only 27 had been 'exposed' to the market. A third of the patients had no connection to the market at all, including the study's 'patient zero', the elderly man with Alzheimer's who fell ill at the beginning of December. Months later, George Gao, the director of the Chinese Centre for Disease Control and Prevention, revealed that all the samples taken from animals at the market had tested negative for the virus. The positive samples had been found in sewage or other environmental sources, which probably meant they had come from humans. The Chinese health authorities began working on a different theory that the market may have helped to disperse the disease among traders and shoppers but concluded it was not where it originated in Wuhan.

It was Monday 30 December 2019 when Shi received the bombshell call on her mobile while she was at the conference in Shanghai. Wang Yanyi, the Wuhan virology institute's director, told her a new pneumonia-causing virus had broken out, which had already been identified as a coronavirus by their colleagues at another of the city's laboratories, the Wuhan Centre for Disease Control and Prevention. 'Drop whatever you are doing and deal with it now,' she recalled the director saying. Shi packed her bags quickly and took the first train back to Wuhan.[4]

By now, concern was growing among staff at the city's hospitals. While Shi rushed back to Wuhan, Dr Li Wenliang, an ophthalmologist at Wuhan Central Hospital, sent a message to medical colleagues in an online chat forum suggesting they wear protective clothing because he had seen several cases of a virus that appeared to be like Sars. His comments were swiftly stamped upon by the Wuhan medical authorities. The Wuhan Municipal Health Commission (WMHC) immediately contacted Li and demanded he sign a letter admitting responsibility for the 'release of false information'.

But as news about the virus was starting to slip out by word of mouth, the Chinese authorities finally decided it was time to tell the world there was potentially a problem. The World Health Organization (WHO) was notified on 31 December that a number of people had been struck down with pneumonia, but the cause was not stated. Alongside the statement, the Wuhan health authority put out a bland public announcement reporting 27 cases of flu-like infection and urged people to seek medical attention if they fell ill. Neither statement indicated that the new illness could be transmitted between humans or that the likely source was already known: a coronavirus.

Indeed, there would be no real openness. The next day Li was summoned to have a serious chat with the authorities, along with seven of his friends. They were warned against 'publishing fictitious discourse related to the confirmation of seven SARS cases at the Huanan fruits and seafood market'. Li was taken in to the police station and forced to sign a letter retracting his claims about a Sars-like virus and was then vilified on the state-run media channel Chinese Central TV (CCTV). Li was allowed to return to work and it was only a matter of days before he picked up a persistent cough, which was the first sign he had unfortunately contracted the virus that he had been warning his colleagues to protect themselves from. Tragically, he died from Covid-19 five weeks later, triggering a furious international outcry. At 34 years old, he was one of the virus's youngest victims at the time he died and a symbol of China's inability to be transparent about the seriousness of the problem enveloping Wuhan. It was clear the virus could not be contained by simply suppressing all talk of it.

In those first two weeks of January, desperate scenes were unfolding at Wuhan hospitals as patients began to flood in. The hospitals were hopelessly ill-prepared and ill-equipped. Medical staff, often in insufficient protective gear, were forced to make life-and-death calls about who they could treat and who they had to turn away. Dr Peng Zhiyong, the director of the intensive care unit in Wuhan University's Zhongnan Hospital, gave an interview to Chinese media outlet Caixin Global describing the horrific scenes. Within four days of the arrival of the first coronavirus patient, he said, all 16 intensive care beds were full and the situation was 'dire'. More than 40 members of his team then contracted the disease from patients. Things were even worse at another of the city's hospitals, where two-thirds of intensive care staff had reportedly been infected. Peng described how the health authorities imposed deliberately 'stringent' criteria that had to be met in order for a case to be diagnosed as coronavirus.[5] 'Very few people would get diagnosed based on those criteria. The head of our hospital told them this multiple times during this period. I know other hospitals were doing the same,' he said. It meant that infected patients were released from hospital, endangering the rest of the community. But it had the desired effect of keeping the official case numbers artificially low.

The doctors fought the epidemic in gruelling conditions. Some wore nappies inside their protective suits to avoid taking breaks during their shifts. Others went without food and drink for 12 hours at a time. Peng said: 'We refrain from eating or drinking during our shift because the gear is no longer protective once we go to the washroom. The gear is thick, airtight and tough on our body.' Few of Peng's colleagues went home after their shifts because of concern about infecting their families. Peng said he frequently broke down in tears when patients had to be turned away from the hospital despite begging for treatment. 'They wailed in front of the hospital,' he said. 'Some patients even knelt down to beg me to accept them. But there was nothing I could do since all beds were occupied. I shed tears while I turned them down. I have run out of tears now.'

* * *

When Shi returned to Wuhan, she immediately checked her laboratory's records to see if any errors, particularly with the disposal of hazardous materials, could have caused a leak from the premises and released the new virus into the city. In her interview with *Scientific American* she claims she was immensely relieved when she says she discovered that the genome sequences for the new virus – which give it a unique identity – were not an exact match with any of the samples her team had brought back from the bat caves. 'That really took a load off my mind,' she said. 'I had not slept a wink for days.'

Shi said she wanted to learn all she could about this mystery coronavirus. Time was short because the virus was spreading rapidly. But in those early days of January, the Chinese scientists did not seek help from international colleagues because the existence of the new coronavirus remained a strict secret. Using a technique to amplify the virus's genetic material, her team swiftly managed to confirm that samples from five patients at the Wuhan Jinyintan Hospital had genetic sequences present in all coronaviruses. These were sent to a team led by Professor Zhang Yongzhen of the Shanghai Public Health Clinical Centre laboratory, which was able to map the virus's full genomic sequence by 5 January. The Shanghai centre then passed its discovery to the country's National Health Commission and urged it to recommend that 'relevant prevention and control measures' be taken in public places because of the severity of the symptoms.

But the veil of secrecy remained. The public release of the genomic sequence to the international scientific community was put on hold, even though it would have been critical to the development of tests for the virus, and no warnings were issued to the Chinese public or the world about its dangers. When the hashtag #WuhanSARS appeared on social media on 6 January, the Chinese authorities immediately censored it. So, Zhang's team in Shanghai took matters into their own hands. On 11 January they shared the genetic code they had sequenced on a

US computer database called GenBank, which is available to scientists around the world. A source close to the team has explained to the *South China Morning Post* that the move was prompted by the urgent need to produce biological test kits, 'especially when a large part of the population [was] moving [across the country] during the Lunar New Year holidays'.[6] As a result, several Chinese companies were able to develop test kits for the virus within a week.

But the release of this information infuriated the Chinese authorities. The day after, the Shanghai Public Health Clinical Centre laboratory was closed for 'rectification' – a term often used for the re-education of employees or institutions after they had incurred the wrath of the Communist leadership. The source from the Shanghai team said: 'The centre was not given any specific reasons why the laboratory was closed for rectification.' By February the team had submitted four requests to the authorities seeking permission to reopen, but received no reply. 'The closure has greatly affected the scientists and their research when they should be racing against the clock to find the means to help put the novel coronavirus outbreak under control,' the source said. The Shanghai Health Commission refused to say what lay behind the decision.

Hours after Zhang's team released the genome sequence, China's National Health Commission was forced to relent and finally announce it would share the critical information with the WHO. It was sent out through Shi's team at the Wuhan Institute of Virology the following day on 12 January. However, it would still be another eight days before China finally admitted on 20 January that there was evidence that the virus was capable of being transmitted between humans. This was vital information that was apparent soon after the coronavirus had been identified at the turn of the year because so many medics in the hospitals were catching it from patients. But it had been recklessly withheld for weeks by the Chinese authorities. If the virus had been transmitted directly from animals in the market, it would have been easy to contain in Wuhan – but human-to-human transmission meant it would inevitably escape the confines of the Chinese city. In other words, the virus could be a global threat. The WHO had simply taken China's earlier claims at face value. On 12 January it endorsed China's claim that there was as yet no proof of human-to-human transmission and passed on the news in a press release on its website. 'The government reports that there is no clear evidence that the virus passes easily from person to person,' it stated. The health body would later be criticised for being so credulous.

By now the overcrowding of the Wuhan hospitals was chronic. It sparked one of the most remarkable construction feats the world has ever seen. Working around the clock, a phalanx of diggers and trucks cleared, dug up and laid a concrete base on a huge area of ground in the Caidian District to the south-west of the city. Then, dozens of cranes moved in to begin positioning hundreds of 10-metre-square prefabricated boxes as if they were children's building blocks. In just 10 days, the new two-storey 1,000-bed Huoshenshan Hospital was completed and staffed with 1,400 medical personnel from the People's Liberation Army. The speeded-up video of the frenzied work on the hospital became a social media sensation. While there was great admiration for the way a state could harness its workers to complete such a project so quickly, it was also sobering. There was obviously a very serious problem – perhaps of a scale not previously witnessed – if such drastic measures were necessary. China's secret was out and there was now enough information to strike fear into the hearts of pandemic planners around the world. This could be the Doomsday virus that experts had been warning about for decades.

Meanwhile, Shi had been writing a scientific paper that described the new coronavirus to the world for the first time. Entitled 'A pneumonia outbreak associated with a new coronavirus of probable bat origin', she submitted it to *Nature*, a respected

British scientific journal, on 20 January and it would later be published on 3 February. The document was ground-breaking. It revealed that the Wuhan Institute of Virology already had in storage the closest known relative of the virus, which it had taken from a bat. The sample was named simply RaTG13. According to the paper, it was a 96.2 per cent match to the new virus and it shared a common lineage with Sars-CoV-2, which was distinct from other Sars-type coronaviruses. In other words, RaTG13 was the biggest lead available as to the origin of Covid-19.

It was therefore highly surprising that the paper gave only scant detail about the history of the virus sample, stating merely that it was taken from a *Rhinolophus affinis* bat in Yunnan province on China's southern border in 2013 – hence the 'Ra' and the '13' in its category name. The researchers would conclude that this close likeness 'provides evidence' that the Covid-19 virus 'may have originated in bats' a thousand miles away in Yunnan. This, of course, raised two simple questions. First, if the Covid-19 virus had originated in a bat in Yunnan, how did it travel all the way to Wuhan without causing a single noticeable outbreak along the way? Second, as the world's only known sample of the closest relative to the Covid-19 virus had clearly been in the possession of the Wuhan laboratory since 2013, could it have had anything to do with the fact that the outbreak started in the city? Shi's paper gave only scant details. There was no further information on where RaTG13 had been found or any detail of the circumstances in which it was collected.

We found this puzzling when we began to look at it while researching an article for *The Sunday Times* on the origins of the virus in early summer 2020. But we spotted a clue. It was in the last letters of RaTG13's name. It turned out that the TG stood for Tongguan, the town nearest the abandoned mine that Shi and her team had tested for coronaviruses after the six miners had been struck by the mystery illness. So, had the closest known relative to Covid-19 come from the mine? If so, it was curious that Shi's paper hadn't mentioned that link, especially as three people had died after picking up what was almost certainly a viral illness there. While we were looking at it, a small band of scientists, academics and enthusiasts from different countries were messaging each other, questioning whether RaTG13 might actually have been the novel coronavirus that Shi had described in her 2016 paper chronicling the results of her team's sampling in the mine. Despite repeated requests Shi and the Wuhan laboratory refused to confirm it for months. However, our research uncovered a series of clues that, when put together, confirmed that the strain that had been labelled RaBtCoV/4991 in the 2016 paper had in fact been renamed. RaBtCoV/4991 and RaTG13 were one and the same. But the renaming had – accidentally or deliberately – obscured the direct link between the closest known relative of Covid-19 and the deaths in the mine. Why were they attempting to hide it?

In our *Sunday Times* article on the origins of the virus in July 2020 we asserted definitively for the first time that RaTG13 was the sample in the mine. The clearest evidence we found was in a database of bat viruses published by the Chinese Academy of Sciences – the parent body of the Wuhan Institute of Virology – which lists RaTG13 and the mine sample as the same entity. It says it was discovered on 24 July 2013, as part of a collection of coronaviruses that were described in the 2016 paper on the abandoned mine. Indeed, researchers in India and Austria have compared the partial genome of the mine sample that was published in the 2016 paper and found it is a 100 per cent match with the same sequence for RaTG13. The same partial sequence for the mine sample is a 98.7 per cent match with the actual Covid-19 virus.

Peter Daszak, a close collaborator with the Wuhan Institute, later confirmed to us that RaTG13 was the sample found in the mine. He claimed there was no significance in the renaming. 'The conspiracy folks are saying there's something suspicious about the change in name, but the world has changed in six years – the coding system has changed,' he said. Daszak confirmed the mine sample had been stored in Wuhan for six years. He said the lab's sample of the virus disintegrated after sequencing the full genome for RaTG13. 'I think they tried to culture it but they were unable to, so that sample, I think, has gone,' he said.

However, Professor Wendy Barclay, head of Imperial College London's infectious disease department and a member of the UK government's Scientific Advisory Group for Emergencies (Sage), was surprised that the virus's link to the mine deaths had not been referred to at all in Shi's January 2020 paper. 'I would expect people to be as clear as they can be about the history of the isolates of their sequencing,' she said. 'Most of us would have reported the entire history of the isolate, [back] to where all that came from, at the time.' This view was shared by the group of scientists and academics debating the issue on social media. They became so exercised about the lack of transparency that they wrote to *Nature* demanding the Wuhan Institute of Virology write an erratum clarifying the sample's provenance. A *Nature* spokesman said in May: 'Concerns relating to this paper have been brought to *Nature*'s attention and are being considered at the moment. We cannot comment further.'

The director of the Wuhan Institute, Wang Yanyi, gave an interview that same month in which she described suggestions that the Covid-19 virus might have leaked from the lab as 'pure fabrication'.[7] She said that the institute managed to sequence the genome of RaTG13 but had not been able to return it to a live virus. 'Thus, there is no possibility of us leaking RaTG13,' she said. Shi briefly referenced RaTG13 in her interview with *Scientific American* a couple of months earlier. She mentions the discovery of a coronavirus that 96 per cent matches the Covid-19 virus, but does not link it to the year-long investigation in the mine. She does, however, separately talk about her team's work in the mine and the fact that several miners had died of a pneumonia-type illness there. She says that there were many coronaviruses found in the mine, with some bats carrying multiple strains, and it would therefore have only been a matter of time before these viruses would have killed other miners if it had not been shut down. Curiously, however, she claims that the miners who actually died had been struck down by a fungus. This claim is not borne out by the two detailed hospital studies on the miners.

Other virology experts believe that it was significant the miners had tested positive for antibodies against a Sars-like virus when they were in hospital in 2012. Professor Martin Hibberd, a professor of emerging infectious diseases at the London School of Hygiene & Tropical Medicine (LSHTM), said the antibodies provided 'a good clue' that the cause of death was 'a proper coronavirus', which was 'most likely' to be Sars-related. '[RaTG13] is so similar to all the other Sars coronaviruses and so I'd imagine all of that family can cause similar disease, so it makes good sense to me that if the miners caught it they would end up with something that looks similar.' Deenan Pillay, Professor of Virology at University College London, said that the antibody test results 'made it more likely that these individuals have come across a virus which may be Sars or look very similar to Sars, in other words, a close Covid-19 relative. And, of course, the data and the clinical picture in terms of lung disease is compatible with having either Sars ... or indeed a close relative of Covid-19.'

Professor Richard Ebright, a US molecular biologist at Rutgers University in New Jersey and a Fellow of America's Infectious Disease Society, is very critical of the Wuhan Institute's failure in 2016 to admit the virus had been linked to Sars-like deaths in the mine. But he is even more scathing about its obfuscation over RaTG13's provenance once the pandemic had begun. 'If there had been a known connection to Sars-like or COVID-like respiratory tract infection that would be of the greatest interest and it would be immediately a question why that wasn't mentioned in the 2016 paper,' he said. 'And in addition, much more important than that, that would make it immediately the case that one would need to entertain the possibility that RaTG13 itself may have been a proximal progenitor to Covid-19 and there was only one place that that virus was located and that was in the Wuhan Institute for Virology.' He added: 'There's the question of why things weren't mentioned in 2016. But a much more pressing, much more urgent, much more obvious question is if there is a possible link between RaTG13 and human infections in 2013, then there's a possible link between RaTG13 and human infections in 2019 and 2020.'

The precise origin of the Sars-CoV-2 virus is one of the most important questions facing humankind today. It may well be that one single infection of a human being somewhere in the world began the spread of a deadly virus to tens of millions of people and resulted in more than a million people losing their lives. So where the virus first infected that person and how the Covid-19 virus managed to initially take a grip in Wuhan are crucial facts that need to be established by the scientific community in the hope that this may one day help to prevent such a mass human catastrophe ever happening again. But the task of searching for the origin of the virus has become bogged down in a minefield of international politics. The aggressive comments by United States president Donald Trump may have jeopardised the possibility of answering these crucial questions. He inflamed tensions early on in the crisis by blaming China for what he has called the 'Kung Flu' and officials only exacerbated this by joking that Sars-CoV-2 was 'Made in China'.

This had made China, its scientists and some of their collaborators abroad even more defensive. Maybe the fear of being wrongly held to blame was the reason for the obfuscation surrounding RaTG13. It is also possible, however, that the secrecy and misdirection surrounding this virus strain is because there is something embarrassing that China wishes to hide. The simple truth is that nobody knows for certain – at this time of writing – where the virus originated. Therefore, nothing should be ruled out. It may be that the virus came from an animal transported to Wuhan. It could also be that it was carried back from one of the coronavirus bat caves by a researcher who was attempting to understand the origin of Sars. There is also the possibility that the virus leaked from a laboratory that was carrying out experiments altering the infectivity of a virus such as RaTG13. All these theories needed to be explored as a matter of urgency and the lack of openness obstructed the quest to discover the truth of the matter.

The least convincing stance taken in the initial months of the virus's spread was adopted by scientists on both sides of the argument who believed they could absolutely rule out some of the possibilities above. During the height of the pandemic, science sometimes became a matter of faith with a disregard for the empiricism that is its foundation. Scientists would claim that it was impossible that the virus could have leaked from a lab or returned to Wuhan through an infected researcher. Yet it is not clear why these theories are deemed less likely than the notion that it entered the city through an infected animal. It could be argued that the infected animal theory is actually far more improbable, given that the virus emerged in Wuhan rather than in the country's south.

One of the loudest voices defending the Wuhan Virology Institute was Daszak, the New York-based Mancunian, who had spent 15 years hunting for viruses alongside the Wuhan Institute's team. He was frequently embroiled in Twitter spats with those who claim that the virus leaked from the Wuhan laboratory. 'The preponderance of evidence on the origin of Covid,' he told us, 'is absolutely crystal clear that this did not originate in the lab.' He argues that this is because there is 'a vast diversity of viruses circulating in rural China, Southeast Asia – one to seven million people getting infected – and this incredible network of movement, high speed rail, good road systems, a wildlife trade that takes people and animals directly connecting into Wuhan's central seafood market'. He says the virus came from a cave in southern China. He claims that the 'best guess right now' is that the virus started within a 'cluster' that includes the area around where RaTG13 was found and the town of Mengla just south of the mineshaft where another bat coronavirus with a 93 per cent likeness to the Covid-19 virus had been discovered in the months after Sars-CoV-2 first emerged. As to how the virus travelled all the way to Wuhan, Daszak says: 'Fair assumption that it spilled into animals in southern China and was then shipped in, via infected people, or animals associated with trade to Wuhan.' But there is a lack of any clear evidence to support his theory at the moment.

In reality, there are other strong possibilities. Professor Hibberd, one of the UK's top experts on emerging infectious diseases, believes Daszak's theory is feasible and the virus may have travelled with an infected animal such as a pangolin, which perhaps passed it on to a human wildlife trader when it was being transported for sale in the market. 'Maybe a young guy moves a pangolin and sold it on and may have had a mild infection but didn't have any disease,' he said. 'It's not impossible for that scenario to happen.' On the other hand, Hibberd believes it is also possible that the virus could have been brought back directly by one of the many scientists who were frequently travelling between the caves and Wuhan. 'If you imagine these researchers who probably did this are students who are probably quite young. It's entirely possible that a researcher might become infected through the study of bats,' he said.

Indeed, the Wuhan Institute was not the only body of scientists from the city who were delving into the virus-laden caves and taking the risk of carrying an infection back with them. On 10 December 2019, as the virus was entering Wuhan, a Chinese state media outlet coincidently published an extraordinary video lionising the bravery of a young researcher called Tian Junhua, who is said to have caught 10,000 bats in studies for the Wuhan Centre for Disease Control and Prevention (WCDCP). Junhua admitted that he knew little about bats when he first started visiting the caves eight years earlier and once had to isolate himself for 14 days after being showered with bat urine while wearing inadequate protective equipment. On another occasion bat blood had spilled on to his hands, but he claims he has never been infected. The young researcher aroused suspicion because one of the offices of the WCDCP is a mere 278 metres from the Huanan seafood market. He has refused to talk publicly about his work since the Covid-19 outbreak, but his friends have firmly denied that he was a 'patient zero' who brought the virus to Wuhan.

The possibility that RaTG13 or a similar virus turned into Sars-CoV-2, and then leaked from the laboratory into the population after infecting, say, one of the scientists at the Wuhan Institute, is an issue that seriously divides the experts. The director of the institute, Wang Yanyi, says it is impossible that a virus could have escaped from the premises and cites the opinion of the Australian virologist Edward Holmes, who believes that RaTG13 would take up to 50 years to evolve the extra 4 per cent that would make it a 100 per cent match with the Covid-19 virus.[8] Hibberd is slightly less conservative and believes it might take less than 20 years to naturally morph into the current pandemic virus. On the face of it, it does appear unlikely that a coronavirus such as RaTG13 could have naturally changed so much in just seven years if these experts are correct about the timing. But their large divergence in opinion suggests that this is not a clear science.

Other experts have pointed out that such arguments about the timing are based on the assumption that the virus develops at a constant rate. The rate at which the virus might have changed has largely been calculated from observations in the months since it was first studied in January 2020. Ebright, the New Jersey-based professor, points out that the virus may not have always progressed at the same speed and sometimes it might have been faster. He accepts that the 'distance' between RaTG13 and the Covid-19 virus could well be in the order of three to five decades, as the other academics suggest. But he cautions that this is 'with the assumption that the rate of evolutionary change has been constant throughout the entire period and equals the rate of evolutionary change of the fully human adapted Sars-CoV-2 in humans, and that is not a valid assumption'. He argues: 'When a virus changes hosts and adapts to a new host, the rate of evolutionary change is much higher. And so, it is possible that RaTG13 – particularly if it entered humans prior to November of 2019 – may have undergone adaptation in humans at a rate that would allow it to give rise to Sars-CoV-2. I think that is a distinct possibility.'

Furthermore, Ebright believes that serious questions should be asked as to whether the Wuhan Institute's work increasing the infectivity of viruses might have created Covid-19 by artificially enhancing the ability of RaTG13 or another coronavirus to become more contagious to humans. A strong opponent of biological weapons, he has also been a long-time critic in the US of 'gain-of-function' experiments in laboratories – especially those that alter the genetic code of viruses to make them, for example, more infectious. Such experiments can be well intentioned because they are designed to help humankind gain a better understanding of how viruses can morph into killers of humans, but they are also hugely dangerous if they ever leak from a laboratory.

Ebright argues: 'It also, of course, is a distinct possibility that work done in the laboratory on RaTG13 may have resulted in artificial in-laboratory adaptation that erased those three to five decades of evolutionary distance.' This is a controversial theory and not one shared by Hibberd. 'Sars-CoV-2 and RaTG13 are not the same virus and I don't think you can easily manipulate one into the other. It just seems exceptionally difficult,' said the London-based professor. Ebright alleges, however, that the work required to create Covid-19 from RaTG13 was 'identical' to work the Wuhan laboratory had done in the past. 'The very same techniques, the very same experimental strategies using RaTG13 as the starting point, would yield a virus essentially identical to Sars-CoV-2.'

The Wuhan virology institute refuses to answer our questions about why the link between Sars-CoV-2's closest known relative and the deaths of the miners was kept secret. A few weeks after our *Sunday Times* article was published revealing proof of the connection, the laboratory did eventually accept that RaTG13 and RaBtCoV/4991 were one and the same. It will not, however, say whether efforts have been made to return to the mine, which is the best clue in the hunt for the origin of Sars-CoV-2. Such obfuscation is extremely hard to understand. It would seem strange that the scientists would not revisit the mine. After all, when they were investigating the origin of Sars they went to caves with the nearest known matches for coronavirus and trawled all over them to see if they could find a near-identical strain. This proved to be a highly successful strategy and therefore would be the obvious way to start investigating the origins of Sars-CoV-2. Unless, of course, the Chinese authorities already knew it had been manufactured in a laboratory.

It was not until November 2020, nine months after the original publication, that an addendum was added to the *Nature* article giving more details about the discovery in the Mojiang mine. The Wuhan Institute revealed that it had kept the blood samples taken from the hospitalised miners and at some point in 2020 had checked them for Sars-CoV-2. The institute claims that the tests came back negative. The addendum says Shi and her team 'suspected' that the miners had been 'infected by an unknown virus' but, inexplicably, it does not say whether any attempt was made to check their stored blood samples for the presence of RaTG13.

* * *

On 23 January 2020 – three days after Shi submitted her paper on RaTG13 to *Nature* – Wuhan became the first city in the world to go into lockdown to combat the new virus. The virus's human cost in the city would eventually be huge, with 4,000 people losing their lives by March, according to official figures. But many people believe those figures to be a major underestimate. Some locals think the true figure should be 10 times as much, based on the numbers of dead bodies that were incinerated in the city each day.

The virus was already well on its way around the world. It would only be another week after the Wuhan lockdown that a Chinese student studying in York and his relative became the first recorded Covid-19 cases in Britain. By then, however, it is almost certain that the virus was already in the country. Since the virus emerged at the beginning of December there had been 901 flights from China to the UK. Of those, 23 flights brought thousands of passengers directly from Wuhan to Heathrow until the route was suspended on 24 January. One of those direct flights had even been allowed to land on the day before the Wuhan lockdown.

The floodgates were open and even in those early days of late January, Britons are thought to have been bringing the virus into the country from Europe. Professor Tim Spector, an epidemiologist at King's College London, who runs the Covid Symptom Study app, reported that he had been contacted by up to 500 people who had returned to the UK over Christmas and January with symptoms. Many of these may have just had some form of flu, but one particular group stands out. A study of the Tyrolean ski resort of Ischgl in Austria has found that 42 per cent of its inhabitants had antibodies, which indicated that they had previously contracted the virus. 'I was interested in the Austrian surveys done in Tyrol because I was quite struck by the stories of all the people that came back from Austrian ski holidays in January, predominantly, feeling ill. It was very convincing because a lot of the stories were the same from different people,' said Spector.

A British IT consultant called Darren Bland, from Maresfield, East Sussex, visited the resort on 15 January and stayed for four days. During his trip, Bland went to the Kitzloch bar, which was known for its lively atmosphere and shoulder-to-shoulder drinking. Many other coronavirus victims would report going to the bar too. 'We visited the Kitzloch and it was rammed, with people singing and dancing on the tables,' Bland told the *Telegraph*.[9] 'People were hot and sweaty from skiing, and waiters were delivering shots to tables in their hundreds. You couldn't have a better home for a virus.' He fell ill the day after returning home on 20 January and may have been one of the first British people to have felt the debilitating effects of this powerful new virus. His symptoms lasted for 10 days and he felt like he was 'wading through treacle'. His wife, two daughters and friends from America and Denmark were all afflicted with the same illness. But they were never tested at the time.

The first British death from coronavirus occurred 10 days later on 30 January, even though it wasn't known at the time and the government did not announce the UK's first fatality until 5 March. But the case of Peter Attwood suggests that the virus had entered the UK much earlier than anyone realised. Attwood, 84, from Chatham, Kent, developed a dry cough on 28 December, which gradually worsened until he was admitted to hospital on 7 January. His daughter Jane Buckland, 46, recalled: 'The doctors did every test under the sun but couldn't figure out what was wrong with him. His blood tests showed a high level of infection but they had no idea what it was. He died on 30 January and the provisional death certificate said it was "heart failure and pneumonia".' The doctors had been mystified by his illness, originally believing he may have died of a lung condition caused by working close to asbestos. But Attwood, who was a retired secretary at a car dealership, had never worked with asbestos. Since possible deaths from asbestosis have to be referred to a coroner, a post-mortem was carried out. During the examination, coronavirus was discovered in his lung tissue and so, in September

2020, the coroner recorded that the cause of his death was 'Covid-19 infection and bronchopneumonia'.

One of the odd aspects about the Attwood case was that he had not left the country in the months before he died, which suggests he must have caught the virus from someone else in Britain. His daughter believes she may have passed the virus to him because she came down with Covid-19-like symptoms even earlier, on 15 December. 'I had all the Covid symptoms – dry cough, fever, aches and pains, diarrhoea – before Christmas, but no one knew what it was,' Buckland told the *Sun* newspaper.[10] 'I went to Christmas parties and was hugging and kissing everyone, even people I didn't know. That's what people do at Christmas.' It is possible that Buckland passed on another virus to her father, who contracted coronavirus elsewhere or after he was admitted to hospital. We will probably never know. But the fact that the virus was found in his lungs in late January does suggest it had spread more widely than was appreciated at the time.

Buckland is highly critical of China's lack of transparency at the beginning of the outbreak, which left her father's doctors in the dark about his illness. 'My father could still be here if we'd known about the threat of this horrible virus earlier. If we'd known we were possibly spreading a deadly virus, things could have been very different. It's no wonder so many people in this country ended up dying from it. My dad was elderly and had an underlying heart condition, so he would have been shielding.' She added: 'If China hadn't lied to the rest of the world and kept this hidden for so long, it could have saved countless lives. Covid has obviously been around for much longer than we know. People have been talking about a cover-up but we don't know the scale of it.'

The cover-up had not worked because the virus was clearly on the move. It was now no longer just China's problem.

PART TWO

SLEEPWALK INTO DISASTER

24 January 2020 to 23 March 2020

3

Wildfire

Friday 24 January 2020 to Wednesday 5 February 2020
UK government's risk assessment: Low

By the fourth Friday of January a silent and stealthy killer was creeping across the world. Passing from person to person and borne on ships and planes, the coronavirus had already left a trail of bodies. The virus had spread from Wuhan to the rest of China and then officially to six countries, but it was certainly in many others, including Britain, as we know from the tragic case of Peter Attwood, who died with the virus in his lungs. Sensing the coming danger, the British government briefly went into wartime mode that day, 24 January, by holding a meeting of Cobra, its national crisis committee.

But it took just an hour that lunchtime for the threat to be brushed aside. Matt Hancock, the puppyish health secretary, bounced out of Whitehall after chairing the meeting and breezily told reporters that the risk to the UK public from the new coronavirus was 'low'. This was despite the publication that day of an alarming study by Chinese doctors in the medical journal *The Lancet*. For the first time, it assessed the lethal potential of the virus and its conclusions suggested it was comparable to the 1918 Spanish flu pandemic, which killed between 17 and 100 million people.

Unusually, Boris Johnson had been absent from the first Cobra meeting. The committee – which includes ministers, intelligence chiefs and military generals – gathers at moments of great peril such as terrorist attacks, natural disasters and other threats to the nation. Cobra is normally chaired by the prime minister, but Johnson decided he was too busy that day to listen to an earnest discussion about a foreign flu bug. He had things to do that he deemed to be more important, such as hosting a Downing Street reception for the Chinese ambassador Liu Xiaoming, as part of the celebrations for the country's Lunar New Year – which doubled as an opportunity to discuss a post-Brexit trade deal. There was an opportunity to steal a quick, jovial, Boris-style photo opportunity as he joined in with the traditional lion dance ritual that was also being held outside the front door of No. 10 Downing Street.

The ceremony started with Johnson prodding the costume lions with a paint brush to stimulate the four senses. The creatures then came to life, rising to 12 foot high, with two male dancers holding the costumes aloft. According to the ritual, the choreography represented the symbolic awakening of the lions, which allowed them to see, smell, eat and hear. The dancers bounced the costume lions back to the ground and shimmied to a drum beat while Johnson swayed from foot to foot on the heels of his black leather shoes. The typically awkward scene ended with Johnson inviting the dancers and the watching members from the Chinese community inside for tea.

Although Johnson had taken so little interest in the virus that he skipped the first important Cobra meeting, the reporters outside had certainly awakened their senses to the key issue of the moment affecting China and the world. When the Chinese ambassador re-emerged from the same door later, he was greeted by a reporter's shouted question: 'Mr Ambassador, are you concerned about the spread of the coronavirus?' Liu replied: 'The Chinese government is very determined to curb this virus. President Xi has already ordered resolute measures to get control of it. We are also working with the international community, with the WHO, with other foreign governments. We think we have put it under control.'

China had been covering up the seriousness of the disease since it began, and the official line was now that the outbreak had been contained. Nothing could have been further from the truth. Whether Johnson asked how China was coping or any other searching questions about the virus of the ambassador during this New Year tea party is not known. Certainly, Johnson's actions over the coming weeks would suggest that the virus was not something he was particularly curious about.

There was, after all, a triumphal mood in Downing Street that day. The years of party infighting and political deadlock that had split the nation in a way rarely witnessed in British history were finally over. Brexit was almost done. The British side of the withdrawal treaty from the European Union was being signed in the late afternoon and Brexit would take place the following week.

It was a personal triumph for Johnson, whose career had been wedded to Brexit ever since he had lent his undoubted charisma and jokey populist appeal to the Leave Campaign four years earlier. Brexit had propelled him into Downing Street and had given him his storming victories in Labour's northern heartland that had proved so decisive in the December general election weeks earlier. That Friday in January, therefore, should have been the defining moment of Johnson's premiership. But this was before the world changed in a way that Johnson did not see coming. In the afternoon his spokesman played down the looming threat of the virus from the East and reassured the nation that the UK was 'well prepared for any new diseases'. The confident, almost nonchalant, attitude displayed that day in January would continue for a lost 38 days.

The prime minister had been sunning himself with his girlfriend in the Caribbean resort of Mustique when China first alerted the World Health Organization on 31 December that several cases of an unusual pneumonia had been recorded in Wuhan. The pair had jetted out on Boxing Day to the millionaires' paradise – an exclusive private island where Princess Margaret used to spend 'X-rated' holidays and the eye-wateringly expensive villas are owned by tycoons and celebrities such as the singers Mick Jagger and Bryan Adams, and the fashion designer Tommy Hilfiger. Towards the end of his stay there was a major ratcheting-up of tensions between the West and Iran as the Islamic country's most powerful military commander, General Qasem Soleimani, was assassinated in an airstrike at Baghdad Airport ordered by the United States president Donald Trump. It prompted three meetings of Britain's Cobra national security committee, but, in a precursor of what was to come, Johnson decided not to cut his holiday short to attend any of them. Instead Mark Sedwill, the cabinet secretary, was left to chair Cobra. Emily Thornberry, the shadow foreign secretary, accused Johnson of 'sunning himself, drinking vodka martinis somewhere else, and not paying attention'. Johnson would not discuss the virus with the health secretary until 7 January, two days after he returned.

Meanwhile, China had claimed the virus could not be transmitted from human to human, which should have been reassuring. But this did not ring true to Britain's public health academics and epidemiologists, who were texting one another, eager for more information, in early January. Was this the virus that the scientific community had feared for years?

Devi Sridhar, Professor of Global Public Health at Edinburgh University, had predicted with extraordinary prescience in a talk two years earlier that a virus might jump species from an animal in China and spread quickly to become a human pandemic. So the news from Wuhan set her on high alert. 'In early January a lot of my global health colleagues and I were kind of discussing, "What's going on?"' she recalled. 'China still hadn't confirmed the virus was human to human. A lot of us were suspecting it was because it was a respiratory pathogen and you wouldn't see the numbers of cases that we were seeing out of China if it was not human to human. So that was disturbing.' By as early as 16 January, the professor was on Twitter calling for swift action to prepare for the virus. 'Been asked by journalists how serious #WuhanPneumonia outbreak is,' she wrote. 'My answer: take it seriously because of cross-border spread (planes means bugs travel far & fast), likely human-to-human transmission and previous outbreaks have taught over-responding is better than delaying action.'

Events were now moving fast. Four hundred miles away in London, on its campus next to the Royal Albert Hall, a team at Imperial College's School of Public Health led by Professor Neil Ferguson produced its first modelling assessment of the impact of the virus. On Friday 17 January its report noted the 'worrying' news that three cases of the virus had been discovered outside China – two in Thailand and one in Japan. While acknowledging many unknowns, researchers calculated that there could already be as many as four thousand cases. The report warned: 'The magnitude of these numbers suggests substantial human-to-human transmission cannot be ruled out. Heightened surveillance, prompt information-sharing and enhanced preparedness are recommended.' At this stage, only 41 cases of illness from the virus had been reported in Wuhan and it was said to have caused just two deaths, which was an astonishing piece of disinformation by the Chinese authorities given the chaos that was taking place in the city's hospitals at that very moment.

The following Wednesday, 22 January, two days before the Cobra meeting, the government convened the first meeting of its Scientific Advisory Group for Emergencies (Sage) to discuss the virus. Chaired by the government's chief scientific adviser, Sir Patrick Vallance, and chief medical officer, Professor Chris Whitty, the committee convenes the top brains who advise the government on serious scientific issues that threaten the UK and its people. The committee had been notoriously secretive over the years for reasons that are difficult to fathom. Science is founded on the principles of openness and transparency, as external independent scrutiny is critically important. Yet the culture of Britain's most important scientific committee was the very opposite. Not only were its discussions held behind closed doors, but even its membership was kept entirely confidential. Vallance claimed this was to prevent 'lobbying and other forms of unwanted influence'. But the logic was hard to comprehend because on that basis the identity of every adviser to the government and decision maker who might be a target for lobbyists should remain secret. It also suggested that Vallance did not believe the Sage members had the backbone to resist being influenced if they were lobbied, which seemed unlikely given their eminence.

It would mean that in the opening weeks of the pandemic the public had no idea whether the committee had the requisite knowledge or the required independence to provide the best advice. The absurdity of the position had already been recognised in 2010 when the inquiry into the swine flu outbreak ruled that there should be transparency about the identity of Sage members. The inquiry's report stated: 'In line with the Code of Practice for Scientific Advisory Committees (SAC), which states that SACs should operate from a presumption of openness, we recommend that SAGE members and their declarations of interest are published once initial membership has been established.' Yet the Conservative government failed to take up the recommendation and continued to protect the committee from scrutiny throughout the following decade. When the government's handling of the crisis later unravelled, the public would become increasingly concerned about the committee's lack of transparency.

More information was emerging about the new coronavirus on the day of the first Sage meeting. Chinese scientists were warning that the virus had an unusually high infectivity rate – known as the R number – of up to 3.0, which meant that each person with the virus would typically infect up to three more people. One of those present at Sage was Imperial College's Ferguson, who was already working on his own estimate – putting infectivity at anything from 2.6 to possibly as high as 3.5 – which he sent to ministers and officials in a report on the day of the Cobra meeting on Friday 24 January. The Spanish flu had an estimated infectivity rate of between 2.0 and 3.0, whereas for most flu outbreaks it is about 1.3. So, Ferguson's finding was a bombshell that should have made people sit up and take notice.

Another alarming fact in the professor's report was that in order to stop the spread of the virus in the UK there needed to be a cut in the transmission rate – direct contact between people – of up to 60 per cent. In layman's terms, it meant a lockdown, a move that would paralyse an economy already facing the risk of a battering from Brexit. At the time such a suggestion was unthinkable to the government and belonged to the world of post-apocalypse movies. But it was an early and cogent warning that this wasn't just any old virus that was about to sweep through Britain.

Ferguson further warned that the Chinese outbreak was far larger than shown in official figures and that 3,300 people a day were flying out of Wuhan, making the spread of the disease highly likely. His report stated: 'Given this evidence for human-to-human transmission, enhancing rapid case detection will be essential if the outbreak is to be controlled.'

The growing trepidation among scientists appears not to have been heard or heeded by policy-makers. The government was relatively relaxed, as Britain had the best pandemic plans in the world, or so they thought. On 23 January, Hancock had told parliament that there had been 571 cases and 17 deaths in China. He said all of the deaths so far had been 'contained to mainland China' but most cases were non-fatal. 'In these cases,' he said, 'most people experience cold and flu-like symptoms and then recover. However, there have been a small number of cases so far where it has proven more serious and fatal.' He added that Professor Whitty did now believe 'there is an increased likelihood that cases may arise in this country'. But Hancock was confident that everything was in hand. 'We are well prepared and well equipped to deal with them,' he said. 'The UK is one of the first countries to have developed a world-leading test for the new coronavirus. The NHS is ready to respond appropriately to any cases that emerge.'

After the 24 January Cobra meeting, the chorus of reassurance was not just from Hancock and the prime minister's spokesman; Whitty was confident too. 'Cobra met today to discuss the situation in Wuhan, China,' said Whitty. 'We have global experts monitoring the situation around the clock and have a strong track record of managing new forms of infectious disease … there are no confirmed cases in the UK to date.'

However, by then the number of cases had jumped to 1,000 worldwide and had caused 41 deaths, mostly in Wuhan. *The Lancet* report that day presented a study of 41 coronavirus patients who had been admitted to hospital in Wuhan, which found that more than half had severe breathing problems, a third required intensive care and six had died. And there was now little doubt that the UK would be hit by the virus. The journal's editor Richard Horton wrote a tweet emphasising the significance of the study and highlighting its finding that an alarmingly high number of people required treatment in intensive care once admitted to hospital. 'The challenge of 2019-nCoV is not only the public health response. It is clinical capacity. A third of patients so far have required admission to ICU [intensive care unit] … Few countries have the clinical capacity to handle this volume of acutely ill patients. Yet no discussion.' He would later say it was a 'national scandal' that this dire information had not been acted on immediately. 'We knew in the last week of January that this was coming. The message from China was absolutely clear that a new virus with pandemic potential was hitting cities. People were being admitted to hospital, admitted to intensive care units and dying and the mortality was growing … We could have acted. [We had] time when we could have ramped up testing, time when we could have got personal protective equipment ready and disseminated. We didn't do it.'

Other scientists were also starting to see the writing on the wall for the UK. Among those expressing concern was Sir Jeremy Farrar, the director of the Wellcome Trust, who was also a member of the government's Sage committee. He said: 'This virus has crossed from animals into people. That does not happen often, and it is, without doubt, very serious. People are scarred by the memory of Sars, and a global outbreak of a novel respiratory virus like this is something experts have warned about for many years.' He was joined by Martin Hibberd, Professor of Emerging Infectious Diseases at the London School of Hygiene & Tropical Medicine, who said it was vital that new evidence should be rapidly obtained over the next few days if the world was to be as prepared as possible. 'I think all of the comments made on the 24 January … reflected the need to prepare as much as possible for this new virus,' he said later. 'While we were still seeking to learn what its full impact might be, we also expected our preparedness plans to be in place and in action, so that we could remain in control of this outbreak as much as possible. This was certainly done by other governments at the time, such as Singapore. We should not be caught unaware, even if we were unsure of the true severity.' Professor Graham Medley, a member of Sage and the chair of the government's influenza pandemic modelling group, Spi-M, would later tell Channel 4's *Dispatches* programme: 'This was obviously going to be the pandemic that we had all been thinking about and talking about. The pandemic that was the basis of the film *Contagion*. This was going to kill an awful lot of people very quickly in the United Kingdom, and indeed everywhere.'

But little was being done to prevent the virus coming from China. This was despite concerns in some quarters of the government about the large numbers of Chinese students returning to Britain after celebrating Chinese New Year on Saturday 25 January with their families. In fact, Professor Paul Cosford, medical director at Public Health England, has since conceded that he would 'not be surprised' if people had come back from China to the UK with the virus. Some countries like Italy would introduce temperature testing at airports and others would ban all flights from China or introduce quarantines. Yet the British government was unwilling to introduce such policies. It was argued that the policies would be 'symbolic gestures' because the virus's incubation period of up to fourteen days would mean that many people would pass through airports while carrying the infection without realising it, because they were not yet displaying symptoms. Instead, information leaflets were produced that were passed to anyone flying to Britain from affected regions telling them to call 111 if they developed symptoms.

A study by Southampton University has shown that 190,000 people flew into the UK from Wuhan and other high-risk Chinese cities between January and March and were allowed to travel across Britain at will. The researchers estimated that up to 1,900 of these passengers would have been infected with the coronavirus – guaranteeing the UK would become a centre of the subsequent pandemic.

Sure enough, five days after the Cobra meeting, on Wednesday 29 January, the first coronavirus cases on British soil were found when two Chinese nationals from the same family fell ill at a hotel in York. That same day, the second emergency Cobra meeting on the virus was held in the cabinet meeting rooms at the back of Downing Street. Again, Johnson was absent even though he was certainly in Westminster that day, appearing at Prime Minister's Questions and declaring he was having a day of ministerial meetings – though apparently not the Cobra one. In the morning, he had also found the time to tweet a jokey video of himself answering questions, such as 'Is Boris Johnson for or against Brexit?' to promote the fact that Britain would be officially leaving the European Union in two days' time. He once again left the responsibility for chairing Cobra to Hancock, a politician who would become an increasingly familiar figure on the nation's television screens as the year wore on.

So who was the man who would find himself in charge of Britain's National Health Service at its hour of greatest need and upon whose narrow shoulders Johnson had placed the burden of tackling the virus in the early days? Matthew John David Hancock, aged 41 at the time of the crisis, was ambitious from an early age. He was brought up in Farndon, Cheshire, in a wealthy family that ran a software business and paid for his private education at the King's School in Chester. A little like Johnson, there was no shortage of confidence. He is said to have announced his desire to become prime minister aged just 10 years old. Academically bright, he took the classic modern politician's route to the top when he was accepted into Oxford University to study Politics, Philosophy and Economics – or PPE, an acronym that would take on a different and more painful meaning for Hancock in the opening weeks of the pandemic. He received a first-class degree.

He became a Conservative activist aged 21. While campaigning for the party in Guilford, Surrey, during the 2001 general election a couple of years later, he committed the first of many gaffes that would blight his career, while not hindering its progress. He managed to send out 50,000 election pamphlets supporting Tory Nick St Aubyn with the confusing message that the candidate wanted to '*untie* the community'.[1] He had meant to write 'unite' but he suffers from dyslexia – a disability he says he has drawn strength from over the years. St Aubyn lost the seat by 538 votes.

In 2005 he was offered the chance to join the Conservative Party's economics team by George Osborne, the then shadow chancellor, after they met at a drinks reception in London, and he later rose to become the future chancellor's chief of staff. He was given the safe Conservative seat of West Suffolk in the 2010 election and became a member of parliament at the relatively tender age of 31. Seen as a rising star with the chancellor's patronage, he was soon promoted to various junior ministerial roles by David Cameron.

As minister of state for energy from 2014 he managed to put his foot in it again – several times. After claiming that protection of the environment was a core principle of conservatism, he returned from a climate change conference in a hired private plane[2] and accepted £18,000 in donations from a key backer of one of the UK's leading climate-change-denial organisations. Climate campaigners rounded on him.[3] In October that year he managed to retweet a poem suggesting the Labour Party was 'full of queers'. He later apologised, insisting it had been a 'total accident'.

In 2017, as minister in the Department for Digital, Culture, Media and Sport, he made an extraordinarily bold promise. He announced that he would ensure that '100 per cent of the UK' would have access to 'fast and reliable broadband by 2020'. In a way, this would become his trademark political gambit during the pandemic: you make a big, seemingly impossible, promise and attach it to a future date, thereby muffling your critics. But while Hancock's broadband proposal might be now forgotten by the millions still struggling with slow and unreliable internet connections, the pandemic pledges would unravel under intense media scrutiny.

Later that year, Hancock's challenging relationship with tech projects continued when he became the first MP to launch his own smartphone app. Entitled the 'Matt Hancock app', it was designed to communicate with constituents, but it was described as 'a fascinating comedy of errors', with privacy campaigners claiming it could collect users' photographs even if they had refused access.[4] One data expert pointed out the irony of a minister of a department responsible for data privacy launching an app that had questionable compliance with privacy law.

But Hancock was still a man on the way up and in July 2018, at the age of 39, he became health secretary – the biggest job of his career and the latest stepping stone towards his childhood dream of reaching the very summit of British politics. He would soon, though, face a key test. When he was appointed to the position, a growing scandal was unfolding in his constituency's local hospital.

There was emerging evidence that executives at the West Suffolk Hospital in Bury St Edmunds were covering up catastrophic medical blunders that were causing serious patient harm. They had placed one of the hospital's most senior consultants under disciplinary investigation after she had voiced concerns about mistakes that had killed a healthy 47-year-old engineer and left an ex-headmaster with an MBE brain damaged and blind. The executives had even paid an expert to examine the consultant's handwriting and attempted to force her to be fingerprinted after a whistle-blower had written an anonymous letter to a bereaved family warning that their loved one may have died due to clinical negligence. The atmosphere in the hospital became so toxic that some medics said they had become suicidal, likening the repressive culture to North Korea.

In early 2019 Hancock was made aware of the allegations that doctors who were trying to speak out were being bullied. Around the same time, *The Sunday Times* was also alerted to the story and we began investigating. We found that, for months, Hancock had failed to respond to repeated appeals for help, including from the consultant herself. This was despite the health secretary having gone on record saying that whistle-blowers in the National Health Service should be protected. Only after the story broke – as the coronavirus was beginning to spread across the world – did Hancock relent to the growing pressure and order an inquiry in early 2020. It raised questions over whether he really believed in protecting whistle-blowers in the NHS or whether such policies were just convenient soundbites for a politician on the rise. It also raised concerns about his ability to hear and heed warnings when a major crisis was on the horizon.

But he had other things on his mind that year, which he perhaps deemed more important. In the Brexit referendum, Hancock had voted to remain and he was a staunch supporter of Theresa May after she became prime minister in 2016. It had done his career no harm. But when May resigned in May 2019, it was time for Hancock to release his naked ambition and go for the top job. Lined up against him was Johnson, the clear favourite in the Conservative leadership contest. Hancock had to find a way to stand out against Johnson, who was cruising to victory, and his opportunity came over his rivals' refusal to rule out proroguing parliament – effectively shutting it down for a period – to end the Brexit paralysis.

It was shortly after the 75th anniversary of the Second World War D-Day landings on 6 June, and Hancock was withering: 'There's this idea from some people that to deliver Brexit we should suspend our parliamentary democracy. That we should prorogue parliament. But that goes against everything that those men who waded on to those beaches fought and died for. And I will not have it!' He even wrote to all of the other leadership candidates, including Johnson, challenging them to say they would not prorogue parliament. He declared: 'England is the mother of all parliaments – respected as such around the free world. To suspend parliament explicitly to pursue a course of action against its wishes is not a serious policy of a prime minister in the twenty-first century.'

These were fine and principled words, but they didn't get him very far. He was knocked out in the first round of the leadership contest after securing only 20 votes, and his only real choice then, as a career-focused man, was to back the eventual winner. So, he vociferously endorsed Johnson's campaign. His reward came when Johnson became the party leader and prime minister, and kept him in the cabinet as health secretary. But this put Hancock into a difficult corner that would have made even the most hardened politicians cringe with embarrassment – because Johnson was determined to press ahead with his plans to prorogue parliament in order to deliver Brexit. When Johnson's intention was announced, Tom Peck, a political sketch writer for the *Independent*, tweeted a link to Hancock's post-D-Day speech and wrote: 'I for one will be very sad to see @MattHancock have to resign, now the Prime Minister has disrespected the war dead in this way.'

The idea of resigning could not have been further from Hancock's mind. With the dexterity of an escapologist twisting himself out of locked chains, he declared his wholehearted support for Johnson's suspension of parliament and gave his reasons for it. He declared that the Brexit debate – in what he previously had called 'the mother of all parliaments' – had been a waste of time. Parliament 'hasn't got us anywhere' he now argued. There was an important distinction, he said. He had opposed a longer prorogation of parliament from July to November, but a shorter one was fine. The letter he had sent to his colleagues while he was standing as a candidate in June made no mention of the length of the prorogation. In fact, it made a simpler point: 'A policy on Brexit to prorogue parliament would mean the end of the Conservative Party as a serious party of government.'

In the end the Supreme Court disagreed with Hancock's new position and Johnson's prorogation plans were ruled unlawful. But the episode did little for Hancock's reputation as a politician with integrity. *The Spectator* editor Fraser Nelson noted that Hancock's critics saw him as a 'sycophant who crawls up to anyone who is in power'. It certainly suggested Hancock was a flexible politician whose adaptable principles were carefully attuned to his own survival. Those powers would be tested like never before once the pandemic struck.

* * *

The Cobra meeting chaired by Hancock on Wednesday 29 January was beginning to recognise the seriousness of the events unfolding in China, but still did not quite appreciate the scale of the coming storm that would eventually reach the UK's shores. The official death toll in China from the virus went up to 170 that week and confirmed infections reached 7,700. Given the rapid spread of the disease, Cobra laid plans to fly British citizens out of Wuhan and into RAF Brize Norton in Oxfordshire. Before getting on the plane passengers would have to sign a contract agreeing to accept a 14-day quarantine, which would be spent in hospital accommodation on Merseyside.

The following day the WHO declared the coronavirus threat to be a global public health emergency because of the spread of the virus outside of China. It was an 'unprecedented outbreak', according to a statement from the WHO, but the health body still continued to express confidence in 'China's capacity to control the outbreak'. This was surprisingly optimistic as the virus had already broken out from China and was now far beyond its borders. There had been eight cases of human-to-human transmission in Germany, Japan, Vietnam and the US, and this was undoubtedly only the tip of the iceberg, because these were only the known cases. Tedros Adhanom Ghebreyesus, a former Ethiopian health minister and the director-general of the WHO, would be accused of being too close to China, having been elected in 2017 with its active support. That month he had been happy to repeat China's reassurances that there was little to worry about. In particular, when Italy and then the United States moved to ban flights from Wuhan, Tedros inexplicably cautioned that this would 'have the effect of increasing fear and stigma, with little public health benefit'. The Japanese deputy prime minister Tarō Asō – angered by the postponement of the 2020 Tokyo Olympics until the following year – would later complain that the WHO should be renamed the 'Chinese Health Organization', such was its readiness to play down the crisis. Donald Trump would also suspend the United States' financial contribution to the organisation over the same issue. Tedros's biggest concern at the time was 'the potential for the virus to spread to countries with weaker health systems, and which are ill-prepared to deal with it'.

The UK complacently believed itself to have the best contingency plans in the world to tackle a pandemic and felt there was no need to panic. On Thursday 30 January the government announced the threat level would be increased – but only from 'low' to 'moderate'. There was, however, good reason for the government's top scientific advisers to feel major unease about the virus. Scientists at the London School of Hygiene & Tropical Medicine had confirmed to Whitty in a private meeting of the government's New and Emerging Respiratory Virus Threats Advisory Group (Nervtag) – the body that informs Sage and ultimately Cobra – that the virus's infectivity could be as bad as Ferguson's worst estimate several days earlier, which indicated a reproductive rate of 3.5.

The responsibility for the virus continued to be delegated to Hancock despite the gravity of the problem, and he was now holding daily meetings to receive progress reports. According to the Department of Health, some initial orders were made at the very end of January for personal protective equipment (PPE) under 'just-in-time' contracts, which were supposed to fill the gaps in times of emergency. These contracts instantly ran into difficulties because the key Chinese suppliers were now prioritising meeting the demand generated by their own country's outbreak. Mostly these were days of drift and meetings. The machinery of government was not fully engaged because, at the top, Downing Street was distracted and saw the virus as a problem that had been blown out of all proportion to the threat.

Friday 31 January was, after all, the big day: Brexit day. It was the official parting from the European Union, which should have happened 10 months earlier on 29 March, but was prevented by a parliamentary stalemate that was only ended by the Conservatives' landslide victory in the December general election. With the government enjoying an 80-seat majority, the opposition fell away and the Brexit bill had breezed through parliament in the first three weeks of January. So, while coronavirus infections in China jumped by 25 per cent in just one day that Friday, Johnson was thinking about his place in history and celebrating with his team in Downing Street. Outside, a neon clock was projected onto the building's wall, counting down to 11 p.m. and the end of 47 years in the European Union. Johnson grabbed a gong and banged it with great gusto at 11 p.m. 'There are very few moments in our lives that really can be called an historic turning point, and this is it,' he told his guests, who included Hancock, his chief adviser Dominic Cummings, trade secretary Liz Truss and the chancellor Sajid Javid. Turning to Cummings, he said: 'It was he, I seem to remember, who came up with the famous phrase that we should "take back control". It was also Dom that came up with the other three-word epigram, that the policy of the government should be to "get Brexit done". And I want you to remember that you were here tonight, after 11 o'clock, when finally, we got Brexit done.' Some of those in the room were in tears. As loyal as ever, Johnson's girlfriend Carrie Symonds took the opportunity to tweet a photo of their Jack Russell cross dog Dilyn wearing a Union Jack coat.

Meanwhile, the crisis that would soon derail the Brexiteer promise of a bright new dynamic dawn was deepening by the day. More detail was emerging on Sunday 2 February about the first known cases in Britain. The York university student from China had been staying in a city centre hotel with his mother, which was where they fell ill on the Wednesday night, and they were being cared for in a special NHS isolation unit in Newcastle. Public Health England (PHE) said anyone who had spent more than 15 minutes within six feet of either patient would receive advice. Health officials were also trying to track down 438 travellers from Wuhan who had entered the country and were still within the incubation period for the virus. More than a third of the 1,561 passengers and crew who arrived before the city was quarantined 10 days earlier were unaccounted for. At the same time, there were further urgent attempts that weekend by the Foreign Office to airlift as many British nationals from Wuhan as possible. The urgency of the situation was clear as cases in China jumped by 50 per cent over the first weekend of February to 14,380, while deaths climbed to 300. A 44-year-old man in the Philippines became the first known person to die from the virus outside China after returning from a trip to Wuhan.

It was against this backdrop that, on the Monday morning, Johnson travelled across London to the Old Royal Naval College in Greenwich to give his first big Brexit speech after signing the treaty. There is a reference to this speech in the prologue to this book, but it is worth repeating the important passage as it reveals much about the prime minister's views on the growing virus crisis at that time, 3 February. The speech was full of optimism that Brexit would herald a new era for Britain as a trading nation, but he warned that there were some obstacles that had to be overcome. In particular, it was important to be on our guard against developing international trade barriers and protectionism, he argued.

'When barriers are going up,' Johnson told the audience, 'and when there is a risk that new diseases such as coronavirus will trigger a panic and a desire for market segregation that go beyond what is medically rational to the point of doing real and unnecessary economic damage. Then at that moment humanity needs some government somewhere that is willing at least to make the case powerfully for freedom of exchange, some country ready to take off its Clark Kent spectacles and leap into the phone booth and emerge with its cloak flowing as the supercharged champion, of the right of the populations of the earth to buy and sell freely among each other. And here in Greenwich in the first week of February 2020, I can tell you in all humility that the UK is ready for that role.'

These words go a long way to explaining Britain's nonchalant approach to tackling the virus in those early weeks and why Johnson had been happy to delegate so much to Hancock. He did not see the virus as a serious problem despite the repeated warnings from the scientific community and the rapid increase in cases within China, which had not been contained and were now spreading around the world. It would cost his country dearly.

Johnson's *laissez-faire* stance was perhaps not entirely surprising. While London mayor, he gave a speech to the press gallery annual lunch in 2011 announcing his admiration for an unlikely fictional character: Larry Vaughn, mayor of Amity Island in the 1975 Steven Spielberg film *Jaws*. In the film, Vaughn places holidaymakers' lives in jeopardy by refusing to close down the beach after a shark attack because he wants to maintain tourism and the local economy. Johnson told the press gallery that the real hero of *Jaws* is the mayor. 'He kept the beaches open … I don't know what happened to his political career thereafter, but he did the right thing,' he said.

The comment suggests that Johnson believed it was worth risking lives to protect the economy and prevent infringements of civil liberties. He would later attempt to wriggle out of the remarks when the pandemic struck. 'The mayor of Amity was only dealing with one shark that had attacked one or two of his constituents. The situation we face now is that there are greater numbers of sharks,' he tried to explain.[5] But his words explain his thinking in the opening weeks of the outbreak and why he might have an antipathy towards any measures to contain the virus that would threaten trade or limit people's freedoms.

In the afternoon following Johnson's Greenwich speech, the mood in the Commons was becoming increasingly serious. 'The epidemic has grown at a pace quite unprecedented in recent history, with the official case count more than tripling in the past week,' warned Labour's shadow health spokesman Jon Ashworth; 'this is a time of considerable strain on the NHS.

How many specialist beds are available across the system to deal with more cases of coronavirus should we need them?' He went on to ask pointedly: 'What plans are in place to ensure that NHS staff are protected over the coming months – because, as he rightly says, this is a marathon, not a sprint?'

Hancock replied: 'In the case that the epidemic here gets much more serious, we have 50 highly specialist beds, and a further 500 beds are available in order to isolate people, but of course, we are working on further plans should there need to be more.' His answer was telling, not only because it showed the small scale of the government's contingency for a pandemic but also because he completely neglected to respond to the Labour MP's question about protecting NHS workers.

By now the scientific advisers on the Sage committee were privately warning the government that the numbers of recorded cases in China were probably a substantial underestimate. They heard evidence in the committee that there could be as many as 200,000 to 300,000 infections across the country, with the total number of cases doubling every four or five days. They were already seeing trends – which were later borne out – suggesting that children were barely affected and most of the deaths were of people above 60 years old. The scientists believed that the case death rate was lower than the 2003 Sars outbreak, which killed around 7 per cent of all those infected, but this was hardly reassuring. The virus was clearly much more infectious than Sars, which had only spread to 8,098 people worldwide. The Sage meeting of Tuesday 4 February advised 'caution' in communicating the fatality rate to the public as it was 'complex'.

There was no doubt that the situation was grave and that the virus was moving at a pace that appeared unstoppable. Nonetheless, the next day Johnson was still missing when Cobra, the key national emergency committee, met to discuss the response to the crisis for a third time. There was no obvious reason for his absence as he was again in Westminster that day holding meetings with ministers and sparring with Jeremy Corbyn, the Labour leader, during Prime Minister's Questions in the Commons. That afternoon he attended a video-linked Facebook Live event with members of the public, which took place in Downing Street just metres away from the Cobra summit rooms. It was a chance for Johnson to rattle on about Queen Elizabeth I and Shakespeare, whose portraits lined the walls around him in the Pillared Room. Shakespeare was one of Johnson's particular preoccupations at the time, as he was in the process of finishing a book about the great English playwright. Having delivered Brexit it was now time to take his foot off the pedal and cruise a bit until his February holiday.

Johnson would also miss the next two Cobra meetings on the virus. It would not be until 2 March – which was another five weeks away – that he would attend a meeting of one of the emergency meetings on Covid-19. It is highly irregular for a prime minister to miss consecutive Cobra meetings. An analysis of more than 40 Cobra meetings on major emergencies in the decade since the Conservatives came to power shows that the prime minister has almost always chaired the high-priority meetings unless they were too far away from London to get to the committee on time. In fact, according to the analysis, there were only three occasions in the last 10 years when a prime minister, who had been in Westminster, had skipped a Cobra meeting. Two occurred in March 2018 when Amber Rudd, the then home secretary, chaired two Cobras on the Salisbury Novichok poisonings instead of the then prime minister Theresa May. But May was already taking personal charge of the crisis by chairing two meetings of the National Security Council on the poisoning that same week. The other instance was when a huge volcanic ash cloud from Iceland drifted towards UK airspace in May 2011 and threatened to cause travel chaos. Philip Hammond, the transport secretary, chaired a Cobra meeting on the crisis, but the prime minister, David Cameron, had an obvious excuse for his absence. He was busy hosting Barack

Obama on only the second ever UK state visit by a US president.[6] On each of those three occasions, the prime minister in question had clear and justifiable reasons for not attending.

When we revealed in *The Sunday Times* in April that Johnson had missed all of the first five Cobra meetings, the government spin machine lurched into action. In an extraordinary 14-page error-strewn 'blog', the government's new Covid 'disinformation' unit claimed that 'it is entirely normal and proper for [Cobra] to be chaired by the relevant Secretary of State', who in this case was Hancock. It argued that it was acceptable for Johnson to miss the first two Cobra meetings in January because, at that time, the WHO 'had not declared Covid-19 a "Public Health Emergency of International Concern", and only did so on 30 January'. That did not account for the other three absences in February.

Indeed, the government's former chief scientific adviser David King told Sky News that during the Blair and Brown premierships he couldn't remember a single Cobra meeting 'when the prime minister wasn't in the chair'. King was backed by Jonathan Powell, Tony Blair's chief of staff for the 10 years when he was prime minister, who said: 'If the government was really firing on all cylinders and getting on with it and taking it really seriously then you expect the Prime Minister to be there ... to miss five in a row at the beginning of this real crisis is a sign of how they underestimated it at the beginning.' Powell could certainly not recall Blair missing a Cobra meeting when he was actually in Westminster.

Lord Kerslake, the head of the civil service between 2012 and 2014, said that the prime minister during his time, Cameron, typically chaired three-quarters of the Cobra meetings and the main reason for non-attendance was that they were away from London. He said: '[Cobra] is there for a national emergency and you don't call it unless there's something pretty serious. And if there's something pretty serious, you would expect the prime minister to chair it.'

In an attempt to prove its point, the government's blog gave three examples of previous occasions when the prime minister had not chaired Cobra. Michael Gove, the Chancellor of the Duchy of Lancaster, was claimed to have chaired Cobra during the summer of 2019 as part of the preparations for a possible no-deal Brexit. However, this appears to have been a new Brexit daily operations committee – codenamed XO – which met regularly in the Cabinet Office's Cobra rooms. The blog also pointed to the fact that Grant Shapps, the transport minister, had chaired Cobra when the travel company Thomas Cook had collapsed early on the morning of Monday 23 September 2019. This flagged another meeting Johnson had missed, although this time he had good cause because the collapse happened as he was on a flight to the United States to meet world leaders at the United Nations. The third example given by the blog was that of Alan Johnson, the then health secretary, who had chaired Cobra at the beginning of the swine flu outbreak in April 2009. Yet this was because Gordon Brown was on a visit to Poland and he had actually taken the time to join the Cobra meeting by phone. In fact, Brown was a particularly poor comparison for the government to make in defence of Johnson.

Brown may not have been Britain's most popular prime minister, but nobody could ever say he shirked his duty. There is an illuminating passage in the highly entertaining book *Power Trip*, written by his former special adviser Damian McBride, in which he describes how Brown cancelled his holiday to attend a Cobra meeting in August 2007, even though it was a much lesser national emergency than the coronavirus crisis. It was Brown's first day of holiday since he had taken over as prime minister from Blair, and McBride was looking forward to having a few pints in the local pub while keeping the press away from his master, who was staying in a Dorset village a couple of miles away. But after dinner with the Browns on the first night, there was a call to say there had been an outbreak of foot and mouth disease on a Surrey farm. Brown immediately sprang into action.

'Within minutes, GB was on a conference call with all his top civil servants (most already on holiday),' recalls McBride. 'He told them he'd head back to Downing Street in the morning to chair a Cobra meeting. I swear I could hear the collective groan from London. I should also have been gutted that this was my summer holiday up the Swanee.' After three hours' sleep, McBride returned to the prime minister's holiday cottage at 5 a.m. for the drive back to London and found that Brown had been up all night preparing for Cobra.

He had been reading the report by Iain Anderson, who chaired the official inquiry into the government's handling of the 2001 outbreak. McBride recalled: 'The journey back to London was a flurry of phone calls from GB, barking instructions and questions at officials and ministers, all lifted from his study of the Anderson report. Footpaths. Bridle paths. Horse racing. Exports. Tax breaks for farmers and the tourist industry. Cull zones. Exclusion zones. Buffer zones. At times he had a mobile at each ear so that two officials could receive the same orders.'

The 'two-hour race from Dorset' back to London, observed McBride, represented 'everything that was good about Gordon as a leader and man of action'. When he got back to Downing Street, Brown convened the meeting in the cabinet room and stood like a general with 'maps of Surrey spread out' on the table, issuing instructions on the size of the cull zones. Brown's prompt action meant there would be just seven further cases of foot and mouth across the country compared with 2,000 infections in 2001. McBride continued: 'When he made his statements to the media that day, he looked a mess, but no one watching him would have been in any doubt that he was in charge, in control and totally the right man for the job.'

They are, of course, very different styles of leadership. Brown was famously a workaholic who – like Theresa May – wanted to understand policy by being on top of every detail himself. On the other hand, Johnson had brought a novel approach to the job: seeing himself as a chairman-style figure who decides the overarching strategy and relies on others to get to grips with the finer points of a policy and execute it without his help. The contrast with foot and mouth disease could not have been starker. It is predominantly an animal virus that ruins farmers' livelihoods and can mean that healthy animals have to be culled. But Johnson was faced with a virus that was highly infectious in humans, had already killed many people and was now spreading fast across the UK.

4

Sleepwalk

Thursday 6 February 2020 to Wednesday 12 February 2020
UK government's risk assessment: Moderate

The news agenda was changing quite considerably. For years the topic of Brexit had dominated current affairs in the newspapers, radio and television, and it may well have continued that way as Britain wrangled with Europe over trade negotiations. On Thursday 6 February the executive editor of *The Sunday Times* popped into our darkened box of an office in the bowels of the newspaper's glass London Bridge headquarters and articulated for the first time the shift we were beginning to witness in the media's attention. 'Coronavirus is the new Brexit,' he said. He was correct. The story was only getting bigger and bigger as its catastrophic and devastating ramifications became clearer. The virus would barely leave the newspaper's front page for the rest of the year. That Thursday was the day when the virus took the life of the Chinese whistle-blower Dr Li Wenliang and the news made headlines around the world. The virus was on the march and was now well and truly out of China. It had reached 24 countries, and those were just the ones that were known about.

The big news in the UK that day came out in a press conference hosted by Professor Whitty, the government's chief medical officer. He announced that the first British person had caught the virus and it was a major development because the case presented a new nightmarish set of complications. 'The person who caught this did not catch it in China, they caught it elsewhere in Asia,' Whitty said. 'That's an important point from an epidemiological point of view because there is now evidence of some limited transmission in a number of Asian countries.' This meant that Britain would have to be alert to cases coming in from other countries and not just China. He added: 'If a doctor in the NHS sees a patient who has travelled from Asia, now they will start thinking about testing from a wider geographical area than would have been the case before. So, we are shifting geography for NHS doctors to test.' It was an approach similar to sticking a finger in a dam spurting open with holes – as the virus was already spreading between people in the UK.

He wasn't named at the time, but the first British case to be detected – who would later be unkindly labelled the 'superspreader' – was Steve Walsh, a 53-year-old businessman from Hove. He had tested positive for the virus at the Royal Sussex County Hospital in Brighton and by that time had already been trailing the infection around for at least two weeks. He had travelled halfway around the world and come into contact with hundreds of people. The previous two cases in the UK – the two Chinese nationals in York – had been swiftly isolated in hospital after falling ill. But Walsh provided a wholly different set of problems that served to illustrate just how difficult it would be to stifle the contagion that had now reached Britain.

Walsh did not display any symptoms, so he was oblivious to the fact that he might be spreading the virus. He had taken a coronavirus test as a precaution because an organiser from the sales conference he had attended at the Grand Hyatt Hotel in Singapore a fortnight earlier had been in touch to say that one of the other delegates had been diagnosed with the disease. More than a hundred people had attended the conference, including one Chinese national from Hubei, the province that includes Wuhan. But the virus could have been spread by one of the other delegates because it was no longer just a Chinese problem.

Walsh had spent three days at the Singapore conference from Monday 20 January before flying to the French Alpine ski resort of Les Contamines-Montjoie, where he is believed to have infected several other British people who were staying in the same chalet. He returned to Britain on Tuesday 28 January on an EasyJet flight from Geneva to London Gatwick. This meant that Public Health England, the government agency charged with handling pandemics, would have to track down 15 people who sat close to him on the plane. While at home in the seaside town of Hove, he visited the local Grenadier Pub on Saturday 1 February. As a result, five of the pub's employees would later have to self-isolate. Walsh then went to a runners' yoga class at a community centre, which led to the entire building later being closed.

Of those thought to have been infected by Walsh, five were hospitalised in France, five in Britain and one on the Spanish island of Majorca. Such was the fear of the virus, four schools in Brighton allowed their children to stay at home or had pupils in 'self-isolation' within days of his positive test being announced. An accident and emergency medic at nearby Worthing Hospital became the eighth person in Britain to be diagnosed with coronavirus, but it was unclear how this connected to Walsh. Indeed, Walsh would have been only one of several people – with or without symptoms – who were already spreading the virus in the UK, especially as many families were returning from peak season skiing holidays in the Alps, where the virus had taken hold.

While the UK's public health officials were tracing Walsh's contacts, the crisis was escalating internationally. The number of cases on the British-registered *Diamond Princess*, a cruise ship moored off the city of Yokohama, south of Tokyo, rose by 60 to 130 on the weekend of Saturday 8 February, demonstrating just how contagious the virus was between people in confined spaces. Tedros Adhanom Ghebreyesus, the head of the World Health Organization, gave a press conference in which he predicted that the small number of cases in the 24 countries outside China 'may only be … the tip of the iceberg', as there were now 'concerning instances' in which the virus was spreading to people who had never been to the country. He warned that it was essential to prepare for the worst now while there was still time. 'All countries must use the window of opportunity created by the containment strategy to prepare for the virus's possible arrival,' he said.

These were vital weeks, but still the British prime minister was not engaging in the key meetings and was leaving the health secretary to deal with what he had described in his speech days earlier at the Old Royal Naval College as the medically irrational panic over the virus. Hancock, meanwhile, was getting on with things. On Monday 10 February he introduced new regulations that gave the government the power to compel people infected with coronavirus in England to isolate themselves, if they did not do so willingly. In order to introduce the new powers in line with the 1984 Public Health (Control of Disease) Act the government had to declare that the transmission of the virus presented a 'serious and imminent threat'. But the health secretary chose not to use those words in his statement announcing the regulations to the Commons the next day. 'The clinical advice about the risk to the public has not changed and remains moderate,' he reassured his fellow members of parliament. Everything seemed fine, but was it?

There was still a strong sense of complacency at the heart of government. Answering questions from MPs, Hancock repeated his message that the NHS had the capacity to treat 50 to 500 coronavirus patients. He was asked by a friendly Conservative colleague, Dr Caroline Johnson MP, whether there were preparations for a wider package of measures – such as supplying fitted masks – to ensure the safety of NHS staff when they came into contact with patients carrying the virus. Hancock replied reassuringly: 'Yes, of course. Making sure that we have the equipment to keep our staff safe is a very important consideration – keeping medics safe is very important not only for them, but for the public, because they provide such an important service.'

Yet the failure to provide personal protective equipment (PPE) would become a major thorn in the government's side when the pandemic struck in earnest over the following months. So, what exactly had the government been doing to make sure it had adequate supplies in those first six weeks since news of a novel virus had come out of Wuhan? Part of the answer would be provided in the government's error-strewn 14-page rebuttal blog in response to criticism from *The Sunday Times* in April. We alleged that the government had lost a vital 38 days from 24 January when it should have been making preparations for the arrival of the virus, and its attempts to justify the few active steps it had taken in the blog suggested that surprisingly little had been done to ensure PPE supplies were available and ready.

NHS England declared the virus its first 'level 4 critical incident' at the end of January, but the government's blog was able to point to just three concrete things it had done in those early days to address the need for protective equipment. In the last days of January, four weeks after the pandemic had begun, the blog says there were internal meetings about the supply chain and the 'first additional orders of PPE was [*sic*] placed on 30 January via NHS Supply Chain's "just-in-time contracts"'. On Friday 7 February the Department of Health gave a seminar over the internet for suppliers in China, the European Union and other countries in which a request was made to carry out 'full supply chain risk assessments and hold on to EU exit stock-piles'. This message was then reinforced in a letter from the department on 11 February – the day Hancock fielded the question about PPE in parliament.

So only one of the actions the blog pointed to was an attempt to actually purchase additional PPE and this immediately ran into difficulties, according to a Downing Street adviser who has given invaluable help in preparation for this book but does not wish to be named. The 'just-in-time' contracts had been put in place with the suppliers years earlier as a safety net in case there was an emergency and there was a sudden need to bring in essential kit. However, the Downing Street adviser says that by the time the requests were being made from late January onwards, it was too late. This was mainly because the contracts were mostly with Chinese manufacturers, which were facing unprecedented demand from the country's own health service and elsewhere because of the virus. The firms also had production problems due to the increasing restrictions on movement imposed in China in an effort to curtail the virus's spread. Even some of the European suppliers were unable to deliver, despite firm contracts being in place. A French mask manufacturer failed to fulfil the terms of a £1.2m contract with the NHS to supply around 7 million masks in the event of a pandemic.[1] Instead, the firm allegedly prioritised more lucrative deals with clients elsewhere – including a Chinese state-owned energy company and the French government – as demand and therefore prices soared.

'All of the comfort blankets we thought we had basically went up in flames,' one UK official said, describing the frustration that would be felt in the coming months when PPE supplies were almost impossible to source. It was noticeable that the government's blog failed to provide any evidence of a single successful delivery of PPE during January and February.

The fact that the health service was relying on 'just-in-time' contracts rather than its own stockpiles was symptomatic of a much bigger problem. Its stockpiles were in disarray. While the prime minister's spokesman, the health secretary and the chief scientific adviser had all declared that the UK was 'well prepared' for a pandemic, the reality was very different. For years a pandemic had been assessed as the number one threat to the nation above flooding, severe weather, biological attack, nuclear accidents or terrorism. Not only was it estimated that a pandemic would have the highest economic and societal impact, but it was also considered a relatively likely occurrence in comparison to other disasters. Britain lauded its pandemic planning as the best in the world, and maybe it was – once. But stockpiles had dwindled in the years of austerity and resources had been diverted to prepare for a no-deal Brexit that had become the country's obsession. It meant that the UK government had to hit the ground running in those early weeks of January and February, but there was a lack of momentum and leadership. Britain was drifting into a catastrophe believing it was well prepared.

'It was a massive spider's web of failing; every domino has fallen,' the Downing Street adviser explained. The members of the government's advisory group on pandemics 'would joke between themselves, "Ha-ha, let's hope we don't get a pandemic," because there wasn't a single area of practice that was being nurtured in order for us to meet basic requirements for a pandemic, never mind do it well,' said the adviser. 'If you were with senior NHS managers at all during the last two years, you were aware that their biggest fear, their sweatiest nightmare, was a pandemic, because they weren't prepared for it.'

The modern era of pandemic planning began in earnest following the 11 September terrorist attacks on the United States in 2001, which caused governments around the world to sit up and take notice. In Britain, the Labour government led by then prime minister Tony Blair responded to the threat by pouring money and resources into systems that might make the country more resilient in the event of such an attack or a natural disaster. 'We were the envy of the world,' said the Downing Street adviser.

Since a pandemic was thought to be the most likely and dangerous threat to life, the first ever major country-wide rehearsal was undertaken in 2007 to see how the UK might deal with a flu-type pandemic. Codenamed Winter Willow, it brought together 5,000 people from across government, including ministers, NHS staff, the emergency services and local officials. The results were a major wake-up call. It had only been simulated as a moderate pandemic scenario, but even so the protective equipment for medical staff had rapidly run out. The government published its first risk register the following year, assessing the devastation a pandemic could cause. 'In addition to the severe health effects,' it said, 'normal life is likely to face wider social and economic disruption, significant threats to the continuity of essential services, lower production levels, shortages and distribution difficulties.' The number of deaths such a pandemic might cause was estimated to be between 50,000 and 750,000. This bleak scenario galvanised the government, now led by Gordon Brown, to make further heavy investments to ensure that by 2010 the UK had an 'incredibly detailed' pandemic plan. 'Every minister was briefed on it and trained on it and educated that a pandemic was our top national risk, and that meant something,' said the Downing Street adviser.

But there were lean years ahead. The Conservatives under David Cameron and then Theresa May made tough decisions on spending as they attempted to reduce the national debt in the wake of the financial crisis. Contingencies for a disaster that might not happen were a low priority. 'Pandemic planning became a casualty of the austerity years, when there were more pressing needs,' the source said. Levels of investment in the government's emergency stockpile of protective equipment for healthcare workers began to slide. A planned mobile phone alert system to warn people of outbreaks was mothballed, according to a leaked Cabinet Office note from November 2014. 'Following the last meeting in June, the Government has since decided to pause implementation of the proposed mobile alerting system,' it states.

The last rehearsal for a pandemic before the emergence of the coronavirus hardly inspired confidence. Run by Public Health England in October 2016, the three-day operation codenamed Cygnus tested how more than 950 officials – including ministers, local emergency workers and prison officers – would react if an influenza pandemic struck Britain. As part of the exercise, ministers held four dummy meetings of Cobra across the 72 hours. The following month, Professor Dame Sally Davies, the chief medical adviser at the time, gave a gloomy précis of the exercise's results at an international health conference. She said the NHS had failed the test and was not ready for a severe flu outbreak. 'We've just had in the UK a three-day exercise on flu, on a pandemic that killed a lot of people. It became clear that we could not cope with the excess bodies, for instance. It becomes very worrying about the deaths, and what that will do to society as you start to get all those deaths, [including] the economic impact,' she said.

It took nine months for the government to produce a formal assessment of its own performance, and the verdict was damning when the report was completed in July 2017. It was sent to the devolved administrations of Scotland, Wales and Northern Ireland as well as to all Whitehall departments and the NHS. It concluded that Britain's preparations were inadequate for the 'extreme demands' of a pandemic. Professor Sir Ian Boyd, one of the UK's chief scientific advisers between 2012 and 2019, wrote about the exercise later in the journal *Nature*. 'I recall a practice run for an influenza pandemic in which about 200,000 people died. It left me shattered. We learnt what would help, but did not necessarily implement those lessons. The assessment, in many sectors of government, was that the resulting medicine was so strong that it would be spat out. Nobody likes living under a fortress mentality.'

Dr Phillip Lee was the justice minister at the time and was also privy to Cygnus's results. 'It was quite a sobering experience. The conclusion at the end was we don't have ventilator capacity to match a pandemic so we need to deal with that or at least be in a position to press the button immediately there's any sense of a threat. The same with PPE kit,' he said. 'I personally would have thought there would have at least been some attempt at building up capacity of quality PPE kit … [that]

would have been the bare minimum that you would have done in response to Cygnus in 2016.'[2]

As part of 26 key recommendations from Cygnus, the NHS was told it needed to make urgent and drastic improvements, which would have to be paid for with money the government was advised to specifically ring-fence for that purpose. That did not happen. A key warning that should have been heeded was a particular concern expressed over the social care sector. The report found that care homes would be unable to cope with the large numbers of old people who would be discharged to them from hospitals in the rush to free up beds for pandemic patients. Marked 'Official – Sensitive', the document was filed away and never made available to the public. When quizzed, ministers would refuse to reveal the report's findings or which of its recommendations they had implemented.

The Downing Street adviser says that most of the list of recommendations was ignored. The main problem was Brexit. Exercise Cygnus had happened in the months after the vote to leave the European Union and by time the report came out there was a new possible emergency to prepare for. The fear of a no-deal Brexit began 'sucking all the blood out of pandemic planning', the adviser said. 'All the blood was flooding to the Brexit planning and we never picked it up. Countries like Germany never took their eye off the pandemic ball, neither did the Middle East and even America had some interest. There should have been a constant watching brief that would have filtered down. But it just fell off.'

One of the effects of downgrading the importance of pandemic planning was that medical staff were not properly trained to use the equipment they would need if a contagious virus took hold in Britain. The adviser said there had been 'a window [of time] to train healthcare staff in the use of PPE', especially following the 2014 Ebola outbreak in West Africa, which demonstrated how important the protective equipment was. 'But it never happened,' said the adviser, who argued that doctors and nurses should have been taught to use protective equipment in the same way that firefighters are given training with breathing apparatus. 'You train them not only to wear the equipment, but how to work it, how to manage it psychologically,' said the adviser. 'All we did once the virus struck was drop off great big bins of gloves, and crappy aprons. There's been no training.'

In effect, the adviser said, 'the UK's pandemic plan had been mothballed around the time the Brexit planning got very intense in 2017.' It meant that in the years leading up to the coronavirus outbreak, key government committee meetings on pandemic planning were repeatedly 'bumped' off the diary to make way for discussions about what were deemed more pressing issues. This continued into 2019. As the stalemate over Brexit continued, there was always a constant threat hanging over the negotiations that the UK could walk away from Europe without a deal – which was predicted to cause pandemonium at the borders and possible shortages of key goods such as medicines. The bed shortages in the NHS were also diverting attention from pandemic meetings. 'I remember by December I started to hear something about Wuhan,' said the adviser. 'But we were still delaying pandemic meetings for bed crisis meetings and other types of meetings … They had been bumping pandemic planning meetings all through the autumn because it was seen as a theoretical risk.'

So when the virus began to spread in January 2020, the adviser was surprised to hear leading government figures such as the chief medical officer Chris Whitty expressing confidence in the UK's preparedness. 'You've got this massive dissonance when you've got people like Whitty saying we're the envy of the world. Well, we absolutely were, but that was before the issue was neglected,' the adviser said. There was much catching up to do when the 'nightmare' that the pandemic might take hold in the UK became a distinct possibility in late January and early February. But there was still no great sense of urgency. 'I remember in February somebody saying to me, this is getting serious now, we're going to need to start prioritising these in the diary,' said the adviser. 'I thought, "Gosh, this is looking like a slightly scary one. But it can't be the big one, because they would have done so much more."' In fact, the pandemic plans did not kick into action even then. 'Almost every plan we had was not activated in February. Almost every government department has failed to properly implement their own pandemic plans.'

The adviser says that one of the key lessons learnt from past epidemics was that it was important to overreact to the crisis, because it was impossible to say how severe the outbreak might become – rather than underreact as the government appeared to be doing. 'In every other epidemic incident we went big. You could say we went too big for H1N1 [the 2009 swine flu virus] and we were too big for Ebola. For all of those we could be accused of going big and it being too much. But what AIDS had taught us was that the sign of a good public health approach is that people later on go, "Maybe you went a bit big." That's success.'

Professor Stephen Reicher, a member of the Spi-behavioural group that reports to Sage, explained how critical it is that governments convey the gravity of crises to their populations. 'The major reason why people die in emergencies is that they don't realise it's dangerous soon enough and then secondly, that they're not given good information about what to do,' he said. 'The problem in emergencies isn't that people overreact. It's that they underreact and they underreact often because they're not given clear enough and strong enough information early on.'[3]

A senior Department of Health insider also described the worrying inertia they witnessed in government during those crucial weeks in February: 'We missed the boat on testing and PPE … I remember being called into some of the meetings about this in February and thinking, "Well, it's a good thing this isn't the big one." I had watched Wuhan but I assumed we must have not been worried because we did nothing. We just watched. A pandemic was always at the top of our national risk register – always – but when it came we just slowly watched. We could have been Germany, but instead we were doomed by our incompetence, our hubris and our austerity.'

So while Hancock was telling the Commons on 11 February that the NHS could cope, he was actually disguising a huge problem: civil servants and medical staff had not been trained in dealing with a pandemic for several years; there was scant coordination within government or with local authorities; there was no provision for large-scale diagnostic testing of people for the virus; and most worryingly of all, the stockpiles of PPE were smaller than anyone realised. It is possible that there may have been enough PPE for the 50-bed-type epidemic Hancock had told the Commons there were contingencies for. But there certainly was not enough for a full-blown outbreak and the situation was becoming increasingly dire.

It was a key part of the pandemic plan – the NHS's Operating Framework for Managing the Response to Pandemic Influenza dated December 2017 – that the NHS would be able to draw on large stockpiles of PPE. The plan states: 'Many of the items are already in place in warehouses (termed "just in case" stockpiles), while others will be procured through "just in time" contracts.'

The stockpiles in the warehouses were the essential element, as the Downing Street adviser explained. 'The nature of a pandemic means you are in a race to manufacture personal protective equipment,' the source said. 'Therefore, you stockpile, you prepare, you refresh that stockpile and you have incredibly good health care logistics. So, you put the stuff that's getting to expiry back into the NHS sector and then you buy again.'

The UK's national pandemic stockpile had been established in 2009 following the swine flu outbreak, with around £500m being spent on protective equipment. By the time the coronavirus pandemic began, the stockpile was mostly housed in a 370,000-square-foot distribution centre in Merseyside that had been built specifically for the purpose. But supplies had been allowed to significantly dwindle over the intervening years. An analysis of official financial data by the *Guardian* found that the value of the stockpile reduced from £831m in 2013 to £506m by March 2019 – a drop of almost 40 per cent.[4] Leaked lists of the stocks showed that by 30 January 2020 the stockpile held 10 per cent fewer respirators, 19 per cent fewer surgical masks and 28 per cent fewer needles and syringes than it had in 2009.[5]

The remaining stock had not been replenished and was in a worrying state of decay. More than 200 million crucial items had expired in the eight months before the virus arrived in Britain in January. This meant that, in total, 45 per cent of the 19,909 boxes holding PPE supplies had exceeded their use-by dates. More than half the national stockpile of facemasks – 84 million – were also past the point where they should have been binned and recycled. The stockpile did contain 26.3 million respirators, which could have been vital to help NHS staff avoid becoming infected by inhaling airborne particles of the virus. But 20.9 million (79 per cent) of these respirators were out of date.

It turned out that many of the out-of-date respirators had been purchased in 2009 with stickers showing that the expiry date was 2012. The solution had been simple. All the stickers were covered with a new expiry label of 2016 to give them four years' extra shelf life. But once those dates had expired, more stickers had been placed on top to pretend that the respirators were fit for use until 2019 or 2020. Some of the hospital medics who later received the respirators shared photographs on social media of the peeled-off labels alongside pictures of the equipment, which showed they had visibly degraded after so much time spent in the warehouse. The hospitals were furious. Dr Matt Mayer, chief executive of the medical committee covering Berkshire, Buckinghamshire and Oxfordshire, called for those responsible to face criminal charges for knowingly putting NHS workers' lives at risk. In its defence, Public Health England claimed all the expired products had passed 'stringent tests' to ensure the respirators and masks had remained fit for use. But when a reporter from *Channel 4 News* approached the main supplier of the masks, a US safety firm called 3M, they were clear that the products should not have been used once they were past their expiry date. The firm says that, over time, the strap and the foam used to give a tighter fit to the nose can degrade, which can adversely affect the seal that is supposed to keep out the virus particles.

Other basic equipment critical to the care of Covid-19 patients was not even a part of the stockpile. There were no gowns, visors, swabs or body bags.[6] This was exactly the type of equipment that should have been identified as a top priority to buy in at the end of Exercise Cygnus. The lack of gowns was particularly reprehensible as the government's Nervtag advisory group had recommended only six months earlier in June 2019 that they should be purchased. The gowns would become one of the items in shortest supply in UK hospitals when infections began, with some hospital staff being forced to use bin bags as a replacement. Indeed, the lack of investment had also meant that there was insufficient eye protection for health workers. This was important because there was concern that the virus could be passed by airborne droplets entering through the eyes. In 2017 Nervtag had recommended 'providing eye protection for all hospital, community, ambulance and social care staff who have close contact with pandemic influenza patients'. But in June of that year the minutes of the Nervtag meetings record a health department official asking the advisory body to reconsider the recommendation because of the 'very large incremental cost of adding in eye protection'. The minutes state: 'A subsequent internal DH [Department of Health] economic assessment has revealed that following these recommendations would substantially increase the cost of the PPE component of the pandemic stockpile four- to six-fold, with a very low likelihood of cost-benefit based on standard thresholds.' So, just as with gowns and respirators, there was a shortage of eye-protection equipment when the pandemic began.

But this wasn't initially made clear to the hospitals in the early weeks. A leading infectious disease expert described how at the end of January a London hospital had asked officials about the levels of PPE reserves and was reassured that 'there was a good stockpile'. The expert concluded: 'So, at some point along the line, whatever calculations were made about the amount of PPE required weren't big enough ... There were clearly supply issues very early on.'

It wasn't just the hospitals that the government needed to be stocking up supplies for in the event of an emergency. Workers in care homes had to be adequately protected to prevent spreading the virus to the vulnerable elderly people they were looking after. Even those who looked after the dead were at risk and needed to be provided for. 'We should have stockpiled PPE, including for staff working in care homes, and also mortuaries because what Ebola taught us is that the handling of the dead is a major issue, and they often run out first,' said the adviser. There had been a dedicated 'PPE stockpile for the dead' and the mortuary staff who handled their bodies, but the source said that it had been mostly decommissioned and sold off in the preceding two years. 'It ended up being absorbed into local hospitals so it just got used,' said the adviser.

These were all key tasks for the government to catch up on in the earlier weeks of the virus, but there was little activity. An example of the government's complacency was its attitude to the threat that the virus might cause an economic catastrophe. In his appearance before parliament on 11 February, Hancock was asked what advice he was preparing for employees on zero hours contracts who would lose wages if they took time off work when suffering symptoms. The health secretary brushed the issue aside, saying: 'That could become an important consideration in due course, but I am glad to say that, at the moment, the impact on employment is very small, because we have only eight cases.' In fact, the pandemic plan suggested that the government should have already been discussing such issues with employers, and the wider impact a virus would have on business. 'There was a duty to get them to start thinking about their cash flow and their business continuity arrangements,' said the adviser.

The other key weapon that the government should have been looking to bolster in those first six weeks was the UK's capacity to test for the virus. A central part of any pandemic plan is to identify anyone who becomes ill, vigorously pursue all their recent contacts and put them into quarantine. The case of Steve Walsh was an early lesson insofar as it illustrated how just one person could potentially infect large numbers of people who all then had to be contact traced and tested.

The importance of contact tracing was highlighted in a report by scientists at the London School of Hygiene & Tropical Medicine, which was published on Friday 7 February, the day after Walsh's infection had been announced – therefore a timely reminder for the government. It argued that the virus could be contained with a rapid track and trace system, but warned that an inadequate system could lead to infections spreading uncontrollably across the country. 'Highly effective contact tracing and case isolation is enough to control a new outbreak of COVID-19 within 3 months,' it said. 'The probability of control decreases with long delays from symptom onset to isolation, fewer cases ascertained by contact tracing, and increasing transmission before symptoms.'

However, if the virus spreads there would have to be a huge production of diagnostic kits to carry out all the tests that would need to take place for contact testing to be successful. The UK had appeared to be ahead of the game initially. It was a badge of great pride to Hancock that Britain had been one of the first countries to develop a new test for the coronavirus in January. 'Testing worldwide is being done on equipment designed in Oxford,' he told the Commons. But the advantage was not pressed home in those opening weeks.

A major problem the UK faced was its inability to produce tests on a mass scale. This was mainly because Britain does not possess a large established diagnostics industry. Germany could call upon a testing giant like Roche, one of the world's largest diagnostics companies, to mass produce tests, but the UK was reliant on importing supplies from abroad. Again, that meant Britain was in competition with the rest of the world for the dwindling supplies that countries engaged in large-scale production could spare. Unfortunately, the government did not act quickly enough to secure even a fraction of the huge amount of testing equipment that was needed.

There was also a critical lack of laboratory testing capacity. According to Martin Hibberd, a professor of emerging infectious disease at LSHTM, a key reason for that had been money. The NHS had moved away from using its own laboratories in the years before the pandemic and had increasingly farmed out its work to privately owned facilities in an effort to cut costs. Yet when coronavirus first emerged, Public Health England had wanted to have control over testing capacity and had been reluctant to use the private laboratories to help ramp it up. 'There was a network of [publicly owned] diagnostic laboratories and I think that's largely disappeared,' Hibberd said. 'Public Health England are still hoping to do all of [the testing] within their own laboratories.' This put a severe limit on the country's ability to boost testing. Again, this was a problem that needed to be addressed with urgency when it became clear that the virus would spread internationally. But too little was done in the opening weeks of the outbreak.

By contrast, countries such as South Korea were already running a highly effective contact tracing regime by activating their well-rehearsed pandemic plan, which involved utilising the nation's laboratories. 'As soon as the first whiff of something came out of Wuhan what the good regimes did was mobilise their testing laboratories,' said the Downing Street adviser, 'but over the last five years, we've made all of ours private and commercial.' It was therefore important, the adviser said, that the government should reach out to Britain's large network of private biochemical laboratories, seeking help in mass producing tests, as countries such as Germany would do so successfully. But there was no attempt to kick-start testing in the private sector in the crucial initial weeks. 'We should have communicated with every commercial testing laboratory that might volunteer to become part of the government's testing regime, but that didn't happen,' said the adviser. It would be more than two months before there was a proper attempt to seek the assistance of the private laboratories. The adviser said: 'The biochem industry was eventually asked for help in April and they said to the government, "You never asked us … we furloughed all our staff."' The adviser believes that Cobra, led by the prime minister, should have taken the initiative in January and offered manufacturers £1m grants to try to produce pregnancy-style kits that people could use to test for the virus at home. 'They could have diverted funding as soon as this was known to be serious in January. Make it a prize. That's the sort of thing Cobra should have been sitting to do.'

The lack of action was described by Doris-Ann Williams, chief executive of the British In Vitro Diagnostics Association, which represents 110 companies that make up most of the UK's testing sector. Amazingly, she said her organisation did not receive a meaningful approach from the government asking for help until 1 April – the night before Hancock bowed to pressure and announced a belated and ambitious target of 100,000 tests a day by the end of that month.

It meant the UK had no infrastructure to continue contact tracing in a meaningful way once there were more than a handful of cases. This was compounded by the fact that there were insufficient numbers of trained people to carry out the tracing. Public Health England, for example, only had 300 contact tracers for the whole of England, which meant it could only cope with five new cases a week because each new infection generated so many contacts that each had to be tracked down. Professor Gabriel Scally, a leading public health expert and a former senior civil servant in the Department of Health, said: 'If I was mobilising as a director of public health for something like the city of Bristol, I would have expected to have maybe between 300 and 500 people just for that place alone working on case identification and contact tracing. I have difficulty understanding why, for example, they weren't even at a pretty early stage talking about really, really stepping up testing to try and find out where the virus was in a country as big as the UK.'[7]

Professor John Ashton, a former director of public health in the north-west of England, says the contact tracing could have been taken up by regional health services but they had been run down and restructured in the years before the outbreak. He argues that the country was ill-prepared because of the 'centralization of public health into Public Health England and the whittling away of public health at the local and regional level'. He says, 'We went from nine regions to four quasi regions, but they were really civil service outposts and the resources and budgets and everything has been dramatically cut.' It meant that Public Health England was highly dependent on its central laboratory in Colindale. 'We used to have a very strong local network of laboratories, but they've allowed many of those to wither away.' He believes the government could have addressed the contact tracing problem by using the thousands of environmental health officers in local councils. Many of those had been 'saying they could have been available for contact tracing but nobody asked them', he said.

There was a similar failure to harness the resources of British private companies to build up the reserves of PPE in those weeks in January and February. The British Healthcare Trades Association (BHTA), which represents almost 500 companies employing more than 17,000 people who make or sell healthcare equipment, was poised ready to help supply PPE in February – but nobody from the government or the NHS contacted them.

In fact, this would continue throughout March and it would not be until 1 April, at the peak of the hospital crisis, that the trade body's offer of help was accepted. Sarah Lepak, the BHTA's director of governance, said: 'From the outset it was very unco-ordinated, very piecemeal contact with industry, which was frustrating.' She said the NHS was 'too slow to commit', which meant they missed critical periods when PPE manufacturers did have supplies available. 'Businesses have been very willing to switch manufacturing where they can. For example, a business that would normally be making specialist footwear switching across to making protective visors,' she added. 'So, the message has been – there's enough equipment out there, it's simply a question of being fleet of foot to get your hands on it.' By the time officials eventually deigned to properly engage with the trade body, the soaring demand from abroad meant disillu-sioned British companies had already begun shipping large amounts of precious PPE overseas. Dr Simon Festing, the BHTA's chief executive, said: 'Orders undoubtedly went over-seas instead of to the NHS because of the missed opportunities in the procurement process.'

So what had gone wrong at the heart of government in those first six weeks that prevented it from getting onto the front foot? There were certainly historical problems from the years of austerity and Brexit, but these made it all the more important that urgent actions were taken as soon as the seriousness of the crisis facing the UK was realised. The government's response when *The Sunday Times* first levelled this charge of inactivity was to say there had been no 'scientific consensus around the fact that this was going to be a pandemic' at the end of January. This may well have been true insofar as nobody absolutely knew whether it would be a pandemic or simply an epidemic. But as we pointed out in the last chapter, experts – such as Richard Horton of *The Lancet*, and Professor Martin Hibberd of the London School of Hygiene & Tropical Medicine and the

Sage committee member Sir Jeremy Farrar – were all saying on the day of the first Cobra meeting on 24 January that the coronavirus outbreak in China represented a serious threat to public health that may well become global.

Horton argues in his book *The Covid-19 Catastrophe* that the ignorance excuse is government disinformation and does not hold water. He recounts how his own words were twisted in a 'Kremlinesque way' by the government's blog rebuttal to our article in order to downplay his warnings. He then makes a reference to a televised address by the prime minister on 10 May. 'Boris Johnson spoke to the nation,' Horton writes. 'He said of Covid-19, "We didn't fully understand its effects." His plaintive excuse will likely become the core defence of his government in the subsequent public inquiry into why the UK failed so spectacularly to protect its citizens. It is a defence that can and must be refuted.' Horton argues that the warnings were clear and strong at the end of January: 'The facts were utterly opposite to the message from Downing Street. There was international scientific consensus. The government had simply chosen to ignore it.'

Horton said of the government: 'They really are scared that the verdict of history is going to condemn them for contributing to the deaths of tens of thousands of British citizens … They are desperately trying to rewrite the timeline of what happened. And we must not let them do that.'

There was no doubt that the threat was being taken more seriously in the Far East in January and early February. Professor Hibberd, an expert in infectious diseases, was in a unique position to compare the UK's response with that of the Singaporean government, for whom he had previously worked as an adviser. 'Singapore realised, as soon as Wuhan reported it, that cases were going to turn up in Singapore. And so they prepared for that. I looked at the UK and I can see a different strategy and approach. The interesting thing for me is, I've worked with Singapore in 2003 and 2009 and basically they copied the UK's pandemic preparedness plan. But the difference is they actually implemented it.'

Hibberd believes the scientists advising the UK government's committees felt too constrained to shout out the warnings to the politicians, who, in turn, were not engaged sufficiently to ask the crucial questions. 'I can imagine that there is a kind of an atmosphere in those meetings where rocking the boat is a difficult thing to do. So, I think the scientists tried to present data in relation to what they expected was feasible politically,' he said. 'And the politicians didn't put any questions or open up anything else that would make them think that other options were possible. So, I think there's a balance [of responsibility] there between the two ... the scientists were modelling what they thought was possible and the government wasn't really thinking through what they were saying.'

By contrast in Singapore, he said: 'The government had a much more joined-up and critical assessment of what was coming out of the scientists. In Singapore, they pushed forward the questions, they challenged the scientists. "Well, what does this mean for beds? What would this mean for care? Can we track these people? Can you do contact tracing? How many tests would we need to do?"' Whereas the politicians' failure to take responsibility in the UK left the country in a 'grey area where nothing is happening', he said.

But the Downing Street adviser was even more critical of the politicians. According to the adviser, Brexiteers at the top of government instilled a culture in which the views of scientists were often dismissed out of hand, a practice developed during the Brexit referendum after multiple experts had argued in favour of the UK remaining in the European Union. 'Whereas the government used to stop play and listen to the scientists, now they had lost the ability to hear expertise,' the adviser said. 'A pandemic was always the one that I wondered about the most in terms of would they stop everything and hear the experts. They demeaned people who sat in front of them and said this is a risk. They had lost the ability to hear scientists.'

In fact, many of Britain's senior politicians displayed little knowledge or curiosity about Britain's pandemic planning even after the crisis. A series of ministers demonstrated their lack of knowledge about Exercise Cygnus when ambushed by the media. Helen Whately, the care minister, was interviewed on LBC radio by presenter Nick Ferrari the day after the *Sunday Telegraph* had run a front-page investigation revealing that many of Cygnus's recommendations had ultimately been ignored. Ferrari said to Whately: 'They spent three days on this exercise, which showed holes all over the place and nothing was done by the Conservative government. Instead the austerity continued. How do you defend that minister?' Whately replied: 'It's not clear at all to me where you're getting your information from.' Ferrari retorted that he was staggered that nobody had alerted the care minister to the issue. On ITV's *Good Morning Britain*, Victoria Atkins, the Home Office minister, was asked directly by presenter Piers Morgan: 'Have you ever heard of Exercise Cygnus? Yes or no?' She said, 'I'm a home office minister. I focus on my portfolio. Questions about the science ...' before Morgan interjected: 'It's not about the science. You're smiling again as if this is all some big joke. Have you ever heard of Exercise Cygnus, yes or no? I'm asking you a simple question.' Atkins replied: 'No I haven't.' At one of the government's daily press conferences, Dominic Raab, the foreign secretary, was asked: 'On Exercise Cygnus ... have you personally read that document and has it been made available to all of your key scientific advisers?' Raab replied: 'I would have to go and check. I've read a huge volume over recent weeks but it's not something that immediately springs to mind.' Even Hancock, who had been health secretary for almost two years, admitted that he had been forced to instruct his officials to find out what happened in Cygnus as a result of reading about it in the media. He told LBC radio: 'I asked my officials to go back when this first came up in the press a few weeks ago and check that everything that was recommended was done and that's the assurance that I got.' He added that the exercise took place 'before my time' – when Jeremy Hunt was health secretary.

At the time of writing, the politicians have already found themselves on the wrong side of history following an initial parliamentary inquiry into the PPE fiasco and the failure to follow the pandemic plan with regard to businesses and the economy. The public accounts select committee concluded in its report in July that: 'There were fundamental flaws in the government's central procurement and local distribution of vital goods and equipment … Despite a pandemic being identified as the government's top non-malicious risk, it failed to stock up in advance.'

The committee was also highly critical of the way the Department of Health had failed to focus on the challenge of how to identify needs in the care sector and ensure supplies of PPE to those looking after the elderly and vulnerable. It went on to say that the committee was 'astonished by the government's failure to consider in advance how it might deal with the economic impacts of a pandemic'. It concluded ministers had plenty of time and ample warning but had done next to nothing. It said: 'Despite the first reported case of coronavirus being confirmed by the chief medical officer in England on 31 January 2020, the Treasury did not announce plans for significant funding to support businesses and individuals until the budget on 11 March, and it did not become clear to the Treasury until the following week that a furlough scheme would be needed.' The former Labour minister Meg Hillier, who chairs the committee, said: 'A competent government does not run a country on the hoof, and it will not steer us through this global health and economic crisis that way. Government needs to take honest stock now, learning, and rapidly changing course where necessary.'

There was also another reason for the government's complacency: besides austerity, Brexit and the prime minister's apparent lack of interest in the virus. The government's advisers had adopted the conventional approach of treating the virus as if it were flu. If no vaccine is available in a flu pandemic, the plan is that a majority of the population would be allowed to become infected to build up a 'herd immunity'. One well-known senior Conservative confided: 'I had conversations with Chris Whitty [the chief medical officer] at the end of January, and they were absolutely focused on herd immunity. The reason is that with flu, herd immunity is the right response if you haven't got a vaccine.' The politician continued: 'All of our planning was for pandemic flu. There has basically been a divide between scientists in Asia, who saw this as a horrible, deadly disease on the lines of Sars, which requires immediate lockdown, and those in the West, particularly in the US and UK, who saw this as flu.' Whitty denies that he has ever been an advocate of herd immunity other than as part of a vaccination programme. But herd immunity was a view that appears to have infected the government. As the weeks wore on, Dominic Cummings, the prime minister's most influential adviser, is said to have taken a strong interest in the herd immunity concept as a solution to the crisis, although this is something he too denies. The concept of herd immunity is toxic politically because it effectively means that the weakest in society – the ill and the elderly – are left to perish. This was, however, by design or incompetence exactly what happened as a result of the government's failure to tackle the crisis in its early days.

In the meantime, on Wednesday 12 February a fourth Cobra meeting was held to discuss the virus. Again, Johnson was in Westminster that day but his seat at the head of the table was once more delegated to Hancock. Watching the scene slowly unfolding, the Downing Street adviser was dismayed that there was no leadership displayed by the prime minister. 'The message loses its potency,' the adviser said. 'It doesn't feel like you've got anybody in charge. Even his own closest colleagues worked on the principle that if this was the big one, he might look like he gave a shit. And he didn't look like he did.'

5

Holiday

Thursday 13 February 2020 to Sunday 23 February 2020
UK government's risk assessment: Moderate

The prime minister was demob happy in the second week of February. On the day before the fourth missed Cobra meeting he was in Birmingham to publicise a government initiative that, unlike the virus, was something that Downing Street had decided to take charge of that week: the new HS2 high-speed rail line linking the north, the Midlands and London. While in the city, he was quizzed by reporters about coronavirus, as the news was becoming even more alarming. The virus had by then claimed 1,018 lives and infected over 43,000 people worldwide, and these were just the known cases. That morning the television news and newspapers were showing eerie shots of public health workers in hazmat suits and masks deep cleaning the County Oak Medical Centre in Brighton. Locum doctor Catriona Greenwood had worked there after contracting the virus while staying in the same skiing chalet as Steve Walsh, the so-called superspreader. The ITV news report caught the mood: 'It's a sight we have all become familiar with in China. But this is not China. This is Brighton.' The *Daily Mail*'s front-page headline sounded the alarm in large capital letters. 'How many more are infected?' it bellowed.

But Johnson was dismissive about the threat of the virus when he responded to the reporters in Birmingham. 'We are a great country, we have got a fantastic NHS, we have got fantastic doctors and advice,' he said. 'People have every reason to be confident and calm about all that kind of thing – on the coronavirus, and any threats from disease.' It wasn't how the government's own scientific advisers viewed the impending crisis. Sir Jeremy Farrar, an infectious disease specialist who sat on the government's Sage advisory committee, has described the sense of unease at that time.[1] 'I think from the early days in February, if not in late January, it was obvious this infection was going to be very serious and it was going to affect more than just the region of Asia,' he said. 'I think it was very clear that this was going to be an unprecedented event.'

Indeed, a team from Imperial College London and Oxford University have since produced back-dated modelling assessing the historic spread of the disease during this period. It was a piece of clever scientific detective work. They were able to make more accurate estimates than were available at the time by using the dates when people died from the virus and then working back to when they must have picked up the infection. Their study suggests that the answer to the *Daily Mail*'s headline question was that at least 70 people were already infected across the UK in the second week of February. By contrast, only eight people had been detected by the track and trace programme.

There would, however, be an increase to nine known cases in the UK when it was announced midweek that a woman who was thought to have flown in from China with the virus had turned up at the A&E department of University Hospital Lewisham in south-east London on Sunday 9 February. She had been driven there in an Uber and later officials descended on her flat in Paddington dressed in the now increasingly familiar white protective suits. It was the first case in London, which was a reason for real concern as the densely populated capital, with its packed trains and tubes, was an ideal breeding ground for the virus. Once in London, the disease could spread quickly to the rest of the country through the city's many transport links.

In interviews that week Dr Paul Cosford of Public Health England warned that more cases of coronavirus were 'highly likely' in the UK. A photo appeared on Twitter of a suited commuter wearing a gas mask on the tube with the caption 'When coronavirus hits London'. It would be the first of many similar pictures in the coming weeks as Covid anxiety gripped the capital.

The Imperial and Oxford back-dated study suggests that the contagion progressed at an alarming rate from that week onwards. Infected people, who had not come onto the contact tracers' radar, were left to unwittingly spread the disease freely among their communities. The research indicates that transmission rates were so high at the time that the number of infections was doubling every three days, just as some of the initial reports from China in late January had suggested they might. The maths was remorseless. One infected person would result in eight others contracting the virus in nine days. After 21 days, the virus would spread to 128 people. As the numbers doubling every three days became larger, the virus would become uncontrollable. It is a sobering thought that one single case could lead to the infection of a million people in less than nine weeks. Time was already running out in those early days of February if Britain was to contain the virus – as South Korea and Singapore would successfully do with an intensive and widespread programme of contact tracing. But Britain did not have a comparable testing capability or even a cohesive plan. It was not even taking any great steps towards gearing up its testing capacity to meet the threat.

Indeed, the prime minister seemed completely relaxed about the virus. The reason he was demob happy that week was because he had decided to take some time off work. It was, after all, the parliamentary recess and he had several pressing matters to deal with resulting from his complicated personal life.

* * *

But there was one last thing Johnson had to do before going on holiday. The press called it the St Valentine's Day Massacre, although it actually took place on Thursday 13 February – the day before the anniversary of the infamous 1929 Chicago gangster killings. Johnson had decided to reshuffle his cabinet for the first time since the election in December and, with a healthy majority in parliament, it was time to get out the Thompson submachine guns once again. The prime minister's first purge of the cabinet had taken place immediately after he had been voted party leader in July 2019 when he stripped the cabinet of ministers whose opposition to a no-deal Brexit could no longer be tolerated. Several had walked before being pushed. As a result, the cabinet lost a number of experienced politicians – safe hands whose wise counsel might have proved invaluable as the government faced its worst crisis in Britain since the Second World War.

Political commentators saw the July 2019 reshuffle as a lurch to the right, as fervent Brexiteers such as Michael Gove, Dominic Raab and Priti Patel were thrust into key positions. The new Johnson regime also displayed a ruthlessness towards some of the more moderate voices in the wider Conservative Party who did not toe the line on Brexit. In September 2019 he expelled 21 members of parliament who had voted against their own government to prevent a no-deal Brexit. These included the former chancellors Ken Clarke and Philip Hammond, ex-cabinet minister Sir Oliver Letwin, former education secretary Justine Greening, the ex-attorney general Dominic Grieve, and Rory Stewart, who had previously been the international development secretary. The party had been streamlined for one purpose: delivering Brexit.

However, once the election had been won with a thumping 80-seat majority and Brexit had been delivered, the process of reshaping the government's top team continued along the same lines as Johnson sought to cement his position. On that Thursday morning reshuffle before Valentine's Day, Julian Smith, secretary of state for Northern Ireland, was sacked despite having played a key role in securing a cross-party deal to restore the Northern Ireland Executive, ending three years without a devolved government in Stormont. It was widely believed that he had been punished for his disloyalty the previous October when he described a potential no-deal Brexit as being 'a very, very bad idea for Northern Ireland'. The theatrical attorney general Geoffrey Cox was also let go, reportedly for using his booming voice one too many times to share his 'independent' views with the rest of the cabinet. Next, Johnson dispatched two ministers who had stood against him in the Conservative leadership contest the previous summer to the backbenches: Angela Leadsom, the business secretary, and Esther McVey, the housing minister. But the ousting of another of the failed contenders for the leadership was the biggest surprise. Had Sajid Javid's departure as chancellor taken place in any normal workplace, he would have had a case for constructive dismissal.

At the heart of it was an internal power struggle with Dominic Cummings, the man who many believed was really pulling the strings in Johnson's regime and who would later be the key figure guiding the government's policy on the virus once Downing Street had finally understood the seriousness of the threat. Johnson had called in Javid, the chancellor of the exchequer, at 11 a.m. on the morning of the reshuffle for a meeting in Downing Street's cabinet room, which was to last for an hour. The prime minister gave Javid reassurance that he was still the best person for the job of managing the nation's money and went on to discuss plans for the upcoming budget. But there was a catch. Javid was told that he could only keep his position if he sacked all of his own advisers and worked with a joint Downing Street and Treasury team. Cummings was not in the room but Javid knew instantly who was behind this move. Javid had been resisting Cummings's desire to relax the Treasury's spending constraints. Cummings wanted money to be lavished on the poorer northern Brexit-supporting Labour seats where the

Conservatives had made ground in the election. The chancellor was determined to follow his own prudent instincts and keep the public finances under control. But Cummings had Johnson's ear.

Uncompromising and often sharp-tongued, Cummings was one of the first people hired by Johnson after he had taken the leadership the previous summer. The 48-year-old chief adviser was already a man of political folklore – admired and despised in equal measure. He had made many enemies in his previous spells working for the Conservatives, but he appeared not to care and was happy to point out the intellectual inferiority of colleagues in the party – once unkindly calling the then Brexit secretary David Davis 'as thick as mince'. Even those who disliked him would have to admit that he was a formidable political strategist who, as the co-founder and chief architect of the Vote Leave campaign, had taken a central role in the defeat of those who supported Remain in the 2016 Brexit referendum. He was depicted as an intense, if socially awkward, political savant bursting with ideas in a television drama depicting his role in the campaign, in which he was played by the actor Benedict Cumberbatch. Johnson had hired him as a master tactician to cut through the thicket of Westminster obstacles that were preventing his government from delivering the Brexit it had promised and Cummings certainly lived up to his reputation. The chief adviser had devised the provocative policy of threatening to suspend parliament, which was taken as proof that Johnson's administration would do whatever it took to deliver Brexit. That was before the courts quashed the move. He had also been instrumental in pushing for a risky election at the end of the year and then masterminded the campaign, giving it a relentless focus on just three words: 'Get Brexit Done'. It won swathes of support in Labour's northern heartlands – a coup the Conservatives had not managed to pull off in decades.

So by February 2020 his stock was so high that there was only ever going to be one winner in his escalating war with the chancellor. Cummings had fired the first shot the previous August when he sacked Javid's key aide Sonia Khan without even having the courtesy to inform the chancellor. The 27-year-old adviser's crime, which she vehemently denied, was that she had allegedly lied about her contact with the office of former chancellor Philip Hammond, who opposed a no-deal Brexit. Cummings summoned Khan to Downing Street, demanded she hand over her phones, and then told an armed police officer to escort her from the premises. Javid was 'absolutely furious' but his protestations were ignored. Javid did not help matters by contacting colleagues in the days before the election suggesting that Cummings should be removed if the result was poor. The enmity continued to bubble over, with allies of the spin doctor briefing that Javid's nickname was 'Chino' – an acronym for 'chancellor in name only'.[2] In late January, there were more media briefings designed to undermine Javid, with claims that Cummings was 'writing the budget' himself.[3]

So the prime minister's ultimatum during the reshuffle was the final straw for Javid and he tendered his resignation. His tenure as chancellor had been the shortest since 1970 – just 204 days. Within hours Johnson had replaced him with Rishi Sunak, who had been Javid's second-in-command as the chief secretary to the Treasury. Smart, confident and only 39 years old, Sunak was a Brexiteer through and through who didn't mind that his advisers would be run from Downing Street. Although he came across as being capable, he cannot have been prepared for the extraordinary decisions he would have to make as chancellor as the virus gathered pace over the next month. Certainly, Johnson did not warn him.

The mood within the cabinet during those February weeks would later be described by Tim Montgomerie, a renowned Conservative activist and blogger whom Johnson appointed in September 2019 as his social justice adviser working out of the Cabinet Office. In an extraordinary article[4] for someone who was a loyal insider at the time, he wrote: 'Long before 40,000

British deaths from this pandemic and the evaporation of the Prime Minister's reputation for competence there were multiple signs that the ship of state was heading for rocky times. Key talents had been reshuffled out of the cabinet because they had committed the sin of independent-mindedness. The top table was left with a very middle-ranking membership. Ministerial special advisers who dared to differ had been dispatched and years of hard-won experience lost in the process.'

Too much power, he argued, had gone to Cummings. 'In February's reshuffle we learnt that earning the disfavour of key prime ministerial adviser Dominic Cummings was fatal, even if you were Chancellor of the Exchequer. Everyone was dispensable. Except Dom.' Montgomerie described how the No. 10 team under Cummings 'often preferred to greet internal dissent with retribution – much of it pre-briefed to favoured journalists. Throughout the Westminster village every Tory had quickly learnt the score: do, say and tweet as you are told – or else.'

Montgomerie revealed that he issued a message to Johnson in mid-February in which he told him 'ministers increasingly fear rather than respect your No. 10 operation'. He says he 'begged' the prime minister 'to anticipate looming problems before it was too late' and expressed his concerns about 'curtailed cabinet meetings' where issues such as the economic impact of coronavirus received just five minutes of 'discussion in January'.

It had often been noted by those who worked with Johnson that he had a habit of disappearing after taking unpopular decisions and leaving his colleagues to smooth everything over. So it was on Thursday 13 February. After axing six ministers, he headed off to the country for a 'working' holiday at his grace-and-favour retreat at Chevening in Kent with his girlfriend Carrie Symonds. The sun had peeped out in the afternoon – a rare glimpse of spring in a February that had been unremittingly rainy with a series of storms that had brought flooding and chaos across the country. But the 15-bedroom 17th-century Grade I-listed mansion was an ideal place to get away from it all, sealed off from the world by 3,000 acres of gardens, parkland and woods, including a boating lake and a maze.

The estate is situated just inside the bottom right-hand corner of the M25, a few miles north-west of Sevenoaks. It had been bequeathed to a board of trustees by the 7th Earl of Stanhope, who did not have children of his own and had lost his only brother in the First World War. Stanhope drafted an act of parliament in 1957 that gave the power to the sitting prime minister to nominate a minister or a member of the royal family as the resident of the grand estate. The earl had been a Conservative politician who had founded the Greenwich Maritime Museum opposite the Old Royal Naval College where two weeks earlier Johnson had given the speech in which he decried the irrational panic over coronavirus.

Chevening had been nominated as the home for Prince Charles before he bought Highgrove in 1980. In recent years it had mostly been used by successive foreign secretaries, which included Johnson, who had held the cabinet position in the two years after Brexit. But the then prime minister Theresa May was not one of his biggest fans. She had initially dispensed with protocol by trying to make Johnson share Chevening with Liam Fox, the international trade secretary, and David Davis, the Brexit secretary, until the trustees intervened to say that only one person could be nominated. However, by February 2020 the prime minister's traditional country retreat at Chequers – the 16th-century mansion set in Buckinghamshire's Chiltern Hills – was being repaired. So Johnson, now prime minister, had himself pulled rank over his foreign secretary Raab and commandeered Chevening.

He would be out of the public eye for 12 days. His aides were thankful for the rest, as they had been working flat-out since the summer: winning the Tory leadership contest; fighting an internecine Brexit battle within their own party; losing the Brexit power struggle in a hung parliament; campaigning in the general election; and launching Johnson's premiership.

Johnson, however, had also managed to squeeze in a 10-day holiday with Symonds in the Caribbean only six weeks earlier – and that was another problem that he was leaving behind as he drove out of London. It had been all over the newspapers that morning.

The prime minister had claimed that the multimillionaire David Ross, the former Carphone Warehouse boss, had covered the £15,000 cost of the Mustique holiday in his declaration for the register of MPs' financial interests. However, Ross's spokesman set hares running by putting out a statement saying that Johnson had not stayed in the villa he owned on the island and he had merely 'facilitated' the prime minister's accommodation. The hunt was on for the mystery donor who had provided their villa free of charge. In fact, what had happened, according to sources close to Ross, was that Johnson had mentioned to the millionaire that he desperately needed a holiday. Ross is said to have asked 'mountains or beach?' and Johnson replied that Carrie preferred the latter. His villa, however, was unavailable for the period after Christmas, but there had been a cancellation of a three-bedroom villa, called Indigo, on the island and the owners had been fully paid as the people renting it out had pulled out too late for a refund. So Indigo was made available to Johnson and Symonds for free. The prime minister's political opponents questioned his judgement in taking such an expensive freebie. While the villa had been paid for, it could have been rented out at full price as the island was fully booked. The cost of the villa was normally £3,400 a day at that time of year, which means that Johnson should have declared a gift of £34,000, rather than £15,000. It is not clear why he didn't as his spokeswoman refused to engage on the matter other than to say 'all transparency requirements have been followed,' and Johnson could not be questioned directly because he was on holiday, again.

Johnson may have been a great crowd pleaser on the Conservative Party's rubber chicken circuit, but he also came with a lot of personal baggage and much of it had to be sorted during the 'working' holiday in Chevening. He was still married to Marina Wheeler, the mother of four of his children, but had secretly become engaged to Symonds at the end of the previous year, possibly in Mustique.

One of his tasks in Chevening was to finalise the terms of his separation from Wheeler, and midway through his holiday it was announced in the High Court that the couple had reached a settlement, leaving Wheeler free to apply for a divorce to end 27 years of marriage. But there was another tricky problem to navigate. Symonds had been carrying their child for more than six months and people were beginning to notice. The news would have to be made known soon, which meant that Johnson would have to prepare his family for the announcement.

Families can be complicated at the best of times but Johnson's many dalliances over the years – often finding their way into newspapers because of his celebrity – had made matters especially difficult for the people in his life who loved him. It had been years since the tabloids had first nicknamed him 'Bonking Boris'. The relationship with Symonds would be his third marriage, his fifth extramarital fling to be made public and the fifth time as a married man that he had made another woman, who wasn't his wife, pregnant. It was a bit of a pattern. Wheeler herself had become pregnant with their daughter Lara in 1993 while Johnson was still married to his first wife, Allegra Mostyn-Owen, who recounted the moment she found out as follows: 'He suddenly blurted out that he wanted a quickie divorce. I said: "Is she pregnant?" and he said: "Yes, how did you guess?"'[5]

While the editor of *The Spectator* and the MP for Henley, Johnson had a four-year affair with Petronella Wyatt, then a columnist at the magazine who was in her early 30s. She twice became pregnant during the relationship, but the babies were lost as a result of an abortion and a miscarriage. The affair ended in 2004 and Johnson, aged 40, lost his job as shadow arts minister and party vice-chairman for lying about it. At first, he had categorically dismissed the allegations with typical rhetorical flourish as an 'inverted pyramid of piffle', but, foolishly, he directly assured the then Conservative leader Michael Howard the stories were untrue. Howard decided Johnson could not be trusted when he learnt the truth and sacked him immediately. Johnson was also thrown out of the family home by Wheeler, a barrister specialising in public law, but she later took him back.

Wyatt later said that Johnson had grumbled to her: 'I find it genuinely unreasonable that men should be confined to one woman.' Her assessment of the man she knew intimately for four years is highly revealing. In an article for the *Mail on Sunday*, she described Johnson as 'a loner' with few friends and 'a compensating need to be liked'.[6] She claimed he was the opposite of vain. 'Boris regards himself as rather ugly, requiring "half an hour to talk away my face".' On his tendency to be economical with the truth, she said: 'Boris never sets out to lie. It is just that he will do anything to avoid an argument, which leads to a degree of duplicity.' In fact, Johnson once said of himself: 'As a general tactic in life it is often useful to give the slight impression that you are deliberately intending not to know what is going on – because the reality may be that you don't know what is going on – but people won't be able to tell the difference.'

In 2006 the *News of the World* reported Johnson was seeing Anna Fazackerley, a 29-year-old journalist, and then in 2009 – a year after he became London mayor – he fathered a child with Helen Macintyre, a 39-year-old art consultant. Three years later a High Court judge ruled the press could report on the child because the then mayor's 'recklessness' in conducting extra-marital affairs called into question his fitness for public office. Wheeler was said to have tolerated Johnson's philandering because she viewed it as a 'childish side of his personality which one day he'll grow out of'.[7] But by September 2018 her tolerance had run out, and the couple issued a statement saying they had separated and begun divorce proceedings after 25 years of marriage.

It was Symonds who was the final straw. Johnson and Symonds had first been photographed together in February 2018, seven months before Wheeler announced their separation. The pair were pictured laughing outside the Conservative Party's fundraising Black and White Ball and dined together on Valentine's Day in Covent Garden. Johnson had first crossed paths with Symonds when the then 22-year-old was helping his campaign in the 2010 London Conservative Party mayoral election. A highly capable young woman, she moved quickly up the party ranks, rising to become the special adviser to Javid before being appointed as the Conservative Party's head of communications at the age of just 29 in 2018. By March 2019 her relationship with Johnson was out in the open and the pair went holidaying together in Italy.

By early June that year, Symonds, now aged 31, was part of the Johnson team when the 55-year-old publicly launched his campaign for the Tory leadership, and they were now increasingly being spotted at public events together. That month, police were called to her flat in Camberwell, south-east London, after neighbours had heard screaming, shouting and banging inside. Symonds could allegedly be heard telling Johnson to 'get off me' and 'get out of my flat'. In a recording of the altercation made by a neighbour, which was reported by the *Guardian*,[8] Johnson refuses to leave the flat and tells Symonds to 'get off my fucking laptop', before a loud crashing noise rings out. Symonds tells Johnson he was ruining a sofa with red wine: 'You just don't care for anything because you're spoilt. You have no care for money or anything.' Both Johnson and Symonds refused to comment on the incident.

For Johnson's family looking on, there were even more embarrassments. In September 2019 the journalist Charlotte Edwardes wrote a column in *The Sunday Times*[9] alleging that Johnson had squeezed her inner thigh under the table while she was sitting next to him at a *Spectator* lunch in 1999. When she compared notes with the woman sitting on the other side of Johnson, she said he had done the same thing to her. Rumours quickly spread that week at the Conservative Party conference that the other woman was Mary Wakefield – the wife of Dominic Cummings. Wakefield issued a denial that she was the other woman at the table. Johnson also firmly denied groping Edwardes, but the allegation put Matt Hancock in an awkward position when he was pressed for his reaction on television. To his credit, he took the brave route and said: 'I know Charlotte well and I entirely trust what she has to say. I know her and I know her to be trustworthy.' In another interview, he answered the question in a more roundabout way, which itself was telling: 'Boris has never lectured other people about their private lives. I think that we should concentrate on delivering on what we are in politics for, which in my view is to serve the citizens of this country.'

In the conclusion to her column, Edwardes made clear how seriously she viewed the matter. 'But what has really changed? It's a reference point, I suppose – I was able to say recently, to a work contact putting his hand on my knee during lunch: "Actually that's illegal now, can you please stop?"' she wrote. 'Then again, the double thigh-squeezer is prime minister. He's seen off mere papery knee-fondlers – two ministers were flung out for this in 2017 – and now he's installed in No. 10, where, I imagine, he man-sprawls the sofas, brushing crumbs from his tie, while, upstairs, his bedroom is a Tracey Emin installation. Happy #MeToo anniversary, everyone.'

While these events must have been excruciating for his children, there was sadder news in the family that added to the complexity of their relationship with their father. In January 2019 Wheeler was told that she would have to undergo hospital tests after a routine screening for cervical cancer detected abnormal cells. It was just four months after it was announced she was divorcing Johnson. The diagnosis of cancer was confirmed in May, which meant she had to undergo two potentially life-saving operations that summer.

So Johnson had a lot on his mind during those days at Chevening. He was preparing to announce his forthcoming marriage and the birth of a child to a woman who was just five years more advanced in age than the oldest of his children – while divorcing their mother who was recovering from a life-threatening illness. Even some in his own party believed that his chaotic personal life was not just a problem for his family; it was also a distraction that was bad news for the nation.

Montgomerie, his adviser during that time, saw first-hand the effect Johnson's personal life was having on his decision making and, in the end, he'd had enough. He would resign when Johnson returned to London later that month. 'On 27 February I told him that, with enormous sadness, I was walking away from his offer to me of a "great project". I could see the car crash coming and I couldn't bear to be part of it,' he said. He believes the upheaval in Johnson's private life and losing the strong stabilising effect of his wife Marina was affecting Johnson adversely. '[Marina had] an extraordinary brain; unafraid to dispense home truths. She was his anchor and, despite everything, had been for most of his adulthood. He's now divorced and, while I wish nothing but happiness for Johnson and Carrie Symonds, I can't make sense of so much of his turbulent time in Downing Street without thinking that the turbulence in his private life does a great deal of the explaining. Few of us would be unaffected in similar circumstances.'

Coronavirus was not the only major issue that did not get the attention it deserved while the prime minister was on holiday in Chevening. People up and down the country were asking where he was when the second big storm hit Britain on the weekend beginning Saturday 15 February, causing misery for thousands of people who were left homeless by the flooding. As the rain from Storm Dennis lashed down outside Chevening, a cosy morning inside with the newspapers might have been highly informative for the prime minister. *The Sunday Times* was reporting on a briefing from a risk specialist predicting that Public Health England would be overrun during a pandemic because it only had the capacity to test 1,000 people a day.[10] It also warned that there were major potential problems about the supply of personal protective equipment to health workers. 'The epidemic containment effort in China has already created a global shortage of essential medical supplies including test kits, protective masks and gloves,' the report stated. 'This shortage is already so severe that China has resorted to using CT-scans as surrogate tests to ensure capture of most Covid-19 patients. Outside China, testing has also been mainly limited to symptomatic and highly suspect cases. It is worth remembering that most factories for these supplies are in China or southeast Asia, and pandemic-related disruption of this supply chain would just feed into a vicious circle.' These were problems that needed to be addressed immediately.

But the government seemed to be blithely sailing on without any sense of urgency. In the case of PPE it had actually decided to give some of its supplies away to the very country that manufactured most of the equipment in its stockpile: China. While it would have been wise to have stored every possible item of PPE in readiness for the pandemic and make it a top priority to buy in more, the government shipped 279,000 items of its depleted stockpile to China in or around early to mid-February. It could be viewed as a kind humanitarian gesture by the government in response to a request for help from the Chinese authorities. However, real-world politics was also involved as Johnson's government needed to curry favour with the Chinese at a time when it was still struggling to strike the trade deals it needed in the wake of Brexit. It would be a matter of weeks before NHS chiefs were giving briefings warning that a lack of PPE left the health service facing a 'nightmare'. But, nonetheless, containers filled with 1,800 pairs of goggles, 43,000 disposable gloves, 194,000 sanitising wipes, 37,500 medical gowns and 2,500 facemasks were dispatched to the Far East. There could not have been a clearer sign that the government had underestimated the threat. When we later revealed this extraordinary giveaway in *The Sunday Times*, the government's defence was to argue that China had later sent large amounts of PPE to Britain. But on closer inspection, the Chinese supplies the government was describing were commercial deals that the British government paid for rather than a reciprocation of the earlier generosity. In fact, Britain was, in effect, buying back the PPE it had given China for free in February. It would also take another six to eight weeks before Britain was able to purchase these supplies from China and, by then, the NHS was already running out of protective kit, with some medical staff having to resort to buying their own makeshift kit from DIY stores.

Indeed, as part of the charm offensive with China, Johnson had to make an important work call during his holiday in Chevening. On the morning of Tuesday 18 February he spoke to Xi Jinping, the Chinese president, who immediately thanked him for the UK's donation of the medical protection kit. Liu Xiaoming, China's ambassador to Britain, later described how Johnson had gushingly praised China in the call and told Xi that he 'loves China and he wants to work with China to elevate the relationship to a new level'. The call is believed to have been set up through an unusual back channel involving Johnson's father Stanley, who had met with the Chinese ambassador in early February. Liu had expressed concern that the prime minister had not shown public support for China over the coronavirus crisis and Stanley had then passed on the message to his son via email to Zac Goldsmith, the minister for international development. The truth was that Johnson had not said anything much publicly about coronavirus at all, apart from playing down its significance. So it wasn't surprising he hadn't talked about China's struggle with the virus.

But the Chinese relationship was important and the call seemed to do the trick. The two countries had set up a working team the previous year to lay the foundations for a trade deal, but this had been stalled by the negotiations with the European Union. On the day following the call, Liu announced that China was ready to restart preparatory work with British officials on a future trade deal. He said China would now engage with Britain 'more positively'. He added: 'We are ready to work with our British colleagues any time.' It was good news for the UK, but it was also another way in which the one-eyed obsession with Brexit had come before preparations to combat the virus.

The fifth Cobra meeting on the virus had taken place on the day of the call to the Chinese leader. Johnson, of course, did not attend, even though it is only a one-hour drive from Chevening to Whitehall. Once again, the post-Brexit dealings had taken precedence. There was a symmetry to Johnson's actions. The first and last Cobra meetings he missed were both on days when he chose to give time to the Chinese rather than the virus. He was paying tribute to a country that had not done the world any favours by concealing the seriousness of the threat in the initial weeks back in January. Remarkably, it would be another fortnight before a further Cobra meeting on the virus would be called, despite the fact that cases in the UK were multiplying exponentially.

While those cases might not have been picked up by the contact tracers, there was real evidence that British people were being caught up in the unfolding disaster across the globe on the *Diamond Princess*, the British-registered cruise ship moored off the city of Yokohama, south of Tokyo. So it was even more remarkable that the prime minister was absent from the 18 February Cobra meeting – many would later describe it as a complete dereliction of his duty. The *Diamond Princess* was being overwhelmed with the biggest cluster of infections outside China. There were now 355 confirmed cases among its 3,900 passengers, who had all been ordered to quarantine in their cabins. Over the weekend, the US government had announced plans to charter a plane to repatriate its 400 citizens held on the ship. There were 80 British citizens on board, but no such plan had been put in place by the British government to help them escape. It was a nightmarish existence on the ship, with passengers cooped up and fearing for their lives. Anger was starting to break out on board.

David Abel, 73, and his wife Sally, from Woodford Halse in Northamptonshire, had been posting regular updates on social media of life on board. Abel had been a staunch Tory supporter but he was starting to direct his frustration at Johnson's government. 'Don't you want the English people home? I am always proud to be British but this now – it's gone beyond a joke, I've never felt less loved by my own country. I thought the UK would be as quick as the USA. But it just shows we're wrong … We are literally being treated like trash.' Directly addressing Johnson, he said: 'When he just says "keep calm, don't panic," I'd like to see you in this situation, mate. I really would.'

It would take another five days for the UK government to repatriate its citizens. By that time, they had been stuck on the ship for more than two weeks. But before the airlift, David and Sally tested positive for the virus, alongside two other Brits, and had to be taken to a Japanese hospital to be treated for pneumonia. They would not return home for many weeks. Fourteen of those on board the *Diamond Princess* died of the disease, including a British man who would become the first known UK citizen to perish from the virus.

Meanwhile, it was clear that affairs of state were on a bit of a back seat at the Chevening country house, despite repeated claims that this was 'a working holiday'. Members of the Downing Street policy unit were told to provide 'weekend reading' for the prime minister on key aspects of policy. But they were told to cut the number of memos in his red box if they actually wanted Johnson to bother to read them. One source told *The Sunday Times*: 'They've been told it should be an easy read: no more than four pages, or he's never going to read it. Two pages is preferable.' Another official said: 'Box submissions have to be brief … if they're overly long or overly complex, Dom sends them back with savage comments.' It led a Whitehall source to accuse Johnson and Cummings of running 'government by ADHD'.[11]

One of the key things that the government missed while Johnson was away in Chevening was the chance to pool resources with the EU to combat the virus. The EU had held a conference call for heads of state to discuss jointly tackling the coronavirus on the first day of his holiday. A key initiative by the EU was to set up a common purchase scheme for ventilators, which were vital to treating the severest Covid-19 cases and were in short supply globally. Britain was invited on to the call, but Johnson had not taken up the opportunity and the UK also missed the deadline to join the scheme. It would be the first of eight such conference calls that he would miss by the end of March. Johnson's spokesman would later blame an administrative error for the failure to sign up to the scheme.

There was by now a growing frustration among the prime minister's own officials about his lack of leadership on the virus and his failure to knuckle down and fully understand the potential crisis. 'There's no way you're at war if your PM isn't there,' the Downing Street adviser said. 'And what you learn about Boris was he didn't chair any meetings. He liked his country breaks. He didn't work weekends. It was like working for an old-fashioned chief executive in a local authority 20 years ago. There was a real sense that he didn't do urgent crisis planning. It was exactly like people feared he would be.'

Johnson was also under pressure to return from Chevening on Wednesday 19 February to chair another Cobra meeting on a separate matter. Storm Dennis had been devastating. By now it had blasted Wales and the south with 90 mph winds and torrential rain, which has caused further severe flooding. Five people had been killed, 400 homes were underwater, and hundreds of people were being evacuated. But water levels were still rising, threatening thousands more people's homes. He was an easy target for the opposition, who questioned why he was refusing to quit his working break to take personal charge of the crisis or even to visit the affected areas. Jeremy Corbyn, the Labour leader, said: 'In refusing to visit flood-hit communities, nowhere-to-be-seen Boris Johnson is showing his true colours by his absence.' He went on: 'Failing to convene Cobra to support flood-hit communities sends a very clear message: if the prime minister is not campaigning for votes in a general election he simply does not care about helping communities affected by flooding.' In fact, one person had been killed and hundreds of homes had been left without electricity in Kent – the county where the prime minister was staying. MPs and council leaders said the lack of leadership had actively obstructed the response in some towns and delayed the release of vital funds. One angry councillor asked: 'Where is Boris? I haven't seen him in his wellies reassuring people whose lives have been ruined.'[12] Johnson would later say he had not wanted to distract from the rescue efforts.

The headaches were mounting for Johnson during his 'working holiday'. On the following Saturday, 22 February, another of his more colourful sexual liaisons from the past came back to haunt him. It was a troublesome matter he had brought upon himself that had been proving yet another diversion as people around him were looking to him for leadership. In some ways this affair was almost cartoonish. Jennifer Arcuri was a blonde bubbly American businesswoman and former model whom he had visited regularly for sex in her top-floor London flat with its silver dancing pole – while he was the city's mayor and still married. But serious matters had arisen from his relationship with Arcuri. We had broken the story in *The Sunday Times* the previous September and it had become the most serious scandal involving a sitting prime minister since Tony Blair was interviewed by the police over the award of peerages to donors in 2006.

Johnson was accused of abusing his position by giving Arcuri taxpayer-funded favours while he was London mayor, and he was facing a possible police investigation into the criminal offence of misconduct in public office. That Saturday, he received an urgent written request from the Independent Office for Police Conduct (IOPC), which was the body tasked with deciding whether to carry out a formal criminal inquiry into his dealings with Arcuri. It instructed him to hand over all of his communications with Arcuri and the records and dates of all of their liaisons. The IOPC had asked him for the information once before. But it wanted to check that there was no mistake and that Johnson was sticking to his claim that he possessed no texts or emails from the affair, which had gone on for years. The messages must have been destroyed or lost, because Johnson and Arcuri had been regularly in touch with each other over a long period.

The story had come about because we had met a source in an airy London hotel in the summer of 2019 and, over tea and biscuits, they told us that the man who was about to become prime minister had been engaged in a passionate affair with Arcuri, a vivacious former model turned tech entrepreneur who had been 26 years old when they first met. Johnson had been 48 years old at the time. The fact that Johnson had been engaged in yet another affair was hardly a story and it would not have made the pages of our newspaper unless there was a more important issue at stake. But there was. The source alleged that while the sexual relationship was ongoing, Arcuri had improperly received sponsorship money and favours from the mayor's office for her loss-making businesses. When we later checked Johnson's register of interests, he had failed to mention Arcuri at all as a potential conflict of interest. On the face of it, there was evidence of wrongdoing, but first we had to establish the facts. It took months to piece together what happened between 'BoJen' – as a friend had once described Johnson and Arcuri – before we published the story on 22 September on the front page of *The Sunday Times*.

The article detailed how Arcuri and her fledgling businesses had been given £126,000 of public money, despite the firms having jointly lost more than a million pounds. Much of that was sponsorship cash from the mayor's promotional agency, London & Partners, which Johnson had responsibility for at the time. Johnson had also attended numerous events that Arcuri had arranged to promote her company in his official capacity as mayor, while declining to attend similar more established events run by other London businesses. She had also received preferential treatment by being given permission to attend overseas trade missions led by Johnson, where she could promote her business. In fact, her businesses had not met the eligibility criteria for any of the three Johnson trade missions she attended in the space of just a year. Arcuri had initially been turned down for trips to New York and Tel Aviv by officials, but these decisions were overturned after intervention by Johnson's close team. One internal email described how she was given access to a New York trade mission after she had discussed the matter with Johnson and he had been happy for her to take part.

As mayor, Johnson was bound by the code of conduct of the Greater London Authority (GLA) 'to declare any private interests relating to their public duties and to take steps to resolve any conflicts arising in a way that protects the public interest'. He was also expressly barred from providing any undue benefits to friends. Yet there is no doubt that Arcuri was a friend and more – as she confirmed to a number of our sources. Arcuri herself gave a series of television and newspaper interviews following the *Sunday Times* story in which she coyly hinted that she had been intimate with Johnson, but it wasn't until a year later, in October 2020, that she finally confirmed their affair.

The relationship is believed to have begun in the autumn of 2012 and lasted until the spring of 2016. Arcuri later showed the television journalist John Ware her diary entries and text messages from Johnson spanning from 2012 to 2018. According to Ware, Arcuri's diary makes clear that she thought Johnson was obsessed with her and she might one day have gone on to be his partner in Downing Street, but she had reservations about whether he was the type of man she would want to start a family with.[13] She decided to end the relationship after he had taken her to his family home in north London when his wife was away. Johnson understood his duties of disclosure as London mayor. He had previously been rapped on the knuckles by the Greater London Authority's Standards Committee for failing to declare his relationship with Macintyre, the mother of his fifth child, when he appointed her as an unpaid City Hall adviser in 2009.

He had expressly told Arcuri that she should not speak to newspapers about their relationship. Arcuri attempted to contact him when she first heard that we were investigating her business affairs in the summer of 2019. She claims he answered the call, gasped when he heard her voice and immediately passed the phone to an aide who spoke in a Chinese accent, presumably to make Arcuri believe that she had the wrong number. From then on, her calls were blocked. She says she was saddened that Johnson had prioritised his ambitions and career over their friendship, which she still valued.

By February 2020 many of these details were in the public domain and the IOPC investigators would themselves uncover evidence that Arcuri and Johnson had been engaged in a sexual affair in 2014. They did not, however, have access to our sources and it was before the admission from Arcuri. For reasons that are unclear, the texts and diaries that Arcuri had shown to Ware were not given to the IOPC investigators and it did not have the powers to seize them since their inquiries were merely a review before a formal investigation. The prime minister deliberated with his lawyers for 10 days before responding to the IOPC's request. On Wednesday 4 March his legal team sent the investigators an email, again claiming that he did not hold any of the information requested.

Outside Chevening, the body in charge of the UK's contact tracing was congratulating itself. On Friday 21 February there was a blog post from Duncan Selbie, chief executive of Public Health England. He was in charge of 5,500 staff who were responsible for running laboratories, developing tests and managing outbreaks in England. When he took on the £185,000-a-year job in 2013, Selbie had joked that his public health credentials could be fitted 'on a postage stamp'.[14] His lack of experience may have contributed to his words that day. 'There have been no new positive cases this week in the UK, which is testament to the robust infection control measures in place, as well as the diagnostic and testing work that is happening in laboratories across the country,' he wrote.

In fact the virus had been spreading like wildfire. According to estimates by Oxford University and Imperial College London, the number of infections in Britain that day had soared to 1,600, which was a 22-fold increase since Johnson had departed for Chevening just over a week earlier. By then, Selbie's track and trace programme had only picked up a total of 23 cases in the UK – just 1 in 70 of the estimated actual infections. Even worse, by now there were reckoned to be 41,000 infections in Italy. With thousands of Britons returning from Italian ski resorts and tourist spots after their half-term holidays, a flood of new infections would have entered the country through the unprotected borders over the final week in February. Nicky Longley, an infectious diseases consultant at London's Hospital for Tropical Diseases, was part of a team that staffed a public health service helpline for those with symptoms. The plan, she said, had been to make all efforts to catch every case and their contacts. 'To start with, it looked like it was working,' she said. 'I don't think anybody really foresaw what was happening in Italy ... and I think, the minute everybody saw that, we thought: "This is game over now."[15]

On the same Friday, the scientists on Nervtag, the key advisory committee to the government specialising in respiratory illness, decided to keep the threat level at 'moderate'. But the decision was not unanimous among the group's members. Professor John Edmunds, one of the country's top infectious disease modellers from the London School of Hygiene & Tropical Medicine, was participating in the meeting by video link, but his technology failed him at the crucial moment. Edmunds wanted the threat level to be increased to high, but could not make his view known as the link was glitchy. He sent an email later making his view clear. 'JE believes that the risk to the UK population [in the PHE risk assessment] should be high, as there is evidence of ongoing transmission in Korea, Japan and Singapore, as well as in China,' the meeting's minutes state. But the decision had already been taken.

Peter Openshaw, Professor of Experimental Medicine at Imperial College and another Nervtag member, was in America at the time of the meeting and also believed the threat to be high. Three days earlier he had given an address to a seminar in which he estimated that 60 per cent of the world's population would become infected if no action were taken and 400,000 people would die in the UK. He feared too little was being done by the politicians, who were failing to heed warnings about the virus's threat. 'It was hard to get people to really take notice,' he recalled, adding that when he had raised concerns they 'were being brushed aside'. A source on the Nervtag committee said the virus was simply a low priority for the government agenda at the time. 'It was clear from looking at what politicians were talking about that they were still very much thinking about Brexit. This wasn't top of the agenda.'

But anyone wondering how disastrous the virus could be would only have to look at China, where it had already infected

75,000 people and caused 2,300 deaths. On Saturday, Tedros Adhanom Ghebreyesus, the World Health Organization director-general, issued a stark warning. He said the opportunity to contain the wider spread of the deadly coronavirus was slipping away. 'The window of opportunity is narrowing, so we need to act quickly before it closes completely,' he declared.

6

Part-Time Prime Minister

Monday 24 February 2020 to Sunday 1 March 2020
UK government's risk assessment: Moderate

For party events in the evening, the Evolution Club in the middle of Battersea Park, south London, transforms into a neon glass palace with laser lights and glitter balls. It was here that the prime minister made his entrance back into the public arena after his 12-day absence – clambering onto the stage at the Conservative's annual Black and White Ball. With microphone in hand, he attempted to sing the opening line of 'Land of My Fathers' for Wynne Evans, the Welsh opera-singing star of the Go Compare insurance adverts, who was on the stage next to him. 'A touch of the John Redwoods,' Evans quipped, referring to Johnson's Tory colleague's memorably comic attempt to mime the Welsh national anthem when he was the secretary of state for the country. There was then the briefest of duets of another Welsh rugby anthem before Evans cut the prime minister short. 'What a singer,' Evans said unconvincingly, and then it was on to the main business of the evening, with Johnson starting off the auction.

The fundraising event for the party on Tuesday 25 February was attended by 700 wealthy Conservative supporters, who sat around tables costing £15,000 each and dined on red mullet, salsa verde and artichoke, washed down with champagne and white burgundy. Johnson was touting a game of tennis as his auction lot – in which he would be the opponent and the Conservative Party chairman would be the ballboy. Two rich supporters won the chance to play against the prime minister by offering an eye-watering £90,000. One was the wife of an ally of Vladimir Putin. It was that sort of party. David Ross, the Carphone Warehouse founder who had arranged Johnson's holiday in the Caribbean a few weeks earlier, auctioned a grouse-shooting party on his country estate. Donors could also dubiously buy access to the new chancellor Rishi Sunak by sharing a box with him at Lord's for an England versus Australia one-day cricket match. The secretary of state for justice, Robert Buckland QC, was offering, somewhat unappealingly, lunch served in a prison. Whether that was the correct use of Her Majesty's prison service was an interesting point. And there was also a reminder of how the world was changing. 'Among the unconventional lots', the society magazine *Tatler* remarked wryly, was 'a trip to a villa in northern Italy – an area currently in the grip of a Coronavirus outbreak'.

The news from Italy was becoming increasingly alarming. The Mediterranean country had become the first in Europe to be hit hard by the virus. It had detected its first known cases on 29 January – the same day as the UK, and just as in Britain they were two people who had recently arrived from China. The number of cases then quickly accelerated for reasons that remain unknown. People speculated that perhaps the Italian cultural custom of social kissing and hugging may have been responsible for the rapid spread of the virus. But it is more likely that the country had a larger number of infections in January than anyone had realised. This is perhaps because it was initially prevalent among younger people in the country's ski resorts, who were either: asymptomatic; mildly affected; or their illness wasn't recognised as coronavirus.

On the day before the Conservatives' ball, Italy had been forced to bring in the first control measures, with the country's sports minister announcing that all upcoming football Serie A matches would be played behind closed doors to combat the virus's spread. Stopping football in Italy was a serious move. The Italian health service was beginning to realise that it might not cope, as it was becoming overrun with the virus much more quickly than anyone thought was possible. In total, over 229 cases had been detected, including a major outbreak in the northern region of Lombardy, which has Milan as its capital. There had been six deaths on the Monday, but this had leapt up to eleven on the Tuesday. 'The details that came from Lombardy were horrible so we had to really focus to help to find ventilators to increase the number of intensive care units, to ask for new doctors and new nurses from other parts of Italy to go into Lombardy. This was really a disaster,' recounts Professor Walter Ricciardi, the Italian government's scientific adviser.[1]

The number of infections was actually a huge underestimate. According to back-dated modelling by Oxford University and Imperial College London, the virus was completely out of control in Italy, the academics calculating that there were already approximately 51,000 people infected. But even the known cases at the time were enough for people in Britain to sit up and take notice. Devi Sridhar, the Professor of Global Public Health at Edinburgh University, had been monitoring the disease as it entered Europe and she was becoming increasingly concerned. 'I remember at the time I was trying very actively to reach out to colleagues, to friends. I was tweeting and saying, "Please try to start physically distancing, pay attention to what's happening in Italy" because we were just a few weeks behind,' she said. 'We had the benefit of time; we should use that time. But some people would come back and say, "You're scaremongering" or "You're inciting panic."'[2]

There were also fears over the sudden spread of the virus in Iran, which had seen a sharp rise in cases to 95 over the previous week. By now, 2,000 people outside China were confirmed to have been infected in 28 countries, but the World Health Organization was still holding back from calling the outbreak a pandemic. Many experts, however, were in no doubt that its spread was worldwide. 'We now consider this to be a pandemic in all but name, and it's only a matter of time before the World Health Organization starts to use the term in its communications,' said Dr Bharat Pankhania, from the University of Exeter Medical School.[3]

But despite the worrying news from around the world and from a European country with close ties to the UK, the prime minister still did not appear to be doing anything proactive. The only meetings in Johnson's official diary over those first two days of the week since he had been back in London were a reception for women's and lifestyle magazine editors and a 'general discussion' with Chris Evans, the editor of the *Telegraph*, whose newspaper had paid him £275,000 to write articles in his time between resigning his foreign secretary job in 2018 and becoming prime minister in 2019. The prime minister's failure to give priority to the two twin emergencies – the virus and the flooding of people's homes – offered an easy target for his opponents. Even Corbyn, the defeated and deflated Labour leader in his last days at the helm of the party, could not miss this open goal.

At Prime Minister's Questions in the Commons, Corbyn accused Johnson of being 'silent, sulking in his grace-and-favour mansion in Chevening' rather than leading on the virus crisis or visiting the parts of the country hit hardest by the floods. 'How can the country trust a prime minister, a part-time prime minister, who last night was schmoozing Tory Party donors at a very expensive black-tie ball instead of getting out there and supporting the people who are suffering because of the floods?' He added: 'Memes are being produced, asking not, "Where's Wally?" but, "Where's Boris?" When is he going to stop hiding and show people that he actually cares, or is he too busy going about some other business? ... He often goes AWOL: he was late to respond to the London riots because he was on holiday; he was on a private island when the Iranian general was assassinated; and last week he had his head in the sand in a mansion in Kent.' Johnson dismissed Corbyn's 'jabbering' and insisted there had been 'a constant stream of ministerial activity' while he was away.

But it was not the end of Johnson's discomfort. It was the turn of his former chancellor Javid, now sitting on the back benches, to give a speech explaining his departure. Javid's attacks were more subtle but cut deeper than Corbyn's. Javid had barely opened his mouth before Johnson was blushing. He did not name the man, but his initial words left no doubt he was referring to the prime minister's chief adviser. He opened up with a jab at the all-powerful position Johnson had ceded to Cummings. 'Conservatives especially believe that no particular person, or even a government, has a monopoly on the best ideas,' he said. 'Advisers advise, ministers decide, and ministers decide on their advisers.' He then said with a smile: 'Now I don't intend to dwell further on the details and personalities. The Cummings and goings, if you will.' His joke prompted laughter across the chamber's political divide and caused Johnson to sink further into his seat in front of the dispatch box.

There were signs, however, that Javid's enemy – the prime minister's chief adviser – was beginning to sense that coronavirus was more of a problem than Downing Street had previously realised. Cummings had sent one of his most trusted lieutenants, Ben Warner, to listen in on the Sage expert committee meetings, which were now taking place regularly in response to the virus. Warner was a data scientist who helped mastermind the computer modelling for Vote Leave's 2016 referendum campaign and Cummings had drafted him into No. 10 to do similar analysis for the Conservative Party's 2019 general election campaign.

He had joined the committee as an observer for the first time on Thursday 20 February – which was the ninth meeting Sage had held to discuss the UK's reaction to the virus. He was also present at a key meeting the following Tuesday, the day of the Black and White Ball, and would continue to attend most of the

Sage meetings until lockdown. Later, Cummings would join him too. Their presence, when it was revealed months later, would cause controversy, with concerns being expressed that they may have inappropriately influenced the discussions. But it did at least mean that Downing Street was listening directly to the scientific debate, even if it didn't always heed the experts' advice.

The Tuesday Sage meeting was held as usual in the drab grey monolith Department for Business building behind Westminster Abbey at 10 Victoria Street. Sitting around the table while Warner watched were: the government's chief scientific and medical advisers, Vallance and Whitty; the NHS's medical director, Professor Stephen Powis; the chief scientific advisers to the Home Office, the Department for International Development and the Department of Transport; the infection director for Public Health England; Sir Jeremy Farrar of the Wellcome Trust; Professors John Edmunds and Graham Medley from the London School of Hygiene & Tropical Medicine; and Professor Neil Ferguson from Imperial College. The minutes of the meeting show the committee noted how effective extreme measures – such as closing schools and imposing social distancing – had been to limit the spread of the virus when they were used in Wuhan, Hong Kong and Singapore.

The total number of infections in China had rocketed to the 75,000 mark by mid-February. But the strict lockdown in Wuhan and other major cities – which also included the closure of public transport and the shutdown of non-essential businesses – had reduced the number of new cases to a few hundred a day. Sage noted that social distancing and school closures appeared to halve the virus's reproduction number, known as R, down to a score of one. This was the crucial tipping point because the R number signified the average number of people that an infected person passes the virus on to. A score above one meant the virus would begin to exponentially spread. A score below one and the outbreak would shrink. The Sage minutes, which were kept strictly secret at the time, state: 'All measures require implementation for a significant duration in order to be effective ... Reduced spread in the UK through a combination of these measures was assessed to be realistic.' In other words, the scientists were beginning to consider the possibility of a lockdown in Britain.

In a sense it is not surprising that such drastic measures were being contemplated as early as 25 February, as it was becoming increasingly clear that the alternative of doing nothing could prove catastrophic. Sage had asked Edmunds – who had been thwarted from saying the threat level should be raised the previous week – to model the latest 'worst scenario' predictions. The following day Edmunds and his team at LSHTM presented the findings to the scientific pandemic influenza group on modelling (SPI-M), which directly advises Sage. The warnings will have made uncomfortable reading when they filtered their way up to Cummings and ministers.

The modelling report predicted that 27 million people could be infected and 220,000 intensive care beds would be needed if no action at all was taken to reduce infection rates. The predicted death toll was 370,000 by December 2021 without any intervention to prevent the spread of the virus. The modelling was still a work in progress. According to Edmunds's colleague Nick Davies, who led the research, the report had suggested the need for wider measures to control the spread of the virus. It had not yet recommended an actual lockdown, but the team were in the process of modelling the effects of a 12-week lockdown involving school and work closures, shielding the elderly, social distancing and self-isolation.

The number of confirmed infections in the UK had by now risen to 13 – after four British people had returned home with the virus from the *Diamond Princess* the previous weekend. In fact, the back-dated modelling research estimated that there were actually probably 2,000 infections by that point. The possibility of large-scale unseen spread had been acknowledged by the government's Spi-M advisory committee more than a fortnight earlier, which warned: 'It is a realistic probability that there is already sustained transmission in the UK, or that it will become established in the coming weeks.'

Yet, inexplicably, Public Health England was giving out confusing advice on the Tuesday of the Sage meeting and the Conservative Party's ball. They issued guidance informing the care home sector, which was looking after Britain's most elderly and vulnerable people, that 'the current position in the UK' was that 'there is currently no transmission of Covid-19 in the community'. Care home staff were told they did not need to wear facemasks and the public health body added that it was 'very unlikely that anyone receiving care in a care home or the community will become infected'. That guidance remained in force for a further 19 days. It seemed clear that Public Health England was out of touch with what was actually happening. The Sage minutes show that the public health body had only begun a surveillance operation that week to gather data that would provide 'sufficient sensitivity to detect an outbreak in its early stages' and might give a 9- to 11-week warning prior to the epidemic reaching its peak. Why this work started so late is a mystery, because there had been clear warnings for more than a month.

The health secretary, meanwhile, was making one of those big claims that would become his trademark during the crisis. Hancock was going to save the world from the virus. 'Plans are in place in case of the virus becoming a pandemic, but it is not yet certain that that will happen … we aim to contain the virus both abroad and here at home, and prevent it from becoming a pandemic,' he proudly told the Commons on Wednesday afternoon. It wasn't entirely clear to the MPs watching on how he was going to do this. He mentioned only a slim package of measures such as advising people to use tissues and wash their hands more, and introducing 'enhanced monitoring' at airports.

But in reality, only a tiny fraction of people coming to the UK were monitored or tested and there was a half-heartedness about the government's approach that raised questions about how seriously it was taking the threat. The approach to the question of Italy, in particular, lacked conviction. That day – the Tuesday of the Conservative's Black and White Ball – the Italian government had put 11 towns in the regions of Lombardy and Veneto into lockdown, with police manning checkpoints to impose the quarantine measures. The UK's response to the deepening crisis there was to ask anyone returning to Britain from the 11 towns to self-isolate. But it was obvious that the outbreak would have already spread far beyond those towns. Indeed, any tourist who had been to those towns would have to return through airports and fly on planes before they came home to self-isolate. So, they would have closely mingled for hours with other travellers heading to Britain with no social distancing. Yet the government did not require people who had been in other areas of northern Italy to self-isolate unless they had already experienced symptoms.

Perhaps even more cavalier was the approach to passengers from China. Flights from Wuhan had been stopped and the city was in lockdown, but there was no requirement for people to self-isolate if they came to the UK from anywhere else in China. This was despite China having more infections than any other country in the world: the official figures were 78,496 cases and 2,744 deaths by that Wednesday. Hancock was challenged over this strange discrepancy between the arrangements for China and the towns in northern Italy by Philippa Whitford, the Scottish National Party's health spokesperson. 'Does the Secretary of State recognise the confusion there is that those returning from certain parts of north Italy must self-isolate, even if asymptomatic, but those coming from China do not need to self-isolate if asymptomatic?' she asked. 'That is causing confusion and we may end up behind the curve. If containment is to work, we must be ahead of the curve.' Rather than give a full explanation, Hancock did as he would often do as the crisis unfolded and hid behind the scientists. 'I do not recognise the idea that we should change travel advice between China and Italy,' he said. 'We should base travel advice on expert clinical evidence.' He did not elaborate on the nature of that clinical evidence.

The main measure that had been put in place at airports was still simply handing out pamphlets to international passengers advising them to get tested if they had symptoms of the virus. To this end an isolation unit had been set up at Heathrow to test anyone who had a flu-like illness upon arrival. But even this was piecemeal. In the Commons that day there was consternation about why such isolation units had not been set up at the UK's many other airports where tourists were also flooding in from northern Italy. Jon Ashworth, the shadow health secretary, asked Hancock to 'explain to the House why that facility is proposed only for Heathrow, and why similar facilities will not be in place at other major airports, particularly the bigger airports such as Manchester?' Hancock replied: 'We chose a facility near Heathrow because that is the point of biggest throughput, but we do not rule out rolling that out more broadly if we think it necessary.' Again, he did not explain the anomaly. Hancock was then pressed by his own Conservative colleague Henry Smith, the MP for Crawley, about why there was no such unit in his local airport, Gatwick, which, he pointed out, 'of course has many flights to and from both Asia and Europe?' Hancock's response was enigmatic. 'We do not need it yet – but that is all part of the plan,' he said.

It was never made clear what the cunning plan was or why Gatwick was viewed so differently to Heathrow. Hancock was asked about what measures were in place for family members who lived with someone self-isolating and were therefore at grave risk of catching the virus from them? Labour MP Hilary Benn enquired: 'Should they go about their normal business – go to work or go to school if they are children – in those circumstances?' Hancock's advice was that 'other family members with no symptoms should go about their normal business in the normal way.' In other words, despite the high likelihood they could have contracted the virus from the infected family member, they would be allowed to go about their lives, potentially spreading it to friends, colleagues and all the other people they met and mingled with in the course of the day. This was especially dangerous because the Chinese health minister had warned about asymptomatic spread at the end of January, and the UK's first so-called 'superspreader' had demonstrated that it was possible for one person to pass the virus on to large numbers of people without showing any symptoms.

Later, a major genetic study by Oxford and Edinburgh universities would show that most of the early infections that had triggered Britain's epidemic had come from people travelling into Britain from Europe. The researchers found 1,356 different strains of the virus in 16,500 people in Britain who had tested positive for the infection in the first half of the year. They then worked out where each strain had originated by comparing it to samples taken in other countries. They found that more than 1,000 different people had brought the coronavirus into Britain, which ruled out the idea that one superspreader or 'patient zero' sparked the outbreak. Most of the infections in February had indeed originated in Italy, although later Spain and France became the main origin countries. In total, 77 per cent of all cases in the first half of the year could be traced back to these three countries.

A separate report by the Institute for Economics and Peace found that Covid-19 outbreaks had been worse in areas with major airports, describing the UK as a prime example of a place where constant domestic and international flights had 'facilitated contagion'. Hancock's 'enhanced monitoring' had been ineffectual. Far from saving the world, his failure to take decisive action had actually helped accelerate the virus's spread in the country he was supposed to be protecting.

* * *

People across Britain were starting to take their own precautions as an anxiety about the virus began to creep in. At least 14 schools had shut their doors by Thursday 27 February, despite government advice to stay open, and pupils from dozens of others stayed at home amid fears they may have been exposed to coronavirus during trips to northern Italy. Among those affected was Thomas's Battersea school in south-west London, which is attended by Prince George, the third in line to the throne, and his little sister Princess Charlotte. Four pupils at the school were told to stay at home after returning from northern Italy. Businesses were also beginning to encourage working from home. The American oil company Chevron sent home 300 workers from its headquarters at Canary Wharf, east London, after an employee returned from Italy with flu-like symptoms.

By now, hospitals were beginning to fear that they might not have sufficient protective equipment for staff if the number of infections began to rise steeply, an outcome that looked increasingly likely. Some of their orders to bulk-buy PPE were blocked by NHS bosses, who imposed a ban on individual hospitals stockpiling equipment such as masks.[4] The NHS was fearful that the national stocks would be quickly depleted if some of the larger hospitals started to amass large amounts of equipment. Dentists and GPs had already experienced difficulties in buying masks direct from wholesalers, who sourced the items from China. NHS Supply Chain, the body that handles equipment stocks for hospitals, announced it was imposing controls on the hospitals to 'maintain continuity of supply across the network'.

Doctors were also beginning to ask questions. Two senior clinicians spoke out in the *Independent* newspaper in order to counter the government's 'dishonest spin' that the health service was well prepared for a major outbreak.[5] The doctors, who worked at hospitals across England, said the health service's intensive care capacity was already overstretched and 'would crumble' under a surge in patients needing ventilation to help them breathe. They warned that weaker patients could therefore be denied life-saving care during a severe coronavirus outbreak, with senior consultants being left in the invidious position of having to decide who would be given access to ventilators and beds. Professor Jon Bennett, chair of the British Thoracic Society, said: 'A severe coronavirus outbreak will be very challenging. I have tried desperately not to think about it because when you do it is a very worrying situation. We would be in serious trouble.'

The assessment of that Thursday's Sage committee meeting was also bleak. It heard evidence behind closed doors that in 'the reasonable worst-case scenario', 80 per cent of the UK population may become infected, which equates to 54 million people. The committee estimated a fatality rate of 1 per cent, which meant more than half a million people would die. The findings were communicated upwards to ministers but not to the public. One of the Sage committee members, Professor Medley, later recalled how unsettling it was to be burdened with this information. 'We were actually going to be in that position where we would have hundreds of thousands of people dying,' he told Channel 4's *Dispatches* programme. 'At that time, I was walking around central London looking at people and I was thinking, "Gosh, this is going to happen. We're going to have a big pandemic and I don't think people really fully understand what's going to happen."' It was becoming obvious that control measures would have to be brought in to prevent so many people dying. The Sage meeting's confidential minutes make this clear. 'Modelling suggests that earlier and/or combined interventions will have a more significant impact,' the minutes say. But it would be another four weeks before this advice was fully implemented.

It was left to the financial markets to reflect the growing sense of unease. By the end of the week there was pandemonium on the stock exchange, with City traders coming round to the view that economically destructive measures would have to be introduced because it was the only way to halt the march of the virus. Around the globe, the markets had their worst week since the height of the financial crisis more than a decade earlier. After a blistering few days of selling, the European, UK and US stock markets had all slumped by more than 10 per cent amid escalating fears that the pandemic would cause a worldwide downturn. Britain's FTSE 100 shed more than £200bn over the week, representing an 11 per cent slump, which was its third-worst week since the recession in the early 1980s. Airline and holiday stocks were exceptionally badly hit, with travel company TUI down 30 per cent. EasyJet, British Airways and Lufthansa were also starting to suffer and had announced cuts in flights due to lack of demand. In contrast, government bonds were hitting record highs as investors sought safe havens for their cash.

The last Friday in February was the moment that the prime minister finally appeared to be starting to take an interest in the crisis that was gripping his nation. That morning he summoned Hancock and Whitty into Downing Street to specifically discuss concerns about coronavirus. Eight weeks after reports of the new virus had emerged and after missing all five Cobra meetings on the subject, the prime minister had finally been persuaded to engage directly with the problems ahead. Gone was the bravado with which, at the beginning of the month in Greenwich, he had dismissed the virus as an irrational panic, and gone was the complacency he had displayed in Birmingham two weeks earlier when he had blithely dismissed the threat, saying there was 'every reason to be confident and calm' about the outbreak. After his meeting with Hancock and Whitty, he called the television cameras into No. 10. 'As you can imagine, the issue of coronavirus is something that is now the government's top priority,' he said. 'I have just had a meeting with the chief medical officer and secretary of state for health talking about the preparations that we need to make.'

His new approach was probably as a result of several factors. It was hard to ignore what was happening 600 miles away in Italy, where the virus had shown how rampant and highly infectious it could be. That morning six new cases of infections had been reported in the UK and among them, for the first time, were people in Northern Ireland and Wales. It took the UK total for known infections to 19. There had also been the first death of a British citizen from the virus that morning when an unnamed passenger from the *Diamond Princess* passed away in a Japanese hospital. It may well have been that something had pricked the prime minister's conscience the night before during a pre-arranged visit he had made to observe the late-night accident and emergency service at Kettering Hospital. The staff at the hospital had discussed with him their preparations for an outbreak. And then there was the serious financial issue of the markets being in freefall – a collapse that threatened his promised new era of prosperity post-Brexit.

The prime minister's television address continued: 'I think people are right to be concerned and they are right to want to take every possible precaution, and we will in the course of the next few days be issuing further advice about how to respond and how we will be dealing with any potential outbreak.' A casual listener might have been forgiven for thinking that the prime minister was addressing the problem for the first time. The TV interviewer was allowed one awkward question about the death of the British national who had been on the cruise ship. 'With hindsight,' the interviewer asked, 'should the government have acted sooner to repatriate those citizens on board?' Like Hancock a couple of days earlier, Johnson blamed the scientists. 'I think we were following the very best medical advice and obviously I, er we, very much regret the loss of life,' he stuttered.

The big news came from the Downing Street press office. 'The prime minister is keen to chair Cobra on Monday to ensure that everything that can be done is being done,' said the spokesman.

The meeting had been convened, the spokesman said, following a sharp increase in the number of cases of Covid-19 in mainland Europe, which had prompted fears it was only a matter of time before they started rising in the UK. Finally, after five weeks, Johnson was going to take charge of a Cobra meeting on the virus for the first time, although he was going to wait until after the weekend. Inexplicably, there had been a 12-day gap since the last Cobra meeting on the crisis on Tuesday 18 February. Over that period the number of infections in the UK had soared from 420 to 11,000, according to the Oxford and Imperial College estimates.

Yet Johnson was planning to take more time off at another of his grace-and-favour country retreats that weekend. This time he was heading to Chequers, the Grade I-listed 10-bedroom mansion set on a 1,000-acre estate just outside Great Missenden, Buckinghamshire. Downing Street declined to disclose any of the prime minister's engagements and said it was unnecessary to hold the Cobra meeting sooner because: 'There are daily meetings between Public Health England and the Department for Health and interested departments, the chief medical officer, the chief scientific officer – those meetings happen daily and will continue to happen.'

The delay was met with incredulity. Ed Davey, the Liberal Democrat's acting leader, said: 'With the NHS already so stretched, it's gobsmacking that the prime minister has delayed chairing Cobra for so long.' George Osborne, the former chancellor, was among those pressing the prime minister that day to introduce much more urgency. 'The British Government now needs to go on to a "war footing" with the coronavirus: daily NHS press briefings, regular Cobra meetings chaired by the PM, ministers on all major media shows,' he tweeted.

The need for urgency was obvious. Over the Channel in France, the government announced a ban on indoor public gatherings of more than 5,000 people that Saturday due to its escalating coronavirus outbreak. The country now had 100 confirmed cases and two deaths, whereas Britain had so far detected 23 infections – after another four people had tested positive for the virus that day. That Sunday, two NHS chief executives spoke out in the *Observer*.[6] 'If you have a coronavirus outbreak it will be a nightmare,' one said. 'How will we create the extra capacity that we will need? All hospitals are already full. It will be really, really difficult if we get loads of people with this.' The boss of another trust said: 'About 17% of people who contract the virus need some sort of medical intervention. So, if this properly catches hold you have an increase in the number of people coming through the NHS's door, and then everything falls over.'

But it turned out that Johnson deemed he had more important matters to attend to in his tangled personal life. He had decided to break a bit of good news that was guaranteed to keep some of the critical headlines of his stewardship of the virus crisis off the front pages. Late on Saturday he and Symonds finally publicly announced that they had become engaged and that she was now several months pregnant. In a post to friends on Instagram, Symonds wrote: 'I wouldn't normally post this kind of thing on here but I wanted my friends to find out from me. Many of you already know but for my friends that still don't, we got engaged at the end of last year and we've got a baby hatching early summer ... Feel incredibly blessed.' The pregnancy had been an open secret in Westminster as Symonds failed to appear for significant events including the Black and White Ball earlier that week, and friends had let slip the couple were planning a baby shower. The baby would be the third born in Downing Street in 150 years. Johnson was about to score a unique hat-trick as the first prime minister in history to have a divorce, a wedding and a baby while living in No. 10.

That weekend the number of known cases of the virus was really taking off, with a 50 per cent increase between Saturday and Sunday. The prime minister had decided to pop into Public Health England's National Infection Service laboratory in

Colindale, north-west London, on his way back from Chequers. From film footage of the visit, he appears to have only just been catching up with his own government's policies to protect the public from the virus. He seems to have believed, wrongly, that far more people were being tested at airports when they entered the country than was actually the case. Pointing at a screen displaying a map of Italy, he enquired: 'Wow, so when a flight comes in from Italy do we automatically test everyone who was on the flight or do we just test people who are symptomatic?' The officials looked at him nonplussed and one explained that they only focused on people from the 'hot zones' in Italy. He also appeared to be just starting to get his head across some very basic information about the virus. With a look that suggested he wanted reassurance, he asked: 'It's not the most serious infection you can get, it's something that the vast majority of people survive very well?' A nodding official replied: 'Yes exactly. We have seen some older age groups more severely affected in China.' Johnson's interest pricked up as if this well-known fact about the virus was a revelation. 'Is that right? The percentages in China of the older age groups, the percentage of mortality is higher?' the prime minister asked. 'Yes,' replied the official patiently.

Meanwhile, his officials were working that Sunday in the bowels of Whitehall assessing more terrifying data that was coming in from abroad. The Sage committee members had gathered together with officials from the Department of Health and the NHS in a meeting that was described as a game-changer by one Whitehall source. The assembled officials and experts were shown fresh modelling based on figures from Italy suggesting that 8 per cent of infected people might need hospital treatment in a worst-case scenario. The previous estimate had been 4 per cent to 5 per cent. 'The risk to the NHS had effectively doubled in an instant. It set alarm bells ringing across government,' said the Whitehall source. 'I think that meeting focused minds. You realise it's time to pull the trigger on the starting gun.'

7

The Action Plan

Monday 2 March 2020 to Sunday 8 March 2020
UK government's risk assessment: Moderate

On Monday 2 March the virus had been in the country for almost five weeks and was multiplying fast. This was an important day, as Johnson had finally decided to get to grips with the crisis by doing something he had notably failed to do since it started. 'I have just chaired a Cobra meeting on coronavirus,' he proudly declared in a video message to the nation. Standing in front of a Downing Street bookcase full of leather-bound volumes, the prime minister warned that the virus was likely to become a more significant problem and added, 'this country is very, very well prepared … we've got fantastic testing systems, amazing surveillance of the spread of disease.' The much-vaunted testing and contact tracing surveillance would be all but abandoned in just over a week.

Outside Downing Street, the clouds were gathering again after a weekend in which the country had already been battered by Storm Jorge. Johnson had agreed on an 'action plan' with his fellow members of the Cobra emergency committee that morning, which he hoped would prevent the spread of the virus. But there would be very little immediate activity, as the new measures were to be introduced later, and only if it was felt they were needed. It would be a notable feature of the prime minister's televised press briefings over the next crucial three weeks until lockdown that key actions would be deferred until future dates. Meanwhile, the virus was spreading rapidly. Inexplicably, the final sentence of Johnson's 2 March video message would later be lopped off the version posted on the prime ministerial Twitter page. It was: 'I wish to stress that, at the moment, it's very important that people consider that they should, as far as possible, go about business as usual.'

Downing Street was keen to foster a mood of buoyancy and optimism as the nation began its new future of self-determination in a world where Brexit had finally been delivered. In the following days Johnson initially epitomised the upbeat spirit, shaking hands and attending sporting events, in a clear signal that life should go on despite the virus. Life did continue as usual at the beginning of March. Many people paid with their lives for commuting on packed trains, drinking in pubs and attending mass events during this period.

Across the world, many governments were grappling with the fast-moving crisis and few would emerge from the coming months without making mistakes. In Britain, the government's response was to replace 'Let's get Brexit done' with a new mantra: 'We're following the science'. But was that what the decision-making team – Johnson, Cummings, ministers including Hancock, as well as the chief scientific and medical advisers – were actually doing?

A few hours before Johnson attended Cobra on 2 March, another leader was holding her own press conference in response to the coronavirus crisis, on the side of the world where the sun rises first. With slow precision Jacinda Ardern, the New Zealand prime minister, read out a raft of measures her small island nation was taking to protect health and business because 'the precautionary approach is best'. Travel from China had already been banned for a month and 8,000 New Zealand nationals returning home from the area and Iran had been self-isolating for two weeks. That day Ardern said travellers from Italy and

South Korea would be required to self-isolate for two weeks. 'It is too early to say what the impact will be, but regardless, we are getting in front of this issue,' she added.

The early intervention would prove highly successful and enabled New Zealand to begin to return to normality in April after a relatively short lockdown with just over 1,500 cases and 20 deaths. By contrast, the island of Britain was in a far more exposed position than New Zealand as an international air hub, with 23.7 million people arriving in the UK in the first three months of the year. So it was perhaps all the more surprising that so little had been done in the five weeks before March to prepare the UK for a pandemic while our borders were kept open, despite the warnings from scientists.

A statement on 2 March by the government's scientific pandemic influenza group on modelling (Spi-M) advised that it was 'almost certain' there would be sustained transmission of the coronavirus in the UK and it was 'highly likely' to be already happening. The Spi-M experts estimated that the time taken for cases to double was about four to six days. However, this rate was much slower than the initial reports suggested had been the case in Wuhan in January, which was the best available data on how fast the disease was likely to spread. In fact, the research from Imperial College London and Oxford University, which was produced later in the summer, calculated that infections had been doubling every three days in the UK during early March in line with the Wuhan figures, and 11,000 people had been infected by the Monday of the Cobra meeting. The virus was spreading at a much faster pace and was being carried by far more people than the government realised.

Nonetheless, given the warning about sustained transmission, it might have been expected that the prime minister would have announced more immediate steps when he returned to Downing Street via the network of corridors from the Cabinet Office briefing rooms where the Cobra meeting had been held. The delay in implementing control measures puzzled Lord Kerslake, the former head of the civil service who would have been responsible for implementing such a plan when David Cameron was prime minister. 'If ministers believe that emergency measures will be necessary, they should act now,' he said that day, adding that the only reason for holding back was if 'you don't believe they are necessary in the end'.[1]

His views were shared by Sir David King, a former chief scientific adviser to the government who was succeeded by Whitty and Vallance. 'The most important thing that anyone who has ever dealt with an epidemic knows is that you want to get ahead of it. And the sooner you get ahead of it, the sooner you get the whole thing under control,' he said in June. 'There are several countries that I think did exactly that. And I don't only have to point to South Korea, Hong Kong, but also Australia and New Zealand where the number of deaths to date is measured in hundreds not in thousands, let alone tens of thousands.'

The full details of the government's action plan were set out in a lengthy document from the Department of Health and Social Care on Tuesday 3 March, which introduced a new 'contain, delay, research, mitigate' strategy. It notes ominously that 'if the disease becomes established in the UK ... it may be that widespread exposure in the UK is inevitable.' The government was intent on pursuing a 'contain' and 'delay' policy of allowing the virus to spread through the population, with the intention of shielding the vulnerable and elderly once infections became more prevalent. It then planned to introduce new measures to slow the rate down – the mitigate phase – at some future point when it looked as if the NHS might be overwhelmed. This approach was based on the flu model, which was designed to cope with an epidemic that was highly infectious in a similar way to the coronavirus. The weakness of this approach was that the virus was far more deadly than the flu and therefore could not be allowed to run rampant because no healthcare system had the capacity to treat all those who would very quickly become seriously ill from the disease. In the Far East, countries such as Taiwan, South Korea, Vietnam and Singapore were basing their approach on lessons learnt from combating the Sars crisis in 2003 and other viral outbreaks that emerged from China. These countries moved fast and deployed mass testing and tracing to stop the virus in its tracks before it could take hold.

Since they had adopted the flu approach, the UK's scientific advisers were effectively accepting that they would have to fall back on a strategy of allowing the virus to spread widely in the population if, as was likely, the limited attempt at contact tracing failed. It was then hoped that sufficient antibody resistance would be built up among the populace to act as a shield to prevent a second outbreak occurring later in the year, which might be even worse because respiratory illnesses are more common in the autumn and winter months. This was what would later become known as the controversial 'herd immunity' strategy.

Officially, the country was still in the 'contain' phase in early March and the contacts of anyone known to be carrying the virus were, in theory, supposed to be tracked down and tested. But that battle had already been lost. The UK's meagre test and trace resources could not cope with even a fraction of the 11,000 people that Imperial and Oxford universities estimated were already infected. Indeed, such was the rapid spread of the virus that it had almost certainly reached one of Johnson's own ministers. Nadine Dorries, a junior health minister, began to suffer symptoms of the virus two days after the 3 March strategy document was published.

The government could have decided to move directly to the delay strategies outlined in its action plan. These included a number of lockdown measures such as closing schools, encouraging greater home working and reducing the number of large-scale gatherings. But, in its document, the government said it needed to be mindful of the trade-off between the 'social and economic impact' of such measures and 'keeping people safe'. It decided to err on the side of the economy and wait before introducing any measures. And wait, and wait.

True to form, the prime minister was in a characteristically upbeat mood on 3 March when he presented the fuller version of the action plan. It was the first of the televised media briefings on the virus in Downing Street's wood-panelled State Dining Room, which would become familiar daily occurrences with the prime minister or a cabinet colleague standing at a lectern flanked by scientific and medical advisers. Johnson told the assembled journalists that the virus was 'overwhelmingly a disease that is moderate in its effects' and the country was 'going to get through coronavirus, no doubt at all, and get through it in good shape'. He repeated his misplaced faith in the UK's testing and surveillance systems, and went on to make clear that the action plan was not a list of measures the government 'will do' but rather something it might 'do at the right time'. In other words, very little would be done until the crisis became even more serious. He made clear that the burden of the decision-making on any future changes to the plan would be borne by the scientific advisers. 'Our plan means we are committed to doing everything possible based on the advice of our world-leading scientific experts to prepare for all eventualities,' he said.

The two most important of those scientists were perched on lecterns either side of Johnson: Professor Chris Whitty, the chief medical officer for England, and Sir Patrick Vallance, the chief scientific adviser, would become household names as the crisis unfolded. Intelligent and articulate, Whitty and Vallance would be used as the government's human proof that it was 'following the science'. It had been Hancock's idea to present government decisions to the public as if they were entirely based on scientific advice, when, in fact, they inevitably involved a huge amount of political calculation. The earnest scientists were taken from their normal habitat in the corridors of Whitehall and thrust into the limelight as an embodiment of this scientific approach in order to gain the public's trust. It was also a way of deflecting responsibility when tough decisions had to be made.

In many ways Whitty was the perfect man for the crisis. Balding, with an oval face and rounded lower eyelids, the 53-year-old looked a little like an aristocrat from an 18th-century Thomas Gainsborough portrait. The oldest of four brothers, he had grown up in northern Nigeria and was educated at a top English school – where aged 17 he learnt the news that his father had been shot dead in his car by terrorists while working in Athens for the British Council. He studied medicine at Oxford University and went on to become one of the country's top experts in infectious diseases as Professor of Public and International Health at the London School of Hygiene & Tropical Medicine. He had been a chief scientific officer to the government for a decade before becoming the chief medical officer in October 2019, less than two months before the first coronavirus case was recorded in Wuhan. He was therefore well versed in the ways of Whitehall and the need for tact and diplomacy when dealing with ministers.

The other half of the double act, Vallance, was less experienced in the ways of government. He had taken a salary drop of almost £600,000 from his job as president of research and development at drug giant GlaxoSmithKline (GSK) to become the chief scientific officer in March 2018 – a role paid between £160,000 and £180,000 a year. A clinical pharmacologist aged 60, he had been with GSK for 12 years and before that was the head of medicine at University College London. Both men presented a united front with the government at those early press conferences, but would this continue as the cases grew and the pressure mounted?

Earlier that same day, Tuesday 3 March, Vallance and Whitty had chaired a meeting of Sage in which the alarming inadequacy of the government's limited action plan had been laid bare. They were shown pandemic modelling from Whitty's former colleague

Professor John Edmunds at the London School of Hygiene & Tropical Medicine and a team from Imperial College London led by Professor Neil Ferguson, who had become one of the government's most trusted academic advisers. The modellers had been asked to assess the effects of strategies to mitigate the virus such as social distancing, school closures, whole household isolation and banning mass gatherings. Ferguson concluded that there could be half a million deaths from the virus if none of the interventions were introduced. The forecast was still frighteningly bleak when they factored in the mitigation measures. No matter how both teams modelled the measures – either singly or in combination – the death toll was huge: more than 200,000 could lose their lives in the LSHTM calculation, and 250,000 according to Imperial. 'We looked at the mitigation strategies one by one and in combination and we realised that they would still likely result in large numbers of deaths,' said Edmunds.

Edmunds's team had been hard at work. That day they also produced a second paper highlighting another cause for concern. The team had examined whether it was possible to estimate how many cases there were in a country, based on the numbers of deaths from the virus. It was an imprecise science but the paper came to an important conclusion. 'By the time a COVID-19 death is reported in a newly affected country, it is likely that there are already hundreds or thousands of cases in the population,' it stated. 'This means containment through contact tracing will likely be very challenging, and alternative control/mitigation strategies should probably be considered.'

As if on cue, the first death from Covid-19 in the UK happened two days later on Thursday 5 March when an unnamed woman in her 70s died from the virus in a hospital in Berkshire. Therefore, according to the calculations by Edmunds's team, the best information available at that time suggested the 'contain' phase in the government's action plan was already a failure as there were likely to be hundreds or thousands of cases. It was actually an underestimate because the true number of cases is thought to have been more than 10,000. However, the calculations by Edmunds's team were a strong indication that it was time for the government to abandon the contain phase and introduce more radical measures to halt the spread of the virus.

Some of those who were across this emerging evidence were becoming anxious that the government was out of step with the science rather than following it. The death toll was going to be huge unless something was done soon. Yet the government seemed intent on its wait-and-see approach. Graham Medley, a professor of infectious disease modelling at LSHTM and another member of Sage, has recounted how he witnessed a deep sense of dread taking hold among his scientific colleagues at that time. He recalls receiving a phone call from one member of Spi-M, the committee that models infection rates for Sage. 'He was really emotionally distraught and was saying, "Do they realise what's going to happen?"' he recalled.[2] 'I think he meant not just policymakers but the country at that point. And they didn't.' Daniela De Angelis, a professor of statistical science at Cambridge University who was also on Spi-M, said: 'I do remember very very vividly sending a message to one of the other members and saying, "Wow, you know, whatever we do here is not going to work. It's not going to be enough."'

However, the ministers did not appear to share the deep foreboding of their advisers. An academic source close to the Imperial and LSHTM teams said the government did not even ask the teams to model the solution that was being used in other countries: a lockdown. This was despite the fact that the city of Wuhan, in particular, was providing a clear example that a lockdown was the proven way of limiting the virus's spread once it had been allowed to take hold. Instead, the government commissioned the modelling teams to look at increasingly finer-grained versions of strategies to mitigate the spread of the virus in early March. 'I think a sense of, "It can't really be that bad" was important in explaining the delay,' said the source. 'The [modellers'] central estimates of severity were viewed as a "reasonable worst case" by the government – not the most likely scenario. It took them a while to be convinced.' The source went on: 'I think an overarching concern – and why so much time was spent looking at alternatives involving mitigation and shielding – was that everyone, especially Chris Whitty, Patrick Vallance and the policy people, knew what the economic and social costs of lockdown would be.' The modellers would later take matters into their own hands.

At the 3 March press conference, Whitty had addressed the issue of whether care homes needed to take precautions to protect their elderly residents. The elderly were, after all, the group who were most vulnerable to serious illness from the virus. But he gave reassurance that care homes did not need to do anything just yet and he explained why. 'We will give some specific advice on care homes but one of the things we are keen to avoid … is doing things too early,' he said. 'Because if you do that you get no benefit … but what you do get is a social cost. So what we want to do is give advice at the point we think it is going to have an effect on improving the lives or reducing the chance of infection of people in those care homes.' This was a major miscalculation. It would be only two weeks before care homes would be hit by the first deaths from the virus and therefore some residents must have already been infected as he spoke. By the following month, thousands would be dying in care homes every week from the virus.

The evidence was already mounting from China and Italy that the elderly would form the bulk of those needing treatment in hospital. On the same day as the press conference, the government's respiratory illness advisory group, Nervtag, held a meeting that prompted a discussion via email afterwards between its members about whether healthcare treatment might have to be rationed. Professor Anita Simonds, a respiratory consultant at the Royal Brompton Hospital, told the committee that a number of elderly patients and those with lung and heart conditions might only be offered a limited amount of health-care. She suggested that some of these patients would have to be given palliative care to help them die painlessly 'should the situation deteriorate', as their beds were needed to give younger or fitter people more critical care such as ventilation. 'I don't think that is what we would do in first instance while some sense of normality remains,' she wrote. However, she acknowledged that 'the bulk of the patients presenting in Italy and China' were older people and those with existing illnesses. Therefore, she argued, they would have to make clear that there would be 'ceilings of care' for some patients. It was an acknowledgement by a government adviser that the NHS could be forced to make tough decisions about which patients to treat because hospitals might not have the resources to cope with the expected numbers of Covid-19 patients during the virus's peak.

Across the world people had been replacing handshakes with awkward waves or the knocking of elbows in an attempt to limit the spread of the infection. In Berlin, the German interior minister Horst Seehofer was filmed rebuffing chancellor Angela Merkel when, without thinking, she offered her hand to him at a meeting. Quickly realising her mistake, the chancellor laughed and threw her hands up in the air as an apology. Shaking hands was no longer a polite social etiquette when it could pass on a deadly virus. In the UK the Spi-behavioural (Spi-B) expert group, which reports to Sage, handed out clear instructions that Tuesday that the 'government should advise against greetings such as shaking hands and hugging, given existing evidence about the importance of hand hygiene'.

The British prime minister, however, was determined to carry on as normal. 'I'm shaking hands,' he told reporters that day. 'I was at a hospital the other night where I think there were a few coronavirus patients and I shook hands with everybody, you'll be pleased to know.' It was reckless behaviour and it demonstrated once again that Johnson had failed to grasp the magnitude of the crisis unfolding around him. Professor Susan Michie of University College London, the academic who set up the Spi-B committee that was advising against handshakes, felt Johnson was setting a dangerous example. 'He was modelling a behaviour that is an undesirable behaviour,' she said. 'He was making light of it – you know, it was a bit of a joke. "Following the science" is one of his mantras. It was not a message or communication that was informed by science … These things are incredibly serious. We're talking about people's lives. It's not a laughing matter.' The Sage scientist Professor Medley was also dismayed. 'We already knew that this was a virus that was going to cause an awful lot of death and disability and would require an awful lot of NHS resource. It was with some dismay that we were watching senior politicians behaving in a way that suggested that this was not something that was too serious.'[3]

Despite the disapproval from many of his own scientists, Johnson was unrepentant. On the morning of Thursday 5 March he was at it again when he made an appearance on ITV's breakfast television show *This Morning*. As he entered the studio, Johnson bounded over to Phillip Schofield as the presenter stood up from the sofa and seized his hand. Schofield asked the prime minister about the greeting later in the inter-view. 'You came straight in here and I kept my hands by my side just to see what happened, and you walked in and you shook my hand,' he said. Johnson's reply just made matters worse. 'I did, and I've been going around hospitals as you can imagine and I think you always shake hands,' he said. 'But you washed your hands before you shook mine?' Schofield quickly interjected.

The prime minister was keen to talk to Schofield and his co-presenter Holly Willoughby about the government's new contain and delay strategy. 'Let me explain what's happening today,' he said. 'The numbers continue to grow, not exponentially, but they are continuing to grow.' He was wrong. Infections from the virus were growing exponentially, just as the first studies in

Wuhan six weeks earlier had suggested they would. He went on: 'So the scientific advisory group for emergencies, or Sage, is meeting and they will consider a range of options that we have to try to delay the spread. And they range from things like stopping big public gatherings, sporting gatherings and so on, stopping schools, that sort of thing.'

Johnson, however, had already made his mind up on this. 'Quite draconian stuff,' he told his two interviewers on the sofa. 'What [the experts from Sage] are telling me is that, actually slightly counterintuitively, things like closing schools and stopping big gatherings don't work as well, perhaps, as people think in stopping the spread. So our advice on school closures remains exactly where it was, which is we don't think at the moment schools should be closing.'

Since he believed the virus was 'mild and moderate' for most people, the prime minister was advocating a different strategy. 'One of the theories is perhaps you could take it on the chin,' he explained, 'and take it all in one go and allow the disease to move through the population without taking as many draconian measures.' This was clearly at the root of the government's approach. However, the prime minister added that there was a 'need to strike a balance' and introduce measures to 'stop the peak of the disease being as difficult for the NHS as it might be'. In other words, the virus would be allowed to spread through the population but the government would make strategic interventions at the right time to ensure hospitals did not become overrun. Although the prime minister did not spell it out, the end goal of such a strategy was to produce 'herd immunity' across the UK.

The optimism that the virus could be managed in this way with a series of cleverly timed interventions had already been found to be hopelessly misplaced. This was, after all, the plan that the government's own scientists had modelled, and they reached the damning conclusion that it would lead to between 200,000 and 250,000 deaths. It suited the prime minister because Britain could keep calm and carry on – with perhaps a small change to hand hygiene. 'The most important message at this stage as we start to see the spread,' Johnson blustered, 'is, number one, wash your hands, but number two is, as far as possible, it should be business as usual for the overwhelming majority of people in this country.' The interview ended with a question that finally seemed to knock the prime minister off his stride. It was about changing nappies for his new baby. After much squirming, Johnson said unconvincingly he expected he would do so. When Schofield observed that Johnson did not talk about his family, the prime minister replied: 'Yes, very sensibly.'

The number of known cases was quickly accelerating. In that first week of March, the tally of officially confirmed cases rose from 36 to 206. At the Sage meeting on Thursday, the scientific advisers to the government finally accepted that there was now 'sustained community transmission' in Britain. The crucial piece of information that convinced them was the increase in the number of people testing positive in intensive care units who had not travelled outside the UK or come into contact with anyone from abroad.

By Saturday 7 March the scale of the catastrophe facing the UK could be seen in Italy, where cases had risen five-fold to 5,800 and deaths had increased eight-fold to 233 in just six days that week. There could not have been a clearer example of how the virus was growing exponentially and there was no obvious reason why Britain would escape the pandemic any more lightly than Italy, especially as UK borders were still wide open.

That weekend the Ireland versus Italy Six Nations rugby match in Dublin was called off because of fears Italian fans might accelerate the virus's spread through the city. But across the UK, hundreds of thousands of people attended sports events as usual. They included the prime minister, who made a further statement about Britain being open for business by joining the 81,000-strong crowd that watched England beat Wales in the

Six Nations. He posted a video of himself on Twitter eagerly shaking hands with five female rugby players at the ground. It was difficult to reconcile this behaviour with Johnson's repeated statements that he and the government were following the advice of the scientists.

On Sunday 8 March France banned public gatherings of more than 1,000 people. Yet, on the very same day, thousands of French fans were allowed to mingle in the 67,000 crowd at Murrayfield, Edinburgh, for their team's Six Nations rugby match with Scotland. The folly of Britain's lax attitude to mass gatherings was made plain just four days later when a French tourist died from the virus in Edinburgh. The unnamed elderly man had travelled to Scotland with his two sons to watch the game and would have brushed shoulders with scores of other supporters while carrying the virus. He reported feeling unwell while staying at the Point A Hotel in Haymarket before being transferred to the Royal Infirmary Hospital, where he died. He was the first person to die from the virus in Scotland.

8

Herd Immunity

Monday 9 March 2020 to Friday 13 March 2020
UK government's risk assessment: Moderate

On Tuesday 10 March the gunmetal skies and threat of drizzle did little to dampen the ardour of the horse-racing enthusiasts as more than 60,000 people flocked to the opening of the four-day Cheltenham Festival. The event had once been cancelled for foot and mouth, a livestock disease, but it was not going to stop for the virus, especially with the prime minister sending out messages that Britain was open as usual. On the opening day of the event, Ian Renton, the racing festival's director, sent a letter to local councillors who were concerned that the virus would be transported to the Gloucestershire town by the crowds of people and spread among the spectators and residents. Renton's letter set out the reasons for going ahead with the event and made clear that the organisers were taking their lead from Johnson.

'As with events from England v Wales attended by the prime minister at Twickenham on Saturday to ten Premier League games around the country this weekend,' it said, 'the government guidance is for the business of the country to continue as usual while ensuring we adhere to and promote the latest public health advice.'

The day before, the government's chief scientific adviser Patrick Vallance had been put forward to express the view that mass gatherings were not a big problem. Standing alongside the prime minister in a press conference, Vallance explained that gatherings 'actually don't make much difference'. He said: 'There's only a certain number of people you can infect. So, one person in a 70,000-seater stadium is not going to infect the stadium. They will infect potentially a few people they've got very close contact with. That's true in any setting: in the house, in a church, in a restaurant.'

His comments were instantly ridiculed. A clip of his explanation was tweeted that day by the BBC politics account and the public immediately expressed their bewilderment at his argument. Annabel Macrae, who works at Aberdeen University, replied to the tweet saying: 'But each of the few folk infected may then go home on public transport infecting as they go, stop off at pub for evening, go home carrying [the] virus. This is how the virus spreads!' Jim Hodges told the chief scientific adviser, 'Patrick get a grip', pointing out that just one infected person could create a chain that would be passed between family, friends and neighbours until someone died. 'We have to fight this as a war. No mercy on the virus. Forget the bloody game,' he tweeted. James Birdseye, who said he was a paramedic, wrote: 'This is completely irresponsible of HM Gov. 1 becomes 4 – 4 becomes 8 then 18 then one of those people dies. Let's not wait. Contain this as much as possible.'

The organisers of the Cheltenham Festival did take some minor precautions. Bottles of hand sanitiser were placed in the washrooms and around the racecourse – but this was hardly going to prevent the virus from passing between the crowds of people who mingled and pressed together in the enclosures, drinking, eating and cheering. One of those people was Jules Annan, a 55-year-old freelance photographer, who worked on all four days taking photographs of celebrities, tycoons and royals who had joined the throng. Ten days after the festival, he found himself struggling for breath and was rushed to Cheltenham General Hospital, where he was given oxygen. 'My lungs basically gave up,' he said. 'I knew I was in a bad way.'

Annan cannot be certain about where he became infected but believes it was during the races. He thinks he was one of many. 'There was a guy in the bed opposite me at the hospital who was at the races too and thinks he got it there as well,' he said.

The surrounding county would experience a spike in hospital death rates in the weeks after the festival and there were reports of cases across the country among people who had attended the event. Two racing enthusiasts who attended the festival died on the same day at the end of March. They were Paul Townend, 61, a racehorse owner from Stratford-upon-Avon, and Cumbrian David Hodgkiss, a 71-year-old chief executive of a steelmaking firm and chairman of Lancashire Cricket Club.

Townend's widow, Geraldine, had also been at the event, as the couple were keen racegoers who owned a share in several prize-winning horses, including the highly rated Surrey Thunder and Forecast. Both she and her husband left the festival on Thursday 12 March and started to feel ill on the following Saturday. While her condition improved, her husband could not fight off the virus, which was clogging up his lungs. A week later he was struggling to breathe and was rushed to Warwick Hospital by ambulance. Within hours he was put into an induced coma and placed on a ventilator. 'I told them not to switch anything off until I'm there,' Geraldine said. Dressed from head to toe in PPE, Geraldine was able to say her final goodbyes at the hospital three days later as Paul's lungs and kidneys failed. Geraldine, who ran a blinds and shutters business, was reluctant to blame the racing authorities for going ahead with Cheltenham. 'Everyone did what the government told us to do,' she said, pointing out that mass gatherings were still allowed. She is frustrated that the government did not move faster to halt the spread of the virus. 'We knew people were getting ill elsewhere in January and February,' she said. 'I don't know why we were so ill-informed. Both our sons live in Denmark and they were already in lockdown when I fell ill ... Other countries were in lockdown well before us. The writing was on the wall.'

One of the last sporting fixtures that was allowed to go ahead was on Wednesday 11 March when 3,000 fans came to the UK from Spain to watch Liverpool play Atlético Madrid in an evening Champions League game. All La Liga fixtures in Spain were already being played behind closed doors without supporters, to prevent the spread of the disease. Yet the Atlético fans were allowed to travel to Liverpool from Madrid even though it was the region of Spain worst affected by the virus. They freely mixed in the 52,000-strong crowd at Anfield that evening. They joined the long queues in and out of the ground, crammed into bars and restaurants, and on to public transport. Officially, Spain had 2,140 confirmed Covid-19 cases on the day of the match. However, the actual number of cases was around 640,000 at the time, compared with 100,000 in Britain, according to the Imperial College London and Oxford University estimates. It is worth noting that it would take just eight days for Britain's infection numbers to equal those of Spain. While the UK took no meaningful measures to stifle the virus that week, Spain announced a full lockdown just three days after the Anfield match.

Edge Health, a company that analyses health data for the NHS, has carried out modelling that estimated that the Anfield match and the Cheltenham Festival are linked to a total of 78 additional deaths at nearby hospitals, compared with similar hospital trusts that were used as a control. And that was just the local hospitals. Sir David King, the former government chief scientific adviser, believes the government made a big mistake in allowing mass gatherings to go ahead that week. His son was at the Cheltenham Festival and later suffered coronavirus symptoms, which took him three weeks to recover from. 'If you've ever been to a race meeting or football match, you would normally meet your friends in a pub beforehand, then you often need to get a train – there are long queues and big crowds. Anyone who has attended any of these events knows you are in contact with a very large number of people. But worse than that, the people at these football matches and horse races come from all over the country and return to all over the country. It's the ideal way to spread the virus. My only sensible interpretation is that is what you would advise if you were aiming for herd immunity.'

The pared-down minutes of the Sage committee meeting the week before – which was attended by the usual government figures plus Dominic Cummings – state simply that the committee had 'agreed' that 'there is no evidence to suggest that banning very large gatherings would reduce transmission'. No reasoning was given. While the committee may not have been aware of any scientific studies to show that coronavirus could spread in crowds at sporting events, it was common sense that it would. And not all of the advisers to Sage agreed that it was wise to allow events with large crowds to still take place.

Professor Michie, one of the Sage advisers not present at the meeting that day, said: 'I thought Cheltenham definitely should not have been allowed to go ahead. And I remember seeing people interviewed and looking at the television images of what was happening there and feeling actually slightly nauseous about it, just feeling, "Oh, my God, this is awful." Given what was happening in Italy and we could see was happening here, it seemed inappropriate.' She added: 'I thought, "Why aren't we learning the lessons of what's been happening in other countries? We've had the time to learn and we don't appear to have learnt, don't appear to have drawn the right conclusions and don't appear to be taking the right actions."'

Johnson had begun the week of the Cheltenham Festival attending to a different crisis. He had finally ventured out to visit one of the flood-hit areas in the aftermath of Storm Jorge. He travelled to Bewdley, Worcestershire, where the River Severn had burst its banks, adversely affecting more than 300 homes and businesses. It was one of those car-crash moments that often happens when politicians meet the public for the sake of the television cameras. While there, Johnson defended his decision to stay away from any of the flooded areas during the height of the storms by arguing that his presence would only have 'diverted' the emergency services from their work. But the hecklers were not listening and one shouted: 'Prime minister, you are about two weeks too late. Traitor.' The word 'traitor' followed him around the town like a distant echo. He made a lame attempt to lift spirits with a pun on his election slogan. 'Get Bewdley Done' he boomed – referring to the promise of new flood defences for the town. But as he paused on the bridge to take selfies with two teenagers, there was a cry in the background of 'Do your f***ing job.'[1]

It is a message that might have saved many lives if the prime minister had applied it to coronavirus policy over the previous six weeks. The government appeared to be sitting on its hands. The reasons for this inertia were difficult for the public to understand and would remain so until the government's strategy would finally be laid bare for everyone to see later that week. It would provoke an outraged and incredulous reaction. In the meantime, Johnson and those around him would spend the next seven days defending their inaction – while the news became grimmer and grimmer.

The week started particularly badly on Monday 9 March, the day before the Cheltenham Festival. The stock market's fear that something seismic was happening was escalating rapidly. That day, the virus caused the steepest global stock market fall since the collapse of Lehman Brothers, which had triggered the global recession in 2008. Almost £125bn was wiped off the value of the FTSE 100 in an 8 per cent plummet that represented the fifth-worst day in its history. The exchange finished the day below 6,000 points, which was the lowest level since share prices had tumbled following the Brexit vote in 2016.

The crisis in Italy was deteriorating further. Intensive care wards were now so overrun that guidelines had been issued to doctors to prioritise those with 'greater life expectancy'. Judgements were being made on age, pre-existing conditions and whether a patient had a family to determine who should receive critical care treatment. As a result, critical care experts in Italy issued a stark message to hospitals across Europe that Monday. In a letter to the European Society of Intensive Care Medicine, they revealed that up to 10 per cent of all those infected with coronavirus in Italy had needed intensive care. This, according to the three authors of the letter – professors Maurizio Cecconi, Antonio Pesenti and Giacomo Grasselli from the University of Milan – was a warning to others to prepare. 'We wish to convey a strong message: Get ready! Increase your total ICU [intensive care unit] capacity. Identify early hospitals that can manage the initial surge in a safe way. Get ready to prepare ICU areas [for] Covid-19 patients in every hospital if necessary.'

The fact that large numbers of people would require intensive care at the height of an outbreak had serious implications for Britain. They were set out by Christina Pagel, Professor of Operational Research at University College London, in an article in the *British Medical Journal*. She wrote that it would only be 'a matter of weeks' before 'the UK too may be facing a situation where demand for intensive care exceeds capacity'. Her article called on both politicians and the NHS to be open with the public about the difficult decisions that would have to be taken by doctors 'when there are not sufficient resources to treat everyone'. Doctors would face agonising triage decisions – the process by which they choose the patients who should be given priority when time and resources are scarce. 'Triage protocols are tough decisions to make … but they are tougher decisions to implement and tougher still to be on the receiving end of. Any triage protocol will lead to tragic choices for some,' Pagel wrote. 'We've arguably missed the opportunity to properly engage the public in decisions on how we use their scarce resources to their benefit, but efforts must be made to ensure that the public understand the purpose of any triage protocol and how it will be applied.' Her words would prove tragically prescient. However, the NHS and government would not be open with the public about the triaging dilemmas that doctors did go on to face over the following weeks. The heart-breaking decisions medics would be forced to make over who should be treated would be one of the most closely guarded secrets of the lockdown weeks.

The worrying news kept coming that day. A meeting of government advisers at the Department of Health in central London was told it was now becoming obvious that infections were far more widespread in Britain than the government had previously realised. Professor Medley, who was present, recalls: 'During the meeting one of the members said, "Do you know what, we've got this wrong" and managed to convince us that, in fact, we were further into the epidemic than we had thought. That was alarming. I personally remember feeling full of a lot of adrenalin, [a] very heightened feeling that we are in the middle of what is going to be a very nasty pandemic.'[2]

Cobra had also been convened that Monday. When Johnson emerged from the meeting, he was forced to make an admission. Attempts to contain the virus through contact tracing were unlikely to succeed on their own and this meant that some measures would inevitably have to be introduced to stifle the numbers of infections. He said he would follow the scientific advice and act when the time was judged to be right. In other words, no action would be taken immediately. Whitty told journalists that the first of these measures would be a request that anyone with respiratory symptoms or a fever should self-isolate at home. But he did not envisage this happening for another 10 to 14 days. Johnson was defensive about the failure to bring in more stringent measures as other countries were doing. 'What's happening in other countries doesn't necessarily mirror what's happening here in the UK,' he said. He did not say what made Britain so special or why it was believed the UK could fight the virus by doing nothing for further days or weeks.

There could only be one conclusion as to why the government was persisting with delay tactics and willing to tolerate mass gatherings where the virus could be spread. The government did, indeed, appear intent on pursuing the managed herd immunity policy that Johnson had alluded to the previous week on the *This Morning* sofa. However, at this stage, it had never been fully explained to the public.

There was a view within the team advising the government that a burgeoning number of cases was inevitable – even desirable – once contact tracing had failed to contain the outbreak. It was, of course, the plan that the government's own modellers had estimated would cause 200,000 to 250,000 deaths. Yet, this appeared to be the strategy the government was following. The young and fit would be allowed to acquire immunity by becoming exposed to the virus as they went about their normal lives while the government hoped to reduce the death rate by shielding the old and the vulnerable. Measures to slow down the rate of infection would be introduced only when it looked as if the numbers of cases might overwhelm the NHS.

A source who was advising Downing Street at the time has confirmed that herd immunity was central to the government's plans in late February and early March. 'There was always this message coming straight down of, "We've all got to get it,"' the source said. 'And I remember having a conversation about how, "I don't like this and this chicken pox party thing." In February and March it was like, we've all got to get it at some point, and that was just a sort of mantra.'

Part of the reasoning behind this approach was that the government was unwilling to countenance a full lockdown, even at this late stage. There had been a brief mention in the Sage meeting the week before that the spread of the virus might be slowed down by 'preventing all social interaction in public spaces, including restaurants and bars'. But the edited minutes said this 'would be very difficult to implement' – although they do not set out the reasoning. The scientists could see the solution but the politicians did not want to implement the draconian measures that would be needed.

The government was also mindful of the prediction that any attempt to shut down the virus completely might have repercussions later, with a likely second outbreak. So some herd immunity was therefore deemed desirable to toughen up the country for the colder months later in the year when these types of virus were known to thrive. This was Vallance's argument, which he articulated very clearly in a press conference at the beginning of the week. 'What you can't do is suppress this thing completely,' he said, 'and what you shouldn't do is suppress this thing completely because all that happens is that this thing pops up later in the year when the NHS is in a more vulnerable stage in the winter.'

There were fundamental problems with this approach. Many countries, particularly in Asia, would demonstrate that it was possible to eradicate the virus without a big second wave. But this required a quick decision to lock down before the number of infections had risen too high and also a commitment to keep the measures in place until new infections were close to zero.

It was also a big gamble to rely on herd immunity. There was no clear evidence at the time that those who contracted the virus actually retained any lasting antibodies. Indeed, Johnson had ducked the question when asked directly whether 'we can recatch it'. So large numbers of people would lose their lives and their deaths would be in vain if it turned out that there was no antibody protection over a longer period. Herd immunity was a dangerous experiment with no proven upside, but Johnson's government was willing, nonetheless, to try it.

One of the most blistering takedowns of this strategy was in a document submitted to the government's key modelling committee, Spi-M, on that very Monday. The document was passed to the key decision makers on Sage a week later but, unsurprisingly given its content, it was not made public at the time. It was written by Professor Steven Riley, one of the Spi-M advisers from Imperial College and an expert in the dynamics of infectious diseases.

Riley's paper made clear that the government was, indeed, following a 'mitigation' strategy with the aim of achieving immunity in the population – instead of the lockdown approach favoured by other countries. 'The UK is currently planning a mitigation response to the Covid-19 epidemic rather than ongoing containment,' he wrote. 'The primary benefit of mitigation is that the epidemic will be over more quickly than might otherwise be the case, with the population having acquired herd immunity.' But he had modelled the government's herd immunity approach using estimates of the recent infection fatality rate, and the results were bleak. He found that the NHS would be rapidly overwhelmed under such an approach as there would be such a high number of infections. 'We show that critical care facilities in the UK would be saturated quickly,' he wrote.

He then pointed out a crucial, but little-recognised point. In theory, a strategy leading to herd immunity would protect the economy, as people could go to work as normal. The epidemic would also be over quickly once the virus had spread to sufficient numbers of the population – provided, of course, there was lasting antibody protection. There was, however, a flaw in this logic, according to Riley. As hospitals would inevitably become overwhelmed, death rates would rise significantly because many people would not be given vital medical treatment.

So Riley argued that people would then take it upon themselves to reduce their risks and take extra precautions. Indeed, this was already happening in those early days of March, with many people starting to work from home, wear masks and avoid public transport. They were, in effect, creating their own lockdown, and this voluntary reduction of economic activity would be hugely accentuated if people knew the NHS was too overrun to save them from the virus. Riley's modelling showed that such a 'spontaneous' behavioural change would so dramatically slow the virus's spread through the population that the advantages of the government's mitigation strategy 'are lost'.

Economic activity would stop and there would be no herd immunity because people would be shielding themselves from the virus at home. The result would be the worst of all worlds. 'The country would then have to either struggle on [until] the availability of a vaccine without a functioning health system or attempt the most stringent possible interventions to lower incidence back to containment levels,' he wrote.

Since herd immunity was self-defeating, the government's strategy of delaying the introduction of measures to suppress the virus was a calamitous miscalculation. Riley pointed out that any lockdown would have to be in place over a longer period of time if the government waited and allowed the number of infections to rise. His argument can be summarised with an analogy to a house fire, which causes more damage and takes more time to extinguish when it is allowed to rage through a building unchecked. Following this logic, the delays in early March would inevitably mean the prime minister would be forced to restrict people's freedom and wind down the economy for a longer period of time. There would be a higher death rate and the economy would suffer even greater harm.

Riley therefore concluded that the herd immunity approach would not achieve its goals and, instead, 'would likely have far greater economic costs than would result from an immediate switch now to ongoing containment'. His findings suggested that the UK was not a unique case as the prime minister had suggested on the day the paper was delivered. Lockdown-style containment policies were being successfully deployed in other countries. 'These results directly support current advice from the World Health Organisation and are consistent with policy decisions made by China, Hong Kong, Singapore, Japan, South Korea and most recently Italy,' he wrote.

There was, he argued, a crucial benefit to bringing in containment measures immediately rather than waiting. 'Even if ongoing containment were to fail, we would have gained time and knowledge with which to decide our next strategy.' It would also buy time to equip the NHS with adequate PPE and improve the swamped testing system.

Later Riley said: 'I was incredibly frustrated with the country's lack of action, as you can probably tell in that paper. We really, really didn't know what's going on and we knew it's really bad everywhere else. So not [locking down] as soon as you can in order to have thinking space was the thing that was frustrating. Even if we wanted to take it on the chin, it was worth three weeks [to think through]. That was the thing I couldn't get my head around. I was going to dinner with doctors in London who hadn't been fitted for face masks. I was properly, properly stressed. I couldn't quite understand it.'

The Sage meeting on Tuesday 10 March was shown new surveillance data – based partly on the numbers of infected people needing intensive care – that ended even the faintest glimmer of hope that the virus could be contained. It suggested there were now 5,000 to 10,000 infections, which were spread across the country. The Sage experts advised that the best way to introduce the different measures restricting the virus was to use them all in combination together, as this would achieve 'maximum efficacy from all interventions'. It would effectively be a lockdown, if the government agreed to it. However, the committee, attended by the chief scientists and observers from Downing Street, still did not believe it was time to act. 'There is some flexibility in timing that would not materially alter the effectiveness,' the minutes state. In the meantime, infections would continue to rise exponentially.

The large number of cases meant that the government had to start abandoning its containment strategy. The first concession came on Tuesday 10 March when it dropped its policy of automatically isolating anybody infected with Covid-19 in hospital regardless of the severity of their symptoms. There were officially only 52 known cases at the time, but the data seen by Sage meant it was soon going to be unsustainable to cocoon all these infected patients in hospital. In future, only those needing urgent treatment would be admitted and the rest would be told to stay at home.

That evening, the news broke that health minister Nadine Dorries had contracted the virus – the first of a number of high-profile people to catch the virus that week, underlining just how widespread infections were now becoming. The actor Tom Hanks and his wife Rita Wilson announced the following day that they had contracted the virus in Australia, and were quickly followed by the Arsenal football team manager, Mikel Arteta, who tested positive in London. Dorries tweeted: 'It's been pretty rubbish but I hope I'm over the worst of it now.' She had been self-isolating since developing symptoms the previous Friday and her mother was also suffering symptoms. In the few days before – when she was probably highly infectious – she had visited Downing Street, voted in packed House of Commons division lobbies and mixed closely with her colleagues in the Department of Health. Inevitably, fears began to swirl around the Westminster village that there might be an outbreak at the heart of government.

Remarkably, however, when the chancellor's budget speech was held in parliament at 12.30 p.m. the following day, Wednesday 11 March, not a single precaution was taken. MPs were crammed together in the green seats shoulder to shoulder, with some standing in huddles at either end of the house. There was not a mask to be seen. Scientists such as Professor Gabriel Scally, president of epidemiology and public health at the Royal College of Medicine, were horrified when they saw the scene on the news. He said: 'If we're not allowed to shake hands, what are senior politicians doing sitting beside each other crowded up on the benches? I got the feeling that they felt it just didn't quite apply to them, as if somehow the virus would be different here from anywhere else.'[3]

Sunak was there to address the coronavirus issue in the wake of the stock market collapse two days earlier. Just hours before his speech, the Bank of England had also slashed interest rates from 0.75 per cent to 0.25 per cent in an emergency move to introduce some confidence and stability. Sunak promised to do whatever it would take to support households and businesses through the worst of the outbreak. He pledged to make £12 billion of emergency spending available to support the economy. It was an illustration of the government's continued inability to gauge the severity of the crisis, as Sunak would have to hastily pull together another emergency rescue package just six days later. The new package to offset the effects of the virus would be 30 times bigger.

That afternoon there was a big announcement. The World Health Organization (WHO) finally declared what everyone had known for some time: that Covid-19 was a pandemic that had spread across the globe. While it may not have been a surprise, it was an opportunity for those who were frustrated with Johnson's delay approach to vent their frustration. They wanted the prime minister to do something now. Anthony Costello, Professor of Global Health at University College London and a former WHO director, tweeted what many experts were thinking. 'We are simply not doing enough now. We shd [*sic*] ban mass gatherings, close parliaments, alert all health workers about protective equipment and hygiene, close schools/colleges, promote home working wherever possible, and protect workers in the gig economy. Every day of delay will kill.' It would still be almost two weeks before lockdown would happen.

Johnson was actually doing something that afternoon. He was sitting by the fireplace in the Downing Street study with the government's deputy chief medical officer Dr Jenny Harries, and a camera crew. Their cosy armchair chat was to be broadcast to the nation on Twitter in a defence of the government's current policy – of doing nothing. The set-up was that Johnson would feed Harries earnest pre-arranged questions and she would give a scientist's view. Therefore, the government would be seen to be 'following the science'. It would start with easy topics such as questions on the well-known symptoms of coronavirus and build up to the point where she would explain why the UK was following a different path to the rest of the world with its delay strategy. It was probably quite a moment for the 61-year-old public health official. She was in Downing Street beneath a portrait of Margaret Thatcher being filmed in a one-to-one interview conducted by the prime minister. Only eight months earlier she had held the relatively low-key position of regional director for Public Health England, and now the prime minister had thrust her into the limelight.

'Tell us about the value of face masks,' Johnson entreated. 'You see face masks all around the place; is there any point to that?' Harries replied: 'If a healthcare professional hasn't advised you to wear a mask, it's usually quite a bad idea. People tend to leave them on, they contaminate the face mask and then wipe it over something. So it's really not a good idea and doesn't help.' Several months later, the government would introduce laws making it illegal for anyone to travel on public transport or enter an enclosed public space such as a shop or a restaurant without wearing a mask. The scientific evidence in favour of face masks was patchy, but even in March it seemed like common sense that face coverings could help prevent people inhaling or exhaling the virus. Masks were used widely in South East Asian countries, which had lived through previous epidemics with the danger of airborne pathogens. But the UK government was facing a problem that there might not be enough masks available for the NHS – let alone members of the public. It was one of the many consequences of the failure to address the shortages of personal protective equipment in the country's emergency stockpiles, and it was not in the government's interest to encourage people to buy up the scarce supplies of surgical masks that were available.

As the cameras continued to roll, the prime minister went on to ask a question that was at the front of his mind. 'It's noticeable that there are some countries where they have banned big sporting events and they've stopped mass gatherings of one kind or another,' he said. Liverpool were playing Atlético Madrid that evening and the Cheltenham Festival was in its second day. 'Tell us why so far the medical advice in this country is not to do that?' Harries replied: 'In general, those sort of events and big gatherings are not seen to be something which has a big effect. So we don't want to disrupt people's lives unduly.'

The government was determined to encourage everyone to continue life as normal and the closing of sporting events would have sent out the wrong message. As it was now accepted that the virus would be allowed to spread to build up immunity, it did not matter whether people were infected at big events or small. Within days, however, the sporting authorities would take matters into their own hands and postpone all fixtures because they did not want to endanger spectators.

Back at the fireplace, Johnson then posed what was supposed to seem like a thoughtful question on a thorny subject. 'There's obviously people under a lot of pressure. Politicians, governments around the world, need to be seen to act,' he said, with little disguise that he was referring to his own predicament. 'So they may do things that are not necessarily dictated by the science?' It was a leading question and Harries knew the script. 'As a professional, I am absolutely delighted we are following the science,' she said – almost as if she were appearing in a shampoo advert as the bespectacled lab technician in a white coat. She continued: 'There are other things we can do in this country and the timing of that is really important.' Johnson interjected, eager to reinforce the point: 'And the timing is very important, isn't it?' Harries was keen to confirm: 'Critical, absolutely critical. If we put it in too early we will just pop up with another epidemic peak later on,' she said. This was a further articulation of the government's intention to allow the virus to spread so that immunity could be built up in the population to prevent a second wave.

Over the next 48 hours the public would start to understand the implications of the government's strategy – and it would prove very unpopular. A few hours after the fireplace chat, one of the government's inner team, Dr David Halpern, gave a BBC interview in which he let the cat out of the bag and spelt out what all the delay tactics actually meant. Halpern was the chief executive of the government's Behavioural Insights Team, known as the 'nudge unit', which had been set up in 2010 to advise the Cabinet Office on ways to influence the public to follow desirable policies. In this role he had been advising the prime minister on the virus strategy, and he was also a member of Sage. 'There's going to be a point, assuming the epidemic flows and grows as it will do, where you want to cocoon, to protect those at-risk groups so they don't catch the disease,' Halpern told the interviewer. 'By the time they come out of their cocooning, herd immunity has been achieved in the rest of the population.'[4]

It was the first public mention of the words 'herd immunity'. Halpern is said to have been 'given a bollocking' by No. 10's communications chief Lee Cain for launching those two incendiary words into public consciousness.[5] The phrase gave the impression that the government was happy for the majority of the population to become infected. Yet the government had preferred to sell its approach as a strategy of allowing an unstoppable virus to spread in order to prevent a worse second wave in the autumn. In practical terms, there was no difference between the two.

As the days ticked by, the lack of activity was causing increasing concern among the government's two university modelling teams – Imperial College London and LSHTM – who were frustrated that their warnings to ministers were falling on deaf ears. So they took matters into their own hands and began crunching the numbers on a lockdown from their campuses in London. The first results were contained in an LSHTM study – co-authored by John Edmunds and his colleague Nicholas

Davies with help from a team from Edinburgh University led by Professor Mark Woolhouse. Their report was communicated to the government's advisory modelling committee that Wednesday. It stated that the death rate could be drastically cut with more severe measures to suppress the virus and predicted that intermittent periods of intensive lockdown-type measures would prevent the NHS from being overwhelmed.

Professor Neil Ferguson and his team at Imperial drew similar conclusions that week in an equally devastating report. The early results of that work were discussed in Sage and were provided to the government before the weekend. A draft was also sent to the White House, as it predicted up to 1.2 million deaths in America under a mitigation strategy. The team estimated that the number of UK deaths could be cut to about 30,000 with a series of lockdowns over a two-year period, whereas the government's preferred mitigation measures could allow hundreds of thousands of deaths. It was a stark choice.

On Thursday 12 March there was a deepened gravity in the prime minister's voice when, standing in front of two Union Jack flags, he told the nation: 'This is the worst public health crisis for a generation … I must level with you, level with the British public – more families, many more families, are going to lose loved ones before their time.' His tone seemed to have changed markedly from the day before when he had described the virus as a 'mild or moderate illness'. But the number of confirmed cases had jumped to 596, there had been 10 deaths and hospitals were filling up. It was also clear that tracing every patient with the virus – the key part of the contain strategy – was proving impossible and the government was forced to abandon it that day. Only hospitalised patients would now be routinely tested for the virus.

The dropping of widespread testing ran counter to WHO advice, but Whitty portrayed the move as all being part of a well-thought-out plan. 'It is no longer necessary for us to identify every case,' he said. It meant Britain would now have to navigate policy on the virus while being unsighted as to where it was spreading. 'I was absolutely astonished,' said Devi Sridhar, Professor of Global Health at Edinburgh University, when she heard that contact tracing had been stopped. 'I didn't fully understand the ramifications of what was being said. And then it hit me that, actually, they're letting the virus go. And so at the time I just felt like we were sleepwalking into disaster.' Professor Gabriel Scally, a former regional director of public health in the south-west, added: 'I didn't think it was possible that they would be abandoning community testing and contact tracing. That's leaving an open playing field for the virus.'[6]

To many observers it seemed obvious that a lack of testing capacity was behind the move, but the government did not present it as such at the time. It would not be admitted until early May, when Jenny Harries finally conceded the point to the health select committee. 'If we had unlimited capacity we would have done differently,' she said. As an illustration of how ineffective the testing programme had been, the Imperial and Oxford back-modelling estimates suggest that 130,000 people had caught the virus by the time it was discarded that Thursday and yet the contact tracing had picked up just 0.5 per cent of those infections.

Sophie and Mark Grenville, a couple from Hampshire, found out just how poor the government's virus hunters were at tracing people when they became ill with the virus. They had been on holiday in Indonesia and began to develop a dry cough in early March after they had returned home. The cough was so severe they compared it to a fox or deer barking. Fearing they might have the virus, they called the NHS helpline and then waited for three days to be tested. During this time they wrote entries in a journal, which they called 'A Diary of a Super Spreader',[7] recording their concern about the scores of people they had been in contact with while possibly carrying the virus. Their contacts ranged from 'High Court judges to football chiefs'. The tests were done by nurses in protective clothing at their home, and on Saturday 7 March they received news that they were indeed infected. Despite offering lists of people they had been in contact with, Public Health England only tested two of the names suggested: their sons, who had joined them for dinner on the night they developed symptoms. So the Grenvilles did their own tracing and persuaded 15 of their friends to be tested. It turned out that four of these people had the virus and had not been picked up by the contact tracers.

As well as abandoning community testing, Johnson also finally introduced the first of the mitigation measures that Thursday. The government told people who displayed symptoms such as a cough or a fever to isolate at home – a move that three days earlier Whitty had said would be introduced in 10 days to a fortnight. The government was clearly becoming rattled and wanted to start slowing the virus without suppressing it completely. Johnson also advised anyone over 70 or with serious medical conditions against going on cruises and discouraged international school trips. Two other measures would also be brought in at some point in the future: the banning of mass gatherings and the isolation of whole households if one person had symptoms. But again the government stressed these would be delayed until later. To justify the delay, Vallance repeated the point he had made earlier in the week about herd immunity – without saying the actual phrase. 'It's not possible to stop everybody getting it and it's also not desirable because you want some immunity in the population,' he said. 'We need to have some immunity to protect ourselves in the future.'

Meanwhile, other European countries were taking much stricter measures. That day the Irish prime minister announced the closure of all schools, and a ban on outdoor gatherings of more than 500 people and indoor gatherings of 100 people. At the time, Ireland had 70 confirmed cases and one confirmed death. Italy imposed a full nationwide lockdown that day, with all shops closed except supermarkets, food stores and chemists.

The country now had more than 1,000 deaths and more than 15,000 cases.

The questions were becoming tougher for the prime minister. Beth Rigby, Sky News's political editor, raised the issue of the government's inaction relative to other countries directly with Johnson. 'Prime minister, the US has stopped flights from Europe. Italy has closed down completely, Ireland has today closed its schools. But your action basically consists of asking people to stay home if they feel ill and avoiding cruises,' she said. 'Can you understand why people watching this might think you are doing far too little to protect their families?' Johnson once again hid behind the scientists. 'Well, first of all we have to look at the efficacy of the measures that we are bringing forward,' he said 'and as I have said throughout, we are looking at the science.'

However, the government's boffins had come up with an ingenious reason to explain why its measures had to be staged over time. Whitty explained that people might tire of social distancing and other restrictive measures if they were brought in too soon. 'If people go too early they become very fatigued. This is going to be a long haul. It is very important we don't start things in advance of need,' he said. He feared that people's enthusiasm might flag. If so, he argued, they might lapse just as the outbreak reached its peak, which was 'exactly the time we want people to be complying with these interventions'. He added: 'That is actually not a productive way to do it.' This, he said, was based on behavioural science. But his comments surprised Professor Michie, whose Spi-behavioural committee was supposed to advise Whitty on exactly such matters. She says the committee had never even been asked to look at psychological factors such as 'fatigue', and she found Whitty's arguments both illogical and lacking in common sense.

In fact, immediate interventions at the early stage of the outbreak would have made far more sense, according to Michie. This would mean there would be fewer infections and therefore the virus could be brought under control more quickly, leaving less time for people to become fatigued. 'The earlier you act, the lower the scale of the problem and the quicker it will be resolved,' she said. 'I hope there is not just a government inquiry but an independent public inquiry. I think that will be one of the things that will be seen as, among many mistakes the government has made, one of the bigger ones.' Even Whitty's own committee, Sage, seemed to disagree with him. The minutes of its meeting the next day state specifically: 'Difficulty maintaining behaviours ... should not be taken as a reason to delay implementation where that is indicated epidemiologically.' It seemed like a rebuke for the chief medical officer.

The mixture of small steps forward and delay was causing exasperation. It was articulated that day by ex-minister Rory Stewart, who had been a Tory leadership contender against Johnson five months earlier. 'The prime minister's job is to choose the strategy and I believe it is patently clear from all the way around the world that we need to act today, today, today, today,' said Stewart. He had some experience of viruses after travelling to the Democratic Republic of Congo in 2019 when he was the minister responsible for Ebola. There, he learnt the crucial importance of acting fast to control a highly infectious deadly outbreak. 'There is a chance of getting on top of this and that's where my biggest disagreement with the government comes,' he said. He was concerned the government seemed to be 'working on the assumption that you cannot contain and reduce the number of cases'.

By contrast, Stewart pointed out: 'In South Korea they've reduced [infections]. In China they've reduced. And I honestly believe there is no reason why what they've done in South Korea, we couldn't be doing here in Britain.' He said schools should be shut, gatherings should be stopped and people needed to start working from home immediately. 'Ultimately you can use the police in order to enforce it and you can call out the military to support it in this kind of emergency,' he observed, 'and when you're dealing with something on this scale – it's a once in a 100-year event – then I believe very strongly you take those measures.'[8]

That night Professor John Ashton, the former regional director of public health for north-west England, appeared on BBC's *Question Time*. He was scathing about the continued prevarication. 'I don't know where to start really. I'm embarrassed by the situation in this country. This talk of four stages, and we're now moving on from the containment thing. We've lost the plot here. We haven't taken the action that we should have taken four or five weeks ago,' he said. 'Boris Johnson should have convened Cobra at the outset when it became clear what was cooking up. Countries that took firm action at the time – if you look at what happened in Hong Kong and Singapore, which had a lot of cases initially but which took firm action and they've got the thing under control. We've lost control here … For reasons which are totally obscure to me we have taken it as policy not to track the people who have come back from Italy, not to test the people who have come back from Italy.' He also told the *Guardian* that day: 'We have a superficial prime minister who has got no grasp of public health. Our lot are behaving like 19th-century colonialists playing a five-day game of cricket.'

This was not just an abstract debate about things that might happen in the future. By that Thursday the crisis had already begun in earnest. Real problems were emerging in London's hospitals, which would prove to be the epicentre of the first wave of the epidemic. In stark contrast to the government, the initial reaction of the emergency services was to take drastic measures to ensure wards would not be overwhelmed, as they were in Italy. That day the London Ambulance Service increased the threshold for the severity of symptoms that a coronavirus patient would have to typically exhibit before they would be taken to hospital. This had dangerous consequences.

* * *

The sense of impatience with the government's wait-and-delay policy was becoming palpable across the country. The next morning, Friday the 13th, the newspapers were withering about the strategy the prime minister had laid out the previous day. 'Johnson's response has not been to lock down entire cities or even the whole country as China, South Korea and Italy have done. He has not ordered the closure of schools, as Ireland and Denmark did yesterday. Nor has he ordered the cancellation of large public events, as France and even Scotland have done,' complained *The Times* leader. 'Instead, his response was to announce that Britain would stop testing all but those exhibiting the most severe symptoms of the virus ... This is a remarkable gamble by Mr Johnson, albeit one that the government insists is informed by science.'

The general unease would only increase that morning when the government's chief scientific adviser dug an even deeper hole for his employers. Vallance was explaining to Radio 4's *Today* programme how the government was hoping to spread the numbers of infections across the peak of the outbreak rather than bring in measures to curtail the virus. This was based on the theory that the virus might come back even stronger later in the year. It was the argument he had used twice before that week, but this time he went even further and used the taboo words 'herd immunity'. Since the majority of people would get a mild illness, he said, the government's aim was 'to build up some degree of herd immunity ... so that more people are immune to the disease and we reduce the transmission'. In the meantime, there would be efforts to protect the vulnerable.

Later, on Sky News, he elaborated further. He said that 60 per cent of the population was 'the sort of figure you need to get herd immunity'. This meant roughly 40 million people in Britain would need to be infected. Since the death rate from the virus was estimated to be between 0.5 per cent and 1 per cent this added up to between 200,000 and 400,000 deaths in order to achieve herd immunity. Even this was almost certainly an underestimate, as such large numbers of patients in a single wave would exceed the NHS's capacity and cause even more fatalities because people would be denied life-saving treatment. The Sky interviewer pointed out this would mean 'an awful lot of people dying in this country'. Vallance looked flustered. 'Well, I mean, of course, we do face the prospect of – as the prime minister said yesterday – an increasing number of people dying. That is a real prospect. This is a nasty disease.'

The comments shocked academics who had been listening to Vallance as he toured the media studios. Vallance appeared to have confirmed Halpern's earlier comments that the policy goal was herd immunity and it was the first time that such a senior figure in the government team responding to the outbreak had been so candid. 'I just couldn't believe it. I don't shout or throw things at the television or radio,' said Professor Scally, 'but this time I was shouting at the radio, because herd immunity can only mean one thing and it means massive numbers of people getting this virus and massive numbers of people dying from it.'[9] Devi Sridhar was so outraged that she reached out to someone she knew who was advising the government on the strategy. 'I basically said, "What is underlying this? What am I not seeing? This seems catastrophic to let the virus go unchecked."' Her government contact replied, she says: '"We know what we're doing. We've assessed the different routes and everything is fine. So, basically, don't worry."'[10]

Indeed, it seems that even Johnson had been discussing herd immunity that day in conversation with his Italian counterpart Giuseppe Conte. Details of a phone call between the two prime ministers were later recounted by Pierpaolo Sileri, the Italian deputy health minister. Italy was already in lockdown and infections were so widespread that Sileri had caught the virus himself. He rang Conte to tell him that he had just tested positive.

'And he told me that he had spoken with Boris Johnson,' recalls Sileri, 'and that they had also talked about the situation in Italy. I remember he said, "He [Johnson] told me that he wants herd immunity."' Sileri thought this was foolhardy. 'I said, "Look, right now I'm in bed with a fever. But this isn't a normal influenza. It's something more." I remember that after hanging up I said to myself, "Today, I hope Boris Johnson goes for a lockdown."'[11] It was also claimed that Hancock discussed herd immunity with Italy's representative during a conference call between the G7 countries. The Italian representative is said to have told him that allowing the virus to run wild would result in thousands of deaths and there was no certainty herd immunity would ever work.[12]

There was now huge pressure on the government to adopt a new strategy. The rest of Europe was starting to go into lockdown and the government's critics were beginning to accuse Johnson of actually wanting people to fall ill. Something had to be done quickly. The Imperial College and Oxford University research suggests that there had been 14,000 infections when Sage had been warned on 3 March by the university modelling teams about the dire consequences of its mitigation and herd immunity approach. In the intervening 10 days, very little had happened to mitigate the spread of infections. By the evening of Friday 13 March, an estimated 160,000 people are believed to have been infected. The virus was unrelenting and infections were doubling every three days. Each day of delay in taking action would now cause many hundreds of avoidable deaths.

9

Dither

Saturday 14 March 2020 to Monday 23 March 2020
UK government's risk assessment: High

At 9.15 a.m. on Saturday 14 March, Johnson and his key advisers gathered in the cabinet room in Downing Street for a crisis meeting. By now the government's strategy was in shreds, ripped apart by its own modelling scientists and looking creepily Darwinian after the unfortunate public utterance of the words 'herd immunity'. More than 200 UK scientists and academics had signed a letter by that morning condemning the delay policy and saying thousands of lives could be saved by introducing stricter social distancing measures immediately. The scientists did not think the government was following the science as it claimed. Their letter began: 'As scientists living and working in the UK, we would like to express our concern about the course of action announced by the Government on 12 March 2020 regarding the Coronavirus outbreak. In particular, we are deeply preoccupied by the timeline of the proposed plan, which aims at delaying social distancing measures even further.'[1]

The scientists said the latest data showed that the UK was experiencing a similar growth curve in numbers of infections to other countries such as Italy, Spain, France and Germany, where the outbreaks were further advanced. 'The number of infected will be in the order of dozens of thousands within a few days. Under unconstrained growth, this outbreak will affect millions of people in the next few weeks,' the scientists warned. This, they argued, would most probably put the NHS at 'serious risk' of not being able to cope, as there would be insufficient intensive care beds. 'Going for "herd immunity" at this point does not seem a viable option, as this will put the NHS at an even stronger level of stress, risking many more lives than necessary.' Instead, the scientists said, 'more restrictive measures should be taken immediately, as is already happening in other countries across the world.'

Much of the world was closing down. France was shutting non-essential public locations, Spain went into lockdown that evening, America had announced a ban on flights from the UK and the Italians were already holding impromptu concerts from their balconies after the whole country had been confined to their homes since Tuesday. By then some of the UK public had actually given up waiting for the government to take action and were already taking measures to protect themselves. More firms had taken the unprecedented decision to encourage employees to work from home to avoid contracting the virus. Saturday's sporting fixture list was looking threadbare as the various leagues cancelled games of their own volition despite the huge losses in revenues.

The key advisers around the cabinet table with Johnson that day had begun to realise that a dramatic change of strategy was required. Crucially, the modelling team's death figures delivered that week had begun to spook the man regarded as the second most powerful figure in government. Dominic Cummings had initially favoured the government's delay-and-mitigate approach, but he changed his mind. 'Dominic himself had a conversion,' a senior Tory said. The 'Domoscene conversion', as it became known, was said to have happened at an earlier meeting with scientists. A government adviser told the *Financial Times* that Cummings had been 'watching, listening and asking questions' in the meeting when he suddenly piped up and said: 'Hang on a minute, we're going to have half a million people die in 16 weeks? Why aren't we locking down?'[2] By the Saturday morning meeting he had become a strong advocate of the kind of suppression strategy that would lead to lockdown. It was clear also that the herd immunity strategy had to be abandoned, given the hostile reaction it received when it was made public. At some point, Vallance too had started lobbying for a lockdown. In an email he sent to colleagues in response to questions from *The Sunday Times*, he would claim that he was more firmly in favour of lockdown measures at the time than others in the room. 'I argued stronger than anyone for action for lockdown,' he wrote in May ahead of our article about the cost of the late lockdown. He even claimed he received 'a telling off' from Whitty and Sir Mark Sedwill, the cabinet secretary, as well as from Chris Wormwald, permanent secretary at the Department of Health, for expressing his opinion on the subject.

However, Johnson was won over at the Saturday meeting. It seems he had finally engaged with the fact that the mitigation measures he had initially planned risked a death sentence for a quarter of a million people. A decision was therefore made in principle to lock down Britain. He told those around him at the meeting: 'We need to be taking all measures necessary.' This was a fundamental pivot in government policy towards more draconian actions. However, there were still nagging doubts. The prime minister is said to have still been uncomfortable with the idea of a full, legally enforced shutdown, which his advisers now saw as an unfortunate necessity. A source who attended Cobra meetings at the time said: 'The libertarian in Boris didn't want lockdown.' The result would be that the following week would see further delays and more drip-feed measures. It was the final week before lockdown and it would be played out in slow motion.

It was clear that not everyone in government had given up on the herd immunity strategy. That evening Nadine Dorries, the junior health minister, retweeted a homemade video stating: 'This video explains the science behind the Gov strategy, using a plastic bucket, a bottle and water. It's very effective.' The video had actually been posted on YouTube by a Kent-based chiropodist called Robert Isaacs. He was in his back garden with a bucket of water and an empty plastic bottle with a cut-off top and a hole an inch from its base. If Isaacs poured the water from the bucket into the bottle slowly, it would leak steadily from the hole. This was his way of showing how the NHS could handle a steady stream of patients. If he sloshed it in quickly, then the water would rise and spill over the sides of the bottle. This depicted how the NHS would be unable to cope if it received too many coronavirus cases at the same time.

He concluded that since there were only 500 known cases in the UK there was no point in slowing the spread of the virus down. Instead, he said: 'The plan over the next few weeks was to allow some infections to happen' until NHS capacity was at the point of being breached – or as he put it, 'at the point when the water is right at the top of the bottle'. The rationale for waiting before taking action was that people would not tolerate a long lockdown. 'What you can't do is quarantine the entire population for eight to twelve weeks,' he asserted. 'That just doesn't work. People won't comply with it.' It was herd immunity for dummies.

Dorries's tweet soon began to rack up critics. One commented: 'You're doing it wrong. Please fill up the bucket exponentially fast. Then see if you can stop it before it spills over the rim.' Another pointed out that the video had neglected to make clear that the government's approach would lead to hundreds of thousands of deaths. A less polite commenter responded to the video three weeks later in April as the first wave of the outbreak approached its height. 'Three weeks later and we have over 7,000 deaths and the NHS is struggling,' it said. 'Take this patronising crap down or I will show you where you can shove that watering can.'

Ironically, Dorries tweeted the video just after 10 p.m. that Saturday evening at around the same moment that the early editions of the *Sunday Telegraph* were being printed, which featured a comment piece written by her boss, Hancock. 'We have a plan, based on the expertise of world-leading scientists. Herd immunity is not a part of it,' he wrote. He described herd immunity 'as a scientific concept, not a goal or a strategy'. It was hard to reconcile this strong denial with the evidence from the preceding days. Hancock's claim was at complete variance with the government chief scientific adviser's remarks on herd immunity that week, his own health minister's understanding of strategy as revealed by her bucket tweet and, indeed, almost everything the government had been saying on the subject up to that point.

But then the comment piece was full of Hancockisms – a word that if it ever made a dictionary would be defined as: *noun – Bold, positive claims with a large dollop of wishful thinking, which turn out to be mostly untrue*. 'We have acted to contain the spread of the virus so far,' he confidently stated, omitting to mention that the containment strategy had been an abject failure and the virus was running rampant across the country that weekend. 'We have carried out some of the highest number of tests in Europe,' even though Germany, France, Spain, Denmark and even Malta were all undertaking more tests per person than the UK in March. 'Our surveillance testing is among the most sophisticated in the world,' he claimed, although the government later admitted it had completely underestimated the speed of the outbreak. He went on: 'The UK's plans for the rapid response to and mitigation of the spread of an epidemic are ranked number one above any other country by the Global Health Security Index.' This was true, although it was actually a ranking from the year before the virus. The UK's presence in the top two of the list along with the US would later be cited by academic studies as proof that the newly created index was an unreliable predictor of how a country would cope in a pandemic. Finally, he claimed that the initial growth of infections had 'slowed significantly' as a result of the UK's tracing efforts. This simply was not true. The cases had been doubling every three

days and the contact tracing system had only managed to identify 1 in every 200 infections before it had to be jettisoned.

The last of the mass gatherings took place that weekend. The
Stereophonics played two concerts to 15,000 fans in the indoor
Motorpoint arena in Cardiff despite pleas from doctors to postpone such events. One of their big fans was David Hepburn, a
consultant working in intensive care at the Royal Gwent
Hospital in Newport, who had tickets but did not attend because
he could see it was a mistake to allow the concert to go ahead
when infections were running so high. He ended up messaging
the organisers to plead with them to call it off. When the
numbers of people with the virus requiring intensive care rose
significantly a few weeks later, he tweeted: 'With retrospect, as
disapproving as I was at the time, the decision of the stereo-
phonic [sic] to play those gigs in Cardiff at the start of the
outbreak seems down right insane now.' In the meantime,
Johnson was spending the rest of his weekend in Chequers hosting a baby shower with his pregnant girlfriend.

On Monday 16 March he was back in London attending
another meeting of Cobra. The key issue of how and when to
introduce a lockdown was still to be resolved. A senior Tory
source said Johnson was now 'bottling' lockdown because of
concerns about the economy. Every day was vital as the UK
already had an estimated 320,000 infections on 16 March,
according to the Imperial and Oxford back-dated modelling,
and it would double again in three days. Any failure to seize the
initiative and go into lockdown would cost many lives.

But a senior political source at the Cobra meeting said they
were shocked that Johnson still did not seem to be on top of the
basics about the virus. 'At Cobra meetings under David Cameron
or Theresa May they knew what was going on. They're on top
of the briefs,' the source said. 'The impression I got was Boris
Johnson was winging it a bit. He hadn't seen the data. He wasn't
fully aware of the number of cases or what was happening

around the world.' The source described a lack of clear-sightedness at the meeting. After abandoning herd immunity, the decision makers were unsure about what kind of lockdown was possible. The source said: 'There was no real game plan, which is also unusual. Usually at a Cobra they've got options and you go through them. There was none of that. It was more like a discursive discussion. It was like a bunch of people having a discussion about this thing. It wasn't a normal Cobra meeting. Johnson was just not on top of his game.'

In attendance that day was Sadiq Khan, the mayor of London. It was the first time he had been allowed to attend Cobra since the virus crisis had begun. His previous requests to be present had all been refused despite the rising numbers of infected patients in London's hospitals. The data presented at the meeting was bleak for the UK's capital city, which was thought to account for more than a third of all the virus cases in the country at the time. Khan was described by the source as being shocked at the data and insisted: 'We've got to do something.'

If the prime minister was agonising with the weight of the lockdown decision that week, it wasn't always entirely obvious to those who met him. Later that day he held a conference call with business leaders in an attempt to persuade them to manufacture ventilators. To the shock of those on the call, the prime minister jokingly described the initiative as 'Operation Last Gasp'. The fact that the prime minister was holding the meeting at this stage in the outbreak was another sign of the lack of preparation. It had been recognised that ventilators would be the main life-saving equipment needed for the most seriously ill patients. They allow doctors to keep malfunctioning lungs breathing while giving the patient time to recover from the virus. A report only that morning by Imperial College – based on data from China, Italy and early cases in the UK – had estimated that almost a third of all patients admitted to hospital with the virus would need to be ventilated. Dr Philip Lee, the former justice minister in the Cameron government who still practises as a GP, was astonished that the ventilator appeal to manufacturers had been made so late. 'You're leaving it until mid-March to say, "By the way, we need a few more ventilators. Can anyone step forward?" It's honestly … Just wow. It's just not good enough. It really was deeply irresponsible.'[3]

That morning the scientific advisers in the great grey, slab-like 1960s building on Victoria Street, London, had hardened up their advice. The meeting of Sage recommended that measures were required instantly. 'On the basis of accumulating data, including on NHS critical care capacity, the advice from Sage has changed regarding the speed of implementation of additional interventions,' the meeting's minutes say. 'Sage advises that there is clear evidence to support additional social distancing measures be introduced as soon as possible.' At the evening's press conference, Johnson recommended that people should increase their social distancing by working from home if possible, avoiding pubs and restaurants, and self-isolating at home if someone in their household was ill. There was no compulsion. It was just advice.

Johnson's further postponement of more stringent measures alarmed government advisers. Professor Peter Openshaw, a member of the government's Nervtag committee, recalls: 'Many of us on the scientific advisory committees were keen that action should be taken a couple of weeks before action actually was taken. I think that critical period of delay made the big difference to the peak numbers, both of hospitalisations and of deaths. I think everyone would accept now in retrospect that if we'd gone for lockdown a couple of weeks earlier that would have greatly reduced the numbers of hospitalisations and deaths.'

The scientists were also starting to pull apart the government's flimsy rationale for delaying action. An open letter signed by 681 behavioural scientists questioned whether there was any empirical basis for the notion that people might become easily fatigued if measures were introduced too soon. 'We are not convinced that enough is known about "behavioural fatigue" or to what extent these insights apply to the current exceptional circumstances. Such evidence is necessary if we are to base a high-risk public health strategy on it,' the letter said. The scientists feared that the fixation on this idea had led the government to 'believe that halting the spread of the disease is impossible'. Instead they proposed 'radical behaviour change', which, if successful, would 'save very large numbers of lives'. They noted that the 'experience in China and South Korea is sufficiently encouraging to suggest that this possibility should at least be attempted'.

The big surge in infections was coming and the hospitals were being forced to get ready. On Tuesday 17 March Sir Simon Stevens, the NHS chief executive, wrote to hospital bosses outlining plans to free up a third of the UK's 100,000 hospital beds. His letter said he had been advised by Whitty and the Sage committee that the NHS would come under 'intense pressure' at the peak of the outbreak. He asked hospitals to assume that they would need to postpone all non-urgent operations by mid-April or earlier, which would save 15,000 beds, and ordered that 15,000 'medically fit' patients should be ejected from the wards and found places in the community. The aim was to send 95 per cent of discharged patients back to their own homes, according to the UK Homecare Association, a professional body that would provide carers for some of them. Hospital staff were instructed to review all patients twice a day and ask themselves: 'Why not home? Why not today?'

Stevens had a long-standing connection with the prime minister stretching back decades. The pair had been unlikely friends after meeting at Balliol College, Oxford, where they studied in the mid-1980s. Johnson, an old Etonian and a former member of the Bullingdon Club, the notorious all-male dining society, was politically centre-right, while Stevens, known as 'Simes', had been educated at a Birmingham comprehensive school and was a member of the Labour Club. Yet their friendship was forged during a trip to America with the Oxford Union debating society.[4] Many years later, when standing to be Conservative Party leader in 2019, Johnson described how Stevens had helped him get elected as union president in 1986. He went on to suggest that together they would sort out the NHS.

Simes was given legislative backing for his move to clear out hospitals when Hancock introduced new laws in parliament that week. All 'regulatory requirements' were slashed to help facilitate the mass discharge and hospitals were indemnified against clinical negligence liabilities arising from the crisis. But the bond between the NHS chief executive and the prime minister would be stretched to the limit as Johnson's delay tactics would leave Stevens in the unenviable position of having to make increasingly difficult decisions to prevent the health service being visibly overwhelmed.

The scramble to free up beds would have a particularly ill-thought-out and reckless consequence for the care homes. There was no mandatory requirement to test patients before they were discharged into the care sector, even though the spread of the virus in hospitals was becoming a big problem at the time. It was an expedient decision because there was a practical difficulty: there simply wasn't enough testing capacity for 15,000 patients. It meant that hundreds of infected people were sent to care homes, where they lived and mingled with those at an age where they were much more likely to die if they caught the virus. Some care home owners refused to accept untested patients. Others relented after the government offered payments as an inducement to accept hospital discharges.

It seemed to experts like Martin Vernon, the NHS's former national clinical director for older people, that this was a policy to protect the hospitals for the sake of 'critically ill younger people'. He believes the NHS clear-out 'sent the message out that many older people really do not benefit from being in hospital'. Some health authorities would actually begin making this exact argument to elderly patients to justify excluding them from hospital. The hospitals were placed in a very difficult position and they would be forced to choose which patients they could treat and which they could not. As the hours of inaction ticked away, the crisis was becoming worse. It is an extraordinary fact that each day that passed that week before lockdown, the health service's burden was increasing by a third.

The complacency that had allowed Johnson to sail through February believing coronavirus to be a medically 'irrational panic' was rapidly dissipating. His government was panicking and nothing showed this more clearly than the chancellor Rishi Sunak's big gesture on the afternoon of Tuesday 17 March. Sunak was the new Clark Kent in town, but he was not acting as the caped defender of libertarianism and free trade that Johnson had spoken about in Greenwich six weeks earlier. He was turning on the money tap with the biggest ever state intervention seen in peacetime. The £12bn support package Sunak had unveiled the previous Wednesday had already been deemed totally inadequate. It was clear that further social distancing measures were inevitable and this would therefore have a devastating impact on the economy and jobs. Treasury officials had worked furiously over the weekend to produce a £350bn package of government-backed loans and cash grants to provide support to businesses and workers. 'We will do whatever it takes,' he repeatedly intoned as he announced the colossal splurge in spending. The sum was three times higher than the annual budget of the NHS in England, and it was only the start of the interventions.

Sunak's dauntlessness, together with his reassuring tone and attention to detail, were praised by his colleagues. Many were even beginning to have idle thoughts that 'dishy Rishi' might one day be their next leader. The parliamentary public accounts committee, however, would later be less complimentary. The committee chastised the Treasury for waiting until mid-March before deciding on economic support schemes – despite the warnings from medical chiefs from January onwards. The MPs on the committee found that the government's economic reaction to Covid-19 had been rushed and, in the process, neglected many sectors that needed help. This would have a long-term negative impact on the economy, it concluded. The sheer scale of the government failings were 'astonishing', the committee said.

The growth of the virus was on a rapidly steepening upward curve. The Oxford and Imperial back-dated estimates suggest there were 81,000 new infections in the UK on that Tuesday alone. That took the total number of people who had been infected with the virus to around 400,000 and this would double in the next three days as Johnson pondered over his next move. The virus's spikey tendrils were lodging themselves even deeper into those who walked the corridors of power. Professor Neil Ferguson, one of the government's key modelling scientists, revealed that he too was self-isolating after developing 'a slight dry but persistent cough'.

The following day, Wednesday 18 March, the prime minister announced that schools would be closed indefinitely – but that would not take place until Friday afternoon, by which time there would be further exponential growth in infections. Vallance later told a parliamentary select committee that Sage had effectively advised the government to bring in lockdown measures by that Wednesday. But still the prime minister agonised. The delays were becoming increasingly costly. Many more people were already working from home and starting to keep their distance from others in social situations, but commuter buses and trains were still packed in central London, which was the epicentre of the outbreak. Google data tracking people's movements suggests the use of public transport was down by only a third across the UK by that morning. Italy's chief scientific adviser, Professor Walter Ricciardi, recalls that he was 'shocked' to see the images on television of life going on as normal in Britain. 'Looking at what was happening in Italy at that time where people were already locked down at home, I said, "What's going on in the UK!?"[5]

The pandemic was now hitting the NHS in London like a hurricane and the hospitals had been left exposed. They did not have sufficient protective equipment for staff and the government's decision to stop contact tracing had blindsided the health officials as to where and when the first wave would crash down. The answer came on Thursday 19 March, when Northwick Park Hospital in Harrow, north-west London, declared a 'critical incident'. Cases had been building at the hospital from the initial days of the pandemic, as it had been designated as the screening centre for people with Covid symptoms arriving at Heathrow. But the population in the surrounding boroughs served by the hospital had also been badly hit by the contagion.

Hundreds of people with laboured breathing, fever and fatigue had been entering the hospital seeking treatment for the virus. In the week before lockdown, more than 30 people in the area died from coronavirus infections. It meant Northwick Park had more patients than it could cope with and it began shipping them out to the surrounding hospitals. The incident was an early demonstration of how harrowing and time-consuming tackling the virus would be for the hospitals. Nursing staff would have to neglect other patients while sitting alongside dying people holding their hands with plastic gloves. They had no choice, as the infection protocols meant that relatives were not allowed on to the wards and otherwise husbands, wives, grandmothers and grandfathers would die alone. The numbers of daily deaths from Covid-19 in the capital hit triple figures that week and would surge even higher.

A major problem faced by NHS health service staff was that use of tests for the virus had to be rationed and mostly only the patients in a hospital could be checked for the virus. The failure to expand Britain's diagnostic capacity meant there were few tests available for doctors and nurses, who were placing themselves in grave danger by treating infected patients at close proximity. Even medical staff who developed symptoms would not be tested unless they became so ill that they required treatment in a hospital themselves. So any medical staff who developed a cough or a temperature were forced to stay home and self-isolate for long periods, leaving wards critically short-staffed.

There had been offers from UK research laboratories to help boost the country's testing capacity, but approaches to the government seemed to flounder in bureaucracy. Among those willing to pitch in was the Nobel prize-winning scientist Sir Paul Nurse, who runs the Francis Crick Institute in London. His institute was willing to process 2,000 tests a day, but he became exasperated when he tried to find someone in government who would put his proposal into action. 'I've talked to quite a number of different people from minister levels and also advisers and it's like talking to a blancmange, really,' he said. 'I mean, you sort of poke it and it wobbles for a while, and then more or less goes back to the original shape it had. The problem started with the failure to have proper planning in place to get going, and ever since then we've been trying to play catch-up.'[6]

On the day that Northwick Park was at critical level, Public Health England made a confusing announcement that sent out the wrong messages. The threat of Covid-19 was being downgraded so it would no longer be classed as a High Consequence Infectious Disease (HCID). This seemed inexplicable, as the virus was fast becoming the deadliest pandemic the world had seen for more than a hundred years. The downgrading, the government said, was a technical matter of terminology. The virus may have killed a lot of people, but it was a low percentage of the total numbers infected, according to the official line. Yet an investigation by the BBC programme *Panorama* discovered the move was at least partly a way to get around the shortage of protective equipment in the NHS. The problem was that the

Health and Safety Executive had earlier ruled that the very top level of PPE should be worn when dealing with a disease ranked as an HCID. The change in classification therefore meant health workers could be kitted out with less protective equipment – making the most of the threadbare stocks available. The government had requested that the Advisory Committee on Dangerous Pathogens remove Covid-19 from the HCID list. Sources on that committee said it had taken the decision pragmatically based on the PPE stockpile shortages at the time. On the same day, NHS staff were told it was fine to wear less protective aprons and basic surgical masks.

There was palpable fear in the health service about the deluge of cases that would be faced in the weeks to come and some of this turned into anger against the prime minister, who was still prevaricating. One hospital doctor sent a doom-laden note to the Doctors' Association UK that week. 'Too few ICU beds; too few hospital beds; poor staffing and resourcing,' it said, before adding, 'crushing underestimation of the potential impact on the part of the secretary of state for health and the PM'.

Back in Whitehall, the atmosphere was becoming increasingly tense and the prime minister was looking 'haunted' as he endlessly wrestled with the big decision, according to one government insider. Pushed by his advisers, on Thursday morning he was still veering towards a lockdown – but had limited his ambitions to London, as the first step. The London mayor, Sadiq Khan, and Cressida Dick, head of the Metropolitan Police, were summoned to Downing Street, where they were greeted by Johnson along with his trusted lieutenants Cummings and Robert Jenrick, the local government secretary. They crammed around a small round table in one of Johnson's private offices to make plans for a London lockdown.

Before the meeting, Khan had been ringing round other mayors of big international cities to find out how they were tackling the virus. He was worried that London was particularly vulnerable because it was two weeks ahead of the rest of the country in numbers of infections, and thousands of people were still flooding into the city by air and Eurostar. According to a well-placed source, Khan said, 'Listen Boris, these other cities around the world are doing this, this and this,' before going on to cite the example of Paris, which was locked down and was backing its restrictive measures with fines. The city was already experiencing one of the problems of local lockdowns, which was that wealthy Parisians were leaving in their droves to head for second homes in the country, and taking the virus with them.

But the situation was so desperate in London that something had to be done. The source said Khan told the prime minister that 'as a former human rights lawyer' he did not wish to restrict people's freedom. 'I don't want to do this voluntarily and you're a libertarian. Neither of us wants to do this,' he reportedly said. But, nonetheless, the mayor believed a lockdown was the only option. Khan said he was 'willing to take the flak and volunteer London because these numbers are really scary', according to the source.

Johnson's participation in the meeting was noticeably muted. 'If you were a Martian that landed at that meeting in his office,' the source said, 'you'd have thought Cummings was the prime minister, not Johnson. Cummings was far more aware and more lucid than Johnson.' However, the prime minister finally made up his mind. According to the source, 'Johnson said, "That's a good idea. We'll do it. And we'll announce it today." They agreed that Khan would join Johnson at a press conference that afternoon and say London is going to go into a form of lockdown.' The preparations began as soon as the meeting ended. Cummings went away to consider whether traffic in and out of London could be restricted to prevent a Parisian-style exodus, and the heads of the army were put on notice in case troops might be needed to enforce a lockdown in the capital.

But then the uncertainty and indecision began to grip the prime minister again. Cummings rang Khan to say the announcement would be delayed until the following day, Friday 20 March. 'They were worried about the impact on the markets if the London lockdown was announced on a Thursday. They wanted the markets to close so they could avoid an immediate run on them,' the source said.

By now it was a national crisis so grave that it was time to wheel out the Queen to rally the nation. From Windsor Castle, where she had decamped with Prince Philip, she released a statement harking back to the unbreakable spirit of Britain during the Blitz. Aged 93, she had lived through the last great crisis to hit London 80 years earlier when enemy bombs had fallen on the city. Her enduring presence was a reassuring reminder that the country would one day get through all this. 'At times such as these, I am reminded that our nation's history has been forged by people and communities coming together to work as one, concentrating our combined efforts with a focus on the common goal,' she said. 'Many of us will need to find new ways of staying in touch with each other and making sure that loved ones are safe. I am certain we are up to that challenge. You can be assured that my family and I stand ready to play our part.'

Curiously, with the whole of Whitehall waiting for a decision, Johnson slipped away for a 'personal engagement' that Thursday evening. It is not known why he considered it necessary to meet the Russian newspaper baron, Evgeny Lebedev, at that moment and disregard his own advice to avoid all 'non-essential contact with others'. The owner of the *Evening Standard* and the *Independent* had in the past been a very generous host to the prime minister, inviting him to a lavish party at his Italian villa. But the purpose of the meeting remains a mystery. Later in the year it would emerge that Johnson had nominated Lebedev, the son of a KGB agent, for a seat in the House of Lords. Johnson's press officers have refused to say who was present at this meeting or why it was so important.

* * *

By Friday 20 March there had been 50 confirmed deaths from the virus in the UK but only 700 people had actually tested positive for Covid-19. It is an illustration of just how poor the contact tracing and testing system had been before it was abandoned. The number of cases had doubled from Tuesday to an estimated 790,000 cases by Friday, according to the Imperial and Oxford back-dated data. Behind the scenes the government had now realised that the virus was so wildly out of control they needed to prepare to take even more drastic measures. Officials recognised that so many infections had spread across the country that the NHS could well be placed in the impossible position of having to cope with an unmanageable influx of patients. Doctors would inevitably be forced to take soul-searching decisions about which lives should be saved in order to protect hospitals. It was against the ethos of the NHS, but many dying patients would be denied life-saving treatment to stop the health service being overrun.

The government's Moral and Ethical Advisory Group (Meag), consisting of academics, medics and faith leaders, met that Friday to discuss how this would be done. They were told that Chris Whitty's office had been working with a senior clinicians group to devise ways to 'manage increased pressure on staff and resources' caused by Covid-19. The government's chief medical officer wanted advice on the ethics of selecting who should be given intensive care treatment – and who should not. Sir Jonathan Montgomery, Meag's chair, who was also a professor of healthcare law at University College London, agreed to help produce guidance on the subject.

That led the following day to a document – entitled 'Covid-19 triage score: sum of 3 domains' – being created by one of Montgomery's collaborators, Mark Griffiths, a professor of critical care medicine at Imperial College London. It was a highly sensitive document because it was intended to be used as a triage tool by doctors, and it effectively advised that many elderly people – who were the vast majority of patients being treated for serious infections of Covid-19 – should not be given intensive care treatment. It was indicative of how dire they believed the situation to be. The document would be presented to a full meeting of the Meag committee the following Wednesday.

At the meeting in Downing Street the previous day, the London mayor had warned that thousands of people were still flooding into the city by air and by Eurostar. While no action had been taken as a result, it was now the turn of the French to express the same concerns, but the other way round. The French were alarmed that people were travelling into their country from London, where the virus was being allowed to thrive unchecked. On Friday morning Johnson picked up the phone expecting some *entente cordiale* in a crisis – only to find an irate Emmanuel Macron, the French president, on the line. Macron had locked down France that Monday and was becoming impatient that the UK had not followed suit, as Britons were still freely coming into France and undermining his country's efforts. The details of the leaders' conversation were leaked to Jean Quatremer, the European affairs correspondent of the French newspaper *Libération*. This is Quatremer's account: 'Macron loses his temper on Friday morning. He calls Boris Johnson. "Look here. Our police have been instructed to close the border with the United Kingdom. Friday evening at midnight. Everything is ready to go unless you announce measures to fight the pandemic."'[7]

Something had to be done. Even the UK's closest neighbours were beginning to regard the country as a rogue outlier spreading disease on the edge of the continent. But that Friday the plans for a London lockdown were discarded. In the afternoon there was a meeting of Cobra – and the prime minister was nowhere to be seen. 'I turn up and Michael Gove is chairing it. Not Johnson. It was odd,' one of those present recalls. 'To miss such a critical Cobra meeting, I just don't understand why. It's inexplicable because this is the Cobra where we decided to bring in nationwide measures and he delegates to Michael Gove. It's just odd. It's literally a five-minute walk from Cabinet Office through the corridor to No. 10 to the press conference.'

The key nationwide measure that had been discussed was the proposal to close all venues where people might normally congregate at night. The question for Cobra was not whether this should be done. The situation was so desperate there was no choice. Instead, the members were discussing when the new rules should be introduced. Gove proposed that all bars and pubs should be shut on Saturday lunchtime, but Khan and Nicola Sturgeon, Scotland's first minister, argued strongly that this would encourage people to go out for one final disastrous Friday-night binge. 'Gove went around the room and all of us besides the Treasury minister agreed,' said the source, who was present. 'To give Gove credit, he had moved from his beginning view to this end view.' Gove accepted the consensus and advised Johnson that the measures should take effect immediately.

Johnson did reappear to front the press conference immediately after the Cobra meeting. It was not entirely clear where he had been, but it is possible he was brainstorming with Lee Cain, his communications director. Cain was a tough former *Sun* and *Mirror* journalist who had never quite lived down the fact that he was once deployed to goad David Cameron while dressed as a chicken as part of a newspaper stunt. Johnson had been working with him on a slogan that he could trot out to reinforce the government's key objectives in the fight against the virus. Advisers from the 'Vote Leave' campaign were also on the phone chipping in. Cain suggested that they use 'protect the NHS', which had been successful for Johnson during December's election. When extra words were added, they produced the message that would later become the government's mantra – almost as much as 'we're following the science'.

The now familiar slogan 'Stay at home, protect the NHS, save lives' was launched by Johnson, his chancellor Sunak and

Dr Jenny Harries at the press conference that afternoon. The bombshell news at the press conference was that the prime minister was ordering all cafes, pubs, bars, clubs, restaurants, gyms, leisure centres, nightclubs, theatres and cinemas across the country to close their doors. However, Johnson had ignored Cobra's advice. He fudged the decision by asking the night-time venues to close that evening, but did not make it compulsory until the following day. It meant there would be a last hurrah in the pubs, despite the lobbying from Khan and Sturgeon.

There was another announcement that introduced a word that would become common currency during the crisis. 'Today I can announce that, for the first time in our history, the government is going to step in and help to pay people's wages,' Sunak declared to the room of journalists and cameras. 'I am placing no limit on the amount of funding available for the scheme ... We're paying people's wages up to 80 per cent so someone can be furloughed rather than laid off to protect their jobs.' The 'furlough' scheme was born. There had been little choice, as people could not be expected to stay at home without any money to put food on the table. Harries, the deputy chief medical officer for England, was there to reassure everyone that the health service was well prepared for the difficult weeks to come – just as she had done during the fireplace chat with Johnson the week before. There was, she said, a 'perfectly adequate supply' of PPE (personal protective equipment) for care workers and any supply pressures have been 'completely resolved'. This was not so. The lack of PPE and the failure to protect the elderly in care homes would shortly become a national scandal that would haunt the government and expose its lack of planning since January. Harries also advised people to stay two metres apart during walks outdoors – while standing at a lectern less than a metre from the prime minister.

It was Mothering Sunday that weekend and Johnson was asked whether he was planning to visit his 77-year-old mother on Sunday. There was no doubt by now that the elderly were in the most danger from the virus. Johnson initially gave the official line: 'My advice would be that people should really think very carefully – irrespective of whether they are going to visit their mothers – about any elderly person who may be in a vulnerable group.' But he then confusingly sent out a completely mixed message, adding: 'I will certainly be sending her my very best wishes and hope to get to see her.'

The country was closing down over the weekend beginning 21 March. Some people had already been working from home that week and the closing of social venues such as restaurants, gyms and bars helped convince a number of large employers to decide it was too unsafe to continue trading. The bookstore Waterstones reluctantly closed despite a 17 per cent upsurge in demand for books from people sensing they would soon have many free hours at their disposal. The department store chain John Lewis had stayed open through two world wars but on Sunday it announced it was shutting its stores for the first time in its 155-year history. Visit Cornwall sent out an unusual message for a tourist board to potential holidaymakers. 'Stay away,' it said. Production of the country's most popular soap operas – *Coronation Street*, *Emmerdale* and *EastEnders* – was halted to protect the crew and actors.

The clement spring weather over the weekend brought thousands of people out into parks and open spaces in the new world where they could no longer congregate in sports clubs, pubs or restaurants. It was an opportunity for people who had been cooped up in their homes all week to get out in the fresh air. Many chose to walk with their families for Mothers' Day instead of going out for Sunday lunch, which was no longer an option. That day saw the popularisation of a new word: 'Covidiots'. The newspapers and television channels were showing crowds of people and vehicles flocking to outdoor venues from Richmond Park in west London to Snowdonia National

Park, which had to close its main car parks 'following the busiest visitor weekend in living memory'. To some it was an extension of the selfish behaviour that had seen people panic-buy toilet rolls and pasta over the previous week. But mostly, people had squeezed into the parks because so many other things they would normally do were unavailable and the importance of social distancing was still little appreciated. This was a highly abnormal weekend.

Johnson attempted to correct his mixed message about Mothers' Day by tweeting a public information video. 'You might want to see your mum today, but think about every other mum. Don't put them at risk,' it chided. His aides quietly briefed journalists that he had meant that he would be seeing his mother Charlotte on Skype. He skipped the daily press briefing on Saturday 21 March and took a break with Symonds at Chequers. Over that weekend, a further 420,000 infections are estimated to have spread across the UK, taking the total to 1.2 million, according to the Oxford and Imperial back-dated modelling.

Johnson was back for the Sunday afternoon press conference, where he revealed that letters were now being sent to 1.5 million people who had been identified from their medical records as being extremely vulnerable because of existing conditions. They had been asked to isolate in their homes for their own safety. For many it would be too late. The scenes of crowds mingling in the sunshine had alarmed the government and Johnson warned that tougher action would have to be taken if people refused to observe social distancing advice. 'We will think about this very actively in the next 24 hours,' he said. 'If people can't make use of parks and playgrounds responsibly, in a way that observes the two-metre rule, then of course we're going to have to look at further measures.' But it wasn't just the crowds. The pressure was coming from all sides. His cabinet, backbench MPs and the opposition Labour Party all wanted him to stop dithering and take action.

On Sunday morning Sadiq Khan had effectively pre-empted the prime minister by instructing London to lock down. Whether the London mayor had the power to do such a thing was questionable but Khan did not care. 'This isn't advice, as far as I'm concerned,' he warned. 'These are instructions and these are rules that we should all obey to stop people dying.' Doctors were also raising the alarm. Rinesh Parmar, the chair of the Doctors' Association UK, went on television to say that many of his colleagues felt like 'lambs to the slaughter' and 'cannon fodder' because they were so ill-equipped. He was one of 5,000 health workers who signed a letter to the prime minister calling for more protective equipment for NHS staff – a direct rebuke to the deputy chief medical officer who had claimed supplies were 'perfectly adequate' two days earlier. The weekend had also seen the death of an 18-year-old – the youngest victim of the virus in the UK. It hammered home the message that this was a disease that could kill people of all ages.

On what would become a day infamous in British history, Monday 23 March, the nation woke up to front-page headlines about the crowds the day before. The impression that people had still not quite grasped the gravity of the crisis was reinforced by figures for commuter traffic, which showed that half of employees were still travelling to their place of work that morning. Inside Downing Street there had been a growing realisation that the UK was now on a trajectory to be 'Italy, at least' in terms of cases and fatalities, according to a source advising the top team. Even worse, Britain was still out on a limb when compared with its major European neighbours. By that Monday, Italy had been locked down for twelve days, Spain for nine, France for a week and Germany, which had far fewer cases, the day before. Johnson had held out for as long as he could, but he had reached the end of the road.

When darkness fell at the end of another fresh bright spring day, millions of people tuned in to watch the prime minister's

Britain's late lockdown

Total estimated infections for major European countries at the point
they imposed lockdown

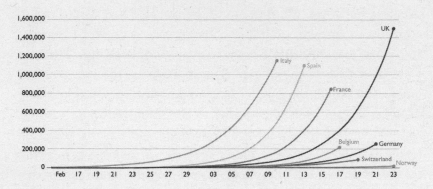

address to the nation. Johnson was at his most headmasterly when he announced with a sombre voice: 'From this evening I must give the British people a very simple instruction – you must stay at home ... You should not be meeting friends. If your friends ask you to meet, you should say No. You should not be meeting family members who do not live in your home. You should not be going shopping except for essentials like food and medicine – and you should do this as little as you can. If you don't follow the rules the police will have the powers to enforce them, including through fines and dispersing gatherings.

'To ensure compliance with the government's instruction to stay at home, we will immediately: close all shops selling non-essential goods, including clothing and electronic stores, and other premises including libraries, playgrounds and outdoor gyms, and places of worship; we will stop all gatherings of more than two people in public – excluding people you live with; and we'll stop all social events, including weddings, baptisms and other ceremonies, but excluding funerals. Parks will remain open for exercise but gatherings will be dispersed.

'In this fight we can be in no doubt that each and every one of us is directly enlisted. Each and every one of us is now obliged

Virologist Dr Shi Zhengli, nicknamed 'Bat Woman', had been researching deadly human pathogens in Wuhan, China, for more than a decade. Her team discovered the closest known match to the Covid-19 virus in a mineshaft on China's southern border in 2013 and brought it back to the city.

The Wuhan Institute of Virology, where Shi's team carried out controversial experiments to boost the infectivity of viruses in the years leading up to the start of the pandemic that was first discovered in the city.

The prime minister paints the eyes of two lions at Downing Street on 24 January 2020 to celebrate the eve of Chinese New Year. On the same day, he missed the first meeting of the national emergency committee Cobra, which was held to coordinate Britain's response to the virus.

Boris Johnson and fiancée Carrie Symonds at Twickenham for the England v Wales rugby match on 7 March 2020. The prime minister was pictured shaking hands with people, infuriating his government's scientific advisers, who felt it sent out the wrong message.

Racegoers cheer at the Cheltenham Festival on 13 March 2020. The four-day event went ahead despite UK infection numbers escalating rapidly and has since been linked to many deaths from the virus.

Epidemiologist Professor Neil Ferguson's pandemic modelling helped persuade Johnson to bring in the first lockdown, which saved huge numbers of lives. Ferguson later resigned from Sage after the *Telegraph* reported he had breached lockdown rules with a lover.

'You must stay at home.' Boris Johnson addresses the nation from
10 Downing Street as he announced the first UK lockdown
on 23 March 2020.

Health secretary Matt Hancock addresses members of the armed forces at
the opening of the NHS Nightingale Hospital in Birmingham on 16 April 2020.
Despite the hospital's £66m cost, not a single patient would be admitted over
the rest of the year due to staff shortages.

Protesters hold a banner reading 'PPE NOW' outside Southend Hospital
on 28 April 2020 during the minute's silence for key workers
who had died from the virus.

Maria Berry (left) with daughter Rebecca McAllister, who lost her father
Brian Noon (pictured on the table) to Covid-19 after they were told
he would not be admitted to hospital even if his condition worsened.

Betty Grove with husband Alan. She died after being sent home from hospital with pneumonia and a collapsed lung.

Johnson's chief adviser Dominic Cummings in the 10 Downing Street Rose Garden, fending off questions during the media inquisition into his 528-mile round trip to Durham while suffering Covid-19 symptoms.

Chancellor Rishi Sunak launches the ill-fated Eat Out to Help Out scheme by serving tables at a Wagamama restaurant. He was criticised for failing to wear a mask.

Chief medical officer Chris Whitty (left) and Patrick Vallance, the chief scientific adviser, arriving at Downing Street on 21 September 2020 for a press conference in which they issued a strong warning about mounting deaths from the second wave after Johnson had rejected their advice to introduce a circuit breaker lockdown.

Sage member Professor John Edmunds repeatedly urged the government to learn from its mistake of the first late lockdown and suppress the second wave swiftly and decisively. His advice was ignored.

Cameron Wellington, a junior martial arts champion from Walsall, died from the virus in November. Aged 19, he is among the UK's youngest known victims of Covid-19. His parents say he might not have died had the government locked down in September.

to join together. To halt the spread of this disease. To protect our NHS and to save many many thousands of lives.'

The lockdown would begin that night, but tragically it had come far too late. The last nine days while Johnson had wrestled over the decision had been particularly brutal. Infections had almost doubled again since the previous Friday, three days before, and had now sky-rocketed to an estimated 1.5 million across the UK. Close to 1.2 million of these infections had happened in the seven days since Johnson bottled the decision to go for a lockdown on Monday 16 March – after he had come to the conclusion that such a drastic measure was necessary at the weekend. It meant that Britain had a higher number of infections than every other major European country at the time they had taken the same emergency measures. Italy and Spain had an estimated 1.2 million when they locked down, France had 890,000 and Germany had 270,000.

It was a welcome move for the government's scientists. 'I have to say that when the lockdown was achieved, was declared or was announced, I was very relieved. I was very relieved indeed,' said Daniela De Angelis, Professor of Statistical Science for Health at Cambridge University and a member of the Spi-M advisory committee.[8] But it was a move that many felt should have happened long before. Sir David King, the former chief scientific adviser, describes the delay as 'grossly negligent'. He said: 'The fact they were short of PPE, the fact they were short of testing equipment. The response of the government has not just been tardy. It has been totally disrespectful of British lives. We created an unmanageable situation.'

The delay was indeed disastrous. The sheer number of people who had been allowed to become infected meant that the country was riddled with the virus and many would be forced to rely on the last line of defence: the courageous doctors, nurses and auxiliary staff of the NHS who had to manage as best they could despite being hamstrung by the lack of testing and protective equipment. Those 20 days of government delay since

Johnson chaired his first Cobra meeting at the beginning of March are the single most important reason why the UK had the most deaths from the coronavirus in Europe and the second most in the world by the end of the first lockdown.

It is a brutal reality that, to this day, the government appears unable to countenance or admit. The terrible cost in lives was just too high. When asked directly on *The Andrew Marr Show* two months later, Hancock claimed he was 'sure' that the late lockdown did not cost any lives – a remarkable untruth. Vallance, the chief scientist, did at least acknowledge that the lockdown should have been earlier. However, it would be left to the government's own top advisers to set out the true and appalling cost of Johnson's dithering. Neil Ferguson, the government's chief modeller during that period, told a parliamentary select committee on 10 June: 'The epidemic was doubling every three to four days before lockdown interventions were introduced. So had we introduced lockdown measures a week earlier, we would have reduced the final death toll by at least a half.'

This was also emphasised by his colleague on Sage, Professor Jeremy Farrar, who later told a Commons committee that the lockdown 'should have come in earlier'. He said: 'Indeed, in the weekend following the [13 March] Sage meeting there was pressure and urgency to lock down immediately, within the next 24 hours of that weekend and the coming week. That delay led to the epidemic expanding faster than if the lockdown had been imposed earlier. That week was a critical week for subsequent events in the epidemic.'

PART THREE

THE RECKONING

24 March 2020 to 26 April 2020

10

Disaster

Tuesday 24 March 2020 to Wednesday 8 April 2020
UK government order: Lockdown

When the sun broke through the misting of dawn clouds on the first Tuesday of spring, the great thoroughfares of Britain's cities, from Bute Street, Cardiff, to Deansgate, Manchester, to Princes Street in Edinburgh, lay eerily silent. An American television network was broadcasting live footage from the Abbey Road crossing in London to the world, without any tourists pretending to be Beatles or indeed anyone at all. Elsewhere in the capital, a solitary man with shopping bags was pictured scurrying across Westminster Bridge. It was the morning after the historic announcement of the night before. Never before had the British people been locked down in such a way. The virus was already in more than a million households and the prime minister may not have known it at the time but he was almost certainly one of those infected. He had been carrying the virus in his lungs when he delivered his address to the nation the previous evening. The lockdown had come too late and he, like many others, would have to fall on the mercy of the National Health Service doctors and nurses who would save his life.

The empty streets on 24 March 2020 were a testament to how seriously the British people took the threat of the virus. For most it would be the beginning of a new life within four walls – when Zoom calls, pyjama working, home schooling and Joe

Wicks exercise classes would become the stuff of everyday exist-ence. But while people nestled into their homes, a desperate battle of life and death was being played out unseen in Britain's hospitals. This was the real and untold story of lockdown.

'We looked on helpless as ambulances brought patient after patient gasping for breath. Older people, younger people; the virus didn't discriminate,' said a senior intensive care doctor in the south-east. 'Thirty-something-year-olds, previously fit and healthy, would go from smiling and talking to fighting for their lives on a ventilator in a matter of hours. We ran ourselves into the ground to try and save them as intensive care units filled up around us at a rate we knew we couldn't keep up with. Looking around us we wondered how this had been allowed to happen. Why had lockdown come so late? Could we have saved more lives? That is a question that will continue to haunt us. The public saw none of this. If you watched the daily briefing you would think it was all under control. But it wasn't. We were sinking.'

The doctor was one of several we spoke to in late summer who requested that their identity was not disclosed because they feared reprisals from NHS managers for telling a different narrative of those lockdown weeks to the one officials wanted the public to hear. Their accounts are distressing. The prime minister's vacillation over whether to lock down forced the NHS into the impossible position of having to cope with an unmanageable deluge of patients. Britain not only had more infections than any other European country when they took the same drastic decision, it also had fewer intensive care beds than most. Before the pandemic hit, the UK had just seven intensive care beds per 100,000 people, fewer than Cyprus and Latvia and half the number in Italy. Germany had 29 intensive care beds per 100,000 people.

As a result, the government, the NHS and many doctors were forced into taking controversial decisions – choosing which lives to save, which patients to treat and who to prioritise – in order to protect hospitals. This included taking unprecedented steps to keep large numbers of elderly and frail patients out of intensive care wards to avoid these being overwhelmed. It would mean many patients would die without receiving the life-saving care they needed. Downing Street was anxious that critical care units should not be visibly overrun as they had been in Italy, Spain and China, where patients in the city of Wuhan were photographed dying in corridors. So a veil of secrecy was now placed over Britain's hospitals. The publication of critical care capacity figures was suspended, which meant nobody outside the corridors of power would be able to tell whether hospitals were being overrun, and a general ban was imposed on information being passed to the media without sign-off from central command. The NHS management had shifted to a war footing.

The first week of lockdown was one of tragic farce in government. While Britain was facing the worst crisis since the Second World War, the corridors of Whitehall were unexpectedly empty. 'I don't think people appreciate the scale of how disorganised things are inside,' one Tory aide told *The Sunday Times* that week. 'It's total anarchy, with everyone working from home. There's no reliable data and people are overwhelmed.'[1] Despite the fact that there had been many weeks to get ready for the pandemic, a minister confided: 'This is the key week in terms of preparation ... Everyone's rushing around trying to build up the sea walls before the tsunami strikes.' In truth, the tsunami had already hit Britain and the lack of foresight by the government was already being felt. In the hospitals there were already reports of NHS workers having to resort to wearing bin bags instead of clinical gowns because of the shortage of protective equipment.

Parliament remained open for a couple of days. In a hearing held online before the science and technology select committee on Wednesday 25 March, Richard Horton, the editor of *The*

Lancet medical journal, was already holding the government to account for its shambolic response to the crisis. He pointed to scientific papers that had been published in late January that had advocated 'the immediate provision of personal protective equipment' at that time and were urging 'the importance of testing and isolation' because the virus had clear potential to become a pandemic. 'That was a red flag,' he said. 'We have had seven to eight weeks since that time, and February was the opportunity for the UK to really prepare, based on testing, isolation, quarantine, physical distancing, ICU capacity and so on … We missed that opportunity. We could have used the month of February.'

The government's ability to sort out such pressing problems would be further hampered by a casual approach to catching the virus inside No. 10. On the first day of lockdown, Nadine Dorries, the health minister, returned to the Commons after recovering from the virus, but the government then lost Ben Wallace, the defence secretary, who went into isolation after developing symptoms. Hancock, like his prime minister, already had the virus. Without knowing they were infected, he and Johnson attended the last session of the Commons. As they were leaving the chamber, they were seen in a huddle of people who had gathered around the Speaker's chair with just inches between them. It was the perfect example of why social distancing was important because they could easily have spread the virus to their colleagues. By failing to follow the very rules they had so stridently instructed others to adhere to, they were setting a bad example. And they were also endangering lives.

In times of extremis, extraordinary things happen with hardly anyone batting an eyelid. That day the Coronavirus Act – the most authoritarian new law since the Second World War, which set out the legal basis for lockdown – raced through parliament with little amendment and scant debate. Meanwhile, there was a row in cabinet over the Home Office's demand to close the country's borders to flights from virus hotspots. It seemed like a no-brainer – a measure that should have been introduced weeks before. Yet the Foreign Office was objecting to the move because it would hinder efforts to repatriate up to a million British people stranded abroad. The lack of a clear-sighted plan had never been more apparent.

The government was now coming up with things on the hoof. Eager to prevent hospitals from being overrun, Hancock had borrowed an idea from Wuhan. The creation of the Chinese city's 1,000-bed Huoshenshan Hospital in just 10 days had created an internet sensation and showed that it was possible to build a hospital quickly from scratch. Britain would do the same by converting the ExCel conference centre, in east London's Docklands, into a hospital that could provide 4,000 critical care beds. Like many ambitious ideas produced in a hurry, it was not particularly well thought out. Doctors wondered, quite rightly, where the thousands of specially trained intensive care staff would come from. They were, after all, needed in their own hospitals, which would have to struggle with their own tides of cases while facing staff shortages because many doctors and nurses were forced to isolate when they or their families had symptoms that might be the virus. Hancock talked of involving the military, but they did not have sufficient numbers of specialist staff to run such an enormous critical care unit. The minister's new NHS Nightingale hospital would be a white elephant.

On that second day of lockdown Chris Whitty dialled in to an important meeting. It was for a discussion with the members of the government's Moral and Ethical Advisory Group (Meag), whom he had asked for guidance on how to select which patients should be given intensive care when there was limited capacity. This had resulted in the production of the 'Covid-19 triage score' document the weekend before. It provided doctors with a framework for determining which patients should be selected for critical care based on three indicators: age, frailty and underlying conditions. Since any total over eight meant a patient would be given ward-based treatment only, the over-80s were automatically excluded because they were allocated a score of nine points for their age alone. It meant that age group would not be given intensive care. Most people over 75 would also be marked over the eight-point threshold when their age and frailty scores were added together. So they too would be excluded. People from 60 upwards might also be denied critical care if they were frail and had an underlying health condition.

The document – or triage tool – was placed before the 20 members of Meag who attended the meeting on Wednesday, with Whitty acting as an observer. The members could see it was controversial. Some of those present expressed concern about the use of age as an 'isolated indicator of wellbeing' and questioned whether such selection might cause distress to patients and their families. One member later said they were horrified by the selection criteria because these discriminated against the weak and disabled. 'It's a horrible little diagram. Disgusting,' the member said. 'It looked really Nazi-like to me, but there are many voices on that committee. The tool was not welcomed because it seemed very primitive. A lot of the members – and I was one of them – thought it was extremely crude.' However, the minutes of the meeting state that Sir Jonathan Montgomery, the committee's chair, responded to the concerns by taking a more pragmatic approach. He said: '[The guidance] may need to be put into practice very soon.' It was 'going to be a living document, which can be updated to reflect changing circumstances. Decisions will be made to ensure that those who receive care are those who will benefit the most from it.'

A second version of the document, entitled the 'Covid-19 decision support tool', was also drawn up and circulated in the days after the meeting. This raised the score for specific illnesses, but lowered the marks given for age. It was still effectively advising that anyone who was over the age of 80 and not at the peak of health and fitness should be denied access to intensive care – as would anyone over 75 years old, even if they were coping well with an underlying illness. A source says a version of this document with the NHS logo was prepared for ministers for consideration on Saturday 28 March.

According to Montgomery, the guidance was not formally approved or published at the time. But he confirmed the tool had been distributed to doctors and hospitals as part of the consultation process. 'We were aware that some of them were looking at that tool and thinking about how they might use it,' he said. 'Some of them were using it,' he admitted. A source involved in drawing up the triage tool from the Intensive Care Society said it was sent to 'a wide population of clinicians' from different hospitals, including specialist respiratory doctors dealing with the most seriously ill Covid-19 patients.

We tracked down several of those doctors working around the country who say they were forced to deploy the tool or a version of it. They had been faced with an impossible situation with far too many severely ill coronavirus patients requiring intensive care when there were insufficient beds or staff available. The government-commissioned age-based 'triage tool' was the only guidance they had been given to deal with such difficult decisions, so they used it to systematically exclude the elderly, the frail and patients with underlying illnesses from critical care. Those patients would not be given life-saving mechanical ventilation regardless of the severity of their condition. This age-based criterion is alleged to have been applied by hospitals in London, Manchester, Liverpool, central England and the south-east. Many of those who died, after being excluded by the triage criteria, might well have survived if they had been admitted to intensive care. Of the few patients over the age of 80 who were given critical care treatment, close to four in ten were discharged alive.

The virus was becoming an increasingly common occurrence in daily life. Most people would know of a friend, relative, neighbour or colleague who had been infected and it had inevitably reached famous figures too. Tom Hanks and his wife Rita were now recuperating after being diagnosed while filming on the Gold Coast in Australia. Hanks suffered 'bone-crushing fatigue' but managed to tweet cheerfully while overcoming the virus in hospital. Wilson was laid low with a high fever, and, before recovering, lost both her sense of taste and smell – a key symptom that doctors were starting to understand was a tell-tale sign of Covid-19. Other well-known people who had been infected by the time of the UK lockdown were: Idris Elba, the English actor who starred in *The Wire* and *Luther*; Placido Domingo, the opera singer; Prince Albert II, the ruler of Monaco; Michel Barnier, the European Union's chief Brexit negotiator; and even Harvey Weinstein, the disgraced Hollywood film mogul, who caught the virus in a New York jail.

It was, however, still quite a shock when it was announced on the second day of lockdown that Prince Charles had tested positive for the virus. The 71-year-old heir to the throne was said to have been 'displaying mild symptoms' and was in self-isolation in Scotland with his wife, the Duchess of Cornwall, who had tested negative. It would later be revealed that Prince William also contracted the virus around the same time. The Duke of Cambridge's illness was reportedly kept a secret because he felt 'there were important things going on' and he 'didn't want to worry anyone'. It may well have caused alarm if it was known that the two closest heirs to the nonagenarian Queen were both in peril, although William's comparative youth at 37 meant he was at low risk from the virus. He was treated by palace doctors and isolated himself at Anmer Hall in Norfolk, his family home.

That week people were still getting used to the new normals: pedestrians swerving on to roads to give people distance on the pavement, loud conversations in the street standing six feet apart, long queues outside supermarkets and empty shelves when they finally entered. Many people seemed to have been shopping for an Armageddon, with pasta, tinned goods, paracetamol tablets and toilet rolls left in particularly short supply. The stockpiling of toilet rolls was a worldwide phenomenon, with one Australian newspaper printing eight pages extra for use in the bathroom and reports of an armed robbery on a supply van carrying loo paper in Hong Kong. Psychologists began writing long articles pondering what it was in human nature that made people buy more toilet paper when gripped by the fear of a pandemic.

The stockpiling would eventually stop and the supermarket supply chains would recover. Hoarding became something that was looked down upon socially. One of the events that pricked many people's conscience was a much-watched video featuring Dawn Bilbrough, a critical care nurse from York. She had filmed herself in her car while angry and tearful. She had just ended a 48-hour shift in intensive care and had attempted to do some shopping, only to find that her local supermarket had no fruit or vegetables. 'People are just stripping the shelves of basic foods,' Bilbrough sobs in the video. 'You just need to stop it. Because it's people like me that are going to be looking after you when you're at your lowest, so just stop it. Please!'

Her words were particularly powerful because health workers were now the new heroes. While the general public remained at home, they were risking their lives to save others. On Thursday 26 March the public began clapping on their doorsteps at 8 p.m. to show their appreciation. It would become a heart-warming weekly ritual throughout the first wave of the pandemic. The gesture was particularly poignant that weekend, as two working NHS doctors, a GP and a surgeon, died from the virus. They would be the first of many health workers to perish.

The death toll from the virus was rising steeply to hundreds each day by that last weekend in March when the clocks went forward. The lockdown had been a success in its first week by swiftly cutting the rate at which the virus was reproducing, but the large numbers of people who had caught the disease before the measures were introduced meant that April would indeed be the cruellest month. One key place where infections remained high was in the hospitals. Minutes from the Sage committee at the time reveal the serious concerns about how hospitals were becoming breeding grounds for the virus because of the lack of protective equipment for staff and insufficient testing capacity to check whether they were infected.

There were reports of NHS nurses in the Royal Free Hospital in north London tying clinical waste bags around their legs, and staff at the North Middlesex University Hospital were said to be protecting themselves by wrapping plastic aprons around their heads. A nurse told the *Guardian*: 'Nurses are making their own PPE. I know friends I trained with doing the same. We have to protect ourselves, some of us have children and babies. We are trying to help people but have to protect families. I don't know why we are not getting PPE.'[2] Other staff were resorting to buying protective items from DIY shops. A healthcare supplies association highlighted the dearth of visors and protective glasses available in the wholesale market by tweeting: 'Do we have to commandeer the stocks of DIY stores?' NHS trusts were even asking schools to donate science goggles due to the shortages. Doctors were threatening to quit the profession altogether unless they were properly equipped.

The lack of protective equipment was causing a large swell in the numbers of staff who were unable to work after contracting the virus. Many had fallen ill but others were self-isolating needlessly because they or their family had symptoms. If there had been tests available, the self-isolating staff might have been cleared to work. But the tests were now chiefly reserved for patients. NHS staff absence rates were at record levels and many hospitals were dangerously understaffed.

Covid-19 was also thriving in the one place that was supposed to be sorting out such problems: No. 10 Downing Street. While doctors and nurses were left in the dark about whether they had the virus, top politicians were able to get tests. On Friday 27 March the prime minister publicly announced that he had tested positive for Covid-19. To deliver the message, he posted a selfie-style video on Twitter in which he looked distinctly pale but had neatened himself up with a suit and tie. It was hard to tell whether or not he was wearing his pyjama bottoms beneath the picture – as many people were doing on their Zoom calls while working from home. The camera framed only his head and shoulders. 'Hi folks, I want to bring you up to speed with something that's happening today, which is that I've developed mild symptoms of the coronavirus – that's to say, a temperature and a persistent cough,' he said. 'And on the advice of the chief medical officer, I've taken a test that has come out positive, so I am working from home. I'm self-isolating and that's entirely the right thing to do. But be in no doubt that I can continue, thanks to the wizardry of modern technology, to communicate with all my top team to lead the national fightback against coronavirus.'

It was not very reassuring news. At that time, no other leader of a major nation had become infected – although Johnson would be joined by two right-wing presidents later in the year: Jair Bolsonaro of Brazil, who had dismissed the virus as 'a little flu', and then, ahead of the US elections, Donald Trump, who in early March had said people could still go to work when infected with Covid-19. But in a sense it wasn't surprising that Johnson was the first. He had adopted a deliberately cavalier attitude to social distancing in the initial weeks in his efforts to suggest life should go on as normal and had been shaking hands in hospitals where he knew there were infected patients. As he was preparing to post his video, the phone rang and Hancock was on the line to say he had tested positive. Neither man had known about each other's infection until that moment. Before long, Whitty was also forced to self-isolate as he too had symptoms. Finally, the man coordinating the whole of the civil service, cabinet secretary Sir Mark Sedwill, was also incapacitated by the virus along with several other Downing Street staff. Covid-19 had truly infiltrated Britain's nerve centre.

The government's own advisers were incredulous that senior politicians had not taken greater precautions to avoid being infected. 'Whilst the PM was telling people to stay at home and keep at least two metres apart from each other, the House of Commons was open for business and face-to-face parliamentary activities were carrying on,' said Professor Michie, a behavioural psychologist who sits on one of the government's key advisory committees. 'Given the transmission routes of touching contaminated surfaces and breathing in virus-laden droplets, it should not come as a surprise to hear that the PM and Health Secretary have tested positive for coronavirus. If leaders do not adhere to their own recommendations, this undermines trust in them which in turn can undermine the population's adherence to their advice.'[3]

That afternoon Johnson's chief adviser, Dominic Cummings – who was directing coronavirus policy – was seen rushing out of No. 10 to attend to his wife, who was ill with the virus. He came back into work later, seemingly ignoring rules that said whole families should isolate at the 'primary home' if just one member was suspected of being infected. He then skirted the rules again that evening by driving his family 264 miles up to Durham to stay on his parents' farm because, he would later claim, he feared he was also infected and neither he nor his wife would be able to look after their four-year-old son if they became incapacitated. On the Saturday morning, he said he woke up 'in pain and clearly had Covid-19 symptoms, including a bad headache and serious fever'. So both the prime minister and the second most powerful figure in Downing Street would be out of action at precisely the time the country needed leadership.

The following Monday – 30 March – Cummings was spotted by his parents' neighbour, who reported him to the police. Durham Constabulary would later say it received 'reports that an individual had travelled from London to Durham and was present at an address in the city'. A police officer spoke to Cummings's father, who confirmed that his son's family were staying at the property and they were self-isolating. The police did not take any further action.

The Cummings motorway dash would be cited widely as a further example of government figures not practising what they preached. Cummings had been part of the team that drew up rules which clearly stated that: 'During the emergency period, no person may leave the place where they are living without reasonable excuse.' The law gave examples of such reasonable excuses. People were permitted to obtain necessities such as food, to exercise, to seek medical care and to travel to work if absolutely necessary. None of this related to going on a long road trip to a far corner of England – which would typically require at least one petrol stop and loo breaks – in a car with someone who was believed to be carrying the virus.

By contrast, most people took the rules at face value because they believed it was for the good of the country. They made huge life-limiting decisions to prevent the virus's spread by separating themselves from loved ones, missing weddings and even reluctantly staying away from the deaths and funerals of close relatives and friends. A general view was taken that if everyone obeyed the lockdown individually, then it would work. But if everyone with children had followed Cummings's example, the span of the outbreak would have been extended and more people would have died. There would be considerable public disapproval when the Cummings trip became known about at the end of May. But, in the meantime, he kept his secret under his hat.

One of those who was said to be unaware of Cummings's whereabouts during his time in Durham was the prime minister. Was Johnson really so unwell that he didn't know where his chief adviser was at this time of great crisis? According to his spin doctors and fellow government ministers, Johnson was still in charge of the country while isolated in his flat above No. 11 Downing Street, with food being left at his door. He was on his own because his pregnant fiancée, Symonds, had also gone down with the virus. She was holed up with their Jack Russell rescue dog Dilyn at the couple's £1.3m house in Camberwell and is said to have been confined to her bed for a week. At 17 stone, Johnson was particularly vulnerable to the disease and it is claimed he was receiving only piecemeal medical care. Unlike in the White House, there is no dedicated doctor in Downing Street for the prime minister. He would occasionally speak to a GP but, all the while, his health was deteriorating.

With the virus sweeping through the cramped Georgian No. 10 building, from the prime minister down, there was a vacuum at the top of government as March ended. There were 13,000 people in hospital with the virus and in London it accounted for almost nine out of ten of NHS staff taking time off for sickness. On Tuesday 31 March a 13-year-old schoolboy named Ismail Mohamed Abdulwahab, from Brixton, south London, died from Covid-19 in King's College Hospital despite having no apparent underlying health conditions. His family were denied the right to be at his side in hospital when he died and were unable to attend his funeral because they were self-isolating. He was one of more than 600 people who were dying each day, and it was only going to get worse.

On Wednesday 1 April Michael Gove, the Chancellor of the Duchy of Lancaster, who was one of the few in Johnson's top team who had managed to dodge the virus, made a shocking admission. Just 2,000 of the health service's vast half a million frontline workforce had been tested for the virus. He blamed the problem on a shortage of the type of chemical agents needed to manufacture the tests – although this brought an immediate rebuke from the Chemical Industries Association, who said little had been done by the government to source these products.

The paucity of tests for medical staff may not have been entirely down to a lack of availability as the outbreak moved on. Others ascribed a more cynical motive. Professor Sir John Bell, the chair of medicine at Oxford University and the president of the Academy of Medical Sciences, would later tell the parliamentary health and social care select committee that there may have been a deliberate policy to avoid testing NHS workers due to staff shortage fears. 'As time went on, there still wasn't a real push to do healthcare workers and indeed, all patients in the hospital. And it sort of went on, and on, and on,' he said. 'Indeed, there was a suspicion, which I think is probably correct, that NHS institutions and the NHS were avoiding testing their hospital workers because they were afraid they would find [high levels of infection] and they would have to send everyone home, and as a result not have a workforce. That in my view is not an ethical approach to the problem … But I think that was a pretty central issue in that failure to test hospitals.'

The concerns about sending staff home were certainly weighing on the minds of the NHS leadership. In that first week of April, Professor Stephen Powis, the NHS's medical director, submitted a paper to Sage laying bare the nightmarish staffing problems being faced by his service. Workforce reports for the London Ambulance Service, he said, demonstrated that 25 per cent of staff were either off sick or in isolation. He warned: 'Staff sickness and self-isolation is increasing, with 89 per cent of NHS staff absences in London reported to be due to Covid-19.'

One of his comments on the staffing problem was controversial. Buried in his report was a recommendation about the steps that should be explored when hospitals were able to start testing more of their staff. He highlighted the arguments against isolating all doctors and nurses who had tested positive but displayed no symptoms. 'Sending asymptomatic [doctors and nurses] home will drastically impact on [the] workforce, and the amount of transmission from asymptomatic is unknown,' his report states. 'Patient outcomes will be impacted due to reduced workforce.' Allowing infected staff to continue to work would be a big gamble to take. The fact that people with infections who did not suffer symptoms in the initial phase of the illness or at all – known as pre-symptomatic and asymptomatic cases – could be infectious was no longer in any doubt at that time. After all, Britain's first big contact tracing exercise had shown that the so-called 'super-spreader' Steve Walsh had passed the virus to several others before realising he was infected. Powis's report even acknowledges that transmission by staff or patients displaying no symptoms was a 'key … risk'. But he appeared to be suggesting it was feasible for doctors to carry on treating patients even when they had coronavirus. Such a move would undoubtedly increase the chances of more staff and patients being infected. There was an air of desperation in the report.

The whole subject of testing for the virus had become a toxic problem for the leaderless government. It was top of the health secretary's to-solve list when he returned to work on Thursday 2 April. Hancock had been barely able to eat or drink for two days but he managed to make a speedy recovery from the virus after sleeping in 12-hour stretches at home. His comments at that evening's daily media briefing showed he had lost none of his boldness. In a bid to reshape the gloomy narrative on testing, he announced breezily: 'Public Health England can be incredibly proud of the world-beating work they have done on testing,' he said. Few people believed that to be true. The minister then went on to say he sympathised with health service staff who wanted more tests 'so that they can get back to the front line'. However, he stood by his decision to prioritise testing of patients over staff. 'I'm proud that every single patient who has needed a test for life-saving treatment has had access to a test,' he said. This actually only applied to patients in hospitals and did not take into account the thousands of people who would die from the virus in their homes or care homes without access to tests or treatment. But his most audacious claim was yet to come. In early March, UK testing capacity had been at around 2,000 daily tests for the virus and this had been ramped up to 10,000 a day by that week. Hancock declared his intention to increase this by 10 times – in just four weeks. 'I am now setting the goal of 100,000 tests per day by the end of this month,' he said, looking directly at the camera.

Many welcomed the fact that the government was now finally going to try to harness the scores of companies in the private diagnostics industry to produce more tests, even if it was many weeks too late. But the target of 100,000, which seemed to have been plucked from thin air, would cause further distrust among the public as it appeared that the government was attempting to deflect criticism by making promises it could not keep. It is also said to have caused consternation inside Downing Street, which feared a backlash if Hancock failed to deliver.

That evening a peaky-looking Johnson emerged from his Downing Street flat to join in the second weekly 8 p.m. clap for carers. Standing on the doorstep of No. 10 in a suit and no tie, he managed to muster a double thumbs up before retreating inside. The next day, Friday 3 April, he made a video from his 11 Downing Street lair in which he claimed he was feeling better. However, he said he had been reluctantly forced to continue the isolation because he still had 'a minor symptom', which was a high temperature. He did not look or sound at all well. A bed had already been booked for him at St Thomas' Hospital just across Westminster Bridge, which he had so far declined to take up. By the weekend his inner circle were wondering how long he could hold out.

On Saturday morning Johnson was well enough to put his name to a letter inviting all the opposition parties to a briefing with the chief scientists the following week so that they could 'work together in this moment of national emergency'. It was optimistic of Johnson to believe that he would be able to recover in time, but the letter was sent anyway as a political manoeuvre.

That morning the results of the Labour Party leadership contest were announced and Keir Starmer, the former director of public prosecutions, was elected leader. The sharp lawyer was much more of a challenge to Johnson than his predecessor Jeremy Corbyn and the prime minister's advisers felt it would be good to try to keep him onside with the government's coronavirus policy. It was hoped that the call for unity in a national emergency might make the political jousting a little less torrid for Johnson when the Commons returned at the end of the month. But it would be a long time before Johnson was fit enough to spar with Starmer, as his condition was deteriorating fast.

It was the Queen's turn to take centre stage again the following evening, Sunday 5 April. It was another rare impromptu broadcast to the country – something she had done on a handful of occasions during her 68-year reign. 'I hope in the years to come everyone will be able to take pride in how they respond to this challenge and those who come after us will say the Britons of this generation were as strong as any,' she said, before praising 'the attributes of self-discipline, of quiet good-humoured resolve and fellow-feeling [which] characterised this country'. She concluded reassuringly with a fitting final line borrowed from Vera Lynn's famous Second World War song: 'Better days will return. We will be with our friends again. We will be with our families again. We will meet again.'

The British public's resolve had indeed been remarkable. The adherence to lockdown had surpassed any of the modellers' predictions and people were showing great self-discipline as well as community spirit. WhatsApp groups were springing up among streets of neighbours who had previously barely spoken to each other, with supportive messages pinging back and forth. People helped isolating vulnerable neighbours with shopping. Amusing videos with gallows humour were also now spreading faster than the virus. One compared the heroes of the First World War, who were forced to endure the wretchedness of the trenches, with the modern-day Covid warriors who plonked themselves on the couch in their pyjamas to watch television while drinking wine and scoffing crisps. Britain hadn't lost the ability to make fun of itself.

While the Queen's speech was being broadcast that evening, more serious events were unfolding in Downing Street. The prime minister was struggling to breathe. There could be no more pretending that he was fit enough to run the country and he urgently needed hospital treatment because his life was now in danger. He was rushed across Westminster Bridge by car to St Thomas' Hospital and received oxygen during the short journey to ease his distress. He was taken to a private room on the 12th floor. In a sense he was one of the lucky ones because, only the day before, Watford General Infirmary had been forced to turn away patients because of problems with its oxygen supplies, which were needed to treat people with the virus. The news of Johnson's admission led the newspapers that morning. 'Downing Street Shock – Boris in Hospital' cried the *Sun*'s front-page headline. By lunchtime, however, Johnson's aides were playing down the seriousness of his condition. A message was sent from his Twitter account claiming he had just been taken into hospital for 'routine tests'. But now people were beginning to take these updates with a big pinch of salt. Johnson was very seriously ill.

It was always inevitable that an intensive care bed would be ready and waiting for the virus-stricken prime minister if he needed it. But elsewhere, the NHS was under severe strain and it was not just the patients in Watford who were denied care in their local hospital. Doctors were now being forced to make heart-breaking decisions. Two days earlier the Doctors' Association UK had received a plea for help from a doctor working on an intensive care ward. 'The system is already on its knees. There are not enough beds, not enough ITU [intensive treatment unit] facilities and little or no goodwill,' the medic said. 'There is simply not the capacity to handle illness at this scale.'

The selection of patients for intensive care was already taking place and the methods being used bore a remarkable similarity to the recommendations in the 'triage tool' document that Meag members had discussed a week earlier. This alarming development had been spotted by two of the country's leading experts in the critical care field: Dr Claire Shovlin, a respiratory consultant at Hammersmith Hospital and Professor of Clinical Medicine at Imperial College London, and her colleague Dr Marcela Vizcaychipi, an intensive care consultant at Chelsea and Westminster Hospital who lectures in critical care at Imperial.

They were shocked to see that in the first week of April large numbers of people were dying from Covid-19 without being given access to intensive care. They did an analysis of the national figures and set out their concerns in a letter to the *Emergency Medicine Journal* two weeks later. Their study showed that only a small proportion – less than 10 per cent – of the 3,939 patients who were recorded as having died of Covid-19 by Saturday 4 April had been given access to intensive care. This was particularly worrying, according to their study, because a separate analysis of those who had survived showed the 'crucial importance' of intensive care in providing support for patients 'most severely affected by Covid-19'.

When they then compared the numbers of deaths from the virus in the normal wards with the number of intensive care beds said to be available in the UK, they came to a disturbing conclusion. Hospitals not only appeared to be withholding intensive care from patients who might benefit from such treatment, but they were actually being too overzealous and rationing it more than was necessary given the available capacity. This led the two experts to question what criteria the clinicians were using to choose which patients should be denied potentially life-saving treatment. In their study they expressed particular concern about 'a Covid-19 decision support tool' that had been 'circulating in March', noting that it used a number of factors that meant men, the old, the frail and those suffering from underlying illnesses were less likely to be admitted to intensive care. Their description exactly mirrors the tool commissioned by Whitty and submitted to Meag.

The medics wrote: 'Implementation of such tools could prevent healthy, independent individuals from having an opportunity to benefit from AICU [adult intensive care unit] review/admission by protocolised counting of variables that do not predict whether they would personally benefit from AICU care.' Their paper concluded: 'Current triage criteria are overly restrictive and [we] suggest review. Covid-19 admissions to critical care should be guided by clinical needs regardless of age.' Their study was published on 4 May, but the highly select-ive triaging would continue – and it was already too late for many patients.

One of the key observations in the study was that two illnesses in particular – diabetes and high blood pressure – were being used as part of the triage score that might prevent access to intensive care. But the authors pointed out that both conditions were very common among patients and those with the illnesses should have been given additional treatment. 'The extremely common states of diabetes, hypertension and male sex indicate patients requiring extra care, rather than less', they wrote. This is not what happened to people such as Raymond Austin.

The ambulance driver had been initially reluctant to take Austin into hospital. But the sprightly grandfather – who still worked as a computer analyst at 82 years old – had a worry-ingly low pulse and eventually it was decided that there was no alternative. His daughter Vivien Morrison remembers the conversation clearly. 'I think they had a direction not to be taking people to hospital if they could help it,' she said. 'The paramedic was pacing around and he said to me, "I don't want to take him to hospital. But I have to think that if we took Covid out of the equation, I would not be hesitating to take your dad to hospital right now."'

After he arrived at East Surrey Hospital in Redhill the doctors discovered he was suffering from fever and possible sepsis because he was infected with coronavirus. Austin, from Horsham, West Sussex, had a history of diabetes and high blood pressure, but is said to have never previously spent a day in hospital. He phoned Vivien from a ward the day after he was admitted, in a state of distress. 'He was saying, "I think I'm going to die," because they'd made him agree to a non-resuscitation order,' said Vivien. 'It was obviously forced upon him.' The hospital denies this. His condition declined over the following week. His oxygen levels dropped below the crucial 94 per cent and yet his doctors decided he would not be given the critical care that might have saved his life. On Saturday 4 April he was moved between wards. Morrison recalled: 'The nurse said, "We're moving him into the other ward because this is becoming an ICU ward and he's not unwell enough to be in here."'

Yet, the following day – the Sunday the prime minister was admitted to hospital – Vivien received a call from a doctor to say Austin's oxygen levels had lowered to 70 per cent and he would not survive the day. Vivien says the doctor told her that her father would not be given intensive care treatment, or mechanical ventilation if that failed, because he 'ticked too many boxes' under the triaging guidelines the hospital was using. His age, sex, high blood pressure and diabetes would have all counted against him under the triage advice that was circulating at that time. Instead, he received ward-based oxygen, which eased some of the discomfort of his breathing. 'He was written off,' said Vivien, who finds it hard to understand how her previously fit and independent father could be treated in this way.

It was a feature of the darkest weeks of the pandemic that patients would be informed of key life-and-death decisions without their families being present, as the wards would be mostly off-limits to visitors because of the risk of infection. This meant that very few people knew what was actually happening in the hospitals while the nation was locked down at home. However, East Surrey Hospital did allow Vivien and her sister to visit their father one last time provided they did so at their own risk, wore protective equipment and scrubbed down afterwards.

What they saw horrified them. Their father had been transferred the day before to the Chaldon Ward, which Vivien, a 54-year-old charity volunteer, described as a 'death ward' for the elderly in a complaint she later made to the hospital. A red 'Do not enter' sign was emblazoned on the ward door and a porter guarded the entrance. Vivien says that inside there were eight elderly men infected with the virus whom she describes as the 'living dead'. They were lying 'half naked in nappies' on their beds in stifling heat looking 'drugged and dazed'. The scene, she says, was heart-breaking: 'To see people just dying, all around you … It was like something out of a Victorian war scene. With nobody doing anything to help them.'

Her father was lying at the far side of the ward. 'I had to just walk through the ward and not look at the other patients because it was just so horrendous,' she said. 'A couple of times I caught their eye, but what can you do?' Austin was dehydrated and appeared to be desperate for food, but it seemed there were no nurses regularly checking in on the patients. While the sisters sat by their father, the man lying in the next bed passed away on his own. 'He was just flopped, and death colour, and not moving. When we first went in he was coughing a little bit. The nurses didn't even know. We just said, "We think that man has died."' An auxiliary nurse was crying outside the ward. 'We said, "Are you all right? What's the matter?" And she just said, "They're all going to die and no one is doing anything about it."' Vivien's sister was furious: 'My sister said to one of the nurses, "Why are you allowing them to suffer? You wouldn't treat a dog like this."' Their father passed away that day without being given the option of intensive care, which the family believes might have saved him.

The family complained to the hospital and received a profusely apologetic letter back written by the health trust's chief nurse Jane Dickson on behalf of the chief executive. 'I want you to know how sorry I am that we let your father down,' she wrote; 'we have been reflecting on our initial response to the Covid-19 pandemic and I regret to say there are aspects of our care that we got wrong.' Dickson conceded that 'routine tasks of supporting our patients to eat and drink suffered' because staff were 'overwhelmed' and there was a shortage of nurses with the necessary skills. The letter stated that the clinical team did not think 'a more intensive level of care was appropriate given [Austin's] level of frailty'. The hospital said later in a statement that he had not been 'denied the care he needed'. It added there was sufficient capacity to treat him in intensive care if this had been appropriate. His family find it mystifying that more wasn't done to get oxygen into his body, however. They fear that he was a victim of the overprotective triaging guidelines that prevented many elderly patients from being given the care they would have received before the pandemic's peak.

The family also queried why Austin or the other patients in his ward were not taken to the Nightingale hospital in London, which was fully equipped with oxygen and ventilators. It would only ever treat 54 people despite its 4,000-bed capacity. 'To me [the Nightingale] was like a bit of a smokescreen, a facade, because I don't understand why they didn't use it,' said Vivien. In fact, all seven of the Nightingale hospitals – in London, Manchester, Harrogate, Bristol, Birmingham, Exeter and Sunderland – would stand mostly empty through the crisis. Those vacant beds would be used by the government to support its claim that the NHS was never overwhelmed.

However, the doctors on the ground say the Nightingale hospitals were beset by problems from the start. There was a struggle to recruit adequately trained staff from other hospitals that were already overstretched, and medics were reluctant to refer patients because of concerns over the unknown standard of care. One ambulance clinician who was drafted to work at the London Nightingale hospital explained that it was mainly set up to treat 'younger patients who were on less respiratory support' and with fewer underlying illnesses. 'But, actually, those patients were few and far between and they got prioritised on hospital intensive care units anyway because they were more likely to have a good outcome,' the clinician said. 'And actually people who are a bit older or had more co-morbidities were the ones we were having those more realistic discussions with [about being excluded from intensive care].' The NHS press office later claimed it had never been the case that Nightingale hospitals were 'mainly equipped' for young patients.

Austin died on the day the prime minister himself was admitted to hospital. Vivien says the contrast in care the two men received could not have been more stark. 'Boris Johnson came out with this whole thing about them holding his hand 24/7. But that's not what I saw. I just felt really angry. They made this really big thing about the nurses holding their hand. There's someone always there, caring. Not for those eight men there wasn't.'

The government was anxious that little should be known about what was really going on in the hospitals during the first wave of the pandemic. While it was great for the public to clap every Thursday and praise health staff to the rafters, too much information was considered morale sapping in a time of national crisis. The NHS withdrew into itself as the waves of cases hit the hospitals. Pressure was applied to medical staff to prevent public disclosure of problems on the wards. Some trusts were alleged to have trawled their staff's social media accounts and given dressings-down to medics who mentioned PPE shortages or staff deaths. One surgeon working at a hospital in west London said: 'There was an active drive by certain trusts to tell doctors to shut up about it because they didn't want the bad publicity.' The almost Soviet-style secrecy meant that while most people in the UK were hunkered down in their homes, few knew what was actually going on inside the hospitals.

The health service workers wanted the public to understand the nightmarish problems they were facing. One support group, Whistleblowers UK, was contacted by more than a hundred healthcare workers who wished to draw back the curtain on what was happening in their hospitals. Many were bitter about attempts by NHS managers to prevent them from speaking publicly about shortages of personal protective equipment. The BBC was given a newsletter that was sent out by an NHS trust instructing medical staff to avoid 'commenting on political issues, such as PPE'. As an alternative, they were advised to tweet glowing tributes to retired health service staff who had returned to help out, and retweet posts from the hospital's official account. Another trust put up posters telling staff not to 'make public appeals for equipment, donations or volunteers'. The lack of protective equipment was clearly an embarrassment to some health service managers.

One doctor, who spoke anonymously to the media, described how he had received a harsh dressing-down from his bosses after daring to post his concerns online about PPE shortages. 'They hauled me up in front of a panel of senior managers – it was very, very intimidating,' he said. 'They kept on feeding me what felt like government type of lines, saying, "This hospital has never had PPE shortages," which I know to be factually untrue. And that essentially I should stop causing a fuss.' He added: 'There have been colleagues who've died at my hospital. And there have been a handful more who've been in ICU. It's very, very concerning that we can't even say our colleagues have died, please don't let us be next.'[4]

An extraordinary allegation was levelled against the management of the Queen's Medical Centre in Nottingham. The hospital had successfully attracted dozens of nurses and healthcare assistants who had volunteered to help out in the crisis. But the volunteers were unprepared for the horrifying number of deaths they would witness. Normally, the experienced palliative care team would see 200 deaths a year, but the hospital had to deal with 185 deaths in just two and a half months. When the team raised concerns about the trauma this was causing, the hospital's management became 'hostile' and locked away PPE 'as punishment', according to the staff's Unison union representative Dave Ratchford, who spoke to the BBC. Another worker said everyone's sickness records were put on display on a board in a staff room to intimidate staff. Ratchford described the treatment of his members as 'absolutely shocking'. He said: 'We're talking about a very high-performing team who fell foul of a culture that permits bullying and fails to address it. Staff were told their lives would be made hell for complaining.' The hospital's trust said, 'to hear of these grievances is very troubling' and 'bullying and harassment are not tolerated.'[5]

The veil of secrecy placed over the hospitals would allow the government to emerge from the crisis of those early spring months to claim complete success in achieving its objective. 'Throughout this crisis, we have protected our NHS, ensuring that everybody who needed care was able to get that care,' the health secretary Matt Hancock proudly declared in an email to Conservative supporters in July. 'At no point was the NHS overwhelmed, and everyone who needed care had access to that care.' This was simply not true for a number of reasons. One was the way elderly people were denied life-saving care when their illness became critical.

While researching what was happening in hospitals during the lockdown, we came across clear statistical proof that thousands of elderly patients were, like Raymond Austin, denied access to intensive care treatment when they most needed it. The evidence was buried away in data collected from 65,000 people who were admitted to UK hospitals with the virus up to the end of May and that had been analysed by the Covid-19 Clinical Information Network (Co-Cin), which reports to the Sage advisory committee. This data produced by the Co-Cin team is the government's best record of how patients with the virus were treated in hospitals during the outbreak.

Overall, it showed that just one in six Covid-19 patients who lost their lives in hospital during the first wave had been given intensive care treatment. This suggests that of the 47,000 people who died of the virus inside and outside hospitals, an estimated 5,000 – just one in nine – received the highest critical care, despite the government claiming that intensive care capacity was never breached. The figures show that, as the outbreak progressed, there was a significant drop in the proportion of hospitalised patients in England and Wales who were given intensive care before they died. In the two middle weeks of March, 21 per cent of those who died of the virus in hospital had been given intensive care treatment. Yet as the pressure on the NHS increased through April, the proportion of critically ill patients who received intensive care before they died dropped and was as low as 10 per cent by the beginning of May. When the hospitals began dealing with far fewer patients in July, those numbers dramatically increased to 29 per cent.

The main reason for this appears to have been that many hospitals were rationing intensive care given to patients over 60 years old – which was the age group that accounted for most of the serious cases. The data shows that the proportion of over-60s with coronavirus who received intensive care halved between the middle of March and the end of April as the pressure weighed heavily on hospitals during the height of the pandemic. In the middle weeks of March, 13 per cent of that age group admitted to hospital with the virus were given an intensive care bed. By the start of May, that figure had more than halved and was down at 6 per cent. The proportion of the elderly being admitted then increased again when the pressure was lifted off the NHS as Covid-19 cases fell in the summer months. By July the figure was back to 11 per cent.

Most deaths happened among the over-80s, but a very small proportion made it to ICU

Percentage of **hospital deaths** and patients receiving ICU treatment by age

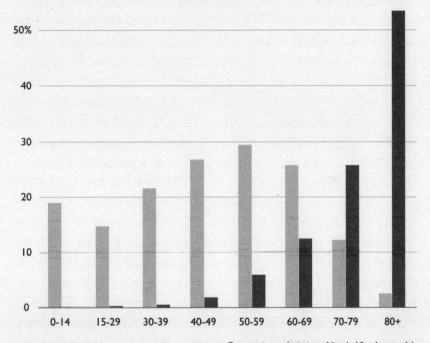

Coronavirus admissions March 10 - August 14

The majority of those who died without the highest level of life-saving care were the oldest patients. More than half of those who died of the virus in hospital during the first wave were aged over 80 and yet only 2.5 per cent of patients of that age group were admitted to critical care. If they had been given intensive care, they might have survived. In the few cases where patients over 80 were given intensive care to treat the virus, 38 per cent were discharged alive during the first wave of the outbreak, according to figures from the Intensive Care National Audit and Research Centre.

Over-60s admissions to intensive care plunged in lockdown

Percentage of all hospital patients aged over 60 who were treated in ICU

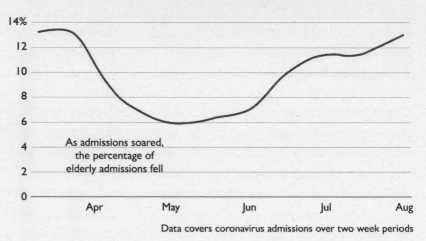

As admissions soared, the percentage of elderly admissions fell

Data covers coronavirus admissions over two week periods

The official version given by ministers and the NHS was that critical care beds were still available throughout the height of the outbreak. This was true for some hospitals in areas less badly hit by the virus, particularly in the north and the south-west. But we have spoken to several doctors who paint a harrowing picture of the extreme choices that were being taken on the wards in the virus hotspots of central and south-east England that were overrun with patients needing intensive care. At their request, we have protected their identity because they are afraid their NHS management teams could take disciplinary action against them for speaking out.

A senior intensive care doctor who was working in the same south-east region as the East Surrey Hospital where Austin died confirmed that medics were forced to choose between patients who needed intensive care beds. Her remarks directly contradict Hancock's claims that everyone received the care they required. 'I don't think the public have ever been aware of just how bad things were and indeed how bad things could get again,' she said. 'Hospitals had to ration intensive care admittance. I hate to use the word "ration", but it's what was happening.' She described how by early April her bosses realised that her hospital's intensive care capacity would quickly be breached if they admitted all the Covid patients who would normally receive that level of care. So they began using the parameters of age, clinical frailty score and co-morbidities to help choose between patients – the same variables recommended by the government-commissioned Covid-19 triage tool.

She said that in normal times those who were very frail would sometimes not be offered invasive ventilation because of their low survival chances and the health complications the procedure can cause. But, she added, what was happening on the Covid wards was very different. 'The respiratory physicians and the ward medics were finding this incredibly, incredibly difficult,' she said. 'They were having to turn people down for critical care and the respiratory physicians were getting upset, because usually we would give those people a shot.' Those unfortunate enough to be excluded from intensive care would be left on the wards without access to invasive mechanical ventilation. Instead, they would receive at best non-invasive ventilation, which she said was 'nowhere near as good' because the oxygen pressures delivered to the patient were considerably lower.

The rationing of intensive care to elderly people was 'wide-spread' within hospitals at the time, she said. 'Colleagues in intensive care reached out to me from across the country for support. They were saying, "This is going on at my hospital, this is feeling really bad."' She and fellow doctors were angered by the government's positive messages about how well the NHS was coping. 'I understand there's a balance between not wanting to panic people, and I also understand about reputation management. But every evening at the [government's televised media] briefing you just couldn't recognise anything that they were saying. It was so discordant with what we were seeing. They'd made it all up. It was completely bizarre – picking certain statistics to highlight how well they were doing versus other countries when actually, particularly in London, it was an absolute car crash.'

This meant that nobody really understood the depth of the crisis in the hospitals and a myth was created that the NHS would be able to cope comfortably with any new wave of the pandemic later in the year. 'The public was shrugging their shoulders and saying, "Oh, it's not that bad" because they hadn't seen it. Some doctors were being called hysterical, just for saying the truth. There needs to be an honest conversation about what exactly was going on,' she said.

Several doctors say that the emergency measures imposed in London, which bore the initial brunt of the first wave with the highest number of intensive care admissions, were particularly harsh. Doctors found the extent of the triaging they were forced to carry out extremely tough. A surgeon working at a hospital in the west of the city said: 'A lot of patients who we will in normal times say, "Okay, we'll admit them to intensive care to give them a chance in the knowledge that they might well not make it" … for those patients that chance was not given.' Professor Christina Pagel, director of University College London's Clinical Operational Research Unit, says the evidence is clear that many people were not offered the full range of treatment. 'There is no doubt that there are people that would have got intensive care at the beginning of March or in June that didn't get it in April because of capacity,' she said. Hancock's claim that everyone received the care they needed simply does not bear scrutiny.

The prime minister was lucky to be in St Thomas' Hospital, which had recently been judged to be the best in the country in a survey of the world's finest medical institutions. On Monday 6 April Dominic Raab, the foreign secretary, told the evening press conference that the prime minister had been admitted the day before 'for tests as a precaution only' because 'some of the symptoms that he had when he first tested positive had persisted.' Raab said Johnson had enjoyed a 'comfortable night' in hospital and was in 'good spirits'. The prime minister was being regularly updated and 'he still remains in charge of the government,' Raab added.

The journalists attending the press conference were sceptical. Raab was quizzed on how Johnson could be so ill he required hospital treatment and yet was still well enough to be running the country. Raab stuck to his line. There were also questions about whether he would lead the country in Johnson's place but the answer was evasive. 'Look, he's in charge, but he'll continue to take doctors' advice on what to do next.' The Downing Street team, Raab said, were working 'full throttle' to make sure that Johnson's directions and instructions were 'being implemented and followed through, whether it's the purchase of ventilators through to the diplomatic effort to return UK nationals who are stranded abroad'.

This was more propaganda straight out of the Soviet era. Johnson had actually been deteriorating since he arrived in hospital and his condition had become so serious that the decision was taken to transfer him to one of St Thomas' two intensive care units that afternoon. He was put in a side room on the east wing's first floor and reporters were later briefed that this had taken place at 7 p.m. – less than two hours after Raab had been telling the press conference that Johnson was in hospital for tests and was still in charge. It appeared his life was hanging on a thread and his chances of surviving were just slightly higher than even. Almost four in ten patients of Johnson's age who were admitted to intensive care during the pandemic's first wave would die there.

His admission to hospital had created a vacuum at the top of government. Since he had not appointed a deputy prime minister, Raab as first secretary of state was given the role of official understudy. But, in reality, Raab would run the country by committee as part of a so-called quad of senior ministers that also included Hancock, Sunak and Gove. Each day they would hold daily meetings at 9.15 a.m., either on Zoom or in person. They had competing agendas and egos, and none had the true authority of a prime minister. At one point Sir Mark Sedwill, the cabinet secretary, is understood to have read them the riot act, insisting that they pull together for the good of the country.

Meanwhile, Johnson was receiving get-well wishes from around the world as his condition remained critical the next day, Tuesday 7 April. Regular updates were being sent to the Queen by No. 10, and his heavily pregnant fiancée Symonds was said to be extremely worried. But help was at hand from the most powerful man in America. 'We're very saddened to hear that [Johnson] was taken into intensive care,' President Trump told reporters. 'He's been a really good friend. He's been really something very special: strong, resolute, doesn't quit, doesn't give up.' Trump revealed that he had asked two companies with 'really advanced therapeutics' to provide treatment to Johnson. 'We'll see if we can be of help,' said the president. 'We've contacted all of Boris's doctors, and we'll see what is going to take place, but they are ready to go.' The nation was on tenterhooks, hoping the prime minister would pull through. 'It was a terribly scary time,' his sister Rachel would later say.

The following day, Wednesday 8 April, the number of people dying from the virus each day exceeded 1,000 and it wasn't just hospitals in the south-east that were forced to take drastic measures. The effects of the rampant spread of the disease in the days before lockdown were now beginning to show in hospital admissions across the country. A senior doctor working in intensive care wards has described how his large hospital in the Midlands was unable to cope. He says his colleagues had no choice but to exclude elderly patients in the same way as the London and south-east hospitals had been doing. 'We were limited by the capacity, the number of beds we had and the worry that if we filled our intensive care units up with frail, older patients we'd be unable to take the younger patients,' he recalled. 'As we got busier, our admission criteria and the people that were being admitted significantly changed to not admitting those that were elderly.'

His hospital's admission criteria were based on a version of the 'Covid-19 Decision Support Tool' that had been prepared for ministers on 28 March. The management of his NHS trust had sent the triage tool to medics saying, 'it had been produced to help guide decision making regarding admissions to critical care,' he said. Many patients were above the cut-off for intensive care when their scores were totted up. 'We got to the point where we almost didn't have anyone in critical care who was over 75,' the doctor said. 'Whereas we had been admitting that age group at the beginning.' Indeed, shockingly, he said the tool was applied so rigorously that the hospital kept dozens of intensive care beds empty. The patients over 75 were not even offered non-invasive ventilation as they died on the non-intensive care wards. It meant that 90 per cent of the hospital's deaths from the virus happened on the regular wards, which were not set up to provide critical care. Just 10 per cent of patients who died received intensive care during the height of the pandemic in April.

To make these decisions acceptable to patients, the intensive care doctor said his colleagues would often have to tell 'white lies'. They would suggest that it was in the patient's best interests to be cared for on the wards rather than in intensive care. 'Convincing patients meant saying to them that this is what we felt on balance was best for them,' he said. 'But the reality was that we were facing multiple admissions of younger, fitter patients at that point, and we just couldn't accommodate the elderly at the rate that they were coming in.' He said the job of breaking the news to patients that they would not be given mechanical ventilation despite their deteriorating condition was extremely difficult and left some staff in tears. But the task was made a little easier, he said, because the need to control infections in the hospital meant very few families were visiting who might challenge the decision. 'Certainly some of the fitter 75-year-olds we could have taken, we should have taken [into intensive care] and we probably would have done as a result of pressure from families,' he said. 'It's much more difficult if you've got to convince the family that you're not going to take their loved one into intensive care than trying to have that discussion with the patient themselves.' Patients who scored too high on the triage tool would have their records marked with a 'Do Not Attempt Resuscitation' (DNAR) so there would be no attempt to revive them if they went into cardiac arrest. 'It was a decision made on their admission,' the doctor said. 'We were encouraged to make a DNAR decision and if you exceeded a score of eight on the Covid-19 triage tool you would be given one.'

This selective policy in the doctor's Midlands hospital continued until May, when patient numbers dropped and the elderly could once again be admitted to intensive care. The doctor blames the prime minister's late lockdown for placing doctors in such an invidious position during those months. 'We wouldn't have had the shortages in PPE. We would have had fewer patients admitted in that short period of time so we would have been able to offer the best in terms of intensive care capacity for each and every single one of them.'

There were a number of versions of the 'triage tool' document being circulated in hospitals during the height of the first wave. The largest health region in Scotland, NHS Highland, even posted a version of the original document – which automatically excluded 80-year-olds from critical care – on the patient information section of its website, with the trust's logo emblazoned on it. The only slight change to the version presented to the Meag committee was that women were given one less point than men to reflect the growing evidence that females were more likely to survive the virus. It meant men would be less likely to be admitted to intensive care than the opposite sex. NHS Highland later claimed that the document had been placed on its website 'in error' and was not used. However, the trust refused to explain the circumstances in which the 'error' was made or which part of the government or health service had passed the document on in the first place.

Even more extreme measures were being prepared elsewhere in the country. On Wednesday 8 April the North Yorkshire and Vale of York Clinical Commissioning Groups issued their own local guidance to doctors in a document entitled 'Ethical Framework for Selecting Patients for ICU Treatment during the Covid-19 Pandemic when Demand Outstrips Bed Availability'. The document drew parallels between the pandemic and a war, arguing that in an armed conflict, patients are selected for treatment 'in order to promote the highest number of survivors'. This might sometimes mean that existing patients would have to make way for new patients who had a greater chance of survival. Indeed, the document has a section entitled 'withdrawing treatment in existing patients' – in other words, turfing them out of their intensive care beds to make way for others.

Under this heading the guidance states: 'It is possible that a patient presents who has a better chance of treatment than someone already receiving ICU support. Should the existing patient have their treatment withdrawn in favour of the new treatment? Withdrawing treatment feels more active than withholding, and can feel more like killing than letting die.' But the document says the ethics of the situation change in a pandemic when resources are limited. 'The intention shifts from the best interests of the individual patient, to maximising the number of survivors,' it states. 'If an existing patient being treated has less chance of survival than a new one presenting, it can be argued that the same principles apply regarding who has priority for a bed. The fact that the existing patient happened to arrive/become ill sooner is not a morally relevant characteristic, and this justifies withdrawing treatment from them and giving it to the new patient.' Dr Nigel Wells, clinical chair at the NHS Vale of York Clinical Commissioning Group, later said the guidance was 'a discussion document' which was not 'approved or implemented'. North Yorkshire's Clinical Commissioning Group failed to respond to questions as to whether the guidance was ever put into practice.

Despite the evidence we gathered from the NHS's own staff and data, the Department of Health has continued to deny there was any rationing of intensive care during the first wave of the pandemic. We approached the department in October 2020 ahead of an article we were writing for *The Sunday Times* and it issued the following statement: 'Patients will always receive the best possible care from the NHS and the claim that intensive care beds were rationed or that patients were prevented from receiving necessary care is false. Doctors make decisions on who will benefit from care every day, as part of normal clinical decision-making.'

A few weeks before our article was published, Simon Stevens, the NHS chief executive, had told an online discussion held by *The Spectator* magazine that the biggest mistake of the pandemic had been the late lockdown, which he blamed in part on 'the absence of testing'. He said seven out of ten people of working age who died from the virus had picked up the infection before the full lockdown. 'So that will turn out to be a crucial period,' he concluded. However, the response to our article from his colleague was furious. Professor Stephen Powis, NHS national medical director, said: 'These untrue claims will be deeply offensive to NHS doctors, nurses, therapists and paramedics who have together cared for more than 110,000 severely ill hospitalised Covid patients during the first wave of the pandemic, as they continue to do so today.' His dismissive comments illustrated why so many NHS doctors, nurses and paramedics had chosen to speak out as whistle-blowers about the scandal of care rationing in hospitals. They were frustrated that Powis, other health service executives and government ministers were misleading the public. The attempt to create an omertà inside Britain's hospitals was shocking. The medical whistle-blowers had described the terrible scenes in the wards to show politicians how important it was to suppress the virus and to emphasise to the public that they needed to follow social distancing rules. They therefore believed the untrue claims that everybody received the care they needed – by Hancock and NHS executives – were dangerous as they could cost lives.

Indeed, the Doctors' Association UK says many of its front-line medics across the country experienced exactly the problems we described. Dr Rinesh Parmar, its chairman, said his members had been traumatised by having to deal with large numbers of dying patients who had been deprived of access to care they would have normally received at the beginning of the pandemic. 'In reality, the late lockdown allowed far more infections to spread across the country than the NHS had the capacity to cope with,' he said. 'It left dedicated NHS staff in the invidious position of having to tell many critically unwell patients who needed life-saving treatment that they would not receive that treatment. Those staff will be mentally scarred for a long time as a result. They dedicate their lives to caring for people and never expected to be left in such a situation.'

Even senior members of the prime minister's own party recognise that the government has not been forthcoming about the extent of the catastrophe that hit the NHS in the first wave. David Davis, the former Brexit secretary, believes his government's strategy had 'fatal consequences for thousands whose lives could have been rescued'. He says damningly: 'The policy appears to have given the least care to those who needed it most. It is profoundly wrong that the government did not come clean to the public about this tragedy.'

11

Left to Die at Home

Thursday 9 April 2020 to Sunday 26 April 2020
UK government order: Lockdown

The silenced Big Ben shrouded in scaffolding could be seen clearly across the Thames from St Thomas' Hospital, where the prime minister struggled for his life in the second week of April. There were many who wondered whether Johnson would ever set foot in the Houses of Parliament again as he spent three nights in intensive care. The country held its breath. Inside the hospital, Johnson continued to be given oxygen. Then, slowly, he started to turn the corner. This was much to the relief of his doctors, who would not, after all, be forced to make a decision over whether to sedate the prime minister in a drug-induced coma – a procedure that would have been necessary if he had required mechanical ventilation. By Thursday 9 April, Johnson was able to return to the normal wards. His condition had been very serious. Stanley Johnson, his father, revealed the next day that things had been touch and go as the prime minister almost 'took one for the team'. His fiancée, Symonds, tweeted a celebratory painting of a rainbow with two lines of clapping emojis. There was relief everywhere. 'Great News: Prime Minister Boris Johnson has just been moved out of Intensive Care. Get well Boris!!!' tweeted the US president Donald Trump.

Downing Street said the prime minister was in extremely good spirits and 'enormously grateful' to his doctors and nurses. He was back in his bed playing Sudoku and watching his old favourite films such as *Withnail and I* and the *Lord of the Rings* trilogy. With some of his old spirit, he insisted that his nurses call him 'Boris'. There is no doubt that the prime minister received some of the best care available and also some special treatment. A source in St Thomas' Hospital speaking to the *Guardian* questioned whether he really should ever have been in intensive care. 'Before the coronavirus crisis you could be in ICU [intensive care unit] without being on a ventilator, but pretty much every bed is now taken by a coronavirus patient with a ventilator,' the source told the newspaper. 'I know people who work in ICU and I know the technicians who prepare all the equipment, and they all say he was not put on a ventilator. He was taking up an ICU bed when he didn't need it. The idea that you would put a patient who didn't need a ventilator on an ICU bed is nonsense.'[1]

However, it is hard to blame the hospital for treating the prime minister as a special case. He was fortunate to have such excellent care at a hospital on his doorstep; many who died from the virus would not be so lucky. The fact that the prime minister had pulled through was a great fillip to the nation at a time when all the other news was gloomy. Stanley Johnson went as far as to say that his son's illness had 'got the whole country to realise this is a serious event'. As if they had not done so already.

His son's delay over lockdown had caused an overwhelming number of infections, which were proving impossible for many hospitals to deal with. Dying people would be placed on normal wards without access to intensive care or would not even be admitted to hospital at all. The scale of the tragedy was almost unimaginable. There would be 59,000 extra deaths in England and Wales compared with previous years during the first six months of the pandemic. This consisted of 25,800 excess fatalities in care homes and another 25,200 in people's own homes. There were actually only 7,800 more deaths in hospitals than in a normal year. The low figure was surprising, as 30,000 extra people had died in hospital as a result of the virus during the same six months. Therefore, there must have been fewer people dying in hospitals from non-Covid illnesses to make that total possible. It is clear that many thousands of deaths that would usually have taken place in hospital had been displaced to people's homes and the care homes.

Deaths at home have soared

Excess deaths above the five-year average in care homes, private homes and in hospital, March 7 – August 28

Care homes
25,833

Private homes
25,215

Hospital
7,846

This huge increase in deaths outside hospitals was a mixture of coronavirus cases – many of which were never diagnosed – and people who were not given treatment for other conditions that they would normally have received had Britain not been in the grip of a pandemic. Ambulance and admission teams were told to be more selective about who should be taken into hospital, with specific instructions to exclude many elderly people. GPs were asked to identify frail patients, who were to be left at home even if they were seriously ill with the virus. In some regions, care home residents dying of Covid-19 were denied access to hospitals even though their families believed their lives could have been saved. The sheer scale of the resulting body count that piled up in the nation's homes meant special cadaver retrieval teams had to be formed by the police and fire brigade to transfer corpses from houses to mortuaries. Some are said to have run out of body bags.

This was the reality of the lockdown weeks, and yet, to date, both the government and the NHS have refused to admit that people were denied care. However, the doctors and nurses knew what was happening. 'It is manifestly the case that large numbers of patients did not receive the care that they needed, and that's because the health service didn't have the resources. It didn't have the infrastructure to cope during the first peak,' said Dr Chaand Nagpaul, chairman of the British Medical Association (BMA).

Drastic measures had been taken to keep the number of patients down in hospitals so that clinicians could deal with the first wave of cases, which had come significantly earlier than the government had anticipated. The numbers of daily deaths from Covid-19 in London had hit triple figures in the last week of March and were now surging even higher.

The London Ambulance Service had prepared by increasing the threshold for the severity of symptoms that a coronavirus patient would have to typically exhibit before they would be taken to hospital. The service uses a simple chart called News2, which scores each of a patient's vital signs and gives marks on breathing rate, oxygen saturation, temperature, blood pressure, pulse rate and level of consciousness. Abnormal indications are given a higher mark. A score of five is usually sufficient for a patient to be taken to hospital. On 12 March that threshold score had been increased to six. 'I believe it was changed because of the volume of calls and the capacity issues,' one London ambulance paramedic explained. 'There were so many people to go to. There was just a period ... where no one really knew how to deal with it.' As a result, many seriously ill people were left in their homes – a policy that was dangerously selective, according to medics.

Dr Jon Cardy, a former clinical director of accident and emergency at West Suffolk Hospital, said that in normal times hospital patients would often be referred for critical care if they scored just five on the News2 scale. 'If I had a patient with an early warning score of six,' he went on, 'I'd be saying: "This person certainly needs hospital treatment." You can't leave them at home with a cylinder of oxygen and a drip. They could easily deteriorate into multiorgan failure.'

It meant that for many people in the initial deluge of cases, it was too late by the time their condition was deemed so serious that a paramedic team would rush them to hospital. Shortness of breath was one of the key criteria for taking people to hospital, but many suffered a condition known as 'happy hypoxia', where their oxygen levels would drop dangerously without them noticing. These people often suffered heart attacks before an ambulance could reach them – and they would not necessarily receive quick treatment. In London the average call-out time for an ambulance almost trebled to more than an hour in late March. An ambulance clinician in south London at the time said: 'I saw a lot of Covid deaths in people's homes. Too many. The critical care paramedics on call would just go from cardiac arrest to arrest to arrest. They were seeing five, six, seven of those patients a day, back-to-back, in their areas.' The guidance continued to be in place until Friday 10 April, when it was advised that people scoring between three and five should be taken into hospital for assessment. The paramedic said it was changed because too many patients who needed urgent care 'were just being left at home'. Deaths from heart problems doubled compared with previous years, according to figures from the Office for National Statistics.

An adviser to the Cabinet Office said mortuary staff were shocked by the number of bodies being delivered from homes by the special police and firefighter recovery teams that had been set up to handle the surging body count. 'The staff were seriously questioning why so many deaths were taking place at home,' the source said. 'We did not explain to the public that this was the delicate balancing act – we've reduced the likelihood of getting an ambulance but we've increased the response teams to pick up bodies in people's homes.' The adviser added: 'The cremations were carried out in these very fast slots, running at weekends, running late into the night. A lot of concessions were struck with both Islam and the Church of England to just rush the bodies through, get them out, get them buried.'

Other methods were being used to keep ill patients out of hospital. On Thursday 9 April an extraordinary document was distributed by the Buckinghamshire NHS Trust asking clinicians and GPs to urgently 'identify all patients who are frail or in the latter stages of life and score them based on their level of frailty'. The purpose was to draw up a list of those who might stay at home when they became seriously ill rather than be taken to hospital. The document made clear that the move was necessary because intensive care was 'expected to far outweigh capacity by several thousand beds over the next few weeks in the south-east region due to Covid-19' and that there was 'a limited staff base to look after sick patients in our hospitals'. It said the approach it was setting out was being adopted by clinical commissioning groups across England.

The trust was asking doctors to scour the lists it was providing from registers of care home, palliative and frail patients as well as those over the age of 80 and give them a score. If the patients scored seven on the frailty scale – which was anyone dependent on a carer but 'not at risk of dying' – the trust recommended that it would be better that they remained at home rather than be taken into hospital. The document said that the decision should take into account the patient's circumstances and family's wishes when deciding on hospital admission, but it was 'ultimately a decision for the clinicians involved'. The Buckinghamshire trust would later claim that every patient who needed hospital treatment was admitted. But it did not explain how that could be true in light of the guidance it had issued.

Indeed, this type of selection made some doctors feel uneasy. One GP in Sutton, south London, who asked not to be named, described how his health authority had made 'inappropriate' demands on his practice to contact elderly and frail patients to discuss their future care plans in a way that would rule them out of hospital treatment. His practice was warned that the health authority would be 'analysing the numbers'. He explained: 'When Covid hit, there was a huge amount of worry about patients being admitted to hospitals and ICU capacity. So there was a huge pressure from health authorities that came on in an inappropriate way, saying, "You need to do this work, but at a faster, quicker pace."' The authority, he said, had identified dozens of his practice's patients who would be asked to accept 'do not resuscitate' orders or agree that they would forgo hospital care in the future. The health authority instructed him to talk to the patients and log their decisions on a centralised system called Coordinate My Care, which ambulance staff could then access to see whether a patient had opted out of hospital care. The Coordinate My Care system had been set up in 2010 and had 79,000 patients signed up at the beginning of 2020 before the pandemic. So, on average, 8,000 patients had been added each year over the decade. Yet in the six months between January and the end of June 2020 the number of patients on the system had rocketed up by 34,000 – a rate eight times higher than an average year.

The Sutton GP said he was 'told to get a certain percentage' of patients on the authority's list 'signed up'. In the end, he only contacted a handful because he felt such conversations were 'damaging to patient–doctor relationships' and he says his practice was ticked off by the health authority for not fulfilling their instruction. Dr Dino Pardhanani, GP lead for Sutton speaking on behalf of NHS South West London Clinical Commissioning Group, later defended the approach. He claimed the discussion of future care plans with patients was 'established best practice and the Covid-19 outbreak did not change that'.

But the anonymous GP said the problem was far wider than just Sutton. Doctors around the country had been issued with similar orders 'to identify patients to have this conversation with during what was a hugely anxious time', he said. The unprecedented escalation of the policy led to complaints. An NHS health board had to apologise after a GP surgery in Port Talbot, South Wales, wrote to patients with serious illnesses at the end of March recommending they accept 'do not attempt resuscitation' orders so that 'scarce ambulance resources can be targeted to the young and fit who have a greater chance'.

On Good Friday, 10 April, NHS England weighed in with its own advice to health authorities, setting out the groups of elderly people across the country who it said 'should not ordinarily be conveyed to hospital unless authorised by a senior colleague'. The list was very broad. It included all care home residents and patients who had asked not to receive an intravenous drip or to be resuscitated. Dementia patients with head injuries were also on the list of those excluded, as well as people who had fainted and appeared to have 'fully recovered' – but only if they were over the age of 70. These were harsh criteria to apply to people who might otherwise have been healthy. A 71-year-old who had once fainted would still benefit from hospital treatment as would a person who had merely expressed a wish not to be resuscitated if their health suddenly deteriorated.

When we asked the NHS national press office about the guidance, it issued a statement claiming the advice had been brought in to make sure that ambulance crews consulted with senior control room colleagues about whether patients could be more safely treated outside of hospital. Yet the NHS withdrew the advice just four days after it was issued, following an angry backlash from groups representing the elderly. Martin Vernon, the NHS's former national clinical director for older people, described the guidance as a 'flagrant breach' of equality laws. 'It seemed to suggest that people in care homes and older people generally have less value, and therefore it's quite reasonable to exclude them from the normal pathway of care,' he said.

* * *

There was no doubt that the measures to protect the NHS had a significant effect. Just 10 per cent of the 4,000 Covid deaths registered in the last week of March and first week of April occurred outside hospitals, according to figures from the Office for National Statistics. Yet in the fortnight spanning the end of April and beginning of May, some 45 per cent of the 14,000 people who died of the virus had not been taken into hospital. They included people like Brian Noon, a 'fit, strong and fun-loving' 76-year-old RAF veteran, who had tested positive for the virus after attending the A&E department at the Lancaster Royal Infirmary on Good Friday with a fever and cough.

The hospital sent the father of five home and arrangements were made for him to be checked twice a day by a rapid response nursing team, who were already visiting to monitor his terminally ill wife Desley, 77. On Easter Sunday his daughter Kerry says she spoke to one of the nurses and was told she needed to talk to him about agreeing to a 'do not resuscitate' order. The nurse warned, Kerry says, that if he deteriorated, an ambulance would refuse to take him to hospital without such an order in place.

The family initially decided not to discuss the issue with Brian because they knew he was afraid of death and it might upset him. The next day the nurse returned to say their father would no longer be sent to hospital if his condition worsened – regardless of whether he signed a 'do not resuscitate' order. 'It was not a discussion,' his eldest daughter Maria said. 'We were told there had been a change to the plan and Dad wouldn't be going to hospital.' They were not aware at the time just how sick their father had become. It was only weeks later that they were shown the rapid response team's logs, which had recorded a plummet in his oxygen levels.

On the Tuesday after Easter weekend Maria received a call from the local GP, who told her he was sorry to hear her father was so poorly. The GP said that Brian's oxygen levels had dropped to 79 per cent and he had been asked to help him with palliative care – treatment that would make his death more comfortable. 'That call was a great shock to the family as we did not know that Dad was dying,' said Maria. 'His oxygen levels had been dropping daily and not once, at any point, did the nursing team communicate this to the family.' The guidance from the British Thoracic Society is that oxygen levels below 94 per cent are abnormal and require assessment for urgent treatment. However, the family later discovered that 'oxygen therapy not required' had been written more than once in his medical records. Despite his desperate condition, the records note that 'no further escalation [of treatment] is intended or considered appropriate'.

The following morning, Wednesday 15 April, the family took a reading of Brian's oxygen levels using his wife's oximeter and it had now fallen to 44 per cent. They called the nursing team at 7.50 a.m. and were told there was nothing that could be done. They were advised to hold his hand, as he would not recover. 'His breathing had got much much worse. He was becoming quite agitated. He was going downhill rapidly. All he kept saying was, "I'm dying, I'm dying,"' Maria said. 'Dad got worse and worse. He became more and more agitated, anxious and distressed. His eyes were glazed and glossy. There was abject fear in his eyes. It was like watching a horror story. My sister called the [nursing team], but it was another hour before they came.'

Brian died at 3.40 p.m. and the nursing team arrived 40 minutes later. 'I'm somebody who's very calm, normally, very patient,' said Maria, 'but I couldn't help ask them, "How could you do this? How could you let someone in this day and age, in a first-world country, die in that condition?"' At the time of writing, the family still do not know why a decision was taken to deny Brian treatment. His GP told them that 'vulnerability scores' were being used by the health service in the area, but it is not clear whether they were applied to Brian. It is certainly the case that he would have been excluded from intensive care if the Covid-19 triage tool or something similar had been deployed to assess him. His age, frailty and diabetes would have tipped his score over the threshold that people would be given intensive care treatment. The family wants answers. 'Dad did not receive timely and crucial medical care and, as a direct result, he died a horrific and excruciatingly painful death,' said Maria. 'We feel like Dad's been murdered. They were killing off the elderly and the vulnerable. If you're elderly, don't you need more care? Don't you need more compassion? We were tuning in to the news and it kept saying, "Protect the NHS, protect the NHS." And we kept thinking, "Why aren't they protecting people?"' When we approached University Hospitals of Morecambe Bay NHS Foundation Trust about Noon's care, Dr Shahedal Bari, the medical director, said it was 'working with the family to answer all of their questions'.

In the south of the country, in Walthamstow, north-east London, another tragedy was unfolding. Betty Grove had been suffering from a cough and was finding it difficult to breathe. The 78-year-old grandmother was diagnosed with pneumonia and a collapsed lung in her local hospital, Whipps Cross, but was sent home four hours later because it was feared she might become infected with Covid-19. She may well have already had the virus, especially given her symptoms. But, according to her daughter Donna, the hospital refused to test Betty for this because they would have to admit her to do so. It was a Catch-22. Over the following days, Betty, a retired Co-op worker of 25 years, 'grew weaker' and began struggling for breath. Donna says she called her local trust's rapid response team repeatedly – sometimes twice a day – asking for help for her mother, but they declined to admit her to the hospital. Betty continued to deteriorate and she eventually died at home of pneumonia in May. The cause of death was given as acute lung injury. Her family believes she would have survived if she had been admitted when she first went to hospital. Donna was furious. 'I get that they did have enough on their plate. They had Covid ... but it doesn't mean to say they can push these people aside and just let them go home to die,' she said. Barts Health NHS Trust has since apologised to the family for Betty's treatment and launched an internal investigation.

The deaths of people like Brian and Betty at home without hospital treatment were part of a much wider national tragedy. From the beginning of March to the end of August, there were 25,200 more deaths in people's homes than in normal years, yet only 2,400 of those were classified as being caused by Covid-19. It is impossible to say how many of the remaining 22,800 deaths were a result of the virus, as there was very little testing outside hospitals. But doctors we have spoken to believe a substantial number were caused by it. Caroline Abrahams, director of the charity Age UK, believes elderly people were 'considered dispensable'. She says the government feared the 'endless news coverage of people dying outside in hospital corridors or banked up in ambulances' and therefore kept many elderly people at home. 'The lack of empathy and humanity was chilling. It was ageism laid bare and it had tragic consequences,' she said.

One of the other reasons that so many people were dying at home was because the mass influx of Covid patients into hospitals was taking an inevitable toll on the care being provided to patients with other health conditions. There were only so many medical staff to go round. 'We could see first-hand the reality that NHS services had to put on standstill large volumes of normal care in order to create the capacity to deal with Covid. Hospitals had to literally become Covid healthcare centres to create that capacity,' recalls Dr Chaand Nagpaul, chair of the British Medical Association. 'It was distressing for doctors because they knew their patients' needs had not vanished.'

The push to prevent hospitals becoming overwhelmed with Covid patients meant there was scant time or space for normal patients. GPs reported that patient referrals to hospitals – including those deemed urgent – were being repeatedly rejected.

Cancer Research UK has estimated that three million people missed vital cancer screenings, tests or treatment in the six months from the start of lockdown, leading to 350,000 fewer urgent referrals. Patients who required scans, outpatient appointments and urgent tests for potentially life-threatening diseases such as cancer were placed on growing waiting lists. 'We didn't have the workforce, we didn't have the logistical arrangements in terms of space,' Nagpaul explains. 'We needed to free up space to create ventilators and critical care facilities that we didn't have before. Wards were transformed into critical care areas. So there was a problem. It was not possible to keep the doors open to patients with Covid illness and non-Covid at the same time, otherwise we would have spread the infection. So the NHS had to really halt its normal service and it was having an impact.'

A neurosurgeon carrying out cancer operations at a hospital in London described how half of his 30-strong team were off work in April because of Covid infections. A further seven were transferred to intensive care to treat patients with the virus, which left him with just eight team members. During this period he could only attend to a quarter of his normal surgical list. There was also a risk of infection, so even operations to remove brain tumours had to be downgraded. 'We want to reduce the amount of time in hospital due to Covid risk, so we had to do smaller operations ... to allow people to get in and out as quickly as possible,' he said at the time. 'That necessarily means that they don't get the best benefit from surgery because, obviously, they have a large amount of tumour still left in their brains.' Some of those who received lesser operations would later die. Operations for breast cancer, hernias and burns reconstruction were all cancelled, he said.

An ambulance clinician working in and around London described how people suffering trauma injuries were also being denied normal levels of care. There were many accidents and suicide attempts related to lockdown. 'We saw a lot of cyclists who'd been run over and lots of people doing DIY at home who are up a ladder, and who wouldn't usually be [if it wasn't for lockdown]. And people who were flouting lockdown and going out and getting pissed and getting in their car. And lots of mental health cases – lots of people jumping from bridges.' But the ambulance clinician says that cases were not admitted to 'a trauma centre unless [they] were really badly injured'. Even older patients who had bleeds on the brain were at times not getting life-saving surgery. 'If patients are a bit older, then we might not intervene,' she said. 'In normal times, the threshold for taking somebody to a trauma centre will be lower. That was really hard for us, having to do that and justify it, knowing that the patient wouldn't have the same chance.'

Many people were voluntarily avoiding hospitals even when they were very ill. There was a mixture of fear of infection and a desire not to overburden the NHS at its time of great crisis. One of the problems was the government's 'Stay at home, protect the NHS' message. Nagpaul says that while the message was 'well meaning', it could also be 'interpreted by the public to not burden the NHS'. He said: 'And what we saw was large numbers of patients then not going to hospital or not calling for medical treatment, who otherwise should have done.' It meant that, ironically, in the midst of the pandemic, many hospitals' Accident & Emergency departments were largely empty. The ambulance clinician from north London describes 'unreal' situations in which the emergency health service workers were 'sitting around' with nothing to do. 'That just never happens normally.' An adviser to the Cabinet Office told us: 'I know a doctor who worked in non-Covid care in hospital who said to me, "I'm just embarrassed to be clapped for. It's never been so quiet."'

Nagpaul says that the thousands of non-Covid patients who had died because the NHS could not cope were the forgotten victims. He believes the government should have acknowledged the extra non-Covid deaths at the Downing Street media briefings. 'What we now know is that the excess mortality in the UK has been tragically high. I believe it's probably the second highest in the world. I think it's the worst in Europe,' he said later in the summer. 'We know that at least 12,000 of those cases are considered to be due to non-Covid causes. So it has had an impact, and people have not survived as a result, but it hasn't been spoken about.'

The seven days from Saturday 11 April were the worst of the outbreak. Over the next week there were an average of 1,350 deaths each day, according to the Office for National Statistics. A Boeing 747 plane carries around four hundred passengers, so the coronavirus death toll over those seven days equated to more than three jumbo jets crashing each day and killing every-one on board.

They were people like Mary Agyeiwaa Agyapong, a 28-year-old nurse. On Sunday 12 April she died from the virus at Luton and Dunstable University Hospital, where she had been work-ing and may have picked up her infection. The hospital's authorities denied claims there had been a shortage of gowns and a rationing of masks while Agyapong had been working there in March. Mary's story was particularly sad. She had been heavily pregnant and doctors had to perform an emergency Caesarean to save her baby shortly before her death. A child that would never know its mother.[2]

That day the prime minister was discharged from hospital after just a week on the wards. He had put on a jacket and tie, but he looked pale in his heartfelt video of thanks to the hospital staff who had looked after him. 'I have today left hospital after a week in which the NHS has saved my life. No question. It's hard to find words to express my debt,' he said. 'I want to pay my own thanks to the utterly brilliant doctors, leaders in their fields, men and women, but several of them for some reason called Nick, who took some crucial decisions a few days ago, for which I will be grateful for the rest of my life.'

He added: 'And I hope they won't mind if I mention in particular, two nurses who stood by my bedside for 48 hours when things could have gone either way. They're Jenny from New Zealand, Invercargill on the South Island to be exact, and Luis from Portugal, near Porto. And the reason in the end my body did start to get enough oxygen was because for every second of the night they were watching, and they were thinking and they were caring and making the interventions I needed.'

His voice caught a couple of times with emotion on those last words. The tone was genuine in a way that suggested he would never underestimate the virus again. But he was still very poorly and headed off to Chequers, where over the next two weeks he would recuperate in the fresh air and pass his hours birdwatching. While the deaths kept coming, the incapacitated prime minister was out with his binoculars spotting red kites, buzzards and woodpeckers on the Buckinghamshire estate. Unsurprisingly, he was banned from riding the second-hand Yamaha TT-R125 motorbike he had been given by Symonds as a Christmas present. But, at least, he wasn't being bombarded with calls from his workaholic chief adviser.

Dominic Cummings had been hit hard by the virus. He woke up on his parents' farm on the outskirts of Durham with a sore head and fever on the Saturday morning at the end of March after he had driven his family up north the day before. His journalist wife Mary Wakefield would later recount in an article for *The Spectator* how 'Dom' was fighting his own battle with the virus as the prime minister's condition was deteriorating in early April. He was breathless, he ached and he couldn't get out of bed. 'Day in, day out for 10 days he lay doggo with a high fever and spasms that made the muscles lump and twitch in his legs ... He could breathe, but only in a limited, shallow way.' But the article cleverly avoided saying where he was convalescing and there was certainly no mention of the 250-mile trip to Durham.

On the day that Johnson had been admitted to hospital, Sunday 5 April, a passer-by had heard some familiar lyrics blasting out from the Cummings farm. 'Friday night and the lights are low, / Looking out for the place to go … / You come to look for a king, / Anybody could be that guy.' It was the Abba song *Dancing Queen* and the guy in the driveway didn't look like just anybody. He looked enormously like the prime minister's chief adviser who had gone AWOL a week before. The passer-by was so intrigued that they decided to call the *Guardian*. A few days later on Good Friday – the day after Johnson left hospital – a reporter from the newspaper contacted Downing Street about the sighting and was fobbed off with a no comment.[3]

Two days later, on Easter Sunday, Cummings was still in Durham. The day also happened to be his wife's birthday. The couple and their son drove out to the market town of Barnard Castle, which was 25 miles away. The trip would become infamous. According to Cummings's account, the family arrived on the outskirts of the town and parked by a river. However, he 'felt a bit sick' and walked around 10 to 15 metres from the car to the riverbank nearby, sitting there for 15 minutes until he felt better. He recalled that an elderly gentleman walking nearby appeared to recognise him. 'My wife wished him Happy Easter from a distance, but we had no other interaction,' he said. The couple resolved to drive back to London the following day. 'We emerged from quarantine into the almost comical uncertainty of London lockdown,' his wife would later write in her *Spectator* article – which was the only hint they might have been somewhere outside the capital.

They returned to a London that was at the height of the pandemic. But the darkest days had passed and on Tuesday 14 April there was some critically important news. Deaths were plateauing, according to the Sage committee. It had been three weeks since the lockdown had been introduced and its effects were now finally being seen in the decline of the death rate. It was a turning point and a relief to the country, the politicians and the NHS that the lockdown seemed to be working. But the vast backlog of infections meant there would still be many deaths from the virus deep into May.

The passing of the peak opened up a tension that would be ever present for the remainder of the year. The lockdown had caused an unparalleled cessation of economic activity and, at some point, people would have to get back to work again. The Treasury could see a deep recession on the horizon and Rishi Sunak, the chancellor, took the view that restrictions needed to be lifted sooner rather than later to avoid financial calamity and mass unemployment. Some Tory MPs on the right of the party were calling for the lockdown to be ended immediately. But bodies were still mounting up in Britain's hospitals and elsewhere, and Hancock, the health secretary, was urging caution. When the prime minister introduced the lockdown, he said it would be in place initially for three weeks, and the deadline had passed that Tuesday. With the prime minister still recovering, the decision over whether to extend it fell to his stand-in, Dominic Raab, who, as commentators pointed out, was always going to play it safe.

At a media briefing on Thursday 16 April, Raab announced there would be three more weeks of lockdown. He pointed out the logical flaw in the arguments being made by some of his more hawkish colleagues in the party. The lifting of restrictions too soon would actually cause more rather than less damage to the economy – while also killing greater numbers of people. 'If we rush to relax the measures that we have in place we would risk wasting all the sacrifices and all the progress that has been made,' he said. 'That would risk a quick return to another lockdown with all the threat to life that a second peak to the virus would bring and all the economic damage that a second lockdown would carry.' It was a simple argument that in the era of coronavirus the economy could not hope to thrive unless infections were under control. But it was a logic his government would later forget.

Prince William opened the second Nightingale Hospital at the National Exhibition Centre in Birmingham that day. The prince praised its hasty assembly as a wonderful example of people 'pulling together' during the pandemic. But local doctors were less impressed because it did not meet their urgent need for more intensive care capacity. 'The Nightingale in Birmingham was never geared up to take intensive care patients,' a critical care expert in the Midlands told us. 'So it was always designed to be a kind of overflow place for people that wouldn't meet the criteria of intensive care. It wasn't designed to have ventilated patients.' As a result, large numbers of people continued to die in the city's hospitals without life-saving ventilation.

By now the virus was making its way through Britain's care homes at a devastating rate. The discharge of up to 25,000 hospital patients into care homes during the pandemic's height was becoming a highly controversial move. Many of these patients had been transferred out of their hospitals without first being tested. Infections in hospitals were a major problem, so the policy had the effect of dispersing the virus into the very place where Britain's most vulnerable were supposed to have been shielded. By Friday 17 April, there had been almost ten thousand excess deaths in care homes since the beginning of March. Yet Hancock would later say that the government had placed 'a protective ring' around the care sector. It was another big but unsustainable claim.

It is one of the most scandalous facts of the lockdown weeks that hundreds of patients who had tested positive for the virus were also deliberately sent into the care homes. In Derbyshire, the county council published a 'good practice for care homes' on its website in late April stating that the owners and staff 'should be prepared to receive back care home residents who are Covid positive' in order 'to ensure capacity for new Covid cases in acute hospitals'. The council claimed it was following guidelines issued by the government. Bradford Council responded to a Department of Health request to free up hospital beds by also instructing care homes to look after infected patients. An email from the council to care home owners set out this policy. It said: 'The tests will have taken place in hospital, and if a positive result is received (this is currently taking 2 days) then we are looking to discharge into (firstly) in-house services, or the independent sector. The length of stay will typically be 5 days (to then total 7 days when they are no longer contagious).' The email reveals that the council even wanted to send people who were dying of the virus out of hospital into care homes for 'end of life support'. After reading the email, David Crabtree, an owner of two care homes in West Yorkshire, wrote to a colleague: 'A deliberate policy to admit live Covid into care homes is just plain stupid.'

Data obtained from NHS trusts by Sky News revealed that just under a third of the 6,435 elderly patients who were discharged from hospitals into care homes between 19 March and 15 April had been tested. This included 623 people whose results showed they had been carrying the virus before being sent to the homes.[4] A month later, the prime minister told the parliamentary liaison committee: 'Every discharge from the NHS into care homes was made by clinicians, and in no case was that done when people were suspected of being coronavirus victims.' Johnson was clearly very badly informed.

One of the other problems was that many care home staff worked for multiple employers. Their shifts took them from home to home and there was no testing available to check whether they were carrying the virus. Some care home staff will have been unaware that they were infected but carried on working while suffering symptoms because they were on zero-hour casual contracts and would not be paid if they took time off for sickness. These staff were equipped with even fewer protective masks and gowns than the medics and nurses in hospital. So the elderly people were dispatched from hospitals into care homes that were completely open to infection and then cross-infection. A third of all care homes declared a coronavirus outbreak, with more than a thousand dealing with positive cases during the peak of infections in April, according to the National Audit Office. Chris Whitty, the chief medical adviser, later acknowledged that it had been a big mistake to have not realised that agency staff working across multiple homes were passing on the virus. This was 'obvious in retrospect', he told a parliamentary committee. 'I don't think any of us would look back on what has happened in social care and say the ideal advice was given.'

Just as people had been left to die without access to hospitals in their own homes, many care residents were also rejected for admission. The West Yorkshire care home owner Crabtree says that many of his residents died without being taken to hospital, which they would have been in more normal times. He describes how one of his homes was forced to accept a patient who was discharged from hospital and then came down with symptoms of the virus at the beginning of April. As the patient's condition deteriorated, the home called an ambulance, but a clinician on the end of the phone refused to send one. 'We were told there was a restriction on beds and to treat as end of life,' Crabtree said. The resident died a few days later in the second week of April. After the patient was taken into the home, the virus then spread to others. A total of seven more residents died from it, and not one was admitted to hospital. 'I couldn't believe what we were being told,' Crabtree said; 'they were denying people because of age.' He said that residents in a similar condition would have always been admitted to hospital 'straight away, no hesitation' before the pandemic.

But in the middle of April, the policy of the hospital changed and infected residents were once again admitted. 'The peak dropped so I don't think there was pressure on beds. After 15 April we were able to get people into hospital,' he said. The hospital then helped save the lives of all five patients who were admitted from his care homes with infections. It suggests strongly that the eight elderly people who had died before the policy switch might have lived if they had been given hospital care. Crabtree said the whole experience had been particularly traumatic for his staff. 'In a care home, you've actually become attached to that person. You've shared holidays, families, Christmases for a number of years, so there is an emotional attachment to coming in every day to see another of your residents die,' he said.

The refusal to admit people from care homes to hospitals was a widespread issue according to the medical staff we spoke to. 'As far as I was aware, patients that were in the care homes if they got Covid weren't then typically taken back to hospital. I can't remember seeing anybody from a care home who had tested positive who was brought into hospital, not a single one,' said the intensive care specialist from the Midlands. A paramedic in London said he would normally be 'in and out of care homes all the time' attending to emergencies. 'We'd typically go in twice a week,' he said. 'But I didn't attend a single care home from the beginning of April to the end of April during that first peak.'

Research carried out by the Health Foundation found that the numbers of care home residents admitted to hospital decreased substantially during the pandemic, with 11,800 fewer admissions during March and April in England compared to previous years. An Amnesty International report concluded that the government had violated the human rights of care home residents via the 'imposition of blanket [do not attempt to resuscitate] orders on residents of many care homes around the country and restrictions on residents' access to hospital'. A Cabinet Office source claimed there had been a 'blanket approach' of refusing admissions to hospitals from care homes and, at the same time, 'encouraging residents to sign "do not resuscitate" contracts' because there were insufficient resources in the NHS. Speaking a few weeks after the height of the outbreak, the source said care homes had been told not to call for ambulances. At the same time, the source said the staff operating 999 emergency phones and NHS 111 were told 'they need to work through the various steps about whether an ambulance needs to be called, and at the moment the weight and the consideration is such that the care homes know not to make the call'. The source said care home residents were being treated as 'collateral damage' and described the strategy as 'mass murder'. Many of those who died had lived through the Second World War, which was being commemorated in the summer as it was the 75th anniversary of victory in Europe. Some had even fought in the war. 'That's what made VE day so difficult,' the source added.

By August almost 26,000 more people had died in care homes than was usual for that time of year.

The scale of the tragedy taking place in the hospitals and care homes had been largely unreported by the time the country settled in for another three weeks of lockdown in mid-April. Both sets of institutions were no-go areas for reporters, and events on the frontline were too frenetic for a broader picture to emerge. The government was therefore enjoying a honeymoon period of relative popularity as the nation rallied around and pulled together at a time of emergency. But doubts were beginning to emerge about the prime minister's handling of the crisis. It was clear that the lockdown would go on for some time, that the number of deaths was remarkably high, and that the country did not appear to have been well prepared for the pandemic, particularly with regard to testing and personal protective equipment.

We – the authors of this book – had been working from home since March and had exposed a 'Harley Street' doctor who stood to make millions by profiteering on the sales of home testing kits for the virus. But we were asked by our editors to take a step back and investigate how well Britain had responded to the coronavirus crisis after the first news about the new disease emerged from China at the beginning of the year. The resulting article, headlined 'Revealed: 38 days when Britain sleepwalked into disaster', was published on *The Sunday Times* website at 6 p.m. on Saturday 18 April. Based on interviews with scientists, academics, doctors, emergency planners, politicians and a Downing Street adviser whistle-blower, it revealed how the government had failed to heed warnings about the imminent threat of the virus, and lost five crucial weeks in January and February when it should have been preparing the country for the coming storm. The article exposed the deep complacency within the government epitomised by the prime minister's failure to attend any of the first five Cobra meetings on the virus. It described for the first time how the government gave China 279,000 items from its depleted PPE stockpile just weeks before the NHS itself began facing critical shortages of protective equipment.

The article struck a chord, possibly because it gave a voice to the unease people were already starting to feel about the government's handling of the crisis. The internet went crazy. Within a day, it had become the most popular online article in the history of *The Sunday Times* and *The Times* and was making headlines around the world. Audience research showed it had reached 24 million people in Britain after being covered more than a hundred times across various television and radio stations that weekend. The government was severely rattled. On Sunday morning Michael Gove, the cabinet minister, appeared on the BBC's *Andrew Marr Show* claiming that it was 'grotesque' to suggest there was anything unusual or irregular about the prime minister missing Cobra. His argument seemed to be that the top-level cross-government emergency meetings were in some way not 'vital to our response to the coronavirus'. He acknowledged that protective equipment had been shipped to China, but said it was justified 'to help with the most extreme outbreak in Wuhan'. In normal times such generosity might have been applauded. But there was little sympathy for a government that sent equipment like this to the world's biggest manufacturer of PPE when NHS staff were now dying because of a lack of protection.

Jonathan Ashworth, the shadow health secretary, told Sky News that Gove had given 'possibly the weakest rebuttal of a detailed exposé in British political history'. There were, Ashworth added, 'serious questions as to why the prime minister skipped five Cobra meetings throughout February, when the whole world could see how serious this was becoming'. That night, a volley of tweets was issued by leading ministers – including Raab, Gove and Hancock – encouraging people to read a 2,000-word government 'blog' that claimed there were 'falsehoods and errors' in the article. A team of civil servants and political aides had been diverted from tackling the pandemic that Sunday to spin a narrative that the government had not put a foot wrong. The claims of errors and falsehoods made in the government's blog were groundless. In fact, a similar 20-point 'blog' had been published four days earlier, attacking a *Financial Times* article, which had quite rightly raised valid questions about the government's failed attempts to procure ventilators. It emerged that a new wartime-style propaganda unit charged with spreading counter disinformation had been set up by the cabinet. Fortunately, it was a bit hapless and would not last for long.

The blog was comprehensively rebutted in *The Sunday Times* the following weekend. We were able to demonstrate that Johnson's repeated absences from Cobra at the beginning of the crisis were unprecedented. The blog had selectively quoted two experts, who had appeared in the article, to make it look as if they had played down the severity of the coronavirus threat in late January – thereby excusing the government's lack of action. One of the experts was Richard Horton, editor of *The Lancet*, who subsequently went as far as to accuse the government of a 'Kremlinesque' manipulation of his words. He had, in fact, published a scientific paper in late January that gave a clear warning that the virus was more infectious than the Spanish flu. The other was Professor Martin Hibberd of the London School of Hygiene & Tropical Medicine, who said the government had used his words out of context and pointed out that, unforgivably, the blog had cut out a sentence from his quote in which he called for urgent action to prepare for a possible pandemic in January.

Nadine Dorries, the health minister, also waded in against the article with some of her own dark imaginings. 'I can smell a bloodstained axe to grind behind it. #IthinkIknowwhoyouare,' she tweeted. We have no idea who she was referring to. It seemed to be a threat to one of our whistle-blowers. But they had no axe to grind. They just thought the government's response to the threat of the virus had been inadequate and incompetent, and needed exposing. Dorries was probably pointing the finger at some poor soul we had never talked to. The first person to reply to her on Twitter was a teacher named Simon Maginn. He wrote: 'Nadine, people are dying today who shouldn't be because of your government's indifference, dogma and delay … This is your disaster. No-one is ever going to forget.'

The first three weeks of April had been both harrowing and gruelling. The late lockdown in March had caused 8,000 deaths a week over those 21 days and although the number of infected patients being treated in hospitals had peaked at 21,683 on 12 April, there was still a frantic battle to keep thousands of people alive on the wards. These were also the weeks when there was a vacuum at the top of government with the prime minister out of action. The small quartet leading the country – Raab, Sunak, Hancock and Gove – had stuck to a limited plan, but without the ultimate decision maker there was no clear strategy for the months ahead. They had not found a solution for the big problems such as care homes, testing and tracing, protective equipment for health workers or the grim statistic that Britain had the highest number of deaths in Europe. Although they would later try to tackle the last of those problems by tweaking the way that deaths from Covid-19 were counted.

At his media briefing on Tuesday 21 April, Hancock did announce some good news. The government would now test health workers even if they did not have symptoms. This should have been in place weeks earlier if only there had been proper preparations, and it would have saved many lives. The testing of NHS staff was now possible, as the government was finally gearing up to try to meet Hancock's ambitious target of 100,000 tests a day by the end of the month. But the progress on PPE was still stuck in a quagmire. The government was talking to 159 firms who might supply the NHS, but it was proceeding with caution as some were fly-by-night organisations. Hancock said: 'We have had some offers, for instance, that have come from companies where, upon investigation, the company has only just been formed in the previous day or two before coming and asking for a cash deal with the government.'

What Hancock did not mention was that some of the suppliers had political connections with the government and their bids for contracts were being dealt with through a 'high priority' channel where they were 10 times more likely to secure the business. The National Audit Office would later discover that almost 500 suppliers with links to politicians or senior officials were referred to the channel. The advantage of this fast stream was that bidding firms were automatically treated as credible by government officials. The departure from standard procurement practice would lead to allegations of cronyism when it was exposed later in the year. Some of the deals would beggar belief. A small loss-making firm run by a Conservative councillor in Stroud was given a £120 million contract to import PPE from China without any competition. A vermin-control company valued at £19,000 was given £108 million to supply protective equipment. When it turned out the protective suits the firm supplied were not tested to the correct standard, 'political' pressure was applied to approve them, according to emails obtained by the BBC. But the procurement scandal would only emerge later.

The PPE issue was dominating the headlines in mid-April for other reasons. Over the previous weekend, unions representing doctors and nurses had expressed their concern about changes to safety guidelines, which meant medics could reuse protective gowns. The measure had been brought in because there were fears that hospitals might run out of gowns entirely within 24 hours. In an attempt to provide reassurance, Robert Jenrick, the communities secretary, said a shipment of 400,000 gowns would arrive from Turkey the following day. It was a farce, however. The shipment was delayed and when it did finally arrive the gowns had to be impounded because they did not meet safety standards.

At the beginning of the month three NHS nurses at Northwick Park Hospital in Harrow had tested positive for the virus after being forced to wear bin bags due to a shortage of protective gowns. One of the nurses had told the *Telegraph*: 'We need proper PPE kit now, or nurses and doctors are going to die. It's as simple as that. We're treating our own colleagues on the ward after they caught the virus from patients. How can that be right? There are so many younger people here on ventilation – many with asthma, or diabetes ... There's little we can do apart from try to help them breathe. Sometimes the body just gives up, and they die. We can't save them.' A senior source at the hospital said that more than half the staff had contracted the virus on one ward and bosses had warned them not to speak to the media about the PPE shortages.[5]

So protective equipment and the safety of health workers was a pressing issue when the opposition was given its first chance to directly question the prime minister's stand-in, Dominic Raab, after parliament returned from the Easter recess that week. Prime Minister's Questions on Wednesday 22 April pitted Raab against the Labour leader Keir Starmer in a near-empty

Commons, with MPs dialling in with questions online for the first time in the history of the Houses of Parliament.

Starmer cited a survey by the Royal College of Nursing revealing that half of nursing staff felt under pressure to work without the correct levels of protective equipment that were set out in official safety guidance. He asked Raab how many NHS workers had now died from coronavirus. Raab had the answer to hand. 'On the latest figures, my understanding is that 69 people in the NHS have died of coronavirus ... I think that we can all agree in this House that every one of those is a tragedy,' he said.

It was more than a tragedy. It was a scandal. Britain's pandemic planning was supposed to have been the envy of the world and yet the previous three weeks had seen mass deaths of people at home who were denied treatment, mass deaths in hospitals and mass deaths in care homes. At the same time, the government's failure to hit the ground running and make preparations in the months of January and February had left those who saved lives and looked after others cruelly exposed. Those who died of the virus included porters, nurses, GPs, care workers, doctors, ambulance drivers, paramedics, cleaners, surgeons, midwives and radiographers. Some were in their 20s and 30s, and many left behind young children. It is impossible to tell all of their stories, but here are a few.

Dr Abdul Mabud Chowdhury, a 53-year-old consultant urologist, wrote a Facebook post just days before he died from the virus on the night of 8 April, asking Johnson to urgently provide every NHS worker with personal protective equipment. Suzanne Loverseed, a 63-year-old care home nurse, died without her family in hospital. 'We might have had another twenty years with her; instead, we had to say goodbye via an iPad, unable to hold her hand,' her son Ian wrote in a blog post. 'At the end, she worked in a care home, with patients dying of this virus. She had no PPE but fearlessly she carried on. That's what killed her.' Mick Gallagher, a 34-year-old Glasgow-based agency care worker, died in his own home on 9 April after an ambulance did not arrive in time. As he passed away, he held the hand of his partner John, who recalled: 'His last words were that he was scared, and I was scared too, but I was there for him. And then he told me that he loved me and I said it to him as well that I loved him and that we were going to get through it.'[6] Father of two Steven Pearson, a 51-year-old mental health nurse from Northumberland, died suddenly at home after just three days of mild symptoms. His wife Anne said: 'Steven was my life, he loved me and the girls. It was the first thing Bethany [his daughter] said, that her dad would never be able to walk her down the aisle or see his grandchildren.'[7] Rebecca Mack, a 29-year-old nurse who treated child cancer victims at Newcastle's Royal Victoria Infirmary, was found dead by paramedics inside her home on 5 April. She had been self-isolating alone after experiencing symptoms and had called an ambulance as she struggled to breathe. It did not arrive quickly enough.[8] Peter Gough, 56, an administration assistant at John Radcliffe Hospital in Oxford, died on 12 May shortly after he had raised concerns about a lack of personal protective equipment. He texted his friend Paul Saville on 7 April to say: 'No PPE for admin staff. Not even sanitizer gel as [there is] not enough for everywhere in hospital.' Saville said his death was 'a scandal'.[9]

More than 650 health and social care service workers would be killed by the virus by the end of the year.

PART FOUR

THE SAME MISTAKE TWICE

27 April 2020 to 2 December 2020

12

Worst of All Worlds

Monday 27 April to Friday 3 July
UK government order: Lifting lockdown

On the cold bright morning of Monday 27 April the prime minister was finally ready to announce his return to work. He had spent a peaceful fortnight recuperating in Chequers free of the burden of official government work, aside from phone calls with the Queen and Donald Trump to reassure them he was on the mend. All the while, the virus had been causing death and devastation on an appalling scale across the country. Since he had tested positive on 27 March, more than 26,800 people in Britain had died with Covid-19. His cavalier approach and then prevarication over lockdown had caused many of those deaths. It also almost cost him his life. Now it seemed inconceivable that he would ever underestimate the virus again.

Johnson still looked slightly ashen when he emerged from the front door of 10 Downing Street into the sunlight. In the windows behind him there were children's paintings of rainbows with the message 'Thank You NHS'. They had been stuck on the glass panes as a heartfelt expression of gratitude from the prime minister. Standing at the lectern, he attempted to deliver his speech with his usual gusto, but a noticeable shortness of breath meant he was more hesitant than normal. 'I'm sorry that I have been away from my desk for much longer than I would have liked,' he said. But the pyrotechnic phrasing was still the same. Johnson compared the virus to an 'invisible mugger' that the country had begun 'to wrestle to the floor'. People were still dying, but the peak of the outbreak had passed. The UK had 'defied so many predictions', he claimed, by 'not running out of ventilators or ICU beds'. This was untrue.

While Johnson had been given an intensive care bed, not everyone was so lucky. There had been many people, such as Raymond Austin, who died without receiving life-saving treatment in the critical care wards. It is possible the prime minister had not been properly briefed and certainly the NHS was keen to give the impression that it had coped during those dark weeks from mid-March into April. This failure to be up front about what really had happened during the outbreak would become a major problem. Conservative backbench MPs were already pressing for the lockdown to be lifted and they, and others, would use the 'NHS was okay' argument to suggest that the hospitals could manage if social distancing restrictions were relaxed and infections started to rise again. This was a dangerously flawed assumption to make.

But that day the prime minister seemed determined to show the nation he had learnt from his mistakes. He acknowledged this was 'the moment of maximum risk' because a wrong step might cause a second spike. The key was to keep the reproduction rate – known as R – under one. The R rate represented the number of infections that were being passed on by infected people to others at a particular time. If R went over the key number 'one', then each infected person was passing the virus on to more than one other, and if it was kept lower than 'one' it would be transmitted to fewer people until it started petering out. Johnson spoke with conviction about the consequences of failing to contain the virus: 'We must recognise the risk of a second spike, the risk of losing control of that virus and letting the reproduction rate go back over one. That would mean not only a new wave of death and disease but also an economic disaster.' He went on to say that: 'We would be forced once again to slam on the brakes across the whole country and the whole economy and reimpose restrictions in such a way as to do more and lasting damage. So I know it is tough and I want to get this economy moving as fast as I can. But I refuse to throw away all the effort and the sacrifice of the British people and to risk a second major outbreak and huge loss of life and the overwhelming of the NHS.'

It was the same argument that Raab had made the previous week. A failure to maintain a grip on infections would leave Britain once again in the worst of all worlds, with escalating deaths forcing another economically disastrous lockdown. Johnson – at least on this Monday morning in April – seemed to have grasped this crucial point.

The government had laid down five conditions that had to be met before the lockdown was eased: ensuring NHS critical care capacity could cope with future demand; registering a sustained and consistent fall in the daily death rate; guaranteeing there would be sufficient supplies of tests and PPE; having confidence there would be no risk of a second peak; and seeing a decrease in the rate of infection to manageable levels. Although the wording was vague and there were no precise targets, most of these conditions were still a good distance from being achieved, including the last one.

That day, 4,310 people tested positive for the virus in the UK – double the number in other major European countries. By comparison, 1,195 positive tests were recorded in France that day, 1,739 in Italy, 1,295 in Spain and 1,144 in Germany. In fact, an estimation of the actual number of infections at the time by Imperial College London paints a much worse picture. Imperial's scientists have calculated that there were 23,000 new infections in Britain that day, which meant that there was a long way to go before restrictions could be safely lifted. In Europe, France was the next highest with 11,000 infections, followed by Italy with 8,400, Spain with 7,400 and Germany with 5,800. They had all locked down earlier than the UK and were reaping the benefits, but still considered infection rates too high to release their lockdowns. The UK had even further to go.

Amid all the gloom and death there was one ray of light for the prime minister. Two days later he was back in hospital again, but for happier reasons. His girlfriend Carrie Symonds had given birth to their son, Wilfred Lawrie Nicholas, at University College Hospital in London. The 'Nicholas' was a tribute to the two doctors credited with saving Johnson's life three weeks before: Dr Nick Price and Dr Nick Hart. Wilfred was Johnson's sixth child or, at least, as far as he has publicly acknowledged. He had been very protective of his complicated private life.

There was one other morale-boosting event that had won the nation's heart. Thursday 30 April was the 100th birthday of a war veteran called Captain Thomas Moore. He had started walking with a wheeled frame around his 25-metre garden in Marston Moretaine, Bedfordshire, more than three weeks earlier, with the initial object of raising £1,000 for the NHS. But plucky Captain Tom had become a media sensation. His efforts broke all records for a single-handed charity fundraising effort. That day there was a Royal Air Force flypast to celebrate his extraordinary achievement in raising £32 million. He was knighted by the Queen – although sadly he would later die after catching the virus.

As May began, it was the day of reckoning for Matt Hancock, the health secretary. He had staked his reputation on an ambitious target: the promise that 100,000 coronavirus tests would be carried out in Britain daily by the end of April. So when he strode to the podium at the press briefing on 1 May there was a certain amount of tension in the room. The target was daunting and there had been much speculation about how he was going to wriggle out of this one if the number was to fall short. But there was a bounce in his step and he began with a liberal use of the first-person pronoun 'I', which suggested he was confident.

'At the beginning of last month I set a goal,' he said, pausing for emphasis, 'that anyone who needs a test should get a test and that as a nation we should reach 100,000 tests per day by the end of the month.' He raised his hands expressively. 'I knew this was an audacious goal, but we needed an audacious goal because testing is so important.' Nobody would disagree. 'I can announce that we have,' he said, missing a beat for dramatic effect, 'met our goal.' He kept a straight face, but he was clearly fighting the urge to punch the air and jig around the room. In case anyone was confused over whether it was his personal triumph, he added modestly: 'It's not my achievement, it is a national achievement.'

The figures announced by Hancock actually smashed the target. He proclaimed that there had been 122,347 tests on the last day of April. However, it was not completely straightforward. It was revealed that only 83,000 tests had been actually carried out that day and the number had been padded out with test kits that had been posted to households and satellite testing locations. Ed Davey, acting leader of the Liberal Democrats, pointed out that Hancock's target 'was always a hostage to fortune, and the truth is, he missed it'. It was disappointing, he said, that the government had chosen to 'massage the metrics', as this undermined public confidence. In fact, there would be questioning of the testing figures even when the number of actual tests did pass 100,000 a day three weeks later. The government drew a lot of criticism for distorting the figures in this way, and the truth is there had been no need for all the jiggery-pokery. Hancock's initiative had ramped up testing almost seven-fold from a starting point of 11,000 tests a day at the beginning of the month. Even at 83,000, it was actually a great personal achievement for the health secretary, who had stuck his neck out and made it happen.

The tension in government in those early days of May concerned when and how the lockdown should be eased. Johnson was coming under increased pressure from his backbenchers to open up the country again. The email inboxes of Tory MPs were stacking up with messages from businesses in their constituencies complaining about the financial pain the restrictions were causing. That weekend, Andrew Rawnsley, the *Observer*'s political commentator, neatly summarised the delicate balancing act that would be required of the prime minister. 'Attempting to ease out of restrictions without reigniting the epidemic will be both the most uncertain and most perilous phase of this crisis,' he said. 'The decisions he makes are ones that will define how he is judged by history. Get it right and he may or may not be rewarded with some public credit. Get it wrong and the blame will likely chase him all the way to the next election.'[1]

Johnson wanted to please his backbenchers and was fighting against his libertarian instincts to lift the lockdown. Two days later, on Tuesday 5 May, the opponents of the restrictions had a small victory when the reputation of the man regarded as the architect of the lockdown was tarnished. Elements of the press had been questioning the work of Professor Neil Ferguson, whose infection modelling team at Imperial University had been influential in forcing Johnson to bring in the lockdown. They trawled through his previous research going back decades, raising questions over the accuracy of his work. Ferguson had become a major media commentator and a powerful voice on Sage since the beginning of the pandemic, and it was a legitimate journalistic inquiry. But in many ways he had been one of the heroes of the outbreak, helping to save many thousands of lives by demonstrating the severity of the crisis. Then, the opponents of lockdown were given a gift.

It was a classic British newspaper scoop. There was some sex, a degree of foolishness and a little hypocrisy. The *Daily Telegraph* reported that Ferguson had been receiving visits at his home from his 'married lover' in contravention of the lockdown restrictions.[2] The paper detailed how his friend Antonia Staats had travelled across London from her family home on 30 March and 8 April to visit the 51-year-old epidemiologist.

Ferguson immediately accepted that it was an error of judgement to have broken the very social distancing measures he was so keen to promote. In his defence, he said he had already contracted and recovered from the virus before the first liaison and believed he was immune. But the lockdown rules made no exceptions for people who had survived the virus – not least because there was no clear evidence at the time that infection conferred full immunity. His principled instant resignation, however, would be in stark contrast to the way another central figure guiding the government's virus policy would behave when caught out bending the rules.

The downfall of Professor Ferguson was certainly useful that day in distracting the public from some bad news for the government. On 5 May Britain's official death toll overtook Italy's to become the worst on the continent and the second worst in the world, behind only the United States. There had been 29,427 reported deaths in the UK compared with Italy's 29,029. In early March, it had been imperative that Britain should avoid ending up in the same situation as Italy. The horrifying advance of the disease in Lombardy had given Britain the advantage of an early warning at a time when the prevalence of the virus here was still relatively low. On 25 March, two days after Johnson had finally introduced the lockdown, Piers Morgan asked Robert Jenrick on ITV's *Good Morning Britain*: 'How are you going to feel if the UK death rate explodes like it has done in Italy because you simply didn't lock down the country properly and because you allowed non-essential workers to all stream out to work. Will you feel responsible as a government for that?' Jenrick replied: 'We believe we're taking the right judgements at the right moment. Of course, we'll only know if that was right in due course.'

The 29,427 deaths meant it was now judgement day and the verdict was damning, especially from the overseas press. The Italian daily newspaper *Corriere della Serra* described a British 'nightmare from which you cannot awake, but in which you landed because of your own fault or stupidity'. The newspaper's opinion writer Beppe Severgnini lambasted the British government for losing 'the advantage that fate and Italy gave it – for example, the first two weeks of the outbreak in Italy when it was obvious the virus was spreading'. The UK government 'did not pay enough attention to what was happening here, while Germany responded very well', he said. The UK's Irish neighbours were scathing. 'Ministers of slim talent have bumbled through daily briefings and now big-business Conservative donors are impatient to reverse a shutdown so contrary to Brexiteer dreams,' Fionnuala O'Connor wrote in the *Irish News* newspaper. 'Boris Johnson needs all his showman's tricks now to sell the phasing out of a lockdown which was less than effective, at least in part, because of his stubborn libertarianism.'

And the criticism went on. Greece's progressive daily newspaper *Ethnos* described Johnson as 'more dangerous than coronavirus', saying one of the crisis's greatest tragedies was that 'incompetent leaders' such as Johnson and Donald Trump were 'at the helm at a time of such emergency'. Criticising Britain's herd immunity policy in March, the columnist Giorgos Skafidas wrote that Johnson 'had gone out and essentially asked Britons … to accept death'. In Australia, the prime minister Scott Morrison pointed out that all countries that had attempted herd immunity had failed to achieve it. He described the strategy as a 'death sentence'. Mike Rann, a former Australian high commissioner to Britain, told the *Sydney Morning Herald* that Britain had 'handled the earliest stages negligently', lamenting 'a shambles of mixed messaging, poor organisation and a complacent attitude that what was happening in Italy wouldn't happen here'.[3]

The government needed to offer some hope. While they were still suffering the fall-out from Britain being top of the wrong type of league table, newspapers were being briefed by Downing Street that lockdown restrictions would begin to be lifted the following week. The *Sun*'s front page on the morning of Thursday 7 May read simply 'HAPPY MONDAY' and the *Daily Mail* enthused 'HURRAH! LOCKDOWN FREEDOM

BECKONS'. Since there were 5,613 positive tests across the country that day, and close to 14,000 estimated total infections, this was a dangerous idea. Britain's infection numbers were significantly higher than those recorded in every other major European country. The country with the closest number of infections was France, which was estimated to have 7,000 that day – half of Britain's total. If anything, the briefings by the government were an attempt to buy time with those in the party who wanted the lockdown to be lifted. Later that day, Dominic Raab, now back in his role as foreign secretary, cautioned that 'any changes in the short term will be modest, small, incremental and very carefully monitored'. He said: 'If we find in the future the R level goes back up or that people aren't following the rules, we must have the ability then to put back measures in place.'

So the new changes announced by Johnson in a pre-recorded video statement on Sunday 10 May were an attempt to signal a way out of lockdown. In the course of the 13-minute video, Johnson introduced his new plan for the country. It was illustrated by a coloured block chart, which looked something like a teaching aid used to help primary school children learn to count. For those who were sitting still and following this new initiative dreamt up by the government's top brains, the red 'number five' block at the top signified the worst alert level in which hospitals were overwhelmed by the virus, and the green 'number one' block at the bottom was an infection-free country. Britain was currently at orange 'four' and, because the nation had been so well behaved, Johnson said the country was 'now in a position to move, in steps, to level three'. He did not explain what level three actually was, although it was clearly coloured yellow and it appeared to rely on the R rate remaining below one. At the time, R may be hovering just below one, he warned. The prime minister said he wanted everyone to 'stay alert' and 'follow the rules' as they went from orange to yellow.

If this was a little confusing, his proposal to keep reducing infections by phasing in relaxations of the lockdown rules was even more so. The major announcement was an instruction that people whose jobs could not be done at home – such as construction and manufacturing employees – should return to work the following morning. 'Work from home if you can, but you should go to work if you can't work from home,' Johnson ordered, while adding that these people should avoid using public transport to get there. That was not going to be possible for many of those workers. This section of the speech was later satirised by the comedian Matt Lucas in a clip that went viral. 'So we are saying, don't go to work, go to work. Don't take public transport, go to work, don't go to work. Stay indoors, if you can go to work, don't go to work. Go outside, don't go outside. And then we will or won't, something or other.' But there was a serious point. Encouraging more people to go back to work was a big change of emphasis and would send the R rate up. People would also be allowed to exercise as much as they liked outside rather than just once per day. This would inevitably lead to people spending more time outdoors, bumping into friends and mingling, even though this was not strictly allowed. Although the risk from outdoor meetings was comparatively small, the combination of these measures would send the R rate up rather than down.

Johnson had a roadmap for easing restrictions in the future if R was controlled. There would be a 'Step two', he said, that would include the reopening of some shops and the return of school pupils at the beginning of June if all went well. Then 'Step three' would be to allow the reopening of the hospitality industry, maybe in a couple of months' time. These were major moves and the scientists wanted each step to be taken individually and slowly so that their effects on infection rates could be assessed. Indeed, Johnson seemed to have accepted that this would be a process determined by scientific monitoring of the effects such measures would have on infections. 'Throughout this period of the next two months we will be driven not by mere hope or economic necessity,' he said; 'we are going to be driven by the science, the data and public health.'

He closed the speech with a new slogan, 'Stay alert, control the virus, save lives', which marked the abandonment of the oft-repeated 'Stay at home, protect the NHS, save lives' that had become so familiar over previous weeks. Unfortunately, this instantly forgettable new slogan did not go down as well as Johnson had hoped. The leaders of Scotland, Wales and Northern Ireland deemed his 'Stay alert' slogan to be a bad idea and stuck with the more cautious 'Stay at home'. Scotland's first minister Nicola Sturgeon was withering about the new wording: 'For Scotland right now, given the fragility of the progress we've made, given the critical point that we are at, then it would be catastrophic for me to drop the "Stay at home" message ... I don't know what "Stay alert" means.' She was not alone in her confusion. Johnson's speech was panned by political commentators as rushed and slightly garbled. Some questioned whether he was back to full health.

Meanwhile, the government had found a solution to all the bad publicity surrounding the country's record high death rate for Europe. On Wednesday 13 May, with no explanation, it dropped the graph comparing the UK's death toll with other countries from its Downing Street media briefings. It had been a constant feature of the briefings previously. At Prime Minister's Questions, Keir Starmer held up a print-out of the government's country comparison chart and said: 'A version of this slide has been shown at the Downing Street press conference every day since 30 March – that's seven weeks. Yesterday, the government stopped publishing the international comparison and the slide is gone. Why?' Johnson was combative. 'The UK has been going through an unprecedented once-in-a-century epidemic, and he seeks to make comparisons with other countries,' seemingly overlooking the point that his own government had been doing so for weeks. He argued that the figures were 'premature because the correct and final way of making these comparisons will be when we have all the excess death totals for all the relevant countries'.

The Office for National Statistics would later report the UK's excess death toll as 49,700 by that day – 50 per cent higher than the government's official figure for virus deaths. The statistics body would also find that England had the highest levels of excess mortality of any country in Europe over the first six months of the year. Starmer said it was obvious the government had stopped talking publicly about the figures because they showed the UK was in an 'unenviable place'. He added: 'Dropping the comparisons means dropping the learning and that's the real risk.' Johnson responded: 'We're watching intently what is happening in other countries and it is very notable that in some other countries where relaxations have been introduced there's signs of the R going up again – and that's a very clear warning to us not to proceed too fast or too recklessly.'

The prime minister had made it clear that he was placing public health ahead of short-term economic concerns, but he was being pressed to do something about the country's financial position. Lockdown was costing the Treasury an awful lot of money. That week, Rishi Sunak, the chancellor, extended the UK's furlough scheme until October. Under the scheme, the government covered 80 per cent of employees' monthly wages up to £2,500 if they were unable to work because of lockdown restrictions. Many employers joined the scheme because they might otherwise have gone out of business or be forced to lay off staff. It was so popular that a quarter of the workforce – some 7.5 million people – were receiving their wages indirectly from the government through the scheme at a cost to the taxpayer of £14 billion a month. The Office for Budget Responsibility had forecast that the total cost of combating the effects of the pandemic in the UK up to that point in May was £123.2bn, with annual borrowing estimated to be 15.2 per cent of the UK economy. This figure was the highest annual borrowing since the end of the Second World War, when it stood at 22.1 per cent.

But the economy could only get going again if the virus was controlled – a point both Johnson and Raab has acknowledged in the previous two weeks. By now, the world's leading economists were crunching the numbers and were also concluding that suppressing the virus down to low levels was better for lives and the economy. The World Bank had scrutinised the outcomes of the different approaches to the pandemic taken by governments across the world and had produced a report entitled 'The Sooner, the Better: The Early Economic Impact of Non-Pharmaceutical Interventions during the COVID-19 Pandemic'. The economists' conclusion was clear from the report's name. They found that countries in Europe and central Asia that had acted earlier to stem the virus's spread and hold infections down at low levels had, as a result, suffered less damage to their economies and fewer deaths. Locking down early was a win-win strategy. The report stated: 'The results suggest that the sooner non-pharmaceutical interventions are implemented, the better are the economic and health outcomes.'

Unfortunately, Britain was an example of how costly it was to have done exactly the opposite. The UK's late lockdown meant it not only had Europe's worst death toll during the outbreak, but also suffered the continent's deepest recession. It really was the worst of all worlds. Between April and June, the UK's GDP dropped by 19.8 per cent compared with the previous quarter – a slump deeper than any other European or North American country and twice as bad as the United States and Germany. It was the worst recession since the government started keeping records in 1955 and it took the British economy back to the size it was in 2003. These dismal figures were impossible to reconcile with the repeated claims by ministers that the government had made the 'right decisions, at the right time'.

In contrast, the benefits of locking down early were plain to see in Australasia, Asia and the rest of Europe. Britain's fellow

Commonwealth island nation New Zealand had locked down on 25 March when it had recorded a total of just 189 confirmed cases and no deaths. Seven weeks later it had suffered just 21 deaths from the virus compared with the UK's 45,000. At the beginning of that week – on Monday 18 May – the country had managed to record no new Covid-19 cases, yet the lockdown was still being maintained. Jacinda Ardern, New Zealand's prime minister, would lift all restrictions in early June, but only after reporting zero new Covid cases for more than two straight weeks. Ardern told reporters she did 'a little dance' when she was told the country no longer had any active virus cases. The economic cost of the ruthless 'Covid Zero' approach had been a 12.2 per cent drop in GDP between April and June, but the country could now begin the repair work. 'Not only have we protected New Zealanders' health but we now have a head start on our economic recovery,' Ardern said. 'We have become one of the most open economies in the world.'

It was a similar story in Australia, which also swiftly brought in lockdown measures on 23 March with daily cases in the mid-hundreds. On 18 May, just nine positive cases were recorded in Australia, which had suffered only 98 deaths. Between April and June, its GDP dropped by just 7 per cent – almost three times less than the UK – because it had been able to lift restrictions more safely as the virus was at such low levels. The outcomes were just as good for countries in the Asia Pacific, which had taken swift action to curtail the virus. South Korea recorded only 15 new cases on 18 May and had lost only 263 people to the virus. Its GDP shrank by 3.2 per cent in the year's second quarter. Taiwan recorded zero cases, seven deaths and a 5.5 per cent drop in GDP over the same timeframe.

Even China had benefited from acting swiftly and decisively at the end of January. Daily positive cases in China had been reduced to double figures before the UK's lockdown. There was no doubt that there was significant under-reporting in China and its death toll was certainly higher than the official figure of

4,634. But the Chinese had suppressed the virus ruthlessly. The country's GDP dropped by 9.8 per cent between January and March compared with the previous quarter, but then grew 11.5 per cent between April and June, which was a clear demonstration of how an economy could bounce back after adopting an eradication strategy. The picture was more mixed in Europe, but some countries brought the virus to heel using similar methods. Norway locked down 11 days before Britain on a day when it had recorded 212 positive tests. By 18 May, there were just eight cases of infection a day and by then the country had lost just 232 people to the virus. Norway's drop in GDP of 6.3 per cent between April and June was around half the 11.9 per cent plummet seen on average across the European Union. It was a similar story in Finland, which registered just 298 deaths and saw its GDP fall by 4.5 per cent. The severity of the outbreak in those countries was a world away from that experienced by their shared neighbour Sweden, which had famously shunned a full lockdown in favour of more relaxed social distancing measures. Sweden suffered more than ten times the number of deaths as well as an 8.6 per cent GDP drop in the year's second quarter.

The international comparisons all pointed to a simple successful formula. The best way to tackle the virus was to act fast and then rigorously maintain restrictions until infections had been stamped out or were mostly eradicated. This allowed countries to avoid a second economically ruinous nationwide lockdown by managing tiny isolated outbreaks using local restrictions and track and trace programmes. A leading member of the Sage committee would later tell us: 'Many other countries basically kept their cases low. They had the same lockdown measures as us but they put them in place earlier than us and they kept the cases low. And they've had less of an impact on their economy. You do less damage to your economy and you save a lot more lives.'

Many of Britain's major European neighbours did not pursue a scorched earth policy on the virus, but their economies did suffer less as a result of locking down earlier. The drops in GDP in the second quarter of 2020 were: Britain minus 19.8 per cent; Spain minus 18.5 per cent; France minus 13.8 per cent; Italy minus 12.4 per cent; and Germany minus 10.1 per cent. By 18 May, the four major powers had all begun loosening restrictions by reopening non-essential shops despite the virus's continued prevalence. France had 492 positive tests that day, Italy 451, Spain 431 and Germany 513. Britain was lifting a major plank of lockdown by encouraging people to go back to work despite recording 2,684 infections on the same day. There were huge pressures on the European leaders to reboot their stricken economies and release their populations from isolation – especially as they could see countries on the other side of the world returning to a semblance of normality. But there was a grave danger of compounding the mistakes of March and starting a second wave of infections. And Britain, which had at least five times more people testing positive than the other major European countries, would be taking the greatest risk of all if it relaxed restrictions too soon.

By the middle of the third week of May, the government's slide in popularity was gathering apace. It was being battered on several fronts. First, there was a public outcry about the highly controversial decision to charge foreign health and social care workers a fee to use the NHS. On Wednesday 20 May the prime minister defended the surcharge as 'the right way forward' to boost NHS funds, seemingly overlooking the fact that many of those workers had risked their lives to prop up the ailing health-care service at the height of the outbreak. However, the decision was reversed the very next day when Johnson appeared to emerge from his temporary amnesia and remembered that it had been foreign health workers who had helped save his own life. The prime minister 'had been a personal beneficiary of carers from abroad', a Downing Street spokesman said in an effort to explain the U-turn.

Then there was yet another matter arising from Johnson's private life. It was mixed news. The Independent Office for

Police Conduct (IOPC) found that there was insufficient evidence to launch a full criminal inquiry over the Jennifer Arcuri scandal. However, it suggested that Johnson may have violated the code of conduct of the Greater London Authority (GLA). This meant that the GLA would now resume its investigation into his failure to declare his relationship with the American businesswoman, which spanned four years while he was the London mayor. The IOPC investigators had been examining how Arcuri was given privileged access to his official trade missions and received thousands of pounds of public money from a body Johnson had been responsible for as the mayor. They had found evidence that confirmed the prime minister had enjoyed an 'intimate relationship' with Arcuri and this had influenced officials who were considering her applications for grants and whether she should be allowed to accompany him on foreign trips. It was now the turn of the GLA to determine whether Johnson's conduct deserved censure.

And third, Dominic Cummings was in the doghouse. On Friday 22 May a joint investigation by the *Guardian* and *Mirror* claimed that Durham police had spoken to Cummings about 'breaching lockdown rules' after he had been spotted at his parents' home at the end of March. They quoted the witness who had seen Cummings in his parents' driveway on 5 April after hearing the Abba song. 'I was really annoyed,' the witness said. 'I thought, it's OK for you to drive all the way up to Durham and escape from London. I sympathise with him wanting to do that, but other people are not allowed to do that. It's one rule for Dominic Cummings and one rule for the rest of us.'[4]

The next day, the Downing Street press office said Cummings had acted in the interests of his child and had kept within coronavirus guidelines. Otherwise, No. 10 was in full denial mode to muddy the waters. 'Yesterday [Friday] the *Mirror* and *Guardian* wrote inaccurate stories about Mr Cummings ... We will not waste our time answering a stream of false allegations about Mr Cummings from campaigning newspapers.'

But the story was broadly true insofar as it revealed for the first time that Cummings had made the 264-mile trip to Durham at a time when his government was instructing people not to travel and to stay in their family homes. It turned out the inaccuracy had been that Durham police had spoken to Cummings's father on the phone about security for the prime minister's chief adviser rather than lockdown rules. It was the transport secretary Grant Shapps's misfortune to take the virus media briefing that Saturday. Shapps attempted to dismiss the issue by claiming Cummings had 'stayed put' on his parent's farm and his family had remained in isolation after arriving in Durham. 'The decision here was to go to that location and stay in that location,' he said. 'They didn't then move around from there.' While Shapps appeared understanding, there was less comfort offered by the previously amenable deputy chief medical officer, Dr Jenny Harries, who was standing at his side in the briefing. When asked whether people were permitted to travel with the virus, she said: 'If you're symptomatic, you stay at home, take yourself out of society as quickly as you can and stay there, unless there's extreme risk to life.'

The story took a further twist as a result of Shapps's comments. Robin Lees, a 71-year-old retired chemistry teacher, had been watching the media briefing and couldn't believe that Shapps was claiming that Cummings had 'stayed put' on the farm. He rang the newspapers to say he definitely recalled having spotted Cummings at Barnard Castle on Easter Sunday. 'I was a bit gobsmacked to see him, because I know what he looks like,' he told the *Guardian*. 'And the rest of the family seemed to match – a wife and child. I was pretty convinced it was him and it didn't seem right because I assumed he would be in London.'[5] The following day Johnson did his best to play down the matter at the Sunday afternoon press conference. He argued that Cummings had 'acted responsibly, legally and with integrity' and had 'no alternative' but to travel for childcare 'when both he and his wife were about to be incapacitated by coronavirus'.

However, he managed to skip answering questions about the sighting of Cummings in Barnard Castle.

The story did not go away that easily. The front page of the *Daily Mail* the next morning, a Monday bank holiday, raged: 'As Boris brazenly backs No 10 svengali who flouted PM's own strict lockdown rules, the question the whole country is asking … WHAT PLANET ARE THEY ON?' So that afternoon an extraordinary drama took place in the Rose Garden of No. 10 Downing Street. It was one of those pleasant sunny days that had made lockdown more tolerable in the early months of summer. A select group of reporters were sitting quietly on socially distanced chairs opposite a plain functional desk and a red chair that had been positioned in front of the shrubbery. They waited for 30 minutes after the scheduled start until Dominic Cummings glided silently across the lawn and sat on the chair for his first public media interrogation since becoming the prime minister's adviser. His voice was surprisingly soft, with a slight Northumbrian lilt, despite his fearsome reputation. 'Hi there, sorry I'm late,' he said. As one commentator noted later, that was the only apology Cummings would make for his actions over the whole hour of questioning. With his glowing white shirt hanging loosely from his thin frame, he had the air of a Jesuit priest who had come to confront the non-believers, armed with only his intelligence and a faith in his own righteousness.

His long opening statement was clearly the result of much thought, as it cleverly avoided most of the obvious pitfalls. On Friday 27 March he had rushed home to attend to his wife Mary, who was vomiting, he said. According to the rules, he should then have remained at home and isolated if he thought that his wife had the virus. Public Health England guidance, published in mid-March, specified that the infected person and 'all other household members who remain well must stay at home and not leave the house for 14 days'. But he said his wife had no cough or fever and she 'urged' him to go back to work at Downing Street. By the evening, he feared that his wife might have the virus and he thought there was a 'distinct probability' that he too might be infected given that those around him in Downing Street, including the prime minister, were dropping like flies. Since, he claimed, there was no childcare available in London, he drove to an 'isolated cottage' on his parents' farm where his sister and two children could look after his son if he and his wife fell ill. He made clear that he had driven 'non-stop', therefore avoiding questions over whether this car full of infected people from London might have spread the disease in a motorway service station.

His justification for not staying at home was a masterstroke. He had found a loophole in the lockdown guidance, which said: 'We are aware that not all these measures will be possible if you are living with children, but keep following this guidance to the best of your ability.' However, his explanation for the drive to Barnard Castle with his family after they had recovered two weeks later would be greeted with derision. He said his wife was worried about the long journey back to London, particularly as his 'eyesight seemed to have been affected by the disease'. So they took a half-hour trip to the 'outskirts' of Barnard Castle to see if he could drive safely. This seemed either implausible or reckless, given the dangers of driving any distance with suspect eyesight, especially with a young child in the car. It was also unclear why his wife would not have driven in such an eventuality.

After his statement, the reporters went one by one to a microphone in the garden and stood as his accusers, asking him if he understood that for the millions of people who obeyed the lockdown rules it seemed like one rule for Cummings and one rule for them. ITV's Robert Peston pointed out that Cummings's actions had undermined the lockdown. 'Your own scientists are worried, and they said this last night: that by introducing an element of personal discretion into the interpretation of the rules you are putting lives at risk,' he said. But Cummings did not give any ground. He conceded that 'reasonable people may well disagree about how I thought about what to do in the circumstances', but was defiant: 'I don't regret what I did … I think what I did was actually reasonable in these circumstances.' He added that he had 'not considered' resigning. The next day, the ITV *Good Morning Britain* presenter, Piers Morgan, summed up the public mood when he said: 'He broke the rules. We know it. Everyone knows it.' Cummings' eyesight test drive was mocked on social media with memes using the Specsavers logo with a slight tweak of its famous catchphrase: 'Should have gone to Barnard Castle.'

The most immediate fall-out from the events in the Rose Garden was the resignation of Douglas Ross, a junior minister in the Scottish Office. He published an open letter criticising the prime minister's chief adviser. 'I have constituents who didn't get to say goodbye to loved ones; families who could not mourn together; people who didn't visit sick relatives because they were following the guidance of the government,' he wrote. 'I cannot in good faith tell them they were all wrong and one senior adviser to the government was right.' On Wednesday 27 May the prime minister appeared before the parliamentary liaison committee, where he was attacked for supporting Cummings by Pete Wishart, a Scottish National Party MP. 'Can I start by saying to you that I actually think you have been quite brave – brave in the way that you have been prepared to sacrifice the credibility and popularity of your own government just to stand by your man,' he said. 'You have done something I have never seen done in the 20 years I have been in the House; you have somehow managed to unite a nation in condemnation and indignation over your handling of Mr Cummings.' He added: 'Eighty per cent of the British public now think Dominic Cummings broke the rules; 63 per cent said you should sack him. But the most worrying thing, Prime Minister, is that 65 per cent say his conduct makes it less likely that the public will now follow lockdown rules. Surely, Prime Minister, no man is more important than keeping this nation safe.' Johnson 'respectfully' disagreed and said it was time to move on. Four days later, Ruth May, England's chief nurse, was dropped from the Downing Street media briefing after refusing to back Cummings in practice questions during a rehearsal beforehand.[6] It clearly remained a sore point at the top of government.

If ever a distraction was needed, it was that week. The prime minister had just the thing. On Thursday 28 May he announced that all five of his tests had already been fulfilled so the lockdown could be eased further. Primary school pupils could return after the weekend, outdoor markets and car showrooms would be allowed to open, and six people from different households would be permitted to meet outside. In addition, all shops could return to business on 15 June. It was puzzling that the five tests could have been met so quickly. But the tests were so broad and undefined, the government could mark its own homework in any way it wished. That evening, Professor Devi Sridhar, the chair of Global Public Health at the University of Edinburgh, tweeted: 'Looking at the estimates for daily new cases in England (8K/day), the openings of shops/schools on Monday, watching carefully what's happening in East Asia & combining this with what we know so far about this virus – feels like mistakes are being repeated from early March.'

The measures were being relaxed before a proper contact tracing system was in place. More than 25,000 tracers had been hired for the tracing system – jobs that essentially involved ringing people who were found to have been in contact with an infected person and instructing them to place themselves under 14-day quarantine. But on the day of the prime minister's announcement, Dido Harding, head of the track and trace programme, had admitted to MPs the system wouldn't be fully operational for weeks. Labour MP Ben Bradshaw tweeted: 'Dido Harding just told me on an MPs' conference call that Test, Trace & Isolate won't be fully operational at local level till the end of June. Not sure where that leaves Johnson's promise of a fully operational "world beating" system by Monday.' Indeed, the hastily assembled track and trace programme was becoming a repeated headache for the government. Dr Jenny Harries was asked a couple of days later how people could be sure calls from test and trace operatives were genuine and not a scam. She replied that it would be obvious because the callers would sound 'professional'. The comment was unfortunate. Nazir Afzal, a former chief prosecutor in north-west England, tweeted: 'I spent a lifetime prosecuting people speaking professionally while taking your money & your lives.'

As the month of June began, Hancock's jiggery-pokery with the 100,000 test figure a month earlier had not been forgotten. He was given a dressing-down by the normally uncontroversial UK Statistics Authority. On Tuesday 2 June the authority's chair, Sir David Norgrove, wrote to Hancock criticising the way the testing figures had been presented. 'The aim seems to be to show the largest possible number of tests, even at the expense of understanding,' he wrote. The letter pointed out that the figures had been totted up by misleadingly combining actual tests that had taken place with those that had merely been posted out to people. This had been one of the key criticisms of the way Hancock had presented the 100,000 figure. Norgrove said the figures used in the press briefings gave 'an artificially low impression of the proportion of tests returning a positive diagnosis'. This, he said, fell 'well short' of the statistics code of practice that Hancock claimed to support.

The government's eagerness to give the impression the country was returning to normal again extended to parliament. Jacob Rees-Mogg, the Leader of the Commons, forced MPs to return to London that Tuesday to vote on his proposal to make them come into parliament when legislation was being passed. Since parliament had returned after the Easter recess, many MPs had been contributing to debates via Zoom and voting online. But Rees-Mogg wanted everyone to attend, even if they were shielding due to an underlying illness that made them more vulnerable to the virus. 'Voting while enjoying a sunny walk or whilst watching television does democracy an injustice,' Rees-Mogg told parliament. 'We ask members to vote in person for a reason: because it is the heart of what parliament is about.' The move prompted fury from parliamentarians, who accused Rees-Mogg of heightening the risk of another outbreak in Westminster and disenfranchising vulnerable MPs. The logistics of observing the two-metre social distancing rule in the Commons while voting created a 'coronavirus conga' in which 523 politicians had to form a queue stretching for hundreds of metres. The queue snaked across the courtyards of the Palace of Westminster and under the road to Portcullis House's glass atrium. The vote passed with a government majority but the continued outrage persuaded ministers to later climb down and allow proxy votes for those with medical issues.

It wasn't the only U-turn the government had to make in those early days of June. The opening of primary schools on the Monday that week had not been a success. So far, the call back to school had only been for reception classes and years one and six, but the plan was for all primary pupils to be in school before the summer holidays. Head teachers, school staff unions and parents had all expressed concern that insufficient time had been given to turn the classrooms into Covid-safe environments. There was, after all, only just over a month remaining before the holidays. By the end of the week, half the schools had complied with the order to open, but only 11 per cent of pupils had returned, which was just a quarter of those who should have been back in the classroom. The following week, the education secretary Gavin Williamson would be forced to announce that the government was abandoning the plans for all primary schools to reopen. Instead, he said that the government would be 'working to bring all children back to school in September', when secondary schools would also be opening.

The concern that Britain was moving too fast with the easing of lockdown was growing. On Friday 5 June a letter from the

Faculty for Public Health had been published in the *British Medical Journal* arguing that it was dangerously premature to relax restrictions, and calling instead for a zero-Covid strategy. 'Several countries – notably New Zealand, Taiwan and South Korea – have managed to reduce the daily number of new cases to zero. That enabled them to respond quickly and effectively to any fresh infections. With powerful mechanisms for surveillance and control in place, their populations are now able to enjoy the economic, social, and health benefits of largely returning to normal life,' the letter said. It went on to argue that the successful countries did not start 'to relax their control measures until the number of new cases was low and falling'. Whereas England, on the other hand, had begun to release its lockdown when the number of new daily cases was falling but still high, the letter continued. 'We believe the urgent priority for the UK is to learn from the success of these countries by setting an objective of having no new community cases of Covid-19 as quickly as possible.'[7]

That evening, however, was the turning point. Johnson held a meeting with Rishi Sunak, the chancellor, and other key ministers that resulted in a decision to throw aside his cautious approach. *The Sunday Times*'s political editor Tim Shipman reported an important story that weekend that Johnson had ordered ministers to lift the lockdown quickly to avoid the possible jobs bloodbath. Johnson had been warned by Alok Sharma, the business secretary, earlier in the week that the failure to reopen the hospitality sector in time for the summer could cost up to 3.5 million jobs. A forecast had been made that some of the Conservatives 'Red Wall' seats in northern England would be among the worst affected by the mass unemployment. Johnson is said to have responded: 'Christ!' At the 5.30 p.m. meeting on Friday, Johnson agreed with Sunak a timetable of 'easements' to the lockdown rules, which would be rolled out over June and July.[8]

There was therefore a positive tone to the next big 'easement' press briefing on Wednesday 10 June in which Johnson breezed through diagrams showing how the country was 'still meeting' the five conditions. Essentially, the conditions were so vague that he only had to demonstrate that infections and deaths were on their way down and that testing had increased. As a result, Johnson confirmed that shops would open the following week along with zoos, drive-in cinemas and places of worship. However, Sir Patrick Vallance, the chief scientific adviser, took the first opportunity possible to puncture the optimism. 'The R is below one but perhaps only just below one, the epidemic is shrinking but not fast, numbers are coming down but they are not yet very low, and the vast majority of the population remains susceptible to this infection,' he warned. 'That urges caution, it urges going slowly with change, and it urges measuring very carefully to see the impact and being prepared to reverse things.'

The questions that day were a little awkward for Johnson. The reporters were effectively asking the prime minister whether he had killed 25,000 people. Two weeks earlier, the second of our investigations into the handling of the coronavirus crisis had revealed how Johnson had allowed more than a million extra infections to spread as he dithered in the last nine days before lockdown and this had been the key reason why Britain suffered the worst death toll in Europe. Professor Neil Ferguson had been asked about precisely this point in a select committee hearing with MPs that afternoon. His view on the subject was put to Johnson by the BBC's political editor Laura Kuenssberg. 'Neil Ferguson, one of the other scientists who was advising the government on lockdown, told MPs this afternoon that if it had been introduced earlier you would have reduced the final death toll by at least a half. Is he right?' she asked. Johnson passed the question to his scientific advisers and tried to move on, but Kuenssberg insisted he answer the question himself – to which he gave a stumbling reply, saying judgements could only be made 'in the fullness of time'. There was no respite, because Beth Rigby, the Sky political editor, returned to exactly the same question. 'Today Professor Ferguson said going into lockdown a week too late cost an estimated 25,000 lives or more,' she said. 'What is your biggest regret and what do you now wish you had done differently?' Johnson repeated his answer about such questions being 'premature'. Vallance, however, was honest. 'I'm sure there are certain things we will have got wrong. And we need to understand what they are, learn from them and get them right next time,' said the chief scientific adviser. Chris Whitty, the chief medical officer, said he regretted the lack of testing in the early stages. But Rigby would not let go. 'Do you not regret going into lockdown earlier ... given what you know now?' she asked the prime minister directly. Johnson again attempted to palm the question off by hiding behind his advisers. 'Well, I'm really going to have to go back to what Chris and Patrick have said.' To which Rigby instantly chipped in: 'But you're the politician. You make the decisions.'

Johnson's final answer was to blame the scientists, including Ferguson. 'We made the decisions at the time on the guidance of Sage, including Professor Ferguson, that we thought were right for this country,' he said. But Vallance would later tell a parliamentary committee that Sage had actually advised Johnson to lock down almost a week before he did so.

The cracks had been appearing between the scientists and the politicians – and more particularly between the prime minister and his chief advisers – for some time. Whitty and Vallance were asked directly whether they were concerned about the pace at which lockdown was being eased. They had no choice but to give diplomatic answers. Whitty accepted that there were risks, but, crucially, he seemed reassured by the fact that it would be possible to 'take a couple of steps back' and reinstate restrictions if the infection numbers were to suddenly increase. They did not know it at the time, but the government would be in no mood to go back on any of the national measures it released over the next three months.

The following weekend, on 14 June, *The Sunday Times* reported that Downing Street was keeping Whitty and Vallance on 'resignation watch'.[9] The prime minister's aides were concerned that the two most prominent scientists in Britain's fight against the virus might walk away over disagreements about the loosening of restrictions. In a clear reference to the frustrated pair, a Sage scientist was quoted as saying: 'We have had enough of being treated as human shields by the prime minister.' It was noticeable that, the next day, Raab appeared at the Downing Street media briefing on his own, unaccompanied by any scientists. His claim that the experts could not attend because they had 'a huge amount of other work to do' was met with scepticism. Sir Ed Davey, the Liberal Democrat's acting leader, sensed that something was wrong. 'The idea that senior experts in government are too busy to answer questions from the public and media is risible. The Conservatives are deliberately turning away from expert advice and, in doing so, dismantling any trust people have in this government.'[10]

This was, after all, the day of the opening of non-essential shops in England. The weekly average for positive tests at that time shows that there were approximately 1,300 each day. This was significantly higher than that of any other major European country at the point they lifted the same restriction. The Imperial College estimates suggest that the number of actual infections was much higher that Monday – around 6,900 new cases a day. Even the World Health Organization had urged caution the day before. The international body advised England to delay lifting its lockdown until its track and trace system was more 'robust and effective'. By now, data had shown that the government had failed to trace the contacts of a third of those testing positive in the system's first week. Dr Hans Kluge, the WHO director for Europe, said: 'The question of lifting the lockdown is as important as going into the lockdown. The key words here are to do it gradually. Do it carefully.'[11]

But the government was forging forward regardless. The following day, Johnson indicated that he might be amenable to relaxing the rule that was helping to reduce transmission of the virus by keeping people two metres apart. The proposal was to cut the distance to one metre. The drive behind the move was to help pubs, cafes and restaurants pack in more customers when they reopened – thereby helping to save some of the 3.5 million jobs in the hospitality sector that the business secretary had warned about. Sunak was seriously lobbying for the distance to be cut and had made his view known in Zoom chats with Tory backbenchers. But when Johnson had been asked about the issue the week before, he had said he wanted to be cautious because infection rates were too high.

However, by Tuesday 16 June the prime minister admitted that the decision was under review in response to a question at that day's press briefing from a member of the public called Trevor from Northamptonshire. Johnson said he fully under-stood the scientific advice was that two metres was safer. But he was softening on the point. 'It is also my view, and I think an increasingly widespread view,' Johnson said, 'that as we get the numbers down and the rate of infection down in the country, then the statistical likelihood, Trevor, of any of us actually being next to somebody – whether two metres or one metre or what-ever distance – who has coronavirus is going down the whole time.' There was a clear flaw in his logic. His scientists were advising that cutting social distancing down to one metre might mean that infections would rise again and therefore there would soon be a greater statistical likelihood of being next to someone with the virus. In fact, Sage had warned 12 days earlier that cutting social distancing down to one metre from two carried between two and ten times greater risk. Downing Street also had access to polling that suggested the majority of the public actually did not want the two-metre rule to be relaxed.[12]

Meanwhile, there was yet another U-turn by the government. Throughout lockdown the government had provided £15-a-week vouchers to less well-off families whose children would normally have received free meals if they had been at school. But the Department of Education had confirmed the vouchers would be withdrawn once the school holidays started. The day before, Marcus Rashford, the Manchester United football player, had written an open letter to MPs in which he drew on his own experience as a child growing up in poverty to impress upon the politicians how important it was to keep providing the vouchers during the holidays. The government had looked quite hard-hearted when Thérèse Coffey, the work and pensions secretary, tried to correct one of Rashford's tweets. He had written: 'When you wake up this morning and run your shower, take a second to think about parents who have had their water turned off during lockdown.' Coffey tweeted a little too cleverly, to say: 'Water cannot be disconnected though.' Rashford's reply was dignified but cutting. 'I'm concerned this is the only tweet of mine you acknowledged. Please, put rivalries aside for a second, and make a difference #maketheuturn,' he wrote. With a rebellion brewing on his backbenches over the issue, Johnson called Rashford personally that day to tell him the government had changed its mind and would continue to hand out the vouchers in the summer.

The screeching U-turns, the enormous death toll and the cavalier approach had not gone unnoticed by an increasingly disillusioned and wary public. Johnson's government was plunging in popularity, especially with regard to its handling of the virus. A YouGov poll found that the government had the joint lowest approval rating in the world over its handling of the pandemic. The British public took an even harsher view of Johnson's stewardship of the coronavirus response than the Americans did of their president Donald Trump, despite the death toll in the USA exceeding 110,000. Perhaps, the only slight consolation for the British prime minister was that the people of Mexico felt similarly aggrieved with their government. Both the UK and Mexico had net approval ratings of minus 15.

Trump's rating was minus 12. On the other hand, the countries that had maintained their lockdowns to try to eradicate the virus all had appreciative populations. Among the highest scorers were the governments of Taiwan (plus 87), Australia (plus 76), Norway (plus 67), Finland (plus 64) and Singapore (plus 61). The recently elected Labour leader Keir Starmer was already overtaking Johnson as the public's preferred choice as prime minister.[13] Rasmus Kleis Nielsen, director of the University of Oxford's Reuters Institute, said: 'I have never in 10 years of research in this area seen a drop in trust like what we have seen for the UK government in the course of six weeks.'[14]

The reputation for incompetence was difficult to shake off. Certainly, the contact tracing fiasco wasn't helping. On Thursday 17 June, the government announced it had abandoned its contact tracing app after spending three months and millions of pounds attempting to develop the technology. Ministers had insisted on using an untested method in which the details of people who fell ill were held on a centralised NHS database so that those who they had been in contact with could be automatically identified and told to self-isolate. But officials admitted the app had only recognised 4 per cent of contacts using Apple phones and 75 per cent of Google Android devices during testing on the Isle of Wight. Hancock was forced to make an embarrassing climbdown after initially championing the app. He announced that his department was now switching to an alternative designed by the US tech companies Apple and Google, which was months away from being ready.

By the final third of June, the scientists were urging caution, the R number was teetering on the brink of exceeding one and there was no proper contact tracing to fall back on if things went pear-shaped. But, nonetheless, the prime minister decided to roll the dice. It was time to open up everything and hope for the best. On Tuesday 23 June, Johnson went way beyond anything anyone expected when he announced the restrictions that would be loosened next. He declared that the anniversary of American independence, 4 July, would be the day of British liberation when the shackles of lockdown would be cast off. Pubs, bars, cafes, restaurants, theatres, cinemas, museums and galleries would all be opened at once. People would be able to get their lockdown pudding-bowl hair cut professionally, have weddings again, stay in hotels, or even head off to the caravan park. Families and cohabitors would be allowed to get together with friends as two households in one home with a limit of up to a dozen people. Johnson had gone the whole hog and had scrapped the two-metre rule by reducing social distancing to just one metre. It meant that more people could be packed indoors in hospitality venues and on public transport.

The *Daily Mail*'s front page the next day captured exactly the spirit Johnson was wishing to foster: 'Summer's back on – Boris unlocks nation and urges: go and enjoy yourselves.' Its mid-market rival the *Daily Express* gushed: 'Cheers Boris – Here's to a brighter future', supported by a photo of the prime minister holding a pint of beer aloft. The *Sun* christened 4 July 'Super Saturday' in an article published alongside a large photo of a man carrying more than a dozen pints of beer under the headline 'Vast Orders'. There was a note of caution in some of the other newspapers. The *Independent*'s headline 'Not risk free' quoted Vallance's comments from the previous day when he cautioned the public about the release of lockdown. While Vallance and Whitty had not directly criticised the boldness of the prime minister's decision, they had again put a dampener on the feel-good mood during Johnson's press briefing. Whitty had warned that it was very likely we would all have to live with the virus as a significant problem throughout winter and into spring. It wasn't going away if the government was intent on heading down this route.

Johnson had repeatedly stressed that it was important to move slowly and with great care since he returned to work following his recuperation two months earlier. So the lack of caution took some of the government's scientific advisers by surprise. They had wanted the measures to be released gradually one by one so that they could monitor infection rates and reverse any relaxation of the rules that seemed to cause an adverse effect. The leading Sage virus modelling expert, Professor John Edmunds, gave an interview to the *Guardian* that day express-ing great trepidation about the move.[15] 'Relaxing the 2-metre rule at the same time as opening bars and restaurants does run the risk of allowing the epidemic to start to regain a foothold,' he said. 'These changes will have to be very carefully monitored and the NHS track-and-trace system will have to be working properly to help keep us safe.'

The virus was still a very serious threat and it was already bubbling up in the Midlands. The city of Leicester had recorded 944 cases in the two weeks before Johnson's announcement. The surge in cases had followed an outbreak in food production plants and the media reported that large gatherings outside takeaway restaurants had helped fuel it. By the last weekend of June, Leicester's infection rate of 135 cases per 100,000 was three times higher than that of any other city in the UK. On Monday 29 June Hancock admitted that localised efforts to tackle the virus had not been a success. So it was announced that Leicester would become the first city to be placed into a local lockdown, which would last for at least two weeks. It would be the only place to miss out on the 4 July free-for-all.

13

A Reckless Summer

Saturday 4 July 2020 to Tuesday 15 September 2020
UK government order: Lockdown lifted

For millions of people, Super Saturday on 4 July was the big release after three months of hibernation. The lifting of the bulk of the lockdown restrictions on a Saturday that also happened to be America's Independence Day was perfect for the upbeat message the government wished to convey. This was the moment for the nation to let its hair down and party, and pursue one of its favourite pastimes again: drinking beer in pubs. It was also the moment when the second wave began.

The chancellor Rishi Sunak had been desperate to foster a summer feel-good factor that would boost consumer confidence and get the cash tills rolling again. His normally sedate Treasury had become a cheerleader for Saturday's party. 'Grab a drink and raise a glass, pubs are reopening their doors from 4 July,' the Treasury's official Twitter account tweeted two days before, using the hashtag '#openforbusiness'. The prime minister was similarly bullish. 'Frankly, I can't wait to go to a pub or a restaurant, even if it's not compatible with the diet that I'm on,' he said. 'I think people need to go out, I think people need to enjoy themselves … I want to see bustle. I want to see activity.' He did, though, urge some caution on the eve of Super Saturday with a fogeyish Johnsonian touch. 'I can certainly tell you I will buy and drink a pint, but not a yard, and I will repeat the message to everybody that this is a big turning point for us – we've got to get it right,' he told the press briefing that evening.

But there were quite a few party poopers. The Treasury's tweet caused a backlash on social media, with some people pointing out that it was insensitive to all those who had died from the virus. An ex-civil servant implored the department to 'read the sodding room', while Labour MP Geraint Davies told the *Guardian*: 'This is wholly irresponsible publicity by the Conservative government, which will fuel a resurgence of coronavirus infection and death in England.'[1] The Treasury quickly backed down and removed the tweet, admitting it had 'got it wrong'.

The NHS high command were worried too. They wrote to hospitals warning them to prepare for New Year's Eve-level surges in demand for emergency services as people hit the pubs. The chief medical officer, Chris Whitty, repeated the concerns that had previously been expressed by his chief scientific adviser colleague, Patrick Vallance, about the relaxing of so many restrictions at the same time. 'None of us believe … this is a risk-free next step,' he said. 'These are environments whose principal job it is to bring people together. That's a great thing to do socially, but it's also a great thing from the virus's point of view. And, therefore, we do have to have a really clear and really disciplined approach to try and maintain social distancing whilst also enjoying pubs.'

For some, the lack of restraint started at 8 a.m. on Super Saturday when the first pints were poured in pubs. Johnson popped out for a pint of bitter with his fiancée Symonds in the garden of the Russell Arms in Butlers Cross, Buckinghamshire. They were again spending the weekend just a mile up the road in Chequers. Sunak made a publicity-seeking visit to the Bell and Crown by the Thames in Strand-on-the-Green, west London. He couldn't quite do his bit by sinking a pint because he is teetotal. 'It's such good news that so many people are able to return to work this weekend, helping us all to enjoy summer safely,' he said in a statement.

But was it safe? The party atmosphere continued throughout the day. 'Brits went barmy on their own version of Independence Day by necking pints in pubs, eating fry-ups, having haircuts – and getting married,' the *Sunday Mirror* reported. By the evening, city centres were heaving with crowds and the television news cameras were screening pictures of people celebrating in the drinking districts of cities such as Bristol, Manchester, Newcastle, Norwich and London. The revelry grew wilder as the night wore on. In London's Soho, there were extraordinary scenes as thousands of people were crushed cheek to jowl in narrow streets. They hugged, they snogged, they bellowed in each other's ears without a thought for social distancing. They were having a great time – but was it too much, too soon?

The scenes terrified those who understood the history of pandemics. Watching the events that day, Professor Devi Sridhar, Chair of Global Public Health at Edinburgh University and a member of the Scottish government's Covid-19 Advisory Group, was reminded of the celebrations in 1918 when people thought the last great pandemic, the Spanish flu, was over after the first wave. 'Back in 1918 there were pictures of parades of people celebrating. So they really thought that was the end.' But the second wave that followed turned out to be even more deadly. She was watching modern Britain making the same mistake. Later, she blamed the government for sending out the wrong signals. 'The messaging was wrong,' she said. 'The idea was that you're celebrating the end of the pandemic, instead of preparing for a hard winter.'

Sridhar was justified in her concern. That week the seven-day average of coronavirus cases fell to just below 600 a day, which was the lowest figure for Britain since the first wave had begun in earnest in March. It would never get lower in 2020. From that weekend onwards, infections began to rise and would increase through July and August – at first little by little and then faster and faster. 'The second wave began on 5 July ... The nadir of the epidemic was that week,' said a senior adviser from the government's Scientific Advisory Group for Emergencies (Sage), who spoke to us at the end of the year when we were investigating the events that led to the second lockdown. He has asked not to be named because he fears he might be stripped of his position if it is known he has spoken out.

The expert is in no doubt that Super Saturday was a reckless error and contradicted all the scientific advice. Until then, the control measures were going to plan. 'Although we did ease restrictions in May and in June, people stayed in lockdown. Even though things were easing up, people remained at home largely and had very few contacts,' said the adviser. 'We stayed very cautious as a nation throughout that period, and the reproduction number stayed below one and cases came down.' Sage had been advising the government to relax the strictest of the lockdown measures incrementally so that they could gauge the effect each one had on infection rates. Minutes of the advisory group's 23 June meeting, which were sent to ministers, had cautioned: 'Releasing a significant number of measures in combination presents a material risk of accelerating transmission.' The rush to open everything up meant the scientists were unable to read which of the measures caused the spike that began in July.

'[Super Saturday] didn't seem like a gradual change to me. That seemed like a lot of things happening all at once,' the adviser said. 'If you have to reverse any of those measures, then which ones do you pick to reverse if you haven't got the data? You don't know which one it was that triggered the spike. We've been in that situation ever since – having to guess.'

The night before Super Saturday, there had been a sobering reminder of what was at stake when a candle-lit vigil was held by NHS staff outside Downing Street in memory of those who had already died from the pandemic. The names of each of the hundreds of NHS workers who had perished were read out within earshot of the prime minister's and chancellor's Downing Street homes.

Many had died as a result of decisions taken inside the building, but Johnson had not so far accepted any responsibility. Indeed, the following Monday he placed the blame on others for the biggest tragedy of the first wave. During a visit to Goole, Yorkshire, he accused care homes of not adequately following safety measures to stem the virus's spread. 'We discovered too many care homes didn't really follow the procedures in the way that they could have,' he said. The care home sector was furious. The National Care Forum, which represents not-for-profit care homes, said Johnson's remarks were 'frankly hugely insulting' to care workers. Mark Adams, who runs the national social care charity Community Integrated Care, said the prime minister's comments were 'cowardly' and a 'travesty of leadership'. He fumed: 'If this is genuinely his view, I think we're almost entering a Kafkaesque alternative reality where the government sets the rules, we follow them, they don't like the results, they then deny setting the rules and blame the people that were trying to do their best.'[2]

On Wednesday 8 July a chastened Johnson refused to apologise but attempted to limit the damage of his words. 'The last thing I wanted to do is to blame care workers for what has happened, for any of them to think that I was blaming them,' he told parliament. He then went on to admit culpability for the first time. 'When it comes to taking blame, I take full responsibility for what has happened.' But it was not a full confession. He had an excuse for his actions. 'The one thing that nobody knew early on during this pandemic was that the virus was being passed asymptomatically from person to person in the way that it is, and that's why the guidance and procedures changed.' This was an extraordinary claim, as the possibility that the virus could be spread by people who presented no symptoms had been recognised since the initial days of the pandemic. Chinese officials had warned about the risk of asymptomatic spread at the end of January and the well-publicised Steve Walsh 'super-spreader' case in early February had demonstrated that many people could be infected by someone who did not feel ill. The Sage committee itself had warned of the issue from the end of January and throughout February. Indeed, the minutes from the committee's 28 January meeting make clear reference to asymptomatic transmission and said 'early indications imply some is occurring.' It was an excuse that did not wash with the House of Commons' public accounts committee, which published a report on the handling of the care home crisis later that month. The report said care homes had been 'thrown to the wolves' and the government's actions were 'at times negligent' due to a series of 'reckless' and 'appalling' policy errors. Committee chairman Meg Hillier said: 'The failure to provide adequate PPE or testing to the millions of staff and volunteers who risked their lives to help us through the first peak of the crisis is a sad, low moment in our national response.'

Yet neither Johnson nor Sunak were in any mood to show caution and take things gradually as they steered the country out of lockdown. This was supposed to be the year in which there would be a new era of prosperity with the exit from the European Union, and yet Britain had lost close to 20 per cent of its gross domestic product in the three months to June when businesses had been shut down. The lockdown shrinkage of the economy was greater than that of any other G7 country in the first half of the year. On the day Johnson had spoken about care homes in the Commons, the chancellor announced a £30bn package to protect jobs because it was feared that unemployment would rise steeply when he planned to end the furlough scheme in October.

Later that day the chancellor headed off to a branch of Wagamama near the Royal Festival Hall on London's South Bank for a stint as a waiter to advertise his new big initiative: Eat Out to Help Out. The discount scheme, which would begin in three weeks' time on 3 August, was intended to prop up the hospitality industry by encouraging diners to return to pubs and restaurants, with the offer of up to £10 off sit-down meals per person from Monday to Wednesday throughout the rest of the month. Staff later said that Sunak was a forgetful waiter, which was a little unkind, but the chancellor was remiss for forgetting to wear a mask while he was serving the tables.

Sunak had been made aware of the risks of persuading a virus-wary public to return to crowded indoor eateries. His communications director, Allegra Stratton, is said to have advised that his spotless reputation might be tarnished if there was a second spike of the virus and it turned out that his initiative had caused it. But he had decided to press ahead anyway. He had not even run the scheme across his ministerial colleagues before its unveiling in an interview with *The Times* the previous weekend. Nor, it appears, did he seek the advice of the scientists from the Sage committee. 'We had nothing to do with it. We were not consulted. We heard about it when the public heard about it,' said the Sage adviser.

The government seemed to be bypassing Sage as it rushed to force more people out of their cocooned lockdown existence and back into the cities and towns. Sage had not been informed in advance about the sudden reversal of another key policy that had been stopping the spread of the virus, which was announced by the prime minister in an online forum with the public on Friday 10 July. 'It's very important that people should be going back to work if they can now. I think everybody has sort of taken the "stay at home if you can". I think we should now say, well, "go back to work if you can",' Johnson said. The government's guidance had changed the day before to encourage businesses to consult with their employees about whether it was 'viable for them to continue working from home'.

The relaxation of the restrictions kept coming. International travel was opened up on the same day as Johnson's online forum. A new 'traffic light' system of 'travel corridors' was introduced that Friday, which allowed people to travel to 59 countries with no requirement to quarantine for 14 days on return to England. The government had belatedly introduced a two-week quarantine for all people coming in from overseas at the beginning of June and this would now only apply to travellers arriving from countries outside the corridors. It meant that over the six months of the pandemic, Britain's borders had only been fully protected for just a month. The new policy permitted British tourists to travel to countries such as Spain with higher rates of infection. In the penultimate week of July, when the air travel corridor was still open, Britain had 6.8 cases per 100,000 people, whereas Spain had 25.9 cases per 100,000.

The wisdom of this move was also questionable, as research would later demonstrate that many people would bring the virus back into Britain from their travels. A study from Basel University in Switzerland shows that a new variant of the virus appears to have emerged in Spain in early summer and then began to spread to the UK by the middle of July. Remarkably, by September the variant was estimated to be responsible for 50 per cent of virus cases in England and 80 per cent of those in Wales and Scotland. Professor Sridhar said: 'We've seen it now in the sequencing data that has come through: that a lot of the new spread in the UK has come from this new strain, which they call the Spanish strain. That's become the dominant one. That means effectively, we re-imported it.'

By the middle of July, most areas of the economy had been opened for business again, with the exception of mass sporting events with spectators. It was a new world with all kinds of unfamiliar protections that had been put in place in an attempt to limit the spread of the virus. Those returning to offices found their workspaces had been reconfigured with one-way floor markings and signage on desktop computers to try to ensure social distancing. Dispensing machines had been set up in the entrance halls and hand sanitiser was provided outside lifts. Perspex barriers had been erected in some restaurants and pubs, similar to those that had already been introduced widely to protect cashiers in food shops. The wearing of masks was now becoming routine.

In fact, the advice on using a mask was yet another screeching hand-brake U-turn by the government in the summer. In March, when there were PPE shortages, Dr Jenny Harries, the deputy chief medical officer, had explained in her fireside chat with the prime minister that it was a 'bad idea' for members of the public to wear masks. In June, mask wearing had become compulsory on public transport, and on Tuesday 14 July the health minister Matt Hancock extended the measure to shops and supermarkets. Hancock said masks were needed because sales assistants, cashiers and security guards had suffered disproportionately during the first wave. 'The death rate of sales and retail assistants is 75 per cent higher among men, and 60 per cent higher among women than in the general population.' It was effectively an admission that the government had previously got it badly wrong on face masks and shop staff had died as a result.

However, even with Perspex screens and masks, the return to a more active world was still a big gamble. As if to emphasise the scale of the risk being taken, a report that had been commissioned by Vallance, the chief scientific adviser, was published that Tuesday setting out what could happen if there was a second wave of the virus in the winter. The report – which was produced by the Academy of Medical Sciences with the help of several Sage members – outlined a 'reasonable worst-case scenario' that might cause as many as 119,000 deaths in a second wave. It warned that numbers of seriously ill coronavirus patients would have an adverse impact on the care given to people requiring treatment for other conditions. Waiting lists for hospitals could increase to 10 million by the end of the year. 'The risk is that a large number of patients will at best have poorer outcomes or at worst die unnecessarily due to delays in accessing care,' the report said.

The tell-tale sign that Britain would be heading towards this worst-case scenario would be if the reproduction number – R

– was to reach 1.7 in September. Indeed, hospital capacity was 'likely' to be stretched even if R reached between 1.1 and 1.5. It was therefore the government's plan to keep R below one. If R was 0.9, for example, then, on average, ten infected people would only pass the virus on to nine others and cases would steadily decline. It was a critically important balancing act because as restrictions were loosened to allow economic activity, as had just occurred, the R number would inevitably rise again. The authors were optimistic, however, that the government would bring in new social distancing measures if R were to rise sharply. 'These would likely be decided on more quickly than was possible during February and March 2020 because of improved surveillance,' it said.

The report drew attention to the example of southern hemisphere countries that had acted swiftly and decisively to stem the spread of the virus in their winter and then retained the measures until the outbreak was almost eradicated. It observed: 'Australia and New Zealand both reacted quickly to the threat from Covid-19 and in doing so have managed to keep virus transmission at very low levels. Assuming that they maintain control, their winter season will be very different from that which is likely in the UK.' The two antipodean countries had both been shining examples of how countries could keep deaths and infections to a minimum by sealing borders and relentlessly driving down the R rate. It had allowed them to return to near normal and open their economies.

New Zealand's economy would recover significantly over the rest of the year. Its prime minister Jacinda Ardern was able to avoid a second national lockdown by acting swiftly to crush outbreaks when they were still tiny by using stringent local restrictions. The country's track and trace programme could then be deployed effectively because the number of cases was low. Daily cases were never allowed to exceed 30 between May and the end of the year. It was a similar story in Australia, where a local outbreak in July, centring on the state of Victoria, was ruthlessly crushed with local measures after reaching a peak of only 721 cases a day. Again the local lockdown worked because the outbreak was nipped in the bud at source. It gave the virus no chance to spread further. While there are some differences between those countries and the UK, there were important lessons to be learnt about how infections needed to be kept at low levels if the economy was to stand a chance of recovering.

Interestingly, the Academy of Medical Sciences' report cited polling showing that a significantly higher proportion of the UK public were suspicious of lockdown being eased than those who favoured relaxing restrictions. It suggested the majority of the public were in favour of the New Zealand and Australia approach of driving the virus down to lower levels. The report also referenced another important reason to keep transmission levels as low as possible: there was a danger the virus might mutate and increase its infectivity or virulence. This was a disturbing prospect.

The following day, Wednesday 15 July, the Labour leader Keir Starmer challenged Johnson in the Commons to say whether he had read the report. Johnson's answer was evasive. He replied merely that he was 'aware' of the report and later a Downing Street spokesman was unable to say whether the prime minister had been through it. A spokesman for the Labour leader said: 'It is deeply concerning that the prime minister hasn't even bothered to read it.'[3]

The government had been well and truly warned about the awful consequences of a second wave but, nonetheless, the good intentions of maintaining an R below one in the UK did not last for long. By the end of July, the scientists on Sage were reporting that they had no confidence that R was not now above the one threshold. During a rainy cool month, the virus had been picking up speed in the north. On Thursday 30 July it was announced that Greater Manchester and parts of East Lancashire and West Yorkshire would join Leicester under new local restrictions. The measures were relatively light: people from different households were banned from mixing at home or in a garden, but pubs, bars and restaurants remained open. Leicester had been under more strict lockdown measures for four weeks and the new rules meant a partial lifting of restrictions for the city.

The figures across Britain left no leeway. Infections were rising and it was only a month before schools and universities would return and inevitably send the R rate even higher. The government's limited room for manoeuvre was acknowledged by Whitty at a hastily arranged press conference the following day. 'We have probably reached near the limits, or the limits, of what we can do in terms of opening up society,' he said. 'So what that means, potentially, is if we wish to do more things in the future we may have to do less of some other things. And these will be difficult trade-offs.' Since getting children back into school was an 'absolute priority', then other freedoms such as going out to pubs and restaurants and mixing between households might have to be curtailed. But the government would continue to disregard the advice of its top advisers and allow R to slide upwards.

The following Monday, 3 August, was going to be the start of Eat Out to Help Out, come what may. According to a Conservative MP source, both Hancock and Michael Gove were concerned about pressing ahead so quickly. He said: 'They were of the view that we were running a very big risk by essentially encouraging schemes like Eat Out to Help Out and pushing the rush back to the offices at exactly the time that infections were starting to tick up nationally.' However, the MP described how 'the voices that were prevailing in government, for whatever reason, were those that were pushing a case that was based purely on economic recovery at all costs as fast as possible.' He blames the hurry on the 'siren voices of the libertarian types' who 'hold a lot of sway over No. 10' and were 'pushing for things to get back to normal'.

Three days later, on Thursday 6 August, Sage held its fiftieth meeting since the start of the pandemic, and it began with Simon

Case, the prime minister's private secretary, reading out a letter of thanks from Johnson for all their hard work. The committee was starting to be concerned about the increases in R and was already anticipating that the brakes might have to be applied to the prime minister's drive to open up the country. The minutes were a reminder to ministers of the simple lesson learnt from the first wave: 'Strong measures introduced early for short periods are likely to be more effective in reducing transmission than less stringent measures which would need to be implemented for longer.'

A group of 58 MPs on the Commons all-party Coronavirus group had come to the same conclusion. The government had refused to hold a public inquiry into the crisis over the summer, despite calls to do so from doctors and bereaved families. However, the MPs had been conducting their own investigation and had received more than a thousand pieces of written evidence from scientists, public experts, frontline medical workers, charities and members of the public. The evidence suggested that the best course of action was for infection levels to be kept to a minimum with prompt interventions. One of the group's vice chairs was the Conservative MP and medical doctor Dan Poulter, who was despairing of his own government's approach to controlling the virus. He would make his views clear to newspapers later that month. There was a danger of thinking, he argued, 'that the coronavirus pandemic presents us with a binary choice between saving the economy or saving lives'. However, he said: 'This is a false dichotomy and the truth is that minimising community transmission will allow a faster and stronger economic recovery.'[4]

By mid-August, positive tests had risen to more than a thousand a day, which was double the number on 4 July. The all-party group was so concerned it broke off from the inquiry and wrote directly to the prime minister on Thursday 20 August. 'It is already clear that to minimise the risk of a second wave occurring and therefore to save lives, an urgent change in government approach is required', said the letter sent by the group's chair, the Liberal Democrat MP Layla Moran. 'With the number of new infections in England remaining stubbornly high and with the risk of a second wave ever present, pursuing a zero-Covid policy in England will provide clarity and reassurance to the UK public, reduce the risk of a second wave and save lives.' The group wanted to maintain compulsory social distancing measures to restrict virus cases to as few as 60 a day. They hoped the prime minister would treat their recommendations 'seriously'.

When the letter arrived at Downing Street, Johnson wasn't there. He and his fiancée Carrie Symonds were on holiday in a place almost as far away from London as you could possibly be while still in the UK. On Sunday 16 August, they had travelled almost the length of the country to stay in a three-bedroom cottage on the north-west coast of Scotland opposite the Isle of Skye. During the week, they had pitched a tent in a neighbouring pasture field to gaze at the stars at night – much to the annoyance of a local farmer who had not given permission for his land to be used in this way. Johnson's ex-mistress Petronella Wyatt had been amused when she read about the prime minister under canvas. 'Boris and Carrie are going to spend part of their Scottish holiday camping … That will finish off their relationship. Boris can't cook and Carrie only likes luxe private villas in hot places,' she tweeted acidly.

But it was a chance for the couple to relax in peace and quiet, and for Johnson to get away from more virus-related trouble back in London, which had kicked off in the days before he left. Since all the school exams had to be scrapped because of the virus, the government had arranged for the A-level results to be predicted by a computer algorithm. It had been a disaster for the Department of Education. Around 40 per cent of results were downgraded from teachers' predictions, with students from disadvantaged areas affected disproportionately by the modelling system. Before Johnson had left that weekend, the media had been awash with furious comments from parents and teachers. Videos of distraught teenagers whose future plans had been dashed were going viral on social media. Gavin Williamson, the education secretary, had stuck to his guns. 'This is it,' he said in an interview with *The Times* on Saturday. 'No U-turn, no change.' However, his tough stance lasted just 48 hours. As the prime minister was pitching his tent on Monday, Williamson announced a U-turn. Teachers' assessments would replace the computer algorithm. 'Over the weekend it became apparent there were real concerns,' he said with a little understatement. Johnson found it easy to resist the many calls to sack Williamson because he was out of the firing line sitting in his tent with Symonds and the baby. It was not his style to return from holidays for work and he was certainly not going to take personal charge of this particular mess.

In the end, however, the prime minister's holiday was cut short after he was tracked down at the cottage by an intrepid newshound with a camera. When photos appeared of the prime minister's hideaway in the *Daily Mail* on Friday 21 August, the couple were advised to leave by their protection team as their safety could not be guaranteed. The letter from the all-party group was waiting for Johnson when he returned to work the following Monday morning. He never replied and went on to ignore the MPs' advice concerning a zero-Covid strategy.

Infections were now rising steeply. But instead of displaying caution, the government was forging on with plans that would only increase the spread of the virus. In the final days of August, Johnson issued a plea to all parents to send their children back to school in September. 'We have always been guided by our scientific and medical experts,' he said, while explaining that schoolchildren would be safe from the virus. Yet he was not following his chief medical officer's recommendations. Whitty had been clear three weeks earlier that there could be no further loosening of restrictions unless other new lockdown measures were introduced to compensate for the effect they would have on the rate of infections. The same applied under the rules that the prime minister had set himself in his speech when he returned to work in April. Government scientists were convinced that a tougher suppression strategy would provide the best platform for keeping the economy open in the autumn. Professor Steven Riley, a member of the government's Spi-M modelling committee, says the evidence that a zero-Covid policy had been the best option was irrefutable. 'From the experience of this pandemic, some countries have had much, much better outcomes by pursuing that [approach]. Even if we didn't achieve it, we should have it as an objective,' he said. 'I don't think that will be controversial. In fact, it's almost silly to suggest otherwise.'

There was a sense in which the lurking menace of the virus had almost been forgotten in those summer months. As September approached, the traditional yearly rhythms crept back in. Many people had managed to get away for holidays abroad, despite running the risk of being recalled quickly as the travel corridors changed to reflect spikes in the virus overseas. But the mellowing sun now signalled that the lazy days of summer were ending and it was time to go back to the daily routine of school and work. Businesses up and down the country had been planning through the summer for their employees to stop working from home at the beginning of September. It was the month when the workforce was expected to return to the daily commute into city and town centres after five months away. There was still much uncertainty and fear of the virus, but it was what the government wanted. One unnamed government minister was quoted in the newspapers as saying that people risked being sacked if they did not go back to the office. The bullying of employees to repopulate desolate city centres became jokingly known as 'Operation Save Pret a Manger', because the businesses that normally served workers at lunchtime were severely struggling and needed help. Since a great number of employees had shown that they were still just as productive working from home, the government really did appear to be encouraging unnecessary risks for the sake of the sandwich shops.

There was an element of wishful thinking in the approach. It was hoped that maybe the virus might one day just ebb away, as the Spanish flu pandemic had once done – albeit after more than two years of death and destruction. Other European countries such as France, Spain and Italy had been gearing up their economies and casting back restrictions with a similar baseless optimism that life might somehow return to near normal with only light-touch controls, despite the virus's continued prevalence. Indeed, infections in those countries had started to rise again and this gave advance notice of what would soon happen in the UK. Surely, Britain was not going to ignore those warnings as it had in the first wave?

When the Eat Out to Help Out initiative came to an end on the August Bank Holiday Monday, it was hailed as a huge triumph for chancellor Sunak. More than 78,000 restaurants and pubs had participated in the scheme before it ended on 31 August. They had claimed back discounts on more than 160 million meals enjoyed by diners over the four weeks the scheme was running, at a cost to the taxpayer of £849 million. But it was too effective, according to researchers from Warwick University, who found that the initiative had increased Covid-19 cases between 8 per cent and 17 per cent. Their research suggested that the strategy of encouraging multiple different households to share enclosed indoor spaces, regardless of the so-called 'Covid secure' measures, had allowed the virus to proliferate dangerously quickly. The report's author, Professor Thiemo Fetzer, concluded that the scheme was a grave mistake. 'Eat Out to Help Out may in the end have been a false economy: one that subsidised the spread of the pandemic into Autumn and contributed to the start of the second wave,' he said. 'Alternative policy measures, such as extending the furlough scheme, increasing statutory sick pay and supporting low-income households through expanding free school meals may well prove to be far more cost effective than demand-stimulating measures that encourage economic activities which actively cause Covid-19 to spread.'

He wasn't alone in taking that position. 'If you look at the use of restaurants in July it's pretty low,' the Sage source explained. 'Yes, you could go to a restaurant, but people didn't typically in July. And it took a bribe from the chancellor to make us go. This was the completely bonkers thing about it. It wasn't about support for restaurants, otherwise it would have counted for takeaways. It was to break our fear and it worked.' He added: 'We were obviously going to have to reverse that. It just seemed insane.'

When the full cabinet returned to Downing Street on Tuesday 1 September following the summer break, they found the prime minister in buoyant mood, enthusing about how life was getting back to normal. 'People are going back to the office in huge numbers across our country, and quite right too,' he told the ministers assembled around the cabinet table. 'Although we know there'll be more [Covid] outbreaks, we're also absolutely confident that we are going to be able to deal with those outbreaks, and bit by bit this incredible country is getting back on its feet.' Johnson was correct, in one respect. According to Google data tracking smartphones, the number of people attending workplaces was now just 35 per cent below normal levels, whereas it had been down 70 per cent during the first lockdown.

But his confidence was entirely misplaced about his government's ability to control the virus. 'Encouraging people to go back to work at the end of August and beginning of September when we hadn't even opened schools yet just seemed to me to be utterly insane,' said the Sage source. This was another measure Sage would have to try to reverse, he said. The effects of the government's strategy were already becoming increasingly evident in the figures for new infections. By that day, the average daily number of infections over a week had passed two thousand for the first time since the initial outbreak in March. They had quadrupled since Super Saturday.

The country's largest study of virus infection by Imperial College, which swabbed 150,000 people, would provide data on how dangerous the reproduction number had become at that time. It found that between 22 August and 7 September, R was estimated to be 1.7, which meant it had already hit the figure identified in the report commissioned by Vallance as the 'reasonable worst-case scenario'. There had been no reason for Johnson's optimism at the cabinet meeting. The scientists had been pinning their hopes on the reproduction number being substantially below the 'one' threshold at the beginning of September, because there had to be a cushion to accommodate the inevitable increases in infections when the schools and universities went back.

With the R number at 1.7, a second lockdown was inevitable from this point onwards. The only question was when.

When the schools went back in the first week of September, the £12bn track and trace system – which had been heralded as a saviour by the government – was still in serious trouble. Over the summer, the system had continually failed to locate potentially infectious people with sufficient speed to keep a lid on the virus. The number of tests being carried out had ramped up significantly from 70,000 a day at the beginning of May to more than 200,000 by early September. But the government's target of reaching 80 per cent of those who were in close contact with someone testing positive within 72 hours had not been hit since June. And there was still no functioning track and trace app.

To make matters worse, the track and trace system became completely swamped as children returned to school. Daily positive tests rocketed from 2,250 to 3,863 in the six days between 1 and 7 September. People began complaining that there were no appointments available at test centres and some were told to travel hundreds of miles for a test. On Tuesday 8 September

Sarah-Jane Marsh, the director of testing, issued an apology and admitted that the laboratories did not have the capacity to cope. 'Can I please offer my heartfelt apologies to anyone who cannot get a Covid test at present,' she tweeted. 'All of our testing sites have capacity, which is why they don't look overcrowded, it's our laboratory processing that is the critical pinch-point. We are doing all we can to expand quickly.'

The tracing system was, however, improving and might have helped control the autumn outbreak if infections had been kept to a lower level. After all, an exponential growth in the virus would quickly expand the numbers of contacts that need to be traced to unmanageable levels. Professor Sridhar believes that if restrictions had been maintained and infections had continued to be driven down, then the testing system might have averted a second wave. 'We might have had a second bump but it would have been manageable because test and trace works at low levels,' she explained.

The rapid rise in infections was causing increasing alarm among the government advisers. On Monday 7 September, Professor Jonathan Van-Tam, England's deputy chief medical officer, told a media briefing that people had become 'too relaxed' about the virus over the summer months. 'These latest figures really show us that much as people might like to say, "Oh well, it's gone away,"' he said, 'it hasn't gone away … and if we don't take this incredibly seriously from this point in we are going to have a bumpy ride over the next few months.' This suggestion that people were not taking the virus seriously prompted an aghast tweet from a public affairs specialist, who pointed out that the government had encouraged such an attitude. 'They were told to shop, take a summer holiday, and it will be over by Christmas,' he wrote. Within hours, the tweeter was slapped down by Nadine Dorries, the health minister. 'No one who knew anything about the pathology of #Covid19 ever said it would be over by Christmas,' she confidently tweeted.

This was unfortunate, as back in the more optimistic days of mid-July her own prime minister had said it was his 'strong and sincere hope' that the government 'will be able to review the outstanding restrictions and allow a more significant return to normality from November, at the earliest, possibly in time for Christmas'. In fact, Johnson had said it 'may conceivably be possible to move away from the social distancing measures' by November. At the same time, he had also offered hope that theatre performances, concerts and business conferences might open in the coming months. This had turned out to be a pipe-dream – with the exception of the odd theatre performance that had gone ahead despite being financially ruinous under Covid restrictions. Many cinemas had reopened, but they too were struggling to make ends meet with the smaller audiences that were necessary to comply with social distancing rules.

But the spike of infections at the beginning of September was making a return to the old world look even further away. On Wednesday 9 September the government's Spi-M modelling committee had concluded that its most pessimistic forecast from July was now a grim reality. 'The current situation is in line with the latest reasonable worst-case scenario, where incidence doubled once in August and once in the first two weeks of September', the committee's minutes noted.

Something had to be done. The prime minister finally gave in to pressure from his advisers and applied the brakes again – but only with the lightest of touches. At a media briefing, Johnson, flanked by Whitty and Vallance, announced that a new temporary law was to be introduced. From the following Monday, people would only be allowed to meet in groups of six, whereas previously, gatherings of up to thirty had been permitted. This was a minor measure. The places where people were picking up the virus would not be shut. Life would otherwise proceed as normal. The new rule of six came as a surprise to members of the Spi-M committee, who would have expected to model the potential effectiveness of such a move before it was implemented. Nicholas Davies, an assistant professor at the London School of Hygiene & Tropical Medicine who sits on the government's Spi-M modelling committee, said his colleagues were not consulted about the new rule, or indeed about Eat Out to Help Out before that. 'They seemed to be making decisions and it wasn't really clear what the rationale for them was,' he said.

Johnson, however, had not lost his *joie de vivre* from the summer and wanted to sugar the announcement that day with some of his famous positivity. By early September it still wasn't clear whether a vaccine could be safe and effective. Worryingly, the much-heralded AstraZeneca vaccine being developed in Oxfordshire had hit a setback that day because a participant in one of the drug's trials had fallen seriously ill. Johnson admitted that there were 'no guarantees' that a vaccine would come along. Instead, his government had devised an ambitious stop-gap. 'So over the summer, we have therefore been working out an alternative plan which could allow life to return to closer to normality,' he said. He called this plan 'Operation Moonshot'. It proposed quick turnaround 'mass testing' so that people could check whether they were infected before attending places where others gathered, such as offices or social events. Johnson hoped the approach would be widespread by the spring, but would begin to be used significantly earlier. 'If everything comes together it may be possible even for some of the most difficult sectors like the theatres to have life much closer to normal before Christmas,' he added. Given that the existing problems with testing were taking months to iron out, commentators found it difficult to understand why the prime minister believed that such an ambitious claim could come true. When Hancock spoke in the Commons the following day about 'verifying the new technology' for the 'moonshot' initiative, parliament's official *Hansard* transcription of the debate recorded a word in square brackets at the end of his sentence. It read: 'Laughter'. Inevitably, the MPs' scepticism would turn out to be well founded. The prime minister had once again over-promised and would under-deliver.

It took just a day for the government's scientists to dismiss the new rule of six as insufficient. The Sage committee minutes the next day noted that the virus was spreading as it had done in February with 'rapidly increasing incidence' and the effects of the return of schools and universities was yet to be seen. Deaths were also rising after reaching a low of eight a day. 'It is highly likely that further national and local measures will be needed to bring R back to 1 in addition to those already announced,' the minutes of the 10 September meeting state. They wanted a lockdown and made it clear they favoured 'an early and comprehensive response' that would have 'more effect and may be needed for a shorter duration' than if the virus was allowed to spread further. But another week was allowed to go by.

There was tension within the government because the economic forecasts were awful. The chancellor had spent hundreds of billions of pounds combating the virus and propping up businesses as the nation's income took an unprecedented dive. But a report by the Institute for Employment Studies on Monday 14 September still predicted that close to half a million people could be made redundant by the autumn. Unemployment would also cause a range of health problems as a result of the stress and poverty. Superficially, this seemed like an argument for avoiding any new lockdown. But the scientists believed this missed the point and that it was important to quickly clamp down on the latest rise in infections. The effect of job losses would not be nearly as deadly as a second wave of the virus and would not overwhelm the hospitals. If the virus was allowed to spread widely again this would ultimately force the government to impose a longer lockdown at some point in the future that would cause even greater unemployment, stress and poverty. It would be the same mistake that was made in the first wave. Yet on Wednesday 16 September, with infections rising to above

4,000, Johnson was still firmly against tougher measures. He had seemingly forgotten his pledge in April to keep the reproduction number below one because otherwise there would be spiralling numbers of deaths and economic disaster. 'I do not want a second national lockdown,' he told the House of Commons. 'I think it would be completely wrong for this country, and we are going to do everything in our power to prevent it.' That evening he received a visit at Downing Street from two tall men in black suits who would later be maligned as Professor Gloom and Dr Doom. The government's chief medical officer and chief scientific adviser were the bearers of even worse news.

14

The Circuit Breaker

Wednesday 16 September 2020 to
Wednesday 2 December 2020
UK government order: Local restrictions

The caramelised light of an early autumn sunset warmed the window panes of Downing Street on the evening of Wednesday 16 September. Inside, Professor Chris Whitty and Sir Patrick Vallance gave their dry and clinical assessment of the progression of the virus to the prime minister, who had firmly ruled out a second lockdown that afternoon. The figures were sobering. In July the government's scientists had tried to picture a worst-case scenario that needed to be avoided to prevent a catastrophic second wave. It looked uncannily like the situation they were now in. Numbers of infections were feared to now be doubling every week and hospital admissions for the virus had increased by 100 per cent since the beginning of the month. Without a drastic intervention, the scientists argued, the country was now on track for 200 to 500 deaths a day by early November. The two top medical and scientific advisers urged the prime minister to impose a two-week circuit breaker lockdown to bring R back under control. The rationale was simple and had been expressed by Sage the week before. A short, sharp, lockdown-style intervention now while infections were relatively low would halt the exponential growth of the virus and bring infections back down to the levels seen in the summer, which were easier to control. The move would both save lives and avoid the longer, more economically damaging lockdown that would be required if the outbreak was allowed to escalate further. It was exactly the type of swift action recommended by the Academy of Medical Sciences' worst-case-scenario planning document that Vallance had commissioned back in July. It was also the approach that had been followed by the countries around the world that had experienced the best outcomes from the pandemic so far.

As darkness descended, the grim reality of the situation began to dawn on the prime minister and his aides. 'That was the moment when he knew we needed to do something,' one aide told *The Sunday Times*.[1] The optimism of the return from the summer holidays had been punctured. Johnson appeared to have accepted the scientists' argument. 'There's no question,' he said as he toured a new vaccine factory two days later on Friday 18 September in his hard hat, '[we] are now seeing a second wave coming in.' Having rejected a national lockdown two days earlier, he was starting to reconsider. 'I don't think anybody wants to go into a second lockdown, but clearly, when you look at what is happening, you've got to wonder whether we need to go further than the "rule of six" that we brought in on Monday.' But he was keeping his options open. He ruled out closing schools and wanted to 'keep all parts of the economy open, as far as we possibly can'.

The proposal for the two-week lockdown went before the Cabinet Office's Covid-19 operation committee that day. Two of the ministers who sat on the committee – Matt Hancock, the health secretary, and Michael Gove, the cabinet minister – were said to be in favour of the tougher measures and plans started to be put in place for a lockdown. Spin doctors briefed journalists that a big announcement would be made on Tuesday. However, one key member of the operation committee was not onside. It was the chancellor, Rishi Sunak. On the Friday evening, Sunak met with Johnson in Downing Street to express deep concern about the damage a lockdown would do to business and jobs. Rumours circulated afterwards that Sunak had threatened to resign if there was a lockdown, but this has been denied. However, his intervention added to the prime minister's own doubts about bringing in new measures. Johnson seemed to have forgotten his own words back in April, when he said that allowing the reproduction rate to go over one 'would mean not only a new wave of death and disease but also an economic disaster'.

The following day, invitations were sent out to a series of experts to join in a clandestine Sunday evening rendezvous with the prime minister. They were told to keep it a secret. The highly controversial agenda of the meeting meant that discretion was vital. When the experts dialled in to the Zoom call at 6 p.m. the next day they found Boris Johnson and Rishi Sunak at the end of the long mahogany cabinet room table in Downing Street. The presence of the chancellor with no sign of other ministers was a little odd, as the experts had been invited to deliver presentations on the coronavirus pandemic and not the economy. It was part of Sunak's attempt to persuade Johnson that there might be a way the country could muddle along with the virus without having to bring in a lockdown.

Three of the four academics who had been invited to speak by No. 10 that Sunday evening were advocates of a far less suppressive approach to the virus. They were from the side of the scientific debate that believed it was desirable to allow immunity to build up in the population by letting the virus run its course with the use of lighter restrictions. By courting the scientists, Johnson and Sunak were opening themselves up to accusations that they were re-engaging with the 'herd immunity' strategy. This had proved highly unpopular back in March, when it was predicted that it would lead to an unacceptable death toll and potentially overwhelm the NHS.

First up was Professor Sunetra Gupta, an Oxford University epidemiologist, who was keen to persuade the prime minister and his chancellor that 'lockdowns were not an option.' She and the second speaker, her Oxford colleague Professor Carl Heneghan, had written a letter to Johnson and Sunak with the backing of several other scientists. They argued that the policy of suppressing the virus was misguided, as the social and economic impacts of lockdowns caused 'significant harm' to people both mentally and physically. Since 89 per cent of deaths from Covid-19 were among those over 65 years old, they urged the government to bring in more targeted measures to protect the elderly. This shielding would also be applied to those with existing illnesses that made them more susceptible to the virus. Describing the meeting later, Gupta says she lobbied for policies that would protect the vulnerable while the virus was allowed to spread through the rest of society, building up herd immunity. She believed that herd immunity would become established in 'the order of three to six months'. If Downing Street had done its homework, they would have realised that Gupta's forecasts had not always been reliable in the past. In March, she led a study that claimed that as many as half the British population could have already been infected with the virus, which was later proved to be wildly inaccurate. In May, Gupta had predicted the epidemic was 'on its way out in this country'.[2]

Next up was Heneghan, whose broad recollection of the Zoom call was that he talked about 'controlling the spread of infection while minimising societal disruption' and using targeted measures to protect those most at risk from the virus. The professor had made his views very plain in a long interview on Sky News' Sophy Ridge programme that very morning, in which he had stated emphatically: 'There is no evidence right now of what's called a second wave.' He believed the government scientists – whom he had described as 'mediocre' in a newspaper that day – were wrongly interpreting the increase in infections, and argued that the country could not afford to bring in harsh measures 'because the impact on the economy is going to be significant'. Heneghan took the view that there would be a resurgence of infections after a short lockdown. Contending that there needed to be 'a level of immunity' in the population for the virus to become manageable, he advocated drawing upon Sweden's approach, which he said was 'creating population immunity'.

During the interview, he called on the prime minister to subtly change his language to 'normalise' the September rise in coronavirus cases, arguing that it was usual for respiratory-type infections to multiply around that time of year. 'This is a seasonal effect now, and if it becomes worse … then, yes, that's the point when we ask for restrictive measures. But that time is not now,' he told Ridge. The professor conceded that it might be necessary to have a lockdown over an extended school holiday at Christmas. But his strongest message to the government was that it should reinforce its messaging to the public by further emphasising the need for people to isolate if they had symptoms. This would mean, he argued, that 'we can go through the winter highly vigilant and not need a lockdown.'

The third speaker was the man viewed across the world as the poster boy for herd immunity. Anders Tegnell, Sweden's top epidemiologist, was calling in to explain his country's controversial policy of avoiding a lockdown. At the time there was a belief that Sweden had been successful in building up herd immunity among its citizens. But there was no clear evidence that it had done so. Sweden's policies were becoming increasingly controversial, as there had been 5,860 deaths from the virus by that day. This was more than fifteen times the number in neighbouring Norway and Finland. These two countries had adopted an aggressive suppression approach to the virus that was broadly similar to the type of policy the Sage scientists now wanted the prime minister to follow. Having clamped down hard and swiftly on the virus, Norway and Finland had seen drops in GDP that were far less dramatic than those in Sweden, in the second quarter of the year. The folly of the Swedish approach would be further exposed in the weeks after the meeting when the country was hit by a new wave of infections that proved it had not achieved anything like herd immunity. Three months later, the Swedish king, Carl XVI Gustaf, declared his country's relaxed policies towards the virus a failure at his end-of-year review. When contacted, Tegnell refused to disclose what he said during the call to Johnson and Sunak. But his presence that evening said much about the way the prime minister and his chancellor were thinking.

Finally, they had to listen to the opposite argument. Professor John Edmunds, the government's leading modeller, was there to articulate the view of his fellow members on Sage that an immediate two-week 'circuit breaker' lockdown was vital. Edmunds has declined to reveal what he said to Johnson and Sunak that evening, but his opinions were clear from a paper he co-authored with other Sage members that weekend. 'Not acting now to reduce cases will result in a very large epidemic with catastrophic consequences in terms of direct Covid-related deaths and the ability of the health service to meet needs,' they wrote.

Edmunds and his Sage colleagues had already exposed the weakness of the herd immunity approach. In their meeting two weeks earlier, they had reviewed evidence that estimated that only 6 per cent of the UK population had gained antibodies against the virus after seven months of the epidemic and 57,000 deaths. They were also concerned by research that suggested that the immunity offered by antibodies appeared to wane after two or three months. It suggested that the chances of the UK achieving herd immunity without a vaccine were slim. They were also in the process of looking into how viable it would be to adopt a policy of sealing off the vulnerable and elderly from the rest of the population. The answer was that it was near impossible. When the work was published the following month, they pointed out: 'To be viable as a strategy, there would need to be complete separation between those over 60 and the rest of the population, as even a small leak would cause many illnesses and death when prevalence is high.' There were an estimated 1.8 million homes where the young and vulnerable lived together, and therefore keeping them apart would be very difficult. There would also be a 'profound negative effect' on the mental health of people who were forced to withdraw from society for a much longer period than the spring lockdown. In addition, Sage noted that an uncontrolled epidemic in younger age groups would still have 'dire consequences for the NHS'. The move would anyway be futile, Sage concluded. The advisory body was almost certain that a further epidemic wave would still occur in older people once they were reintegrated back into society, because not enough immunity would have built up in the population to adequately protect them.

Michael Gove, the Cabinet Office minister, would also later set out the considerable pitfalls of a policy based on only shielding the elderly and vulnerable. In an article for *The Times*, he wrote: 'How, practically, could we ensure that every older citizen, every diabetic, everyone with an underlying condition or impaired immune system was perfectly insulated from all contact with others for months to come? How many are we expected to isolate completely and for how long? Five million? Ten? No visits by carers or medical staff, no mixing of generations, the eviction of older citizens from the homes they share with younger? No country has embarked on this course, with no detailed plan for implementing such a strategy ever laid out.'

After listening to the arguments that evening, the prime minister had a big call to make. There was a great weight of pressure upon his shoulders. He had made the mistake of underestimating the virus during the first wave in March and then delaying measures to restrict its spread. This had caused many thousands of extra deaths. He had promised that he would not allow the country to return to such a dire situation again when he emerged – seemingly as a convert to the cautious approach – from his convalescence in late April. There had been passion in his voice when he said on 27 April that he would not risk a second spike in the virus by 'letting the reproduction rate go back over one'. This was the speech in which he seemed to have accepted that losing control of the virus would cause a new wave of 'death and disease' and also an economic disaster, because the government 'would be forced once again to slam on the brakes across the whole country'.

The reproduction number was well over one by that day in mid-September. If Johnson had stuck to his pledge, his priority should have been to save the country from 'death and disease' by bringing R back under one with a second national lockdown that would avoid a longer economically damaging clampdown at a later date. But the experts invited that evening may well have rekindled some of his libertarian instincts. Maybe his own scientific advisers on Sage were wrong and there was a way forward that could avoid a second lockdown?

Johnson had been a gambler throughout his career. Following the Zoom call, he summoned his top team and put a stop to the preparations for a circuit breaker lockdown.

He was taking the political path of least resistance. By choosing not to lock down he appeased his chancellor and a band of Conservative MPs who felt the economy's short-term prospects should be the priority. That option would minimise the introduction of tough measures that would restrict liberty and harm businesses. For now. But mostly, he was winging it. Maybe he preferred the arguments of Professor Heneghan – that there was no second wave – over the advice of dozens of the government's own experts on Sage. If so, he was cherry-picking an unproven point of view that justified his desire to keep the economy active. Heneghan would still be tweeting his doubts about the evidence for a second wave four weeks later when deaths hit 200 a day again. Subsequently, Johnson would justify this big call by claiming that he wanted to avoid being locked down all year and that it was easy for people – after the event – to assess his decisions with what he called a 'retrospectoscope'.

If he had some slim hope that the second wave of infections might not be so bad, then his own scientific advisers were telling him exactly the opposite. The only proven way of reversing the virus's spread was by fully locking down, as it was clear by now that local restrictions were insufficient to contain the virus when it was already at such high levels. It was obvious to many people at the time that the economy would be hit even harder with a longer lockdown if infections were allowed to rise to the point where hospitals would be overrun again. Johnson's decision flew in the face of all the advice over the summer from the World Bank, the cross-party group of politicians and leading international public health experts that, in the era of Covid, the virus had to be kept under control before the economy could thrive. Otherwise, Britain would be left with the worst of both worlds: an economy that would be shackled by lengthy restrictive measures and a high death toll once again. And that is exactly what happened.

Some of Johnson's own advisers were incandescent with rage about his decision that week in September. 'I don't have sympathy for the government making the same mistake twice,' said a senior source on the Sage committee whom we interviewed extensively about the lead-up to the second wave. 'We told them quite clearly what they need to do for it to work. They don't do that ... It's been wishful thinking all the way through. I think that probably characterises Boris Johnson, frankly.'

The split between No. 10 and its chief medical and scientific advisers had never been more apparent. At 11 a.m. the next morning, Monday 21 September, Whitty and Vallance took the unprecedented step of holding their own press conference – in front of a sombre grey background with no politicians present. It was presented as a briefing for the nation, but it was a clear attempt to make the prime minister change his mind and draw attention to the folly of failing to act decisively. 'As we see it,' Vallance said, 'cases are increasing, hospitalisations are following, deaths unfortunately will follow that. And there is the potential for this to move very fast.'

In order to illustrate how quickly infections were rising, Vallance gave an example of what might happen if the current levels of infections were allowed to carry on doubling every week – as they appeared to be doing at that time. While stressing that this wasn't a prediction, his example showed how the number of infections would quickly rise to 50,000 each day by mid-October. This, he said, would lead to around 200-plus deaths per day by the middle of November. It was a shocking prediction that drew scathing criticism from some newspapers. Whitty and Vallance were accused of 'scaremongering', they were labelled 'Professor Gloom and Dr Doom', and one newspaper quoted an unnamed Tory MP unkindly describing them as Messrs 'Witless and Unbalanced' for greatly exaggerating the figures.

However, time would vindicate the two advisers, as the situation would soon prove to be just as perilous as Vallance had warned. In fact, Vallance had hugely downplayed the predicted November death figures, which would be nearer the 500 daily fatalities upper estimate he had given Johnson a few days earlier. By mid-November the official daily death toll would average at around 430 a day, which was more than twice the number he had indicated in public. The infection figures were more complicated. When mid-October arrived, the opponents of lockdown would argue that Vallance's prediction of 50,000 infections a day was an overestimate, because the daily positive test results, which he appeared to be using as the basis for his calculations, turned out to be 20,000. But they were splitting hairs. According to Imperial College – which has now drawn together official statistics and the results of mass population sampling – infections reached around 45,000 in mid-October, and other official studies have suggested they may have been as high as 73,000. Time has now proved that Professor Gloom and Dr Doom were justified in presenting such a bleak picture. They were certainly in the right ballpark that day. There were big problems ahead.

But Vallance and Whitty had lost the battle over the circuit breaker lockdown in September. Their disappointment with the prime minister's decision was further underlined that day when the Sage meeting – which they jointly chair – endorsed the alarming report from Professor Edmunds and his colleagues warning of 'catastrophic consequences' unless immediate action was taken. The report said that more than 90 per cent of the UK's population remained susceptible to the virus, so measures needed to be swiftly brought in to slow down its spread. 'The more rapidly these interventions are put in place the greater the reduction in Covid-related deaths and the quicker they can be eased,' the Sage minutes state.

The government had spent months repeatedly saying it was following the advice of its scientists. But on such a crucial matter, Johnson ignored them. The next day, Tuesday 22 September, he announced that there would be minor extensions to the rules banning more than six people from meeting and a new 10 p.m. curfew on pubs and restaurants. There was also a request that people now work from home if they could. That was it. The new curfew was a symbolic gesture that, if anything, would help transmit the virus by causing overcrowding on public transport as people were forced to spill out of pubs and restaurants at an unusually early time. The request to work

Slow return

Footfall in workplaces compared to normal levels, selected parts of the UK

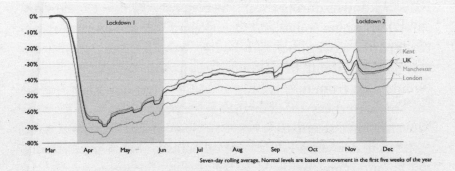

Seven-day rolling average. Normal levels are based on movement in the first five weeks of the year

from home was welcomed by the scientists, but was not considered anything like tough enough. Their concerns were borne out by Google tracking data that showed that the number of people attending workplaces continued to rise in the weeks afterwards.

Our Sage adviser source says that the new restrictions were woefully inadequate. 'Literally days before, [Johnson] had still been encouraging people to go back to work,' he said. 'The [Edmunds] document on 21 September makes it obvious that you need a package of interventions to keep the reproduction number below one. Just picking one and saying we're going to try and get people to work from home a bit in some half-hearted way isn't going to be enough. The epidemic will just come back.' He blames the chancellor for his 'one-eyed' approach in putting the nation's finances first. 'I thought the chancellor was in charge. He was the main person who was responsible for the second wave … My view was all along we are going to have to take these measures, so it's better to take them early, and get the cases right down. Same old, same old,' he said. 'Take the stringent measures early, reset the clock, put the epidemic back, and then hold it at a lower level. And then, holding it at a lower level, life is way safer for everybody.'

The effects of the prime minister's decision would also be the beginning of the end for the most gossiped-about relationship in Downing Street. Johnson's chief adviser Dominic Cummings had become a strong believer in the necessity of swift and decisive lockdowns during the first wave of the pandemic following his 'Domoscene conversion'. Sources in No. 10 say he strongly backed the government's scientists in the argument over the September circuit breaker. Relations between the two men would sour from that point onwards.

The bitterness of the conflict between Johnson and the government's scientists spilled out into the public domain the following day when Edmunds expressed his burning frustration in an interview on BBC Radio 4's *Today* programme. He described Johnson's latest measures as 'trivial' and went on to predict – with remarkable accuracy – what would happen as a result. 'I suspect we will see very stringent measures coming in place throughout the UK at some point, but it will be too late again. We will have let the epidemic double and double and double again until we do take those measures,' he said. 'And then we'll have the worst of both worlds, because then to slow the epidemic and bring it back down again, all the way down to somewhere close to where it is now or where it was in the summer, will mean putting the brakes on the epidemic for a very long time, very hard.' Edmunds saw a clear parallel with the first wave. 'We didn't react quick enough in March, and so I think that we haven't learned from our mistake back then and we're unfortunately about to repeat it.'

Britain's failure to come out of the first lockdown successfully was now attracting international academic interest. On Thursday 24 September a powerful study entitled 'Lessons learnt from easing Covid-19 restrictions' was published in *The Lancet* medical journal by academics from seven universities across the world, with input from the London School of Hygiene & Tropical Medicine, King's College London, Edinburgh University and the World Health Organization. The study compared the health and economic outcomes of Japan, Singapore, South Korea, New Zealand and Hong Kong in the Asia Pacific region – which had all sought to eradicate infections – with countries in Europe where virus cases had been allowed to build up in a second wave. 'At the time of writing, Spain, Germany and the UK have offered a reminder of the enormous potential for resurgence if comprehensive safeguards are not in place', the study warned.

By controlling the virus at very low levels with strict measures, such as border controls and lockdowns, all five Asia Pacific countries had suffered less damage to their economies and lower death tolls than Britain. Indeed, a few weeks after the report was published it would be announced that the Sydney Opera House was to reopen for audiences in Australia and the All Blacks rugby team would play to a near-capacity crowd in Auckland, New Zealand. The academics concluded: 'The argument is strong for countries adopting a so-called zero-Covid strategy, which aims to eliminate domestic transmission.' There was still hope that Europe could regain some control over the virus. 'It is not too late for the ... lessons to be learnt and applied now,' their report said.

One of the reasons for keeping infections low as 'an important aspiration', besides the number of deaths, was because of 'the growing burden of so-called long Covid', the study observed. As the summer months had passed since the first wave, it had become clear that the effects of the virus were not something people always shook off easily after a few weeks. In fact, this was another argument against those who wanted to achieve herd immunity by allowing the virus to spread through the healthy younger section of the population. An alarmingly high number of patients were suffering serious long-term health consequences from the infection and the NHS was poised to launch a network of 40 'long Covid' specialist clinics because there were estimated to be 60,000 sufferers. People were complaining of fatigue, brain fog, breathlessness and pain for many months after contracting the infection. The complications could be very serious and were hitting relatively young people. Dr Soumya Mukherjee, a neurosurgeon working at Leeds General Infirmary and Addenbrooke's Hospital in Cambridge, described how higher rates of strokes, brain haemorrhages and heart damage were being seen even among patients who had only initially experienced mild symptoms. 'We're seeing 30- to 50-year-olds having strokes,' he said. 'We don't normally see that with that age group. The percentages are much higher.'

Scotland had followed something nearer a full-suppression approach in the summer by maintaining restrictions for longer than the rest of the UK. It is one of the reasons the country had a lower death rate than England by the end of the year – 115 deaths per 100,000 compared with 125 per 100,000. But by September a second wave was emerging in Scotland that appeared to be the result of its government's failure to control its borders. This was illustrated by the fact that 80 per cent of the country's new infections were found to be caused by the new Spanish strain of the virus. The problem would be exacerbated by the reopening of universities.

As the leaves began to turn, there was a new accelerator that would help the virus spread even faster. Two and a half million students were returning to higher education and many were criss-crossing the country to start the new term in faraway university cities. The social whirl of drinking and late-night parties during Freshers' Week was the ideal climate for the dispersal of Covid-19, just as it had always been for various flu-type illnesses in the past.

In August, Jo Grady, the general secretary of the University and College Union, had warned that cramming so many young people back into halls of residence 'could lead to universities being the care homes of any second wave of Covid'. Many of the government's own advisers regarded the return of university and college students in the autumn as a step too far. 'We were concerned that, in particular with the opening of the universities, things could escalate very, very rapidly,' said Daniela De Angelis, Professor of Statistical Science for Health at Cambridge University and a Spi-M committee member. A colleague on the committee, who asked not to be named, shared her foreboding. 'I thought university should be taught online,' the source said. 'I didn't see why we were opening universities. I felt that would be very high risk and I didn't see any real need for it. It was not fair on the students either. I thought they'd end up being charged to be taught online and locked up in their halls of residence.'

But the government pressed ahead with the opening of universities that month despite the escalating number of infections. It did not take long for students to pass on the virus. By the weekend of Saturday 26 September, thousands of students had been ordered to isolate themselves following outbreaks at Manchester, Glasgow, Aberdeen, Dundee and St Andrews universities. Nicola Sturgeon, Scotland's first minister, reacted by banning all students in Scotland from going to the pub and threatened disciplinary action if they did not comply. In Manchester, police and security staff began patrolling halls of residence to make sure students stayed inside out of harm's way. In response, the disgruntled students put up signs in their windows saying: 'Locked up – thanks Boris'; '£9k well spent'; and 'Send drink'. The virus was spreading throughout the big university cities. More outbreaks would occur within weeks at Oxford, Cambridge, Durham, Nottingham, Northumbria, Leeds, Sheffield, Bristol and Newcastle.

The return of the universities fanned the flames of the outbreak, which had already been spreading fast. There had been a five-fold increase in September. By the end of the month – Wednesday 30 September – daily cases across the UK exceeded 12,500 and were still rising. In a statement to the Commons the following day, Hancock claimed that despite all the bad news there were 'early signs that the actions that we've collectively taken over the past month are starting to have a positive impact'. It was more wishful thinking.

Something like a quarter of the UK population was now under local restrictions of one form or another as the government sought to quell the virus with just regionally targeted measures. The city of Leicester had been under restrictions since the end of June and people were joking that the local measures were a little bit like the final lines from the song 'Hotel California': 'You can check out any time you like, / But you can never leave.' Infections had fallen in the city during July and August, but cases had shot up again at the beginning of

September after the restrictions had been gradually eased. Areas such as West Yorkshire, the West Midlands, Lancashire and Greater Manchester had also been placed under local restrictions.

As the days sped by, it was becoming obvious that the limited local control measures were having little effect. Wednesday 7 October was the hundredth day since the local restrictions had first been imposed. Their failure to control the virus meant they could not be lifted in those areas and this was now becoming a major political issue, breeding resentment and frustration in the pockets of the country where compliance with the rules was most critical. In the House of Commons, the Labour leader Keir Starmer pointed out that infections had continued to rise in 19 of the 20 local areas in England that had been placed under restrictions for two months or more. In Bury infections had risen by 13 times over that period; in Bolton they had increased by 14 times; and in Burnley they had rocketed by 20 times.

That day the number of daily deaths from the virus hit 100 again for the first time since June. It was clear the government had to change something. But there was a fierce fight within cabinet about what should be done. Hancock and Gove, nicknamed 'the doves', were pushing for firmer measures, which were being resisted by the more hawkish Sunak. His approach went against the findings of the World Bank that early strong lockdowns and control of the virus were the best hope for a country's economy. Even if he didn't want to listen to the government's scientists, it might have been thought that he would have taken notice of the World Bank.

Instead of introducing a circuit breaker lockdown, the government continued to fiddle around the edges with lesser measures. That week it was announced that social mixing between people in different households in all settings except outdoor public spaces would be forbidden by law in parts of the north-east, Liverpool City region, Warrington, Hartlepool and Middlesbrough.

The surveillance of the virus was now ringing more and more alarm bells. On Thursday 8 October Sage received evidence that infections and hospital admissions were exceeding the worst-case scenario. Just as in the first wave, the experts were taking to Twitter to express their exasperation with the lack of action by the government. On Sunday 11 October Professor Anthony Costello, a former WHO director, tweeted a damning assessment of where the UK had ended up. 'We missed our chance in July to keep the epidemic controlled,' he wrote. 'We're in a mess. Cases, hospitalisations and deaths are rising. It's too late for test and trace to stop it. Things will just get worse.' He argued that the risk of persisting with 'local restrictions only' was that 'cases and deaths rise, with possible exponential spread (as in March)'.

The next day, 19,400 positive tests were recorded, which was another 50 per cent increase since the beginning of the month. That afternoon, Johnson addressed the nation once again to provide more grim news. 'There are already more Covid patients in UK hospitals today than there were on 23 March when the whole country went into lockdown, and deaths, alas, are also rising once again,' he admitted. 'These figures are flashing at us like dashboard warnings in a passenger jet. And we must act now.' But the prime minister was still holding out against bringing in a lockdown.

Instead, he announced that he was 'simplifying' and 'standardising' the local rules – even though they were clearly proving to be ineffective. He announced that there would be three tiers of restrictions. Tier one was to be for areas with low infection rates, which would be able to continue life as normal limited by only the existing national restrictions such as social distancing, the rule of six and the 10 p.m. curfew. In tier two, people from different homes could only meet outside, and could visit pubs and restaurants only if they bought a meal with their drink. Tier three was the highest alert level, in which pubs, cafes and leisure centres would be closed.

The rift between Johnson and his scientists was clear at the media briefing. Whitty, who was standing alongside Johnson, admitted he was 'not confident, nor is anybody confident' that even the third tier would be enough to curtail the spread of the virus. In other words, the government's chief medical officer was sceptical that the plan could fulfil its sole objective. And it wasn't even as if there were any immediate plans to deploy the inadequate tier three widely. Liverpool was the only region that would be placed into it at that time.

Again, the scientists were flabbergasted that they were not consulted about the new tier measures. Assistant Professor Nicholas Davies, the Spi-M member, did not believe the tier system would control the virus and was convinced that this meant there would be 'incidence at a high level everywhere'. He recalls: 'It was a moment of increasing concern and worry for a lot of us because it just felt like the decision making was disconnected from the science … It does sometimes feel like shouting into the void.'

The impatience felt by the scientists was now turning into rebelliousness. Sage broke with protocol and rushed out the minutes of the key 21 September meeting from three weeks earlier. The publication was released out of sequence, as there were a couple of other earlier meetings that would normally have been posted on the website first. But this was the meeting at which the scientists had urgently recommended a circuit breaker lockdown. The chairs of Sage, Vallance and Whitty, were clearly desperately worried and evidently attempting to influence public opinion to put pressure on Johnson. Sure enough, the release caused a furore. Until then, very few people had known just how strongly the government's scientific advisers had lobbied for a lockdown in September.

The next day, the leader of the opposition added to the pressure by backing the scientists' call for an urgent shutdown across England. Keir Starmer accused Johnson of having no 'credible plan to slow infections', 'losing control of the virus' and 'no longer following the scientific advice'. He was backed by city mayors across northern England, including Andy Burnham, the mayor of Greater Manchester, who was resisting his city being singled out by the government to join Liverpool in the strictest 'very high' tier. Starmer reinforced the point by warning Johnson that further delay would bring both more deaths and the 'unavoidable' introduction of even more economically damaging restrictions further down the line.

But Johnson and his chancellor Sunak refused to accept the criticism. In the Commons on Wednesday 14 October, the prime minister mocked Starmer. 'Opportunism is, I am afraid, the name of the game for the party opposite,' he said. 'The whole point is to seize this moment now to avoid the misery of another national lockdown, into which he wants to go headlong, by delivering a regional solution.' Sunak still had not appreciated that failing to control the virus would ultimately cause more damage to the economy. He took Labour to task for wanting a lockdown that could be 'counted in jobs lost and businesses closed' and would 'cause needless damage to parts of our country where virus rates are low'. The chancellor was determinedly set against a lockdown. 'Any responsible party of government would acknowledge the economic cost of a blunt national lockdown,' he argued. 'The Labour Party may say it has a plan, but be under no illusion: a plan blind to the hard choices we face – a plan blind to and detached from reality – is no plan at all.' There was no way, he said, that the UK would be allowed to 'blithely fall into another national spring-style lockdown, as the Labour Party wants to'. He accused Labour of 'political games and cheap shots from the side-lines' and rounded off his attack by saying, 'The Labour Party can either be part of this solution or part of the problem. It is called leadership, but from them, I am not holding my breath.' This was just three weeks before Johnson and Sunak would perform another extraordinary U-turn by introducing the very lockdown they had so vehemently repudiated. The continued delay would mean the shutdown was twice as long as the scientists had deemed necessary in September, which precisely proved Starmer's point.

The scientists, meanwhile, had not given up on the hope that they might be able to change the prime minister's mind about an immediate lockdown, which they believed would save thousands of lives. Sage member Professor Graham Medley had teamed up with three Warwick University members of the government's Spi-M committee to publish a paper calling for a two-week circuit breaker lockdown to start during the October school half-term, which was only days away. The paper pointed out the fundamental law in dealing with the coronavirus, which Britain had learnt so painfully in the first wave. 'We consistently find that the optimal time for a break is always now; there are no good epidemiological reasons to delay the break as this will simply push back any benefits until later, leaving more time for additional cases to accumulate,' they wrote. The paper added: 'Additionally, a short lockdown period would limit the economic costs of such a measure.' It was the fundamental point that Johnson and Sunak still seemed to be failing to grasp. In the era of coronavirus, an economy could only begin to flourish if it controlled the number of infections at low levels. Otherwise, the virus would swiftly make its way through the population, and hospitals would become so overrun that economic activity would have to be halted for longer, with a lengthier lockdown.

But still the prime minister held out against making a stronger intervention. In Northern Ireland, the first minister, Arlene Foster, added to the pressure on Johnson by announcing that a circuit breaker lockdown would be introduced within 48 hours – even though the country had only recorded 1,217 new cases and four deaths in the previous 24 hours. The following week, Wales said it too would bring in a 'short, sharp' national lockdown. On Monday 19 October a YouGov poll found that 67 per cent of the public were in favour of a circuit breaker lockdown also being introduced in England. More than 60 per cent of those polled said they did not trust the prime minister to make the right decisions on the pandemic going forward and were fearful of the virus's impact over the winter.

The next day, deaths surpassed the 200-a-day threshold. It was the figure that – in his example a few weeks before of how the virus could quickly spread – Vallance had estimated might be reached in mid-November. The tragic milestone had arrived almost a month earlier than he had predicted. His critics stayed silent. Two days later, the Spi-M committee estimated there were up to 90,000 new infections a day spreading across the country.

The scientists were becoming increasingly despairing about the way the virus was being allowed to make its way rampantly through the population. 'My concern at that point was [that] they introduce something soon, because at that stage we could see that if nothing happened there could have been devastating consequences for the NHS,' said Professor De Angelis. Her fellow government adviser, Nicholas Davies, says he watched on feeling scared, as Johnson appeared to be making the same mistake as he had in the first wave. 'It seemed like a repeat of the situation in March,' he said. 'I would have thought the idea of letting things get to where they were in March and April was enough of a disincentive on its own that would hopefully drive any government to act, because that was awful.'

The terrible consequences of the second wave were already being witnessed in the hospitals, especially in the parts of the country that had been hit hardest by the rising numbers of infections. We spoke to a doctor treating Covid-19 in Manchester, which had been under restrictions since July. The hospitals in the city were admitting so many new patients each day by the final week of October that, as in the first wave, seriously ill coronavirus patients were starting to die without getting access to life-saving mechanical ventilation.

The doctor, who asked to remain anonymous because he fears he might be disciplined for speaking out, said that from the end of October onwards 'a good 70 per cent to 80 per cent of Covid patients' were denied intensive care treatment when they needed it. 'We haven't got the capacity,' he declared. This included patients in their 30s and 40s. 'That is pretty scary,' said the doctor. One was a 31-year-old female Covid-19 patient who died after being admitted to hospital at the end of October. 'She didn't get the care she needed and she passed away,' he recalls.

One of the problems was that large numbers of staff were having to self-isolate because they or their contacts had symptoms of the virus. The doctor told us that the situation became so desperate during that period that a quarantining colleague awaiting his test result for the virus was ordered by managers to treat vulnerable patients undergoing chemotherapy on a cancer ward. 'That is obviously not best practice,' the doctor said. Remarkably, the Manchester hospital was still short of protective masks even though this was supposed to have been sorted out in the summer by the government. 'It's basically a mess,' he said. 'Sometimes they're on the wards, sometimes they're not. It's only a minority of us doctors who haven't had the virus now.'

The doctor says his colleagues were angry about the government's delay in locking down. He said: 'I was really frustrated at the point where Sage was saying they should have done the circuit breaker much earlier, similar to what Wales did.' The economy, he maintained, would only have to be 'locked down longer' as a result of the failure to bring in measures to suppress the virus in September. 'So where was the argument for delaying it? It was clear there was going to be an issue,' he said. 'We were just baffled.'

This lack of specialist staff in his Manchester hospital was clearly not an isolated issue. A survey of doctors in October by the Faculty of Intensive Care Medicine found that four out of five intensive care consultants believed their expanded units were inadequately staffed. This was the critical problem that would be experienced by many hospitals. It might be possible to expand bed capacity, but there were insufficient staff with the training and qualifications to look after the extra patients.

Kim Astwood-Wainwright described the scenes in Fairfield General Hospital in Bury, Greater Manchester, in mid-October when her 67-year-old father Don Astwood was admitted with Covid-19. The hospital was 'overwhelmed', she said, and her father was forced to remain in a bed in A&E for 48 hours because there was no space on the wards. Her father, a wedding DJ nicknamed 'Disco Don', was later placed on a Covid ward with six other men aged between 40 and 90. Kim, a recruitment consultant, went to visit him on the night of 25 October dressed head to toe in protective equipment. 'We went in not expecting to see anything great, but we didn't realise what we were going into,' Kim said. 'The sounds alone of the coughing … it's a whole different sound of chest rattle and all the oxygen machines and everything. It's something I won't forget. We saw the nurses receiving calls from A&E saying, "We've got more people coming up." They were moving patients around because there wasn't enough space.' Kim says the staff's faces were drawn and tired. 'One of them got emotional because she was on the nurse's station when they rang up from A&E. She said to one of the porters, "I don't know where we're going to put them." The porter put his arm around her and said, "It's all right. We'll get through it." And I thought, "My god. If everyone could see this."' Her father died the following morning.

Kim says she feels 'let down' by the government. She believes that Don might still have been alive today if ministers had not been pushing for people to return to normal life. She said: 'We were so encouraged to mix together, eat out to help out, all these schemes, people going back to university, back to schools. We were so encouraged for all this to happen.' Her father might not have caught the virus in mid-October, she says, 'if restrictions had been introduced in September'.

* * *

On Wednesday 28 October, with deaths now topping more than 300 a day, the scientists on the Spi-M committee made one final appeal. They produced a report setting out the dire consequences of the government's continued inaction. As if to emphasise the point, they had written 'not government policy' in large red capital letters on the first page of their report. While the modelling committee had previously avoided making overt economic projections, the gloves were off now. The scientists wanted to show that the delays in bringing in a 'rapid and decisive' lockdown were both killing people and would damage the economy.

The report repeated the same straightforward arguments. While a lockdown would always be bad for the economy in the short term, the scientists made clear that they believed driving infections down would cause less harm to the nation's finances over time. They argued that the test and trace system would be more effective when the virus was brought down to much lower levels and therefore fewer restrictions would be needed. The report also pointed out how self-defeating it was to try to keep the economy open while the virus was growing fast. It would ultimately lead to a 'de facto lockdown' because people would isolate themselves out of fear once the hospitals had been overrun and it was clear there was no available treatment. This effect had been seen during the first wave in March when people started working from home and sports leagues cancelled fixtures before the government ordered them to do so.

That day, both Germany and France announced national lockdowns to curb their own second waves of the virus, leaving Britain's inaction looking increasingly reckless, as it had done in the first wave. The pressure on the government was becoming too much. The following day, Friday 30 October, the operation committee met again in Downing Street. Johnson, Sunak, Gove and Hancock were all present to listen to a presentation from Sir Simon Stevens, head of the NHS, who delivered an unequivocal message: hospitals would be overrun in every part of England within weeks if nothing was done to stem the rate of infections. Gove later wrote of the meeting in *The Times*: 'That afternoon we were confronted with what would happen to our hospitals if the spread of the virus continued at the rate it was growing. Unless we acted, the NHS would be broken. Not just administratively at full stretch. But physically overwhelmed. Every bed, every ward occupied. All the capacity built in the Nightingales and requisitioned from the private sector too.' He added: 'All the arguments against lockdown came up against that harsh, brute reality.'[3]

The prime minister had no choice. He had to finally give in – despite everything he and his chancellor had said about their determination to avoid locking down. A decision was taken to announce a lockdown after the weekend. But there would be one last twist. Fearing that Johnson might wobble again and change his mind, someone in the prime minister's close circle leaked the news to the press that there would be another national shutdown. The story was broken by *The Times* on the Friday and Johnson was forced to call a press conference the next day. The evening of Halloween Saturday saw another momentous announcement. Johnson told the nation: 'From Thursday until the start of December, you must stay at home.' It was to be a four-week lockdown. As the experts had warned, the economy-damaging measures would have to be imposed for twice as long as the proposed September circuit breaker. But as infections had been allowed to climb to such high levels, would even four weeks be enough?

Johnson's delay had an enormous human cost. The prime minister, this time with strong encouragement from his chancellor, had led the country into another tragedy. According to estimates from Imperial College, more than 2.5 million people were infected between the day the prime minister ignored his expert advisers' calls for a circuit breaker on 22 September and the end

UK Covid cases

New **daily cases** by specimen date and seven-day rolling average

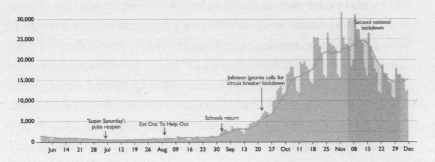

of the second lockdown on 1 December. The figures suggest that if Johnson had brought in measures to just hold daily infections level between those two dates, 1.3 million fewer people would have been infected. With the virus's death rate estimated at between 0.5 per cent and 1 per cent, it suggests that between 6,700 and 13,400 people might never have lost their lives had stricter measures been introduced earlier. And this was only the start of a winter outbreak that had been allowed to spread so widely that it would continue to take lives and place a huge strain on the economy over the months ahead. A poll of 11,080 *Times* and *Sunday Times* readers published on 1 November asked whether they had confidence in the government's handling of the Covid-19 crisis. Just 11 per cent of those polled said 'yes'. An overwhelming 89 per cent said 'no'.

While people retreated to their homes, the hospitals bore the brunt of the government's indecisiveness once again, as they had in March. When the second lockdown began just after midnight on Thursday 5 November, the doctor in Manchester we talked to described how even more patients in his hospital were being denied intensive care treatment due to a lack of space. Some were not even being offered non-invasive ventilation – known as Continuous Positive Airway Pressure (CPAP) – on the standard wards because of a shortage of specialist nurses. 'We haven't got a functioning CPAP ward,' the doctor reported. 'So, we're at the point where if somebody can't get into intensive care and they can't get CPAP then they are in trouble.' The lack of access to intensive care was difficult to explain to seriously ill patients, especially as some were healthcare professionals who were all too aware they needed to be ventilated. 'You have difficult conversations about how there's no beds,' the doctor explained. 'You have to feed their hope there will be a bed available at some point. Generally, by this point they're very sick anyway, and they're very exhausted, so they're not really in a state to put up much of a fight.'

In November Dr Rinesh Parmar, chairman of the Doctors' Association UK, described how medics' morale was 'shot to bits' as they attempted to cope with the effects of the delays before the second lockdown. Doctors were reporting that bed capacity was running dangerously low and protective equipment was still often in short supply. 'Boris Johnson had not learned from his mistakes in the first wave at all,' he said. 'He was clearly ignoring the scientific advice given to him in September. We can see the impact of the second late lockdown. And the impact is that we're having to deal with many more people that are sadly dying from Covid. And that's the bit that we can't stomach. That's the bit that we find incredibly upsetting and difficult to deal with.' The group representing the relatives of many of those who died share the doctors' anger. Jamie Brown, a spokesperson for the Bereaved Families for Justice group, said: 'Essentially the choice the prime minister was presenting between saving lives and protecting jobs and the economy was false all along. It was a total lie. If you wanted to protect the economy you had to first deal with the virus. We've been saying since June the government needs to be forced to recognise the mistakes that have been made in a public inquiry. But they ignored us and repeated the same mistakes. It has been unbelievably, excruciatingly painful.'

The family of 19-year-old Cameron Wellington now live with that torment. A junior martial arts champion from Walsall in the West Midlands, he had been living at home and applying for jobs when the virus struck. His father Norman was the first to test positive for Covid-19 on 8 November. Two days later, it was confirmed that Cameron and his mother Jane were also infected. The family believes the virus entered their home from shopping trips for groceries or through Cameron's siblings, who were attending school. Jane drove Cameron to hospital on 14 November because he was struggling to breathe, but she could not go into the A&E department because of her own infection. Jane recalls: 'As he was getting out, I just said, "You'll be OK, stop worrying." I said, "I love you and I'll be straight back down for you." He said, "OK, Mum, love you." And he walked in.' It was the last time she spoke to her son. Within minutes of her making it home, the phone rang. 'It was a nurse asking me to go straight back down because he was really poorly,' Jane said. When she arrived, doctors told her that Cameron's oxygen levels had dropped to dangerously low levels. 'They were amazed he'd even made it through the doors.' He died on 19 November after suffering multi-organ failure and a blood clot on his lungs. He is among the youngest known victims of Covid-19 in the UK. Jane describes Cameron as 'one of the kindest people you'd ever meet'. She now feels 'totally let down' by the government for doing too little too late to prevent the spread of the virus.

She said: 'We followed the rules and it still got us. They should've shut the country down in September, as soon as the scientists said to. Now we're sorting out our son's funeral. I never dreamt I'd be doing that for Christmas.'

PART FIVE

THE FINAL RECKONING

3 December 2020 to January 2021

15

Plague Island

A modern version of Charles Dickens's famous story, *A Christmas Carol*, might depict Boris Johnson on the night of Thursday 24 December 2020 in his nightshirt tossing and turning in a four-poster bed. There would have been champagne that evening, as the Brexit trade deal had finally been sealed. But a deep unease remained in the pit of the prime minister's stomach.

The hour bell sounds at 1 a.m. With a flash of light, a ghoulish apparition appears. The Ghost of Christmas Past takes the prime minister on a journey back in time. The months flip by like pages of an open book turning over and over in the wind. December, November, August, April and then finally the rush of time comes to rest. It is early January 2020. A happier time. There he is in his pink Bermuda shorts and a baggy long-sleeve shirt with his beautiful young fiancée. They are sipping cocktails next to a gently lapping Caribbean Sea. But no sooner has he felt the warm sun's glow than the picture changes. From a bird's-eye view, he and the spectre swoop down into a grey concrete building. Inside is a room with harsh fluorescent lighting. On a bed is a woman struggling for breath. It is a nightmare. The wards and the corridors of this Chinese hospital are full of such people: coughing, wheezing and dying.

And then, steadily, they tread back through the year in a series of snapshots. Warnings flash up from scientists that there was something uniquely dangerous about this virus from China. The health secretary bounces out of the Cobra meeting to say the risk to the UK is low. The audience laughs in the grand hall of the Old Royal Naval College as he tells them he will don his Superman outfit and fight the fools who are in an irrational panic about the virus. The rain storms rattle against the windows of his Chevening country retreat as he goes missing from public life in February. Politicians are standing up in the House demanding to know why the prime minister has not attended any meetings of his key national security committee, Cobra. There is a terrible sinking feeling in March. Like a recurring exam dream, he turns up and realises he is not prepared. There is no proper plan, no time left to boost testing capacity or personal protective equipment for the medical staff who are about to die. One by one, offices and sports events are closing down voluntarily as fear grips the nation. There is the loneliness in the small hours of night as he agonises over lockdown. Then it is too late.

The blue ambulance lights are flickering all over the country. The hospitals are filling up with breathless patients – just as he had seen in China. He is among them. Pristine black hearses carry thousands of bodies from the care homes to the incinerator. A man in a black top hat shakes his head as he bears coffin after coffin. Sons and daughters crumple in tears. The staff at Downing Street are clapping in the hallway as they greet his return in late April. There is a kumbaya sense of calm – a thankfulness for being given another chance. He will do the right thing now. But there is a fog of pressure in the early summer. The faces of his backbenchers and his chancellor are closing in on him, along with graphs and figures. Beating back the virus will be expensive, they say. Instead, there is now a big party. It is 4 July, Independence Day. People are hugging. The war on the virus is over. Then the summer sun with its long days of hope melts into autumn. There are schoolchildren with satchels heading back to the classroom. But the plague is on the march again. In September, the faces of his chief medical and scientific advisers look deadly serious in the orange half-light as they beseech him. The dominating image now is of another Dickens character. 'Something will turn up,' says Wilkins Micawber. But it doesn't. There are new graphs that show numbers of infections rising higher and higher. And deaths. The days go slowly by. People are urging action, again and again. His legs are inert; there is no running away. There is no choice. It is now the night of Halloween and another lockdown. But it is too late again. Then the lights go out at Christmas. There are queues of yellow and green ambulances outside the hospitals. The doctors have thousand-yard stares. Many hundreds of souls are departing each day. The night terrors go on. In the background there is a ghostly chorus whispering over and over: 'To make the same mistake again is unforgivable.'

History is unlikely to be kind to Johnson and his government's stewardship of Britain's response to the pandemic. Leaders across the world were presented with some of the most unique and difficult problems they will ever face. The virus was a silent killer that forced everyone to forgo that most basic of human instincts: to be together. But some leaders quickly grasped the new reality and took tough decisions when they were necessary. Others tried to muddle through by putting off difficult decisions until it was too late and, as a result, repeated and compounded their errors. By doing so, many more lives were lost. In Britain there was a wishful thinking by the prime minister that everything would turn out to be okay, and it did not. The Ghost of Christmas Present would have presented a bleak vision. In the week between Christmas and New Year, Britain had the highest number of daily infections in Europe and the greatest number of deaths each day – by some distance. A year that had begun with people clamouring to halt all flights to and from China had now turned full circle. China had banned all flights to and from the UK because they feared importing the virus. The hospitals, particularly in London, were brimming over with patients, many of whom were being denied life-saving care. There was a new strain of the virus that was more infectious. The government's own winter-planning document published in July had warned Johnson of precisely such a risk: that if the virus was allowed to persist it might develop into something more dangerous. The discovery of the new strain led to many countries closing their borders to the UK, and it would lead to Britain's third national lockdown – again called too late after the crisis was out of hand. The *New York Times* described isolated Britain as 'Plague Island'.

The government's Christmas nightmare had been inevitable since the end of the four-week second lockdown in England on Wednesday 2 December. The lockdown had significantly reduced infections, but that day the testing stations across the country recorded 16,170 new cases. This was still more than three times the number of daily cases in September when the government's scientists had wanted a circuit breaker lockdown. As if to emphasise that the virus had not gone away, there were also 648 reported deaths from the virus on that Wednesday. Nonetheless, England was moving back into the tier system, which meant that non-essential retail shops would be opened in time for the festive period. In many places deemed to be tier two – such as London, Somerset, York and Cheshire – restaurants and pubs were also permitted to serve up meals again. The meal had to be 'substantial' to justify also buying a drink, and two or more households could not sit around the same table unless they ate alfresco. But the move brought people together in warm indoor environments at a time when infections were still very high. The opening of shops in all the tier regions for the busy festive period seemed reckless to many of the scientists who had argued for the lockdown. Imperial College estimates suggest that there were actually 48,000 new infections across the country on 2 December, whereas there were 6,900 in June on the day the shops were opened after the first lockdown. A massive gamble was being taken for the sake of Christmas shopping. Remarkably, the government had become even more cavalier despite everything that had been learnt from almost a year of fighting the virus.

But, at last, an end seemed in sight. That day there was an announcement that was probably the best news since the pandemic began. Britain was the first Western country to give emergency approval to a vaccine for Covid-19. The Medicines and Healthcare products Regulatory Authority (MHRA) was satisfied that the Pfizer/BioNTech vaccine was safe, which meant that a vaccination programme could begin the following week. The new drug had been found to offer 95 per cent protection against the virus and the government had backed a winner by ordering more than 40 million doses. There were complications, however. The vaccine was cumbersome to handle as it had to be stored at −70 °C, and Britain would only receive 800,000 doses in the initial batch. It would take some time before the company could fulfil its complete order. Two more highly effective vaccines, one from the US company Moderna and the other developed by Oxford University and the British–Swedish firm AstraZeneca, were also on the brink of being approved. The Oxford vaccine would be the game-changer, as the government had ordered 100 million doses and it could be transported more easily because it could be stored at room temperature.

Back in the summer, the prime minister had hoped that the country might have returned to normal by Christmas, but his failure to keep his April pledge and hold R under one meant this was a distant dream. Yet Johnson did not wish to take on the mantle of Scrooge and cancel Christmas. So the government created a five-day amnesty from social distancing restrictions that would allow families to get together at Christmas. Despite warnings from scientists that this was dangerous and would increase infections, three-household groups of any size – called 'Christmas bubbles' – would be permitted to gather between 23 to 27 December. The bubbles meant people could hug relatives and pack closely around tables for the festive feast. The measures were agreed with the devolved governments of Wales, Northern Ireland and Scotland, but there were reservations. 'Just because you can mix with others indoors over this time, that doesn't mean you have to,' cautioned Scotland's first minister Nicola Sturgeon. The chief medical officer Chris Whitty gave similar advice, and the health secretary Matt Hancock put it more simply when he said: 'Don't kill your gran.'

Many people took the government at its word and were planning for big Christmases filled with family and friends. But by mid-December an alarming upturn in infections, especially in London, was starting to make the 'Christmas bubbles' look increasingly foolhardy. The tier system was clearly again not stemming the virus's spread as the government had hoped. On Monday 14 December the capital and parts of Hertfordshire and Essex were put into tier three in an attempt to halt the sudden upsurge since lockdown had been relaxed. It meant that around 34 million people would be in tier three at Christmas, with pubs and restaurants closed. The rest of the country could still go out and buy a drink as long as they also bought a substantial meal – that ministers, in their anxiety to help the hospitality sector, said could be as little as a Scotch egg. Suppliers to pubs reported a boom in demand for the pork and breadcrumb covered snacks.

The prime minister was determined that Christmas would go ahead. He reassured people that they could carry on making arrangements to see family and friends – and buy all those big turkeys. 'I want to be clear we don't want … to ban Christmas, to cancel it,' he told a media conference. 'And I think that would be frankly inhuman and against the instincts of many people in this country.' On 16 December Johnson tried to depict Keir Starmer as the killjoy who wanted to ruin the festive party when the two leaders clashed in the Commons. Starmer had pointed out the sobering news that attempts to control the virus were not working, as three-quarters of tier two regions and half of tier three regions were witnessing a rise in infections. 'All he wants to do is to lock the whole country down,' Johnson chided. 'He is a one-club golfer; that is the only solution he has.' He went on: 'I wish he had had the guts just to say what he really wants to do, which is to cancel the plans people have made and cancel Christmas.'

But it would take only three days before he would make yet another humiliating U-turn and would, after all, be forced to play the role of Scrooge. There had been a truly alarming development. Hancock had announced earlier in the week that a new strain of the virus had been detected in 60 local authorities – mainly in London and the south-east – which was being studied by experts in the government's Porton Down microbiology laboratories in Wiltshire. The research confirmed initial fears that this mutant strain was much more infectious than the original variant. Not even the second lockdown had stopped its exponential progress. On Thursday 17 December 35,400 positive tests were recorded across the UK, which represented a doubling in the daily rate since the beginning of the month. More than 2,000 infected people a day were also flooding into Britain's hospitals, with total admissions fast approaching the figure of 21,700 seen at the peak of the first wave when so many had died without life-saving treatment. On Friday afternoon, the government's scientists briefed the prime minister that he had no choice but to act, because the new strain, known as VUI-202012/01, was up to 70 per cent more transmissible.

The following day, hundreds of thousands of shoppers mingled in the city centres on the traditionally frantic last Saturday before Christmas. As darkness fell in the afternoon, many were still out buying their presents when the prime minister held a media briefing. Having pilloried the Labour leader for supposedly wanting to cancel Christmas, he was going to do it himself. 'Given the early evidence we have on this new variant of the virus, the potential risk it poses, it is with a very heavy heart that I must tell you we cannot continue with Christmas as planned,' he said. Large swathes of London and the south-east were placed under new tier four restrictions and were effectively in a third lockdown under another name. Non-essential shops were closed from midnight and people were forbidden from mixing with other households or travelling outside the area. But for the rest of the country, the three-household mixing would be allowed to continue, albeit on Christmas Day only.

Johnson's government became the first since the Long Parliament during the English Civil War in the 17th century to clamp down on Christmas celebrations. In some ways, Britain had been unlucky to be struck by a mutant virus. But you make your own luck. By allowing the virus to proliferate across the country for almost the entire year, the government had significantly increased the risk that it could mutate into something more dangerous.

Word of the new virus strain led to swift action around the world as countries rushed to ban travel to and from Britain. The failure to get a grip on the pandemic had turned the United Kingdom into the Wuhan of Christmas 2020. Except, while the Chinese city had managed to effectively eradicate the virus in nine weeks, Britain had failed to do so in nine months. Now it was the international pariah, with hospitals overflowing and a terrifying new mutant virus running rampant. The international press was damning. The French newspapers declared Britain as 'cut off from the world' and the *Washington Post* pointed out that Johnson should have 'acted sooner' to put the brakes on 'the runaway train' of infections.

There was a further irony. The travel ban had resulted in exactly the chaos around Dover that had been feared from a no-deal Brexit. France refused to allow lorry drivers to cross the Channel without a negative test for the virus and this led to a gargantuan backlog. Thousands of lorries had to be parked up on the verges of the M20 motorway and on the runway of Manston Airport. Many drivers spent their Christmas parked up in their cabs.

Meanwhile, the Brexit trade deal negotiations were going to the wire. Inevitably, it was in the interests of both the UK and the European Union to come to a compromise after the years of posturing. So on Christmas Eve, with just a week to go before the end of the Brexit transition period, a 2,000-page document was agreed, setting out a new tariff-free arrangement for trade. It was a relief, as the British economy was already heavily damaged. Johnson declared the deal to be 'glad tidings of great joy' for the country. This should have been his crowning moment. It was the reason why he had been made his party's leader and won the election. But the post-Brexit euphoria was overshadowed by the tragedy that was now unfolding around him in the nation's hospitals.

More than 16 million people were in lockdown over Christmas. But there was another ray of hope in the darkest days of the year. The day after Boxing Day, the Oxford University and AstraZeneca vaccine was given emergency approval by the MHRA. The company said it would begin shipping the vaccine at the beginning of January and hoped to ramp up production to two million doses a week. In theory, a substantial proportion of the population could be inoculated by the spring if all went well. The Pfizer vaccine was already being injected into people's arms across the country and the speed of the roll-out was the one aspect of Britain's pandemic strategy to receive praise from overseas commentators. It was now a life-and-death race, because the huge rise in infections, especially in London, was already overwhelming the NHS.

In the days leading up to New Year, almost a thousand people were dying every day from the virus. The numbers of infected patients in UK hospitals had overtaken the numbers seen at the April peak and were rising every day. Doctors in London were comparing the crisis to a war zone, as seriously ill patients were again being denied access to intensive care. For the third time in a year, hospitals did not have the qualified staff to handle the deluge of infected patients flooding through their doors. Hugh

Montgomery, Professor of Intensive Care Medicine at University College London, described how whole families were being wiped out by the virus on the wards. Queues of ambulances were pictured outside the Royal London Hospital in Whitechapel and Queen's Hospital in Romford, with patients waiting for hours inside the vehicles because the wards had run out of beds. Dr Gareth Grier, a consultant with London's air ambulance, tweeted that paramedics were now having to resort to the 'terrible option' of treating patients outside hospitals. 'No one wants to do this, it is a red line for all of us, but we've now had to cross it,' he said. 'The impact on ambulance services is inevitably that patients will come to harm while waiting for a response. This is awful, truly awful.'

Patients were being transferred from hospitals in Kent to as far afield as Yorkshire and Plymouth because of the lack of capacity. Dr Megan Smith, a consultant anaesthetist at Guy's and St Thomas' NHS Foundation Trust, said medics were facing 'horrifying' decisions because patients were now 'in competition' for ventilators. 'Deciding the outcome of, effectively, a competition for a ventilator is just not what anyone signed up for,' she told ITN. 'In terms of the emotional trauma for those individuals, it's horrifying. We shouldn't be having to do it, but we are.'

Despite the crisis rapidly deteriorating, with daily infections cases soaring over 50,000, the government was still adamant that large numbers of schools would reopen in the first week of January. Rachel Clarke, a palliative care doctor in Oxford, tweeted that this would make a dire situation even worse. 'Pupils will transmit Covid to each other and into their homes and families. No-one wants school closures. But a toll of avoidable deaths will follow.'

The scientists on Sage had warned the government before Christmas that the new virus strain was highly unlikely to be controlled if schools returned, even if there was a full national lockdown similar to the four-week clampdown in November.

The virus was simply too infectious. A report by scientists from Imperial College was released on New Year's Eve containing evidence that the mutant strain had actually tripled in numbers of infections while the second national lockdown was in place. By contrast, the number of new cases caused by the old less-infectious strain dropped by a third over the same period. There was also a possibility that the vaccines might be less effective against this new variant, and another highly transmissible strain that had been discovered in South Africa that had already been detected in the UK. This was an extremely worrying development.

The situation in the hospitals was far worse than when the previous two national lockdowns were introduced. There had been fewer than 7,000 Covid patients in hospital when the country was shut down in March, and around 14,000 at the start of the second lockdown in November. By 28 December there were close to 24,000 people in hospital. The country was on the brink of a human catastrophe on a scale even more nightmarish than anything that had come before. Yet Johnson's inertia was growing exponentially. He was still resisting a third national lockdown, even though it was now clear the local tier system was again proving to be woefully inadequate against the tide of infections.

Many could not understand why Johnson had failed to introduce a national lockdown nine days earlier when he had first been informed about the high infectivity of the new mutant virus. Among them was a doctor in west London whose hospital was now coming under pressure. He told us that he and his colleagues were bewildered by the prime minister's failure to bring in tougher measures to combat the mutant strain before Christmas. 'It's very reminiscent of what happened in the first wave in terms of ignoring the problem and not locking down,' he said. 'The prime minister is ignoring the scientific advisers, ignoring the frontline. It's scarily familiar.' The leaders of Scotland, Wales and Northern Ireland had all announced blanket tier four national lockdowns by Sunday 20 December – within two days of the shocking news about the extent of the mutant virus's heightened infectivity. In contrast, Johnson had announced that he was leaving more than two-thirds of England under weaker restrictions over Christmas.

In a sense, the roll-out of the vaccine made shutting the country down a third time even more of a moral imperative. People who had been previously sceptical about lockdowns were now changing their minds, because the vaccine offered a way out. Herd immunity could be achieved without the mass casualties that would have followed if the virus had been allowed to make its way through the population. There was an end in sight and it would be negligent to leave people exposed to a life-threatening virus when they were just weeks or months away from being vaccinated. On Wednesday 30 December executives at the Royal London Hospital issued a written warning to staff that 'disaster mode' had been activated. 'We are no longer providing high-standard critical care, because we cannot,' the message read. Yet, still no new restrictions were introduced and the government was insisting that children should return to school the next week.

The following evening, the last of 2020, was the most muted New Year celebration since the Second World War. The streets of London – which in any other year would have been heaving with crowds – were mostly empty, although an eagle-eyed photographer did spot a woman being ticked off by police for drinking a glass of champagne in the street. That was big news on a very quiet evening. By contrast, on the other side of the world, there were packed crowds watching the fireworks in Melbourne and Auckland to bring in the New Year. Both those cities had adopted scorched earth policies in response to the virus in their winter and had been reaping the benefits ever since. On New Year's Eve, there were more deaths reported in Britain from the virus in 24 hours than there had been in the whole of Australia over the year. In fact, there were more fatalities from the virus recorded in the

UK in just an hour than the total death toll from the pandemic in New Zealand. That evening, there was also a large gathering of revellers to let off balloons at the front of the old Hankow Customs House building as its clock struck midnight. This was in Wuhan, the place where it had all begun a year earlier.

One day there will be an inquiry into the mistakes and missteps during 2020. They have been chronicled at length in this book. By the end of the year, more than 90,000 people had perished in Britain with the virus given as a cause of death on their death certificate, and the country suffered one of the largest falls in economic output ever. The toll was felt most harshly by the poor, the disadvantaged and the disabled. One in three low-paid workers was furloughed or lost their jobs compared with one in ten of the higher-paid. People with learning disabilities were four times more likely to die than those without them. Black people were three times more likely to die than white people.

There have already been some attempts to evaluate what happened and where everything went wrong for Britain. In November, the government's own Office for Budget Responsibility summed up the key elements of a truly disastrous year. 'During the first wave of the pandemic, the UK experienced one of the highest rates of infections, hospital admissions and deaths among advanced economies,' the report states. 'In addition, the UK introduced more stringent public health restrictions later but maintained them for longer than in many other European countries. The combination of the severity of the outbreak and the length and stringency of the first lockdown in the UK saw output fall by over a fifth between the fourth quarter of 2019 and second quarter of 2020 – its sharpest contraction on record and one of the largest among advanced economies.'

This was Britain's reality in 2020: the highest death toll in Europe and a devastating economic slump. The country's gross domestic product is estimated to have dropped by 11.2 per cent over the year, according to the Organisation for Economic

Cooperation and Development. This was a bigger fall than any of the other G7 nations and was close to being the worst of any major economy in the world. However, the first lockdown, which had caused the recession, had been absolutely necessary. It had saved a staggering 470,000 lives, according to a paper commissioned by the government in the summer. The problem was, of course, the length of the lockdown. Johnson's delay in introducing restrictions in March had caused so many infections to build up that Britain had been forced to have one of the longest lockdowns in the world, and it had still failed to bring the virus down to a controllable level.

The All-Party Parliamentary Group on Coronavirus finally published the results of its own inquiry into the handling of the pandemic in the first week of December. The committee had heard from 65 witnesses in over 200 hours of live public evidence sessions and had received almost 3,000 separate evidence submissions since the summer. The MPs' conclusions would be quite familiar to readers of this book. Their inquiry found that the government's flawed approach of holding back restrictions until it was too late in an attempt to protect the economy had caused the UK to have the highest death toll in Europe as well as suffering one of the deepest recessions. It recommended that in future the government should recognise that saving people's lives was the best way to safeguard jobs and the economy.

The government's attempt to claim that the NHS had coped during the first wave was also undermined in a report by the Coronavirus Clinical Characterisation Consortium, which went to the Sage committee in December. The consortium – which is made up of some of the country's leading health experts including Sage member Professor Calum Semple, who received an OBE for his work on the pandemic – accepted that there may well have been 'rationing' of life-saving critical care for coronavirus patients. It had carried out an analysis of the outcomes of 64,000 coronavirus patients in British hospitals, which was close to half of all infected in-patients admitted between March and August. The report says that 'at the peak of admissions, NHS trusts were stretched beyond capacity.' It found that a lower proportion of elderly and co-morbid patients were being ventilated compared with later stages of the outbreak when there was less demand.

In October we had revealed evidence that access to intensive care had been rationed in hospitals across England, which had led to patients being denied life-saving ventilation. This had sparked an intemperate reaction from Professor Stephen Powis, the NHS national medical director, who claimed our story was 'untrue' and was 'deeply offensive' to health service workers. Powis was adamant that 'even at the height of the pandemic there was no shortage of ventilators and intensive care.' The consortium's findings suggest he was very badly informed. Its report also found that survival chances of some Covid-19 patients decreased because there were not enough specialist staff to cover 'the rapid expansion of intensive care beds'. This avoidable reality contributed significantly to the more than 55,000 deaths from the virus in the first wave.

Great calamities in history can have multiple causes. Sometimes they are a result of political movements, demographic shifts and economic change. But sometimes they can simply be the result of decisions and actions by individuals. There is no doubt that Britain was hit by the pandemic at one of its worst and most vulnerable moments. A country divided by Brexit had voted in a government shorn of many of its more experienced hands. But, as this book has covered in detail, the weight of responsibility does fall heavily on the shoulders of the prime minister himself. He would almost certainly agree that individuals do shape history, as is attested by his biography of Winston Churchill in which his hero saves his country from the scourge of Nazism. Unfortunately, Johnson's decisions – in particular the delays to the lockdowns – had a cataclysmic impact on his country, leaving it viewed internationally as a 'plague island', to borrow the words of the *New York Times* again.

Any inquiry will also question the role of his chancellor, Rishi Sunak. The new 'golden boy', Sunak was influential in persuading Johnson to reject the call for the circuit breaker lockdown in September. Johnson preferred the chancellor's anti-lockdown arguments to the advice he was being given by his chief advisers, the Sage scientists and some of his other leading ministers. You can add to that list the world-leading public health experts, the All-Party Parliamentary Group on Coronavirus and the World Bank, who were all clear that the virus had to be kept under control if the economy was to stand any chance of flourishing. Sunak seemed not to have appreciated or understood the growing consensus around this point, which was based on research into the impact of policy decisions on economic and mortality data in countries around the world since the start of the pandemic. There was a telling moment in the Commons in November when he claimed it was a 'misapprehension' to say that the second lockdown had been brought in too late. He claimed the shutdown had been introduced because 'the NHS was at risk of being overwhelmed in a matter of weeks' and that the government 'should only enact such measures when it becomes truly unavoidable'. Did he really mean that it was desirable for the government to wait until hospital capacity was over-brimming before intervening decisively? The consequence of doing so would be a huge loss of life and an inevitable third national lockdown that caused even greater economic damage. This flawed strategy is the single most important reason why the UK would end up locked down for almost the entire winter.

As the year progressed, many other members of Johnson's top team appear to have learnt the lessons from the first wave. For all his inability to admit mistakes, the health secretary Matt Hancock is understood to have constantly pushed for restrictions to limit the spread of the virus, in opposition to some of his more hawkish cabinet colleagues. The prime minister's chief adviser Dominic Cummings was also an advocate of firmer measures before his star waned. Both Patrick Vallance and Chris Whitty did a difficult job with great dignity. They tried hard to push the prime minister into acting, but were not always successful.

Michael Gove was one of the few ministers to clearly articulate an understanding that the economy could only thrive if the virus was kept in check. In a frank article in *The Times* in November, he explained why lockdowns were unavoidable. 'Just as we want to reduce Covid-19 infections to save lives, so reducing them is the key to saving the economy,' he argued. 'Think for a moment what would happen to our economy if we allowed infections to reach such a level that our NHS was overwhelmed. Would families seek out crowded bars and buzzing restaurants if they knew they could be infecting friends and relatives who could not be treated if they fell ill? Would we flock to the January sales if the doors to our hospitals were shut? Would investors, entrepreneurs and tourists make a beeline for Britain if we could not even guarantee the lives and welfare of our existing citizens?' There was no other rational choice in the era of Covid-19. He described a dystopian vision of what might happen if the NHS was overwhelmed. 'It would mean Covid-19 patients who could be saved would die; cancer patients who could be cured would be lost ... the economy would grind to a halt, as a population we could not protect sought to save their loved ones; and the world would hang an indelible quarantine sign over our nation's name.' Although he did not know it, he was depicting all the elements of the crisis that would actually happen in Britain as this book was being completed.

Over the year, it was a regular feature of our investigations for *The Sunday Times* that we would send out long letters to Downing Street explaining our findings and seeking a response. None of the responses from No. 10 ever acknowledged that the government had made any mistakes. This defensive attitude was summed up by Priti Patel, the home secretary, on 22 December when she declared on BBC Radio 4's *Today* programme: 'The government has consistently throughout this year been ahead of the curve in terms of proactive measures with regards to coronavirus.' Johnson claimed sarcastically that the criticisms against him amounted to people being wise after the event, when he appeared on BBC One's *Andrew Marr Show* on Sunday 3 January. 'The retrospectoscope is a magnificent instrument,' he quipped. He dismissed all criticism of his failure to lock down in September when his scientists were urging him to. 'From March onwards you could have spent the entire year in lockdown,' he said. It was a redundant argument. As the New Year celebrations on the other side of the world showed, other governments had successfully eradicated the virus by acting promptly to stop the outbreak at source. This enabled their leaders to open up the economy and let people go back to their normal lives. Those nations spent far less time in lockdown than Britain. Johnson had previously pledged to keep the R rate under one to protect lives and the economy, but he had then abandoned that strategy during the reckless months of summer into autumn. Nobody had asked the prime minister to lock down all year. His advisers had just wanted him to intervene at the right times to keep the virus under control and therefore minimise the period the extreme restrictions needed to be in place. Ironically, by ignoring the advisers' pleas to act quickly and delaying until the last minute, Johnson had trapped the country in a vicious cycle of protracted shutdowns. People in the UK would be locked down for longer than almost every other nation in the world as a direct result of his actions.

The judgement of experts who once worked at the top of government is withering. Sir David King, the former government chief scientific adviser, says Johnson and Sunak bought into the 'totally false dichotomy' that there was somehow a trade-off between the health of the nation and that of the economy. 'If in the interests of the economy you allow the disease to spread it only means you then have to go into a longer more expensive lockdown. The government has been trying to deal with this pandemic in a grossly inefficient manner,' he said. 'Now we've got the worst of all possible worlds. It is not just thousands of people who have died unnecessarily, it's tens of thousands. It has also caused an unprecedented hit on the economy.'

Rory Stewart, the former international development secretary and Conservative Party leadership contender, argues there was a smugness and arrogance about his own government's approach to the virus. He said there was a 'cultural problem' with the belief that 'Britain was the best country in the world at public health response and that we didn't really have anything to learn from other people'. His ex-colleagues, he continued, failed to take on board the way the Chinese managed to eradicate coronavirus. 'China has somehow got itself in a situation, despite having a population much larger than us, where they have got almost zero Covid cases at the moment. Their economy is growing. Britain has nearly 20 times the number of cases per head of population and 40 times the number of deaths, and somehow we've concluded that we can't learn from that.'[1]

The final assessment comes from Lord O'Donnell, who would have been in charge of mobilising the civil service if a pandemic had happened when he was cabinet secretary from 2005 to 2011. 'I think we have to accept the fact that a country that was ranked second in the world for its preparedness for a global pandemic has done very badly on virtually every front. If you look at the health side our outcomes are very poor in terms of excess deaths. On the economic side we've got bigger falls in GDP than almost everybody else. If you look at individual well-being, which is the best overall measure, we've had a very large fall, bigger than in other countries.'[2]

The death toll from the pandemic's first year left tens of thousands of families across the country in mourning. For many the sadness became anger as they began to find out more about how their loved ones had died. Could their lives have been saved if the NHS had not been so overrun? The families we spoke to had nothing but admiration and sympathy for the health service staff who worked night and day under enormous pressure risking their own lives. More than 600 health and social service staff were killed by the virus, and there are likely to be many more before the spring. Instead, the families want to understand the mistakes made by the government, which allowed so many people to be exposed to the infection.

In the summer of 2020 the Covid-19 Bereaved Families for Justice UK group, representing more than 2,000 sets of relatives, wrote to the prime minister and the health secretary demanding an immediate statutory inquiry into their handling of the pandemic to learn lessons so future lives could be saved. They argued that there was a legal obligation to carry out an inquiry under human rights law, as the government had failed to take reasonable steps to safeguard life. They also asked to meet Johnson and Hancock to put their questions in person. Both requests were refused by the government's lawyers. Johnson has said an inquiry will be held 'in the future' but has declined to say when.

The families are now seeking a judicial review to force an inquiry, and have enlisted Pete Weatherby QC and the human rights lawyer Elkan Abrahamson, who have previously represented bereaved families of those who died at Hillsborough, Grenfell Tower and the Manchester Bombings. The lawyers say the prime minister's actions during the pandemic have left the government vulnerable to civil claims being brought for negligence and the violation of human rights. Weatherby and Abrahamson believe that Johnson's conduct could also amount to 'the criminal offence of gross negligence manslaughter', although they believe it is unlikely that the Crown Prosecution Service would take up such a case. That may change, they note, if further evidence emerges at a future public inquiry.

The lawyers say one of the key elements of a case against the prime minister would be evidence that he was aware of the correct strategy for preventing a second wave and had sacrificed more lives by not following it. They point to the passage from Johnson's speech on the steps of Downing Street on 27 April when he had returned to work after recovering from his illness. He said the following: 'We must also recognise the risk of a second spike, the risk of losing control of that virus and letting the reproduction rate go back over one. That would mean not only a new wave of death and disease but also an economic disaster, and we would be forced once again to slam on the brakes across the whole country and the whole economy ... I refuse to throw away all the effort and sacrifice of the British people and to risk a second major outbreak and huge loss of life and the overwhelming of the NHS.' When the moment came, he did, of course, resist bringing in restrictions that would have kept the R rate under control and, as a result, the disastrous scenario he had warned about then came to pass. Abrahamson says the government's lawyers are 'ferociously' fighting attempts to hold an inquiry that would get to the truth. 'If you're not entirely confident, you can justify your actions, you don't want them to be scrutinised,' he observed. 'We as the public are entitled to know why decisions are being taken and are entitled to answers and entitled to challenge those decisions ... but we're not getting any of that.'

> The Phantom slowly, gravely, silently approached. When it came near him, Scrooge bent upon his knee; for in the very air through which this Spirit moved it seemed to scatter gloom and misery ... The Spirit answered not, but pointed onward with its hand. (Charles Dickens, *A Christmas Carol*, 1843)

As we were writing the last chapter of this book it was becoming increasingly clear that the coronavirus crisis was escalating to new levels of horror. The hospitals had been rapidly filling up over several weeks until they were past breaking point, with more and more coronavirus patients being admitted. The numbers of new positive tests for the virus were also setting record daily highs by the end of December. The Ghost of Christmas Yet to Come was indeed pointing onwards to gloom and misery. There is a time lag between people testing positive for the virus and their symptoms becoming so severe that they need hospital treatment. So the huge numbers of new infections would undoubtedly worsen the biggest emergency the health service has ever faced in its 71-year history over January and February 2021 and guarantee that Britain would easily surpass the appalling milestone of suffering 100,000 deaths from the virus. Yet, at the beginning of January, the government was still telling parents to send their children back to school and was continuing to vacillate over a lockdown.

When we began writing this book, we had witnessed the consequences of the decision to lock down late in March, but did not expect the government to make the same mistake again by delaying in the autumn. We certainly did not think that Johnson would commit the same error for a third time. By prevaricating again over Christmas and into the New Year, 1.6 million more people are estimated to have been infected over the 17 days from the time the cabinet agreed that something had to be done about the mutant virus on Saturday 19 December and the inevitable national lockdown on Monday 4 January. That brought the total number of infections allowed to spread across Britain over the combined 68 days that the prime minister had delayed bringing in the country's three lockdowns to an extraordinary 4.5 million, according to Imperial College modelling. On each occasion, he had been advised to act immediately. Those infections then set off chain reactions seeding more infections and deadly outbreaks long after the lockdowns were finally brought in. Such was the lack of clear decision making that Monday that the schools actually returned from holiday for one day before being closed until at least half-term. Johnson had caused mass worry and confusion by claiming, on the

Sunday, that schools were 'safe', but then, the following day, admitting they may be 'vectors for transmission' between households. Announcing the third national lockdown at 8 p.m. that Monday evening, in yet another television address to the nation, the prime minister said it would take months to protect all the elderly and vulnerable with mass vaccinations. In the meantime, the situation was dire. He revealed that hospital numbers and daily positive tests for the infection were even higher than anyone had known.

Looking dishevelled and crestfallen, Johnson explained: 'As I speak to you tonight, our hospitals are under more pressure from Covid than at any time since the start of the pandemic. In England alone, the number of Covid patients in hospitals has increased by nearly a third in the last week, to almost 27,000. That number is 40 per cent higher than the first peak in April. On 29 December more than 80,000 people tested positive for Covid across the UK – a new record. The number of deaths is up by 20 per cent over the last week and will sadly rise further ...

'This means the government is once again instructing you to stay at home.'

References

1: The Best Clue to the Origins

1. 'Beijing told doctors to hide SARS victims', *The Washington Post*, 20 April 2003.
2. 'How China's "Bat Woman" hunted down viruses from SARS to the new coronavirus', *Scientific American*, 1 June 2020.
3. 'State Department cables warned of safety issues at Wuhan lab studying bat coronaviruses', *The Washington Post*, 14 April 2020.

2: Outbreak and Cover-Up

1. 'Coronavirus: Fact-checking claims it might have started in August 2019', BBC News, 15 June 2020.
2. 'Why DID so many athletes fall sick in Wuhan in October? More competitors reveal they were ill at the World Military Games months before China admitted coronavirus could be passed between humans', *Mail on Sunday*, 16 May 2020.
3. 'Coronavirus: China's first confirmed Covid-19 case traced back to November 17', *South China Morning Post*, 13 March 2020.
4. 'How China's "Bat Woman" hunted down viruses from SARS to the new coronavirus', *Scientific American*, 1 June 2020.
5. 'Coronavirus: Doctors are reduced to tears as they turn away patients', *The Sunday Times*, 9 February 2020.
6. 'Chinese laboratory that first shared coronavirus genome with world ordered to close for "rectification", hindering its Covid-19 research', *South China Morning Post*, 28 February 2020.

406

7. 'Director of Wuhan Institute of Virology says, "Let science speak"', China Global Television Network, 25 May 2020.
8. Ibid.
9. 'UK patient zero? East Sussex family may have been infected with coronavirus as early as mid-January', *Telegraph*, 25 March 2020.
10. 'Brit was first to die of Covid outside of China last Xmas – daughter says "he'd still be here if Beijing hadn't lied"', *Sun*, 9 September 2020.

3: Wildfire

1. 'How a simple spelling error nearly cost me my political career: Matt Hancock opens up about his dyslexia', *Telegraph*, 17 May 2019.
2. 'Energy minister under fire for hiring jet to fly back from climate change deal', *Guardian*, 2 April 2015.
3. 'Energy and climate change minister accepts £18,000 from climate sceptic', *Guardian*, 10 April 2015.
4. 'Hi I'm Matt Hancock – culture secretary launches own app', BBC News, 2 February 2018.
5. 'No 10 at breaking point over the coronavirus', *The Sunday Times*, 27 September 2020.
6. 'Obama, Bush only U.S. presidents given UK state visit', Reuters, 24 May 2011.

4: Sleepwalk

1. 'Revealed: NHS denied PPE at height of Covid-19 as supplier prioritised China', *Guardian*, 20 July 2020.
2. 'Coronavirus: Did the government get it wrong?', *Dispatches*, Channel 4, 3 June 2020.
3. Ibid.
4. 'Revealed: Value of UK pandemic stockpile fell by 40% in six years', *Guardian*, 12 April 2020.
5. 'Revealed: PPE stockpile was out-of-date when coronavirus hit UK', *Channel 4 News*, 7 May 2020.
6. 'Has the government failed the NHS?', *Panorama*, BBC One, 27 April 2020.
7. 'Coronavirus: Did the government get it wrong?', *Dispatches*, Channel 4, 3 June 2020.

5: Holiday

1. *The Andrew Marr Show*, BBC One, 12 April 2020.
2. 'Boris Johnson and his "chino chancellor"', *Politico*, 13 February 2020.
3. 'Dominic Cummings said to be "writing budget" for Sajid Javid', *The Sunday Times*, 19 January 2020.
4. 'Why I broke with Boris Johnson', *New Statesman*, 10 June 2020.
5. '"He's a better ex than he was a husband", says Boris Johnson's ex-wife', *Evening Standard*, 29 May 2012.
6. 'The Boris I know: A loner who wants to be loved', *Mail on Sunday*, 27 March 2016.
7. 'Bonking Boris', *Sun*, 7 September 2018.
8. 'Boris Johnson: Police called to loud altercation at potential PM's home', *Guardian*, 21 June 2019.
9. 'Charlotte Edwardes on Boris Johnson's wandering hands', *The Sunday Times*, 29 September 2019.
10. 'Hospitals prepare for coronavirus epidemic to sweep Britain', *The Sunday Times*, 16 February 2020.
11. 'The prime minister's vanishing briefs', *The Sunday Times*, 23 February 2020.
12. 'Where the floody hell is Boris? Angry residents blast Boris Johnson for refusing to visit flooded communities ravaged by Storm Dennis', *Sun*, 18 February 2020.
13. 'Boris and Jennifer Arcuri: Case not closed', *The Critic*, 30 May 2020.
14. 'Duncan Selbie: The new face of public health in England', *The Lancet*, 6 April 2013.
15. 'Special Report: Johnson listened to his scientists about coronavirus – but they were slow to sound the alarm', Reuters, 7 April 2020.

6: Part-Time Prime Minister

1. 'Coronavirus: Did the government get it wrong?', *Dispatches*, Channel 4, 3 June 2020.
2. Ibid.
3. 'Coronavirus outbreak a pandemic "in all but name", says expert', *Guardian*, 24 February 2020.
4. 'Coronavirus: NHS hospitals banned from stockpiling protective masks', *Independent*, 24 February 2020.

5. 'Coronavirus: Weakest patients could be denied lifesaving care due to lack of funding for NHS, doctors admit', *Independent*, 26 February 2020.
6. 'NHS plans to deploy "Dad's Army" of retired doctors if Covid-19 spreads', *Observer*, 29 February 2020.

7: The Action Plan

1. 'UK has plans to deal with pandemic causing up to 315,000 deaths', *Guardian*, 6 March 2020.
2. 'Coronavirus: Did the government get it wrong?', *Dispatches*, Channel 4, 3 June 2020.
3. Ibid.

8: Herd Immunity

1. 'Boris Johnson heckled during visit to flood-hit Bewdley', *The Times*, 8 March 2020.
2. 'Coronavirus: Did the government get it wrong?', *Dispatches*, Channel 4, 3 June 2020.
3. Ibid.
4. 'Coronavirus: Care home residents could be "cocooned"', BBC News, 11 March 2020.
5. 'Haunted, exhausted and under attack as coronavirus death toll doubles', *The Sunday Times*, 15 March 2020.
6. 'Coronavirus: Did the government get it wrong?', *Dispatches*, Channel 4, 3 June 2020.
7. 'Special Report: Into the fog – How Britain lost track of the coronavirus', Reuters, 29 June 2020.
8. 'Rory Stewart interview: Deploy the army to combat coronavirus', *Joe*, 12 March 2020.
9. 'Coronavirus: Did the government get it wrong?', *Dispatches*, Channel 4, 3 June 2020.
10. Ibid.
11. Ibid.
12. 'How the alarm went off too late in Britain's virus response', Bloomberg, 24 April 2020.

9: Dither

1. 'Public request to take stronger measures of social distancing across the UK with immediate effect', 14 March 2020.
2. 'Inside Westminster's coronavirus blame game', *Financial Times*, 16 July 2020.
3. 'Coronavirus: Did the government get it wrong?', *Dispatches*, Channel 4, 3 June 2020.
4. 'How the future PM, Boris Johnson, and NHS boss, Simon Stevens, formed an unlikely bond at Oxford', *Telegraph*, 7 August 2019.
5. 'Coronavirus: Did the government get it wrong?', *Dispatches*, Channel 4, 3 June 2020.
6. Ibid.
7. Ibid.
8. Ibid.

10: Disaster

1. 'Coronavirus crisis: Sickness, fear and now isolation for Boris Johnson', *The Sunday Times*, 29 March 2020.
2. 'NHS staff feel like "cannon fodder" over lack of coronavirus protection', *Guardian*, 22 March 2020.
3. '"No surprise" Boris Johnson got coronavirus when he failed to "practise what he preached", scientists say', *Evening Standard*, 28 March 2020.
4. 'Coronavirus: Doctors "told not to discuss PPE shortages"', BBC News, 15 May 2020.
5. 'Coronavirus: NHS nurses told "lives would be made hell"', BBC News, 21 July 2020.

11: Left to Die at Home

1. 'Boris Johnson and coronavirus: the inside story of his illness', *Guardian*, 17 April 2020.
2. 'Hospital says baby of nurse who died from Covid-19 doing well', *Guardian*, 16 April 2020.
3. 'From evasion to evisceration: How the Cummings lockdown story unfolded', *Guardian*, 29 May 2020.
4. 'Coronavirus: More than 4,000 hospital patients discharged into care homes without test', Sky News, 17 July 2020.

5. 'Three nurses forced to wear bin bags because of PPE shortage test positive for coronavirus', *Telegraph*, 8 April 2020.
6. 'Coronavirus: Carers in Scotland not eligible for death in service payment', Channel 4, 7 May 2020.
7. 'Cramlington mental health nurse dies after contracting coronavirus', *Chronicle Live*, 17 April 2020.
8. 'Mum of Northumberland nurse killed by Covid makes heartfelt Christmas plea for families to stay apart', *Chronicle Live*, 12 December 2020.
9. 'Oxford hospital worker's PPE fears before coronavirus death', *Oxford Mail*, 21 May 2020.

12: Worst of All Worlds

1. 'The government is flying half blind into the next phase of the coronavirus crisis', *Observer*, 3 May 2020.
2. 'Exclusive: Government scientist Neil Ferguson resigns after breaking lockdown rules to meet his married lover', *Telegraph*, 5 May 2020.
3. '"Complacent" UK draws global criticism for Covid-19 response', *Guardian*, 6 May 2020.
4. 'Pressure on Dominic Cummings to quit over lockdown breach', *Guardian*, 22 May 2020.
5. 'New witnesses cast doubt on Dominic Cummings's lockdown claims', *Guardian*, 23 May 2020.
6. 'Chief nurse dropped from Downing Street coronavirus briefing "after refusing to back Dominic Cummings"', *Independent*, 12 June 2020.
7. 'Serious weaknesses in the UK's current plans for suppressing covid-19 risk a second major outbreak', *BMJ*, 5 June 2020.
8. 'Coronavirus lockdown: Now it's the economy, stupid', *The Sunday Times*, 7 June 2020.
9. 'Boris Johnson is tied up in knots over the coronavirus', *The Sunday Times*, 14 June 2020.
10. 'Coronavirus: Government accused of ignoring experts as top advisers absent from press briefings', *Independent*, 15 June 2020.
11. 'Coronavirus: WHO warns against further lifting of lockdown in England', *Guardian*, 15 June 2020.
12. 'Boris Johnson is tied up in knots over the coronavirus', *The Sunday Times*, 14 June 2020.

13. 'Starmer overtakes Johnson as preferred choice for prime minister', *Guardian*, 27 June 2020.
14. 'Public trust in UK government over coronavirus falls sharply', *Guardian*, 1 June 2020.
15. 'Coronavirus: Easing several lockdown rules at once could boost virus, say UK scientists', *Guardian*, 24 June 2020.

13: A Reckless Summer

1. '"Raise a glass": UK Treasury faces backlash after hailing pubs reopening', *Guardian*, 2 July 2020.
2. 'Coronavirus: Boris Johnson criticised over "cowardly" care home comments', BBC News, 7 July 2020.
3. 'Boris Johnson indicates at PMQs he has not read winter coronavirus report', *Guardian*, 15 July 2020.
4. 'Saving lives or UK economy from Covid a "false choice", MPs warn', *Guardian*, 26 August 2020.

14: The Circuit Breaker

1. 'No 10 at breaking point over the coronavirus', *The Sunday Times*, 27 September 2020.
2. 'Sunetra Gupta: Covid-19 is on the way out', *UnHerd*, 21 May 2020.
3. 'Lockdown was the only way to stop the NHS being broken', *The Times*, 28 November 2020.

15: Plague Island

1. 'No Fit State', *Tortoise Media*, 15 December 2020.
2. 'Times Radio Breakfast', *Times Radio*, 24 September 2020.

Acknowledgements

It would be fascinating to travel back in time to December 2019 to see how people would react if they were told that 2020 would be the year of the much-feared global virus pandemic and Britain would emerge with the worst death toll in Europe. They would no doubt want to know what on earth had happened to make Britain one of the most severely afflicted countries in the world. They might also ask why the British economy had been hit harder than any of the other G7 nations and, indeed, suffered more damage to its GDP than almost every other major country. This book has been our attempt to explain those difficult questions. When we originally planned it, we agreed with our publishers that we would write until the end of the year. And what a tragic year it turned out to be – with Britain suffering its highest number of excess deaths since the Second World War. However, we broke with the plan and stole into 2021 by a few days so that we could include the third lockdown. Inexcusably, the restrictive measures had been introduced too late once again. As we end this book, Britain is now facing an unprecedented crisis in its hospitals that will inevitably lead to tens of thousands more deaths through January and February into spring. It looks likely that the country will remain in an economically shattering lockdown for most of the winter. The scale of the

413

death toll and length of the lockdown were both avoidable. They are the result of the poor decision making that we have documented in the preceding pages: an awful final reckoning of a year of recklessness, dither and delay.

We would have obviously not been able to write this book without the help of our sources, who gave us eyes and ears across the country as the deadly virus spread, retreated, and then came back again more aggressively than ever. They allowed us to see the government's handling of the pandemic for what it is: the most scandalous failure of political leadership for a generation. Our contacts gave us a window into the most momentous scenes of the pandemic: the Sage meetings with their terrifying projections; the paralysed Covid-ridden corridors of Downing Street; the life-and-death struggles in intensive care wards; and the agonies endured in the nation's care homes. There are too many sources to thank by name here, but many are referenced throughout this book. We are immensely grateful for the time they took to give us some perspective on events, especially as several did so despite fearing they might lose their jobs if they were caught telling us the truth. So to our whistle-blowers: thank you for the texts describing the heart-breaking scenes on the wards just before you put on your protective clothing for another day helping patients who were gasping for breath; for the long interviews stretching into the night after harrowing shifts picking up sick people and bodies in London's ambulances; and for the snatched early-morning phone calls before you headed into Westminster for another day of fraught decision making. We are indebted.

We also owe a huge debt of gratitude to our brilliant friends and colleagues at *The Sunday Times* who worked alongside us throughout 2020. Their work represents a major contribution to this book. Philip Sherwell, who covers Asia for the newspaper, gave us invaluable assistance with our enquiries into the origins of the virus. He linked us up with a talented local journalist on the ground in China, who reported bravely and translated crucial documents accurately and swiftly. The reporter has wisely asked to remain anonymous for their own safety. Jonathan Leake, the former *Sunday Times* science editor, uncovered many of the warnings given to the government about the virus's seriousness in the first three months of the year. The political reporting team of Tim Shipman and Caroline Wheeler provided invaluable help chronicling the drama in Westminster. We drew on Tim's work, in particular, several times over the year. Dipesh Gadher, the newspaper's home affairs correspondent, tracked down the victims of the virus who attended the ill-fated Cheltenham Festival. News reporter Shanti Das did some terrific work uncovering documentary evidence and chilling human stories that helped prove what really happened in the hospitals and care homes as a result of the first late lockdown. She also did some top-notch reporting on the reckless decisions made by the government in the lead-up to the second wave of the virus. George Greenwood and Tom Calver, from our data team, helped crunch the numbers and draw up the graphs included in this book that, among other things, show the systematic nature of the healthcare rationing during the first wave. Andrew Gregory, the *Sunday Times* health editor, provided important evidence of the appalling cost to patients suffering non-Covid conditions. Lily Russell-Jones, a talented up-and-coming journalist, painstakingly produced international comparisons showing that those countries that took swift and decisive action went on to have less damage to their economies and lost fewer lives. Lily also scoured the parliamentary records to pick out the important rhetoric from the decision makers and provided great help with proof-reading. We also want to thank our inspirational editor Emma Tucker, her deputy Ben Taylor and executive editor Ben Preston. They first commissioned us to examine the government's handling of the pandemic back in March, and their wise counsel and encouragement have been invaluable. Georgina Capel, our literary agent, provided great help and advice, and our lawyer David Hirst carried out the all-important legal checks. And, of course, we are indebted to Joel Simons, our editor at HarperCollins, whom we have actually never met in person because of the weirdness of Covid year. Joel has always been wonderfully cheerful and positive in helping us to shape the direction of the book. He was ably assisted by Nick Fawcett, Mark Bolland and Simon Gerratt, whose intelligent and meticulous subbing and editing were really appreciated. Our thanks also to Sarah Burke, Mark Rowland, Orlando Mowbray, Jessie Meenan and Graham Holmes. Furthermore, we have been fortunate enough to be able to stand on the shoulders of the reporting giants across the British media, who have produced some fantastic work over the year. You'll find their work listed in the references section. A particular mention must go to our friend Antony Barnett at Channel 4's *Dispatches* programme, who did some sterling work on the countdown to the first lockdown, which we drew on in the early chapters.

From George

Inevitably, I need to say a huge thank you to my family. First and foremost, to my wife Clio, who looked after me so well after I came down with symptoms of the virus in early April. In a mask and science laboratory goggles, she fed and cared for me in our spare room while also looking after our children Benji, aged three, and Skye, one. She has at times, I'm ashamed to say, acted almost like a single parent to give me time to write this book. She also put on hold her own plans and dreams. I can't thank her enough. To Benji and Skye, I'm sorry I wasn't the best of dads in 2020. I promise to remedy that in 2021 and play rockets, train tracks and watch *PAW Patrol* together far more often. I must also thank my mother-in-law, who, unfortunately for her, had to live with us for almost the entire year because of the travel restrictions, having just popped over to visit for Christmas 2019. We would not have got through without her love, kindness and homemade dumplings.

ACKNOWLEDGEMENTS

To my parents, thank you for spending my whole life encouraging me and giving me every opportunity to follow my passions, which led me to become a journalist in the first place. And thank you for looking after the kids at crucial moments and providing invaluable feedback on the book. Thanks also to my gran Lizzie, my siblings Rose, Flora and Ned, and his fiancée Kitty, for all your love, encouragement and support. Ned and Kitty, whatever form it takes, your wedding will lift our hearts and light up 2021.

From Jonathan

I am always thankful to my children, Will and Grace, for just being plain lovely, and for growing up into such remarkable and wonderfully huggable young adults. It's been a tough year for my mum because she, like so many people her age, has been forced to adopt a certain degree of isolation. And yet you would never know it from her sunny disposition and positive outlook. Roll on the vaccine. I owe an apology to the many friends I have neglected in the push to get this book delivered on time. It was especially difficult to watch my friends heading off to the Surrey hills on their bikes on a Sunday morning when I was head down writing. And also an apology to George's wife, Clio, as he has spent far too many evenings and weekends with me on the phone. George tells me that one morning he came across his three-year-old son Benji talking into a calculator, which he was pretending was a phone. When George asked him what he was doing, he replied: 'I'm phoning Jonathan.'

Index

Page references in *italics* indicate images.